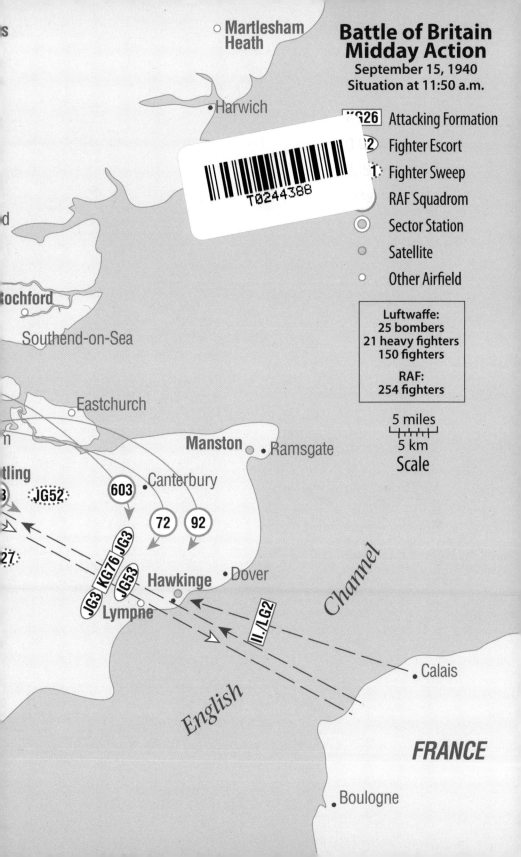

Battle of Britain
Midday Action
September 15, 1940
Situation at 11:50 a.m.

KG26 Attacking Formation

2 Fighter Escort

1 Fighter Sweep

RAF Squadrom

◎ Sector Station

○ Satellite

○ Other Airfield

Luftwaffe:
25 bombers
21 heavy fighters
150 fighters

RAF:
254 fighters

5 miles

5 km
Scale

Martlesham Heath

Harwich

Rochford

Southend-on-Sea

Eastchurch

Manston   Ramsgate

tling

JG52

603

Canterbury

72   92

JG3 KG76 JG3

JG3 JG53

Hawkinge   Dover

27

Lympne

II./LG2

Channel

Calais

English

FRANCE

Boulogne

BATTLE OF BRITAIN

BATTLE OF BRITAIN

CANADIAN AIRMEN IN THEIR FINEST HOUR

TED BARRIS

sh.
SUTHERLAND
HOUSE

TORONTO, 2024

Sutherland House
416 Moore Ave., Suite 304
Toronto, ON M4G 1C9

Sutherland House and logo are registered
trademarks of The Sutherland House Inc.

First edition, September 2024

If you are interested in inviting one of our authors to a live event or
media appearance, please contact sranasinghe@sutherlandhousebooks.com
and visit our website at sutherlandhousebooks.com for more information.

We acknowledge the support of the Government of Canada.

Manufactured in Canada
Cover designed by Gordon Robertson
Book composed by Karl Hunt

Library and Archives Canada Cataloguing in Publication
Title: Battle of Britain : Canadian airmen in their
finest hour / Ted Barris.
Names: Barris, Ted, author.
Description: Includes bibliographical references and index.
Identifiers: Canadiana (print) 20240389301 | Canadiana (ebook)
2024038931X | ISBN 9781990823930 (hardcover) |
ISBN 9781990823947 (EPUB)
Subjects: LCSH: Britain, Battle of, Great Britain, 1940. |
LCSH: World War, 1939-1945—Aerial operations, British. |
LCSH: World War, 1939-1945—Aerial operations, Canadian. |
LCSH: Fighter pilots—Canada—Biography. |
LCSH: Great Britain. Royal Air Force.
Classification: LCC D756.5.B7 B356 2024 |
DDC 940.54/211—dc23

ISBN 978-1-990823-93-0
eBook 978-1-990823-94-7

For my grandchildren—Layne, Sawyer,
Coen, Wyatt, Huxley, and Tully.

May you only experience war by reading
my stories of Canadian warriors.

LIST OF MAPS

Contents

CONTENTS

A S FOR MANY OF MY GENERATION, I FIRST LEARNED OF THE Battle of Britain when my father took me to the see the blockbuster film late in 1969. I was nine years old. I well remember what an exciting show it was, filled with aerial dogfights, explosions, and crashes. And, of course, in the sky, it featured a whirling, swirling, deadly dance of airplanes. It was right up my nine-year-old, aviation-obsessed alley. While the film was generally panned by critics on both sides of the Atlantic, I was much less discerning in my review. I just wanted to see it again.

At the time, I utterly failed to appreciate that the movie portrayed a real, historic, and pivotal campaign of the Second World War—the allied victory that thwarted the feared invasion of Britain by the German Army. Now, having read *Battle of Britain* by Ted Barris, I have a much clearer understanding of this extraordinary story, what was at stake, and what it cost. The film pales in comparison.

When Ted asked me to write this foreword, it was not because of my credentials as a military historian—I have none. It was not because my father was a fighter pilot in the Battle of Britain; he was only ten years old in July of 1940. And it was not because of the deep research I'd done for a novel about this particular campaign—I've never written about any war, let alone WWII. No, I think Ted asked me because of my love for airplanes, and my life as a novelist. I was honoured.

In *Battle of Britain*, Ted does what he has done so well for so many years, in twenty previous books and counting. He takes a big, important, life-altering—and sometimes life-ending— event, like the battle for Vimy Ridge, for instance, and tells the story through the eyes of many of its participants. He brings critical, sometimes cataclysmic moments in history to life by telling the stories of those who were there. And I don't know of any writer who does it better.

This particular approach to military history is not typical of the many, many books written about war in general, or this campaign in particular. There are plenty of academic histories of major conflicts and individual battles that provide important historical perspectives, excellent military analysis, and fascinating geopolitical commentary. We need those texts. Ted Barris brings us all of that in his books, but he also delivers what so many others do not. He gives us compelling stories about real people on all sides, and at all levels, of the conflict.

But that's not all. Ted is just about the only writer out there who shines such a brilliant spotlight on the contributions Canadians have made in the military conflicts that shaped the twentieth century. Many war histories gloss over, or fail to mention at all, the important roles Canadians have played from one end of the chain of command to the other. This is one of Ted's special gifts to his country.

We know, often only obliquely, of Canada's place in military history, particularly in the two world wars. But *Battle of Britain* gives us the names, faces, feelings, families, and heart-stopping exploits of individual Canadians who left their mark on the conflicts in which they served. Ted excels in illuminating these often-unknown tales about unknown Canadian combatants performing astonishing feats of skill and bravery. Well, we now know their names and faces and stories. We also now know that Canadians were stalwart vanguards in the Battle of Britain, arguably the most critical air campaign of WWII— the one that derailed Germany's planned invasion of Britain.

Finally, I can't conclude this without noting Ted's skill as a storyteller. If you've ever seen one of his book talks, you'll know what I mean. And if you haven't, move heaven and earth to get to one of them. Storytelling has its roots in the oral tradition. I've known Ted for years, but I still can't decide whether he was born with a pen or a microphone in his hand. Perhaps it was both, one in each hand.

Reading his books, or seeing him present at festivals, libraries, and Legions across the country, you can arrive at only one conclusion: Ted Barris knows how to research, write, craft, and tell a story that not only catches your attention but holds you spellbound until you turn the final page, or the curtain falls. It's a rare gift. Ted Barris has it, and it's on full display in *Battle of Britain*. More to the point, Ted Barris *is* a rare gift.

—Terry Fallis
Toronto, June 2024

ACKNOWLEDGEMENTS

LONG BEFORE I KNEW THE DIFFERENCE BETWEEN A RUDDER and an aileron or between active and passive verbs, I met an English teacher named Bill Sherwood. He taught us Shakespeare and compositional writing at my high school in Agincourt, Ontario, back in the 1960s. Sherwood's reputation for challenging his students preceded him. We learned from others that when it came time for the major English composition assignment—writing an original short story—he would issue each student a single word. And that word or idea had to be at the core of the composition. Our turn came in the winter term.

"Mr. Barris," he announced early in his challenges (one of the disadvantages of having a surname near the top of the alphabet), "your composition word is"—adding a dramatic pause—"pickles!"

At first, I was distraught. But then an idea came. I loved aviation stories. As a teenager, my bedroom showcased the keepsakes of that fascination. Atop my bookshelf sat plastic models I'd built of a Hurricane fighter, a Spitfire, and other Second World War aircraft. On the shelves below, I'd filed editions of favourite air magazines and my aviation book collection, including titles such as: *Boys' Book of Flight*, *The Courage of the Early Morning*, *Reach for the Sky*, *Duel of Eagles*, and *Fighter*

Pilot by R.J. Childerhose, a novel about a young Canadian pilot dogfighting over Britain. I'd always thought about writing my own version of a story about a group of misfit fighter pilots who punch above their weight during that summer of 1940. Why not name the maverick leader of the group Flight Lieutenant Dill? I dug into my bookshelf for research and recreated their sortie over south England in a short story that I titled "Dill's Pickles."

So, the subject has been in my marrow a long time. The real spark to retrace the paths of real Canadian airmen in the Battle of Britain, however, occurred in a conversation, in 2022, with friend and aviation art and book collector Mike Parry. With the one-hundredth anniversary of the Royal Canadian Air Force approaching in 2024, I asked Mike which aviation story he thought was missing from the Canadian canon of Second World War aviation history? He responded instantly, "Canadians in the Battle of Britain." And with that thought in mind, he shared his library of files, paintings and books, and his own memories of meeting so many of this country's Second World War aviation veterans. Mike had either met or known on a first-name basis such former Canadian fighter pilots as Paul Pitcher, Hartland Molson, John Milne, Dal Russel, Charles Trevena, and others. His insights on this manuscript were second to none.

Other military historians stepped up to assist me in this project as well. I'm particularly grateful for the vital support and access to material gathered and published by Hugh Halliday (*242 Squadron: The Canadian Years*); Keith C. Ogilvie (*You Never Know Your Luck*); David L. Bashow (*All the Fine Young Eagles*); Ellin Bessner (*Double Threat: Canadian Jews, the Military, and World War II*); Diane Bishop, on behalf of her father Arthur Bishop

(*The Splendid Hundred*); Dick Bourgeois-Doyle (*Her Daughter the Engineer*); Greg Kopchuk, who supplied research (*Alberta in the 20th Century: The War That United the Province*) on Battle of Britain pilots from Alberta; Vera Lynn's family (*We'll Meet Again: A Personal and Social History of World War Two*); Carl Christie (*Ocean Bridge: The History of RAF Ferry Command*); Norm Christie (*For King and Empire* documentary series); and Michel Lavigne for his exhaustive documentation of Canadian fighter pilots from 1939 to 1945.

The most overlooked preservers of our military history—the families of those who witnessed and those who served—have always eagerly assisted me in my writing endeavours. Special thanks this time to Blair Russel (for access to his father Dal Russel's papers), Jay Warner (for background on grandfather Arthur Hicklin Warner), Brian Johannesson and Cathie Eliasson (for photo material of Konrad Johannesson); and Mary Shenstone and David Fleury (for assistance to secure images of Bev Shenstone); and while he is no blood relation to Shenstone, Dave Brooks directed my attention to the Shenstone story.

For their personal memories of life on the ground in and around London (as civilians) during the Battle of Britain and the Blitz, I am immensely grateful to Dorothy (Firth) Marshall and her daughter Helen Beauchamp, Anne (Shore) Reed, and Jill (Brown) Mason. In 1993, my father, Alex Barris, interviewed Bill Brydon, another British-born Canadian with memories of the Blitz in England that summer. And on three different occasions, I had the pleasure of interviewing Dame Vera Lynn about surviving and singing through the Blitz in 1940. They were/are proof that Londoners could take anything life (and war) threw at them.

I remain indebted to administration and staff at libraries, museums, and archives, and historical societies and their volunteers, for their knowledge and wisdom continue to provide a beacon for my work. I'm particularly indebted to the Canadian Aviation Historical Society (CAHS), especially Norman Malayney for his meticulous compilation of Floyd Williston's papers (and permissions), as well as Winnipeg chapter members Alan Parkin and Bill Zuk, for their personal libraries and time spent assembling research on Manitoba aviators. CAHS Vancouver chapter president Jerry Vernon supplied original papers (in his trust) from Paul Pitcher's family.

Similarly, many thanks to Dave Birrell (Bomber Command Museum of Canada); Al Mickeloff and Shawn Perras (Canadian Warplane Heritage Museum); Alex Fitzgerald-Black (Juno Beach Centre in France); Kevin Windsor (National Air Force Museum of Canada); and Michael Virr (Vintage Wings of Canada) for their assistance and support. At the University of Victoria Archives, I met library assistant John Frederick, who assisted my retrieval of recordings from their Military Oral History Collection, in particular the interview Cameron Falconer conducted with Beverley Evans Christmas. I also wish to acknowledge the staff at both the City of Toronto Archives and Lakehead University Archives for assistance in sourcing periodicals on this subject.

Special thanks to film archivist Wojtek Deluga at London's Polish Institute and Sikorski Museum in London for delivering unique material on RAF No. 303 Polish Squadron—its pilots, its environs, and one of its dynamic flight commanders, Canadian Johnny Kent. Thanks to Sebastian Wainwright, Andrew Webb, and the Imaging and Film Licensing Team for their help at the Imperial War Museum and to Jacqueline

Vincent at Brechin Group for securing images from Library and Archives Canada. Sincere gratitude also to publishers Carl and Elizabeth Vincent for their enthusiastic response to my queries about photographs of RAF No. 242 All-Canadian Squadron in the Battle of Britain. I am often the recipient of out-of-the-blue stories provided by friends and acquaintances who know that I throw nothing away; thanks to George Hutchison and especially John Kennerley for trusting me with gems from their personal libraries.

Whenever I complete a new manuscript, I often turn to those closest to the story to read my work before publication, and (if necessary) correct elements of my storytelling. This time I turned to two RCAF pilots who flew fighter aircraft during the Second World War. Pilot Officer Ken Raven and his two brothers—Flight Sergeant Harold Raven and Aircraftman Second Class Vern Raven—all served in the RCAF; Harold died in action. Ken flew Spitfires through the end of the war. And Richard H. Rohmer—a.k.a. the General—flew Mustangs with No. 430 Squadron conducting photo reconnaissance. In his 101st year, he continues to serve as major general in the Royal Canadian Air Force. As well, friends and respected authors Charlotte Gray and Terry Fallis gave precious time to read the manuscript, and composed meaningful endorsements. Sincere thanks.

The production of this book—as with many of my past efforts—has depended on the brilliance of production specialists, including mapmaker Mark Smith, copy editor Linda Pruessen, photographer David Laurence, and book designer Gordon Robertson; they have given this work the sparkle I've envisioned from the start. Friend and know-it-all (literally) of things military Malcolm Kelly, as he has for several books, helped me avoid the flak I might otherwise encounter had he not proofread the book for technical accuracy. As well, my thanks to publisher Ken Whyte and his team at Sutherland House for believing in this work from inception to publication.

While I do it occasionally at public-speaking events, I never sufficiently thank the members of my two vital families—my blood relatives, who bolster me when I need bolstering the most, and my family of veterans and their kin for their correspondence and loan of reference material, their generous compliments, their attendance at my public-speaking events, and their steadfast belief that we must share these stories and remember service and sacrifice.

By the way, back in 1964, Bill Sherwood, my high school English composition teacher, gave my short story "Dill's Pickles" an A. Thanks, Bill, wherever you are.

—Ted Barris
Uxbridge, Ontario, May 2024

RANKS OF RAF/RCAF AND LUFTWAFFE EQUIVALENTS

Air Chief Marshal (ACM)	Generaloberst
Air Vice-Marshal (AVM)	Generalleutnant
Air Commodore (AC)	Generalmajor
Group Captain (G/C)	Oberst
Wing Commander (W/C)	Oberstleutnant
Squadron Leader (S/L)	Major
Flight Lieutenant (F/L)	Hauptmann
Flying Officer (F/O)	Oberleutnant
Pilot Officer (P/O)	Leutnant
Warrant Officer (WO)	Stabsfeldwebel
Flight Sergeant (F/Sgt)	Oberfeldwebel
Sergeant (Sgt)	Feldwebel
Corporal (Cpl)	Unteroffizier
Leading aircraftsman/woman (LAC)	Obergefreiter
Aircraftman 1st class (AC1)	Gefreiter
Aircraftman 2nd class (AC2)	Flieger

Glossary of Terms and Abbreviations

Admiralty—Royal Navy

"Angels"—thousands of feet of altitude (as in "Angels 18," meaning 18,000 feet)

AASF—Advanced Air Striking Force

ACT—army co-operation training squadron

Adlerangriff—Eagle Attack

AFC—Air Force Cross

Air Ministry—British government department that managed the affairs of the Royal Air Force

AOC—air officer commanding

ARP—Air Raid Precautions, guidelines to protect UK civilians against air raids

batman—valet in RAF assigned to attend to flying officers' housekeeping needs

BCATP—British Commonwealth Air Training Plan, organized by Britain, Canada, Australia, and New Zealand for instruction of aircrew principally in Canada

BEF—British Expeditionary Force

big wing—tactic of two or more squadrons of fighters airborne to overwhelm enemy aircraft (employed principally by Squadron Leader Douglas Bader)

blitzkrieg—lightning war, a swift, focused blow against the enemy

Brylcreem Boys—term associated with members of the Royal Air Force for their not-a-hair-out-of-place hairdos

CAN/RAF—Canadian Royal Air Force pilot officer

Caribou Squadron—Royal Canadian Air Force No. 1 Fighter Squadron

CEF—Canadian Expeditionary Force

Chain Home radar station—high-frequency radio direction-finding transmitter tower with a receiver hut at its base for identifying enemy aircraft approaching the south and east coasts of England

Chequers—country residence of Winston and Clementine Churchill

Cromwell—code word alerting Home Guard for "readiness for immediate action" against an imminent German invasion

CORB—Children's Overseas Reception Board, which organized the evacuation of British children via passenger liners to Canada

CNE—Canadian National Exhibition in Toronto

CO—commanding officer

DFC—Distinguished Flying Cross

DFM—Distinguished Flying Medal

DSO—Distinguished Service Order

DHist—Directorate of History, National Defence Headquarters

DND—Department of National Defence

E/A—enemy aircraft

Einsatzgruppen—Nazi death squads

erk—short-form term for aircraftman, or "airc"; often ground crew (airframe and aero-engine mechanics, instrument technicians, wireless and electrical mechanics, armourers, carpenters, fabric workers, and metal workers)

Fliegerkorps—air corps

Geschwader—group

Gruppe—wing

Guinea Pig Club—social and support club for Allied airmen with catastrophic burn injuries at Queen Victoria Hospital in East Grinstead

HMCS—His Majesty's Canadian Ship

Home Guard—volunteer citizen army, previously Local Defence Volunteers

Jagdgeschwader (JG)—fighter squadron

Kampfgeschwader (KG)—bomber units

Kanalkampf—Channel Battle

Krzyz Walecznych—Polish Cross of Valour

Lehrgeschwader (LG)—teaching squadron

LDF—Local Defence Volunteers, later Home Guard

Luftwaffe—German Air Force

Mae West—life jacket with bulging front

Maginot Line—280 miles of defensive works built by France in the 1930s along its border with Germany to pre-empt a German invasion

MAP—Ministry of Aircraft Production (UK)

NCO—non-commissioned officer

nickelling—also known as nickel raids, when bombers dropped propaganda leaflets ("bomphlets") over Germany

OBE—Order of the British Empire

OKW—Oberkommando der Wehrmacht (German High Command)

OTU—Operational Training Unit

PDU—Photographic Development Unit

probable—enemy aircraft probably destroyed

RAF—Royal Air Force, previous to 1917 known as the Royal Flying Corps

RAE—Royal Aircraft Establishment, formerly the Royal Aircraft Factory, which designed, built, and tested aircraft engines and aircraft; name changed to avoid confusion with the Royal Air Force

RDF—radio direction-finding, later radio detection and ranging, or radar

RFC—Royal Flying Corps

riggers and fitters—airframe and aero-engine mechanics with air force ground crews

rhubarb—low-level attack on ground targets

R/T—radio telephone

Runnymede Memorial—inscribed monument with names of 20,450 Commonwealth aircrew lost during the war but with no known graves

scramble—quick takeoff

SIS—British Secret Intelligence Service

SSC—Short Service Commission or Direct Entry Scheme, enlisted recruits into military aviation training in return for officer status and Royal Air Force service

Sicherheitsdienst—German Security Service

Seelöwe—Operation Sea Lion, Hitler's plan for invading Britain

sortie—operational flight by single aircraft

sprog—rookie aircrewman

Staffel (Staffeln)—fighter squadron(s)

Stalag Luft III—prison camp for captured Allied aircrew at Żagań, Poland

Stukageschwader (StG)—dive-bomber units

tote board—column of light bulbs inside operations rooms reflecting status of Royal Air Force fighters as they engaged Luftwaffe attackers

Treaty of Versailles—June 28, 1919, its signing ended the Great War between Germany and the Allied Powers

Ultra—British military intelligence code for Enigma decrypts

vics—"V" formation of airborne aircraft

VE Day—Victory in Europe Day, May 8, 1945

Virtuti Militari—Poland's highest military decoration for courage in the face of the enemy

Völkischer Beobachter—Nazi Party newspaper

WAAF—Women's Auxiliary Air Force

Zielwechsel—Target Switch, the operation to intensely bomb British urban centres

CHAPTER ONE

"FIGHT LIKE HELL TO GET INTO IT"

E'D NEVER BEFORE CONSIDERED THE PURCHASE OF A Royal Air Force (RAF) officer's dress uniform. But when his name appeared on the King's New Year Honours list of 1939, Johnny Kent suddenly had to visit Gieves & Co. on London's fashionable Savile Row to do just that. Altogether, the busby, tunic, sword, and belt cost him two guineas, or the equivalent of two weeks' wages for the average Briton at that time.

Next, the young Winnipegger did two other things he'd never considered before. He hailed his first black cab in London and directed its driver, "Buckingham Palace, please!" Kent and fellow Royal Air Force (RAF) officer Henry Hall arrived at the palace gates on February 14, 1939. They received clearance to pass and were escorted smartly into the investiture anteroom "feeling a little nervous and conspicuous."[1]

Recently appointed to a non-specialist permanent commission in the Royal Air Force, Flying Officer (F/O) Kent was to receive an Air Force Cross (AFC) for his military service as a test pilot; F/O Hall would receive an AFC for his service in meteorological flying. And making the investiture all the more exciting, King George VI himself would be presenting the awards. The palace anteroom was full of award recipients. They were joined by palace staff, who briefed them about proper procedure during the ceremony. One staffer circulated around the room sticking hooked pins on the recipients' tunics, so that the King merely needed to hang the decoration on the hook and not fuss with pinning each award on each man's uniform.

Eventually, the line of airmen, arranged in order of seniority in rank and status of decoration, began to advance toward the actual investiture hall. Kent would remember spending these moments collecting his thoughts and taking in the experience of passing through a centuries-old royal residence with its lavish furnishings, picture galleries, and artifacts of royal history. The calm before the investiture also gave him time to reflect on his own short history of service to date.

Only eight years before, in 1931, the sixteen-year-old Kent had convinced his father (less so his mother) that flying offered a worthwhile career. His family agreed to pay for flight instruction at the Winnipeg Flying Club. Under the tutelage of former Royal Flying Corps pilot Konrad "Konnie" Johannesson, Kent received lessons in the club's aging Cirrus Moth. Conditions at the club—extremes in temperatures, regularly gusty winds, and an often unserviceable Moth—made teaching and learning a stop-start affair all summer long.

In late September, Johannesson suddenly had to leave Winnipeg to requalify at a distant Royal Canadian Air Force (RCAF) instructor's school. He rushed Kent to fly solo: taking off, completing a series of airborne manoeuvres, and landing safely back at the airfield, manoeuvres Kent thought could be "relied upon to produce an accident."[2] In weather that had turned cold and blustery that day, Kent found himself ricocheting about the sky and struggling to keep his aircraft straight and level. On landing, he bounced the Moth violently off the grass field, launching pilot and plane seemingly out of control, back into the air, before falling heavily to earth again and braking the plane to a final stop.

"The most Gawd-awful landing I've ever seen," Johannesson declared. "A mystery how in hell the undercarriage took it."[3]

Despite these inauspicious beginnings, while his mentor was away requalifying, novice pilot Kent spent every available minute practising for his flight tests, learning Air Regulations for his written exam, and preparing for the required medical checkup. That fall he was awarded Private Pilot's Licence No. 919 and became the youngest licensed pilot in Canada. As he wrote later, even "the great Billy Bishop received his licence *after* I did!"[4]

Within two years, Kent had completed commercial instruction and become the country's youngest commercial pilot, too. But the Depression strangled all aviation in Canada— military, recreational, and commercial—at a time when Kent needed more hours in the air to advance his competence and employability. That's when Kent spotted a Royal Air Force ad in *The Aeroplane*, a British magazine, offering Short Service Commissions in a Direct Entry Scheme that would give successful applicants the benefit of Air Force training in return for six years of military service.[5]

In January 1934, Kent's application was accepted, and once again his parents bankrolled his career aspirations, paying his passage to Britain. On arrival, he reported to Air Ministry in London and immediately found himself among other Canadian pilots, including a fellow Winnipegger, Alf Bocking, and John "Moose" Fulton from Kamloops, British Columbia. The three Canadians immediately joined scores of other recruits beginning RAF flight training. Over the next two years, Kent advanced from sprog (green recruit) and a top-of-the-class "exceptional" assessment, to training in operational Hawker Furies, to a posting at RAF No. 19 Squadron at Duxford flying the Gloster Gauntlet, at the time the fastest fighter in the world. By 1937, he was achieving top scores in all manner of drills: scrambles, battle climbs, flying in formation, spin recovery, enemy interceptions, air firing, and night flying.

* * *

Immediately after the 1918 armistice in the Great War, the British government assigned on average only 17 percent of its defence budget to Air Force; the number of operational RAF squadrons fell from 188 to twenty-five. And between 1922 and 1935, the lion's share of defence spending supported a strategy of self-defending formations of bombers. Hugh Trenchard, chief of air staff of the Royal Flying Corps (the RAF's predecessor), was the author of that strategy. He insisted that the best form of defence lay in attacking the enemy's bases, machines, hangars, and, if necessary, civilian targets from the air. Years before 1939, Trenchard and company figured another war was coming against the Germans.

"Unless we are determined to go one better than the Germans," he explained to the British war cabinet, "it will be infinitely better not to attempt reprisals at all."[6]

The legislation officially creating the Royal Air Force, a force independent of the British Army and the Royal Navy for both offence and defence in the air, received royal assent on November 29, 1917. The RAF went operational on April 1, 1918. As Trenchard saw it, the RAF could simply serve "as a means of conveyance, captained by chauffeurs," or it could truly operate as an air service to "encourage and develop airmanship . . . and make it a force that will profoundly alter the strategy of the future." He chose to be ambitious, designing an independent air force that would have its own strategic role and technical experts for research and the development of aeronautical science. He envisaged training colleges for officers and technical apprentices; the colleges would produce permanently commissioned officers, or about one-third of the RAF's strength, with the remaining two-thirds comprising "short service" officers with five-year commissions. Trenchard insisted that this would inexpensively build a reserve of "weekend flyers" as a backup to regular force squadrons. Indeed, by the mid-1930s, this model had smoothed the rapid expansion of the RAF and attracted the likes of young Canadians such as Bocking, Fulton, and Kent.[7]

If Trenchard was the principal architect of the Royal Air Force, Hugh Dowding, air chief marshal (ACM) at Air Ministry and eventually the air officer commanding (AOC) RAF Fighter Command, was its tactician. Dowding understood all aspects of training, research, development, and air defence, and thus, in the 1930s, helped decentralize the Air Defence of Great Britain's ponderous system into specialized separate commands: Training, Coastal, Bomber, and Fighter Command. His thinking differed from Trenchard's "attack is better than defence" focus on the bomber force, preferring a well-trained fighter force responsible for ensuring the "security of the base."[8] He conceived and oversaw an integrated air

5

defence system including radar,* human observers, raid plotting, radio control of fighter aircraft (specifically Spitfires and Hurricanes, each equipped with eight guns and bullet-proof windshields), and experienced fighter pilots.

* * *

About the time Dowding became AOC of Fighter Command, the RAF posted provisional officer Johnny Kent to the experimental section at Farnborough airfield (southwest of London) in the Royal Aircraft Establishment (RAE) as a test pilot. At age twenty-three, a flight commander, and now proficient at flying at least sixteen different military aircraft, Kent began testing the efficiency of barrage balloons, Britain's primary defence against raiding enemy aircraft. He realized that intentionally flying aircraft into the cables tethering the balloons to the ground was the only way to test their effectiveness. At the very least, the tests invited disaster. Nevertheless, in two years, Kent conducted over three hundred planned collisions to determine how much damage the cables delivered to inbound enemy aircraft and, conversely, how vulnerable the defensive system might be to enemy cable cutters breaking tethers and scattering the balloons. He did so without a single mishap. Hence his recognition on the King's New Year Honours list and his investiture scheduled for Valentine's Day, 1939.

After what seemed like an endless queue inside Buckingham Palace, Kent stepped into the investiture room and saw the

---

* Robert Watson-Watt, of the National Physical Laboratory, initially called the system "radio direction-finding" or RDF; later in the war, the American term "radio detection and ranging," or radar, became universal.

King dressed in the uniform of a field marshal. Behind him stood the aides-de-camp of the Navy, Army, and Air Force, and in front of him the Lord Chamberlain and the gentlemen-at-arms, resplendent in plumed helmets, breastplates, red tunics, white buckskin breeches, high Wellington boots, and curved sabres. The pomp and circumstance was mesmerizing.

"Right. Your turn," an officer standing inside the entrance told Kent. "March in straight to the Lord Chamberlain. Halt. Turn left and wait for your name to be announced . . ."

Arriving at the appointed spot in front of the Lord Chamberlain, Kent heard the citation read aloud: "To receive the Air Force Cross, Flying Officer John Alexander Kent, Royal Air Force."

Remembering to incline his head and neck only, he bowed; then, as prescribed, he stepped three paces toward the King, who seemed a much shorter man than Kent expected. The King shook Kent by the hand, congratulated him, and hung the cross on the receiving hook. Again, following the protocol he'd been given, Kent took a pace to the rear, bowed again, and marched out past the line of gentlemen-at-arms, "feeling as proud as Lucifer with this great piece of silver dangling from my left breast."[9]

Just as quickly as he'd seemed on top of the world, he was returned abruptly to earth. A short man in a dark suit (Kent surmised a government employee) snatched the Air Force Cross from his chest, plunked it into a case, handed it to him, and said, "This way out!"[10]

* * *

As it turned out, neither the King nor the AFC awardee had much time for formalities. On September 3, as Adolf Hitler's armies marched into Poland and Prime Minister Neville Chamberlain declared war against Nazi Germany, Kent was preparing for his officer's promotion exam, scheduled for September 5. The declaration pre-empted the exam, and Flight Lieutenant (F/L) Kent returned to Farnborough, where he test-flew the Rothermere Bomber, precursor to the Bristol Blenheim light bomber. By the time Hitler had launched his spring offensive in 1940, ending the phoney war,* Kent had reported to RAF Heston to join the Photographic Development Unit (PDU), where his first job was to familiarize himself with the new Supermarine Spitfire fighter aircraft.

For Kent's planned reconnaissance sorties over enemy territory, PDU ground crew had altered his Spitfire away from its front-line combat configuration; they'd lightened the aircraft by removing its guns, its armour plating, its night-flying equipment, and even its radio, "leaving the pilot with no protection except his speed and height."[11] In other words, Kent would have to rely on the Spitfire's exceptional velocity (nearly 370 miles per hour), its rapid rate of climb (2,100 feet per minute), its high service ceiling (more than 37,000 feet), and his piloting skills to photograph images of enemy installations and get them home safely. PDU's airframe specialists had at least painted the exterior of Kent's aircraft with a bright blue, high-gloss finish to help him disappear into the daytime sky.

Even with its high-performance Rolls-Royce Merlin engine, the Spitfire was not infallible, and Kent nearly crashed

---

* The period between October 1939 and March 1940, prior to either side launching land attacks.

twice in his first weeks of reconnaissance flights. During one of his high-altitude photo trips over the Dutch coast, Kent's engine failed at 29,000 feet; he dropped 11,000 feet before it sputtered back to life.[12] On another trip, over Germany, he noticed a thumping noise behind him that was getting closer and louder; he turned to see bursts of German anti-aircraft shells overtaking him along his high-altitude vapour trail. He learned to alter his course frequently to avoid being shot down by flying in straight lines and at the same altitude.

Then, with Allied troops, tanks, and artillery making a last stand to defend Paris—France had capitulated in June 1940—Kent received orders to reconnoiter crossing points along the Seine, or routes of escape for retreating British Expeditionary Forces. Flying at much lower altitudes, and therefore a more obvious target for German fighter aircraft and anti-aircraft guns, Kent's Spitfire had at least been re-equipped with its eight guns. It was during this reconnaissance sortie in late June that Kent scored his first kill, without firing a single shot. He'd climbed to 15,000 feet and was approaching the river to check its bridges when he spotted eleven Messerschmitt 109s (Me 109s) flying in formation below him about a mile away. They were on a course to cross into his gun sights. Without warning, four RAF Hurricanes whizzed past him and dove to attack the leading five German fighter aircraft.

"Everyone seemed to go mad and aeroplanes whirled around in crazy gyrations," Kent wrote in his journal. "I latched onto the last one."[13]

Both he and his German prey plunged earthward, the Messerschmitt pilot trying desperately to elude Kent's Spitfire. The Me 109 suddenly pulled out of its dive and levelled out at 3,000 feet. Kent was just a few plane lengths behind and about to open fire when the German suddenly sent his aircraft into a wild half-roll. Kent followed in kind, but the ground loomed quickly and he aborted the chase for fear of crashing into the riverbank. Kent credits the Spitfire's forgiving response to unorthodox attitudes—flying upside down, climbing stalls, or uncontrolled spins—for his quick recovery. He managed to return the aircraft to straight and level flight literally between the banks of the Seine.

"I saw a red flash out of the corner of my eye," Kent reported, "and . . . a column of smoke coming out of what looked like a bomb crater about 100 yards from the river-bank." Kent guessed that the Messerschmitt pilot had never been chased by a Spitfire before and took violent evasive action as a reflex, or perhaps because the Spitfire's bright blue paint job told him that "the British ace of aces" was on his tail. That he could not claim an enemy aircraft destroyed was a frustra-tion for Kent, but he was "satisfied that the flash and the crater were caused by the German machine."[14]

***

Meanwhile, the RAF Advanced Air Striking Force (AASF) was in a state of rapid retreat and evacuation. The German blitz-krieg had forced RAF pilots to abandon aircraft and entire bases along the front in France. It had all happened so fast, with German bombs falling on his squadron's airfield at Bricy, outside Paris, that Johnny Kent only had time to throw a hand-ful of belongings into a single Tiger Moth and take off to save himself and his aircraft.

The RAF had committed twelve squadrons to France—four at the outbreak of the war and eight more during the blitzkrieg that spring,[15] leaving twenty-two modern single-seater fighter squadrons (approximately 331 Spitfires and Hurricanes) plus nine squadrons with obsolete planes to defend the British Isles,[16] despite the fact that ACM Dowding had recommended fifty-two squadrons be kept at home. Of the 261 Hurricanes dispatched to France, only sixty-six had returned.[17]

The sorry state of Fighter Command back in Britain came into sharp focus when Kent arrived for additional combat training at RAF Hawarden station on the border between England and Wales, in July 1940. With rainy weather, the station had become a sea of mud, and soggy tents were the only accommodation available for aircrew. In the air, few could tell the difference between teachers and students.

Despite all of his high-altitude photo-reconnaissance work in Spitfires, Kent had never flown the Hurricane fighters in use at Hawarden. He was eager to learn actual combat techniques in them and get a posting to a front-line combat squadron. Although his instructors had logged plenty of hours flying Hurricanes, none had actually experienced air combat. In some respects, it was the blind leading the blind. Kent found the training syllabus at Hawarden painfully basic; it consisted merely of formation flying and the simplest of dogfighting exercises.

Kent had never fired eight guns in a fighter aircraft all at once; he had no idea what that sounded like, nor how so much rapid firing would affect the response of his aircraft. During one shooting exercise, he dove at his target—a spit of sand in the Dee Estuary—and fired a short burst, maybe half a second. He dove a second time at the spit and pressed the firing button, but nothing happened. He tried a third attack. The guns appeared to fail again. He landed back at Hawarden, fit to be tied over the poor armament performance of his Hurricane.

"What kind of an installation could produce stoppages in all eight guns at once?" Kent complained to Flight Commander Bill Kain.

"There weren't any stoppages in those guns," Kain explained calmly. "That's all the ammunition we can spare you."[18]

Making simulated combat more complicated, Kent and his RAF aircrew comrades learned that the Germans might soon be using British aircraft captured during the hasty retreat from France to fly unnoticed across the English Channel and attack installations in England. Overnight, Air Ministry ordered all British aircraft be changed to a new set of markings on their wings and fuselages. Thus, any aircraft—potentially captured Whitleys and Lysanders—spotted with old markings would be considered hostile and should be shot down.

A short time later, leading three Hurricane fighters in a defensive operation and with guns fully loaded, Kent spotted a Whitley flying west over the Irish Sea. It showed the old markings, giving Kent every right to shoot the bomber and its crew out of the sky. He chose to lead his section of Hurricanes in close formation, line astern, along the port side of the Whitley, signalling its pilot to turn back to the coast and land. Tension-filled minutes passed before the Whitley navigator flashed the "letter of the day" with his Aldis lamp. Kent considered this an inadequate reaction. Nevertheless, he withheld fire, but escorted the bomber down to the station at Hawarden.

"Why did you take so long to send a recognition signal?" Kent quizzed the Australian flying officer as he emerged from the grounded Whitley. He noticed that the man also had a pocket full of signal cartridges that he could have used to give a "colour of the day" signal for quick identification as an alternative.

"My instructions are not to use these cartridges except in cases of emergency," he responded.

Kent pointed at his three Hurricanes parked beside the Whitley and fumed, "You had twenty-four fully loaded Brownings up your 'chuff' and only one more false move on your part and you'd have had the lot. If that's not an emergency, I'm damned if I know what is!"

Upset he'd been forced to detour from his flight path, the Whitley's navigator was also clearly shaken to learn that his crew might well have died of friendly fire that day. Kent fussed over the incident, too, perturbed that the RAF directive to change aircraft markings had gone astray, and that he could have shot down one of his own. But as vexing as the Whitley incident seemed, Kent's operational frustrations were just beginning. He still hadn't received a posting to combat operations at any of the front-line 11 Group fighter stations defending southern England. The vagaries of RAF decision-making kept thwarting him. On July 18, 1940, he was finally assigned to a combat squadron, RAF No. 54 Squadron at Hornchurch with 11 Group. But five days later he was rerouted to the Royal Aircraft Establishment and back test flying. Then they told him he'd fill the vacancy left by Henry Hall, his fellow AFC recipient in 1939, who had been moved out of RAF No. 257 Squadron at Northolt.

"The extraordinary difference between the First World War and this one," Kent wrote, was that "in the first you had to fight like hell to keep out of it, while in this one you had to fight like hell to get into it."

* * *

Four days after being posted to 257 Squadron, Kent got new orders yet again. He was to remain at Northolt station, but instead of joining the fighter pilots of 257 Squadron, he was to commence flight commander duties with a new squadron about to be formed and soon to share quarters with 257: RAF No. 303 Polish Squadron.

Kent was pleased with the outcome, but when he arrived at the station west of London, all he found was Squadron Leader (S/L) Ronald Kellett, two flight commanders, an intelligence officer, an orderly room corporal, and three non-commissioned officer (NCO) ground crew. There was no other staff, no operational fighter aircraft, and no Poles. When the Polish pilots did arrive, only two of them spoke any English. They all were fluent in French, at least, and Kellett, the commanding officer (CO), spoke French.

So, while Kent brushed up his French, he and the Polish pilots in his flight concocted a third means of communication, a phonetic combination of Polish and English words. Kent began by taking a couple of his new charges to one of the Hurricanes on the flight line and pointing at it.

"Ae-ro-plane," he said slowly and distinctly.

"Sa-mo-lot," they said in response.

Kent wrote the Polish word down phonetically and continued around the aircraft until he had a list of key aircraft parts, a glossary of terms written in phonetic Polish. He put the list on a pad that he planned to strap to his knee when giving instructions via radio from the cockpit of his aircraft.

Language barriers posed one problem. Teaching the idiosyncrasies of a British fighter aircraft was quite another. The Polish pilots had to learn to measure speed in miles per hour, not kilometres per hour, and fuel in gallons, not litres. More confusing, in the cockpits of Polish or French aircraft, the pilot increased power by pulling back on the throttle, while in a Hurricane he did it by pushing forward. Some of the Poles had no experience flying planes with retractable undercarriages—landing gear that folded into the belly on takeoff and vice versa on landing. When one of the Polish pilots landed his aircraft during an exercise with the undercarriage still retracted, Kent lost his temper.

"How in the hell do you think you're going to fight the Germans if you can't even fly the ruddy aeroplane?" he stormed.

"*Oui, mon commandant,*" said the young pilot apologetically.

Missteps and miscommunication at Johnny Kent's No. 303 Polish Squadron seemed a microcosm of the dysfunction facing much of RAF's Fighter Command in the middle of 1940. When the air defence of Britain required total preparedness, maximum precision, abundant aircraft with ground support, and, perhaps most important, battle experience, Fighter Command was lacking on all counts. Neither the time allotted nor the training accumulated seemed enough for the task at hand. An air force striving for independence from the two senior services still managed to misplace vital orders, couldn't post its aircrew efficiently, and kept running out of ammunition in training. And, in part because of setbacks in the retreat from France, serviceable fighter aircraft and ops-ready pilots always seemed in short supply.

Through the pivotal summer of 1940, the RAF's Fighter Command faced the prospect of defending four hundred miles of shoreline along England's south coast, as well as London and other major inland cities, and strategic air bases from Dover in the east to Plymouth in the west. It had to do so with precisely 768 fighter aircraft spread across four command groups and fifty-two combat squadrons. On paper, the Luftwaffe (German Air Force) had a commanding three-to-one advantage against the RAF, with an attacking force of about 2,250 bomber and fighter aircraft deployed across occupied western Europe.

On June 16, the very day France sought an armistice with Hitler, Winston Churchill addressed the British House of Commons for the third time in a month as prime minister. In thirty-six minutes, he delivered twenty-three pages of oratory, reiterating his comradeship with the French people, relaying messages of support from Canada and other Commonwealth Dominions, and acknowledging the fury that his enemy would soon unleash on Britain. He noted French general Maxime Weygand's pronouncement that the Battle of France was over, and coined the name for the next phase of the war when he said, "the Battle of Britain is about to begin."

"Let us therefore brace ourselves to our duties," concluded Churchill, "and so bear ourselves that, if the British Empire and its Commonwealth last for a thousand years, men will say, 'This was their finest hour.'"[19]

The Battle of Britain, as the Germans visualized it, would be fought in steps. The first would be *Kanalkampf* (Channel Battle) in July, as the Luftwaffe and Kriegsmarine (German Navy) eradicate all Allied shipping from the English Channel. Next, in August, *Adlerangriff* (Eagle Attack) would destroy fighter bases across southern England and eliminate the RAF fighter aircraft and their pilots from the battle. Then, if necessary, intense bombing of urban centres such as London would demoralize the British civilian population; this became known as *Zielwechsel* (Target Switch) and began in September. Finally, with the skies and seas clear of opposition, Hitler would launch

Seelöwe (Sea Lion), the full-scale invasion and conquest of the British Isles.

It must have occurred to newly minted flight commander Johnny Kent that the tumult of that first solo flight in a Moth over Winnipeg back in 1931, and the intentional collisions in his test aircraft with barrage balloons at Farnborough, and his unarmed reconnaissance flights at altitude over enemy installations all paled by comparison with the challenges of training a squadron of Polish fighter pilots to defend British skies from the Luftwaffe, whose bomber and fighter aircrew had earned decisive battle honours over Norway, France, and their native Poland. On reflection, rushing to Savile Row to buy that officer's dress uniform to receive a decoration from the King at Buckingham Palace, or fussing over his unrecorded victory versus that Messerschmidt pilot over the Seine, must have seemed frivolous in July 1940.

Now F/L Johnny Kent, like other fighter pilots from the United Kingdom, the Commonwealth, and the now-occupied nations of Europe, had to prepare himself and his squadron to face their enemy in mortal combat in the first great test of air endurance and survival of the Second World War: the Battle of Britain.

CHAPTER TWO

APPETITE TO FLY

I N THE WAKE OF THE GREAT WAR, AS MANY AS 2,500 CANADIANS
returned home from military service in the Royal Flying
Corps and the Royal Naval Air Service. Smitten by the
novelty and romance of flight, many of these First World
War veterans took to barnstorming and exhibition flying. The
Canadian public was curious enough to show up at aviation
exhibitions, and sometimes even to pay for the chance to spend
a few daring minutes aloft as a passenger. The creation of the
Air Board in 1919 gave the federal government a mandate
to establish regulations and standards for Canadian civil aviation, including the licensing of pilots and certification of their
aircraft. By 1920, the Air Board had issued fifty-six private
pilot certificates and 161 commercial certificates,[1] a modest
number considering what seemed a voracious postwar appetite
to fly.

Within a decade, however, everything changed. Aviation
exploits such as Charles Lindbergh's solo flight across the
Atlantic in 1927, Juan de la Cierva's travelling exhibit of his
anti-stall autogiro airplane in 1928, the transatlantic flight of

the British dirigible R100 to Canada in 1930, and Amelia Earhart's solo non-stop flight from Newfoundland to Northern Ireland in 1932 had Canadians clambering to get airborne. All forms of commercial flight—bush flying, barnstorming, airmail delivery, aerial mapping, passenger air service, and hobby flying—boomed across the country. Between 1926 and 1930, the number of companies operating aircraft in Canada increased to one hundred, the number of civil aircraft rose to 527, and distances flown and number of passengers carried multiplied some twenty times.[2]

In marked contrast, Canadian military authorities had let the country's air force wither. There were no replacements for retiring veterans and no money to upgrade semi-obsolete fighter aircraft. Journalist Leslie Roberts remembered listening to Alexander Maclean, then cabinet minister in the government of Robert Borden, comment to reporters on the "big cut" policy for the Canadian Air Force.* "Tell your young friends to keep their money and get themselves jobs," Maclean told them. "Canadian fliers have done remarkable work . . . But aviation is a war business. There'll never be a place for it in a world of peace."[3]

Meanwhile, to meet and regulate pent-up demand for civilian flying, the federal government in September 1927 passed an order-in-council approving the formation of private flying clubs. Ottawa agreed to donate two light aircraft (such as de Havilland Moths) to any community with an approved and

---

* In expectation that Canada would one day need air defence, within a separate service in case of war, the Air Board endorsed a request that King George V allow Canada's military air service to be renamed "Royal Canadian Air Force." It became official on April 1, 1924.

incorporated flying club. In return, those clubs had to procure an airport (with hangar and workshop), hire a pilot-instructor, and engage an aeromechanic. Each club seeking certification had to promise membership of at least thirty prospective pilots, plus ten licensed pilots wanting to continue flying. Clubs fulfilling those requirements would also receive from the government a $100 grant for each *ab initio* pupil who qualified for a private pilot's certificate or a commercial pilot's licence, up to $3,000 a year per club.[4]

Enthusiasm across Canada surpassed all expectations. The flying club movement opened facilities in Halifax, Granby, Ottawa, Montreal, Toronto, Hamilton, London, Winnipeg, Regina, Moose Jaw, Saskatoon, Calgary, Edmonton, and Victoria. The Montreal Light Aeroplane Club, at Saint-Hubert, Quebec, attracted such novice flyers as twenty-year-old Blair Dalzell "Dal" Russel.

"I learned the fundamentals of flying from veteran flyers of the Great War, earning a living as flying instructors," he said. "I completed my flying tests in 1938 and flew from time to time, just for the fun of it."[5]

Russel's family had moved from Toronto to Montreal in 1918, when he was less than a year old. He attended Selwyn House, an independent boys' school in Westmount, and later moved to Trinity College, a private boarding school in Port Hope, Ontario. He wasn't the best of students, but he excelled in sports, a "four-colour boy"[6] leading by example whatever hockey, football, cricket, or gymnastics team he joined. That ran in the family. Russel's father had played for the Montreal Victorias, earning him a place in the Hockey Hall of Fame.

Russel had nurtured his love of flying at the Montreal Light

Aeroplane Club. It was based at the Saint-Hubert aerodrome,[*] where the other principal tenant was No. 115 Non-Permanent Squadron of the RCAF's active reserve air force. It was at Saint-Hubert in 1939 that Canada's civil aviation and military aviation traditions intersected, with a profound impact on each.

"[When] war came again to the Canadian people, Canada was virtually unarmed . . . *sans* equipment," Leslie Roberts wrote. The RCAF's regular strength was just 3,048 officers and men.[7] Almost all of the RCAF's non-permanent (renamed "auxiliary") squadrons, including No. 115, suffered from a lack of equipment, insufficient training time, and a perpetual shortage of manpower. "But on the credit side of the ledger," continued Roberts, was "the known flair of Canadian youth for aerial combat clearly established in the world's first war in the air."[8]

As soon as Britain declared war on Germany in September 1939, Russel left his sales job with Dominion Steel and Coal Company to train full-time as a fighter pilot at the Saint-Hubert aerodrome. He joined fellow trainees who up until then "were weekend flyers, doing their training on little Fleet biplanes which were slow and light primary trainers. I was commissioned in [No. 115 Auxiliary Squadron] on September 15, 1939, and started intensive training."[9]

Six weeks later, Pilot Officer (P/O) Russel had advanced from biplane Fleet Finches at Saint-Hubert to faster, more

---

[*] Among numerous aviation firsts, the Saint-Hubert aerodrome was the first port-of-call for the British dirigible R100 in 1930, and home of *Pou du Ciel* (Flying Flea), a single-seat, single-engine hobby aeroplane (1933) flown locally by Montreal physician Dr. Georges Millette.

powerful, monoplane Harvards at Camp Borden, in central Ontario, where Canadian members of the Royal Flying Corps had been training for military service as far back as 1917. Under instruction, he followed a training syllabus based principally on the RAF model: day and night flying, air pilotage, bombing, reconnaissance and report writing, photo operations, fighting tactics, ground and air gunnery procedures, and signals.[10]

Several of Russel's classmates had also arrived at military training from the Montreal Light Aeroplane Club. George Gordon Hyde, from west-end Montreal, was the middle child of three. There wasn't a camera young George didn't like, or vice versa. At Westmount High and Trinity College his broad and frequent smile earned him the nickname "Kewp," from the Kewpie dolls of Rose O'Neill comic strip fame. Like Russel, Hyde had joined the flying club as a hobby and, at the outbreak of war, left his investment dealer's job in Montreal to join the 115th.

Engineering graduate Arthur Deane Nesbitt was twenty-three in 1933 when he joined the Montreal Light Aeroplane Club. He had been deemed the most competent pilot in the club, winning the James Lytell Memorial Trophy in 1936.

Other volunteers working their way into the fledgling RCAF had come from different military backgrounds around the country. Eric Beardmore, from Kitchener, Ontario, had served in the Victoria Rifles. He convinced the RCAF recruiting officer of his qualifications, claiming to have been "born in Berlin,"[11] the previous name for Kitchener (but residents had chosen to disassociate themselves from Germany during the Great War). Ross Smither grew up in an active and competitive family in London, Ontario. One brother, Walter, was working toward a medical career, while another, Sydney, had worked with the city's YMCA before enlisting in the RCAF. Ross attended H.B. Beal Technical School in the city, while also serving two years in the local militia. His technical training caught the eye of Air Force recruiters and, in 1930, Smither joined the RCAF as an aeromechanic (fitter). Not satisfied with working solely in ground crew, he next qualified as an air gunner and eventually for pilot training at the London Flying Club, which had received its federal charter two years before.[12] "Above average pilot with a good air sense," his instructor's assessment noted, and by the time the war broke out in 1939, Smither had received his flying officer's commission as a pilot in the RCAF and was ready for overseas posting. Until 1936, Charles Trevena had worked on the business side of the daily newspaper in his hometown, the *Regina Leader-Post*. Then, with enough savings for flying lessons on weekends, he took instruction with an RCAF auxiliary squadron. Early in 1940, the Air Force posted him overseas to an Army Co-op Training Squadron (ACT) flying Westland Lysander aircraft in Britain. He would eventually be transferred to RCAF No. 1 Fighter Squadron at Northolt air base.[13]

Hartland Molson, of the wealthy Quebec brewing family, had studied in Canada and in England before attending the Royal Military College in Kingston, Ontario, and serving with a field battery in the militia. When the war broke out, he was working as an accountant in Montreal but, like Russel, promptly quit and joined No. 115 Auxiliary Squadron. Beverley Christmas had grown up in the Quebec village of Saint-Hilaire and joined a long line of prospective air force volunteers in Montreal in 1938; however, his uncle procured an endorsement letter from the Great War ace Billy Bishop, and that helped Christmas gain a spot training with No. 115.

There were also several McGill law graduates in Russel's advanced trainee group, including Paul Pitcher, who had also studied in Switzerland. Pitcher noticed the common makeup of the auxiliary trainees, most of whom were racing against a ticking clock. "Most of us were professionals or business men in our late twenties and early thirties, some married, and quite conscious of the validity of the then current philosophy that, 'The ideal age for a fighter pilot in the [coming] Battle of Britain was nineteen years. After that you had more sense.'"[14]

* * *

While young Canadian aviators were chomping at the bit to go to war, their federal government had little appetite for an overseas military commitment. Four years into his third term as prime minister, William Lyon Mackenzie King, who'd initially come to power after the Great War by unifying pro- and anti-conscription factions within the country, had long emphasized domestic policies to stay in power. Through the 1920s and 1930s, he had championed lower taxes and social welfare policies such as old-age pensions, unemployment insurance, and family allowances, while asserting diplomatic independence from Mother England.* His government had led the "big cut" initiatives of Canada's air force in the 1920s,

---

* In 1922, when the Turkish military threatened to oust Greek armies by force from Chanak, a city on the Allied-occupied, neutral side of the Dardanelles Strait, Canada, France, and Italy refused military support to Britain against the takeover. War was averted when the Turks overwhelmed the Greeks and reached a negotiated settlement for the territory. This was Canada's first major assertion of diplomatic independence from the United Kingdom within the British Commonwealth of Nations.

suggesting to parliamentary opponents that "an air service for military purposes is the height of absurdity."[15]

Even four weeks into the war, in October 1939, when King and his government hosted a strategic war conference of British, Australian, New Zealand, and Canadian representatives to plan the training of Commonwealth airmen in Canada, he uttered out loud that the new war in Europe "was not Canada's war in the same sense that it was Great Britain's."[16] Notwithstanding these attitudes, King would build the RCAF into the world's fourth-largest air force by 1945.

The idea of joint training of pilots had been negotiated by the RCAF and the RAF as early as July 1938. Both air forces had worked out a common syllabus, the kind of aircraft to be used, how to acquire them, and how to integrate civilian flying clubs into the training pipeline. In the process, the Canadian government gained a greater appreciation of the importance that Air Ministry in London attached to air training in a rearmament race with Germany. Meanwhile, because of Prime Minister King's outspoken views about preserving Canadian sovereignty, the British recognized that any aircrew training in Canada would need to happen under the auspices of the RCAF.[17]

The relationship between the two air forces was nevertheless characterized by dithering and gamesmanship until Britain declared war against Nazi Germany on September 3, 1939. Canada officially joined the war on September 10. The same day, two RCAF officers in London—Wing Commander (W/C) F. Vernon Heakes, a liaison officer, and Group Captain (G/C) A.E. Godfrey, who was attending a course at the Imperial Defence College—were invited to a hastily arranged meeting at the Air Ministry. The British let on that they were worried about the RAF meeting personnel requirements if intensive air operations against the Luftwaffe commenced over western Europe. They wondered if Canadian air training systems could graduate as many as 2,000 military pilots a year, and just as many air observers and air gunners, to meet RAF demand. Air Ministry also wondered whether winter flying in Canada might limit instruction, where instructors and training aircraft might come from, as well as the availability of airfields to produce such vast numbers of military graduates. RAF Air Vice-Marshal (AVM) Charles Portal left nothing to the Canadians' imagination when he told Heakes and Godfrey that sending a Canadian expeditionary air force to Britain was *not* the priority.

"All Canadian resources should be concentrated on training [aircrew,]" Portal declared. He was even more blunt in his memoirs, explaining that Britain's "requirement" right then was for "bodies."[18]

The two Canadian air force officers met with Vincent Massey, Canadian High Commissioner to the United Kingdom. They told him that Air Ministry planned to send a mission to Canada to emphasize the need for air training on a grand scale.

"It occurred to me," Massey wrote later, "that Canada might be able to make a decisive contribution . . . by training Commonwealth airmen."[19] The next day, he elaborated on the idea with Stanley Bruce, his Australian counterpart, and the British government's dominions secretary, Anthony Eden, asking that "consideration be given to a scheme whereby Canadian, Australian, and New Zealand airmen should be trained in Canada . . . and sent to the front as distinctive Canadian, Australian, and New Zealand air forces."[20]

On September 26, 1939, British prime minister Neville Chamberlain sent an official request for aircrew training in Canada to Mackenzie King, emphasizing that an overwhelming air force was needed "to counter German air strength and . . . bring ultimate victory."[21] King had just finished supper and was resting in his library at Laurier House. Britain's plea for training pilots in Canada seemed to play into his hands perfectly. First, the proposed British Commonwealth Air Training Plan (BCATP) was significant—it would have to produce tens of thousands of aircrew annually (about half to be trained in Canada)[22]—and, given Canada's penchant for generating heroic fighter pilots in the Great War, an easy sell to the public. Second, a Commonwealth training plan based in Canada would likely not result in long casualty lists. Nor would there be the political risk of conscription for a large army, because the Canadian airmen in the scheme would all be volunteers. Finally, in wiring Canada's acceptance in principle to Britain, King recommended that additional discussions regarding the plan should take place in Ottawa, further emphasizing that the projected BCATP would happen largely on land and in air space sovereign to Canada.

Less than three weeks later, delegates from Britain and the three participating Commonwealth dominions gathered in Ottawa to hammer out details of the plan. The British arrived first. On October 31, Arthur Balfour (Lord Riverdale), leading the United Kingdom air training mission to Canada, met King's cabinet to present the BCATP proposal. It called for the training of 850 pilots, 510 air observers (or navigators), and 870 wireless radio operator/air gunners, or WAGs, every four weeks, or about 29,000 aircrew per year. While some elementary training would occur in Australia and New Zealand, pilot training in Canada would occur at twelve elementary flying training schools and then twenty-five advanced or service flying training schools. BCATP instructors would teach navigators at fifteen air observer schools and three navigation schools, gunners at fifteen bombing and gunnery schools, and wireless radio trainees at one large radio school. The more than seventy training locations would require 54,000 support personnel and an estimated 5,000 aircraft.

The British delegation estimated the total capital and maintenance costs for three years, the length of time the war was expected to last, at just short of $1 billion. The United Kingdom, explained the British delegates, would contribute its share of the cost in kind, with aircraft, engines, spare parts, and accessories worth about $140 million. Canada would be expected to cover $375 million in costs, as would Australia and New Zealand combined.

Prime Minister King's minister of finance, James L. Ralston, blanched at the price tag, saying Canada could not come within "shooting distance"[23] of affording 40 percent of the projected budget. He reminded the conference participants that the BCATP had to be considered within the context of Canada's other financial commitments. King almost insulted Lord Riverdale and company by calling the plan "a scheme suggested by the British government," and adding that "the British must be mainly responsible" for it.[24]

Clearly the principal players in the plan, Canada and Britain, had some tough negotiating to do. King presented two conditions for acceptance: first, that the British buy more Canadian wheat, and second, that the amount of credit Canada offered the UK for war purchases be restricted. That left Riverdale in the position of deciding whether training aircrew was militarily important enough to sacrifice purchasing credit, and whether Britain could dip deeper into its gold and securities supply to purchase weapons and Canadian wheat. In return for such concessions, Riverdale requested that Canada should give the training scheme the highest priority of all its war programs.

The horse trading continued when the Australian and New Zealand delegations arrived. The southern dominions feared the astronomical costs might bankrupt their governments. They also worried that they were contributing too high a proportion of aircrew to Commonwealth operations, given the ratios of 48 percent from Canada, 40 percent from Australia, and 12 percent from New Zealand. Those numbers were adjusted, based on population, to 57, 35, and 8 percent, respectively. The number of training sites was also recalculated, as was the total cost from inception to March 31, 1943, at $607 million. The question of who controlled this massive scheme was ultimately determined by politics and geography. King required that the overall administration of the BCATP would remain with the Canadian government, and its military command with the RCAF.

One stumbling block remained. When King reviewed the British draft of the BCATP announcement, he balked at article fifteen, which stated that "The United Kingdom Government undertakes that pupils of Canada, Australia and New Zealand shall, after training . . . be identified with their respective Dominions, either by organizing Dominion units or in some other way . . . The United Kingdom will initiate inter-governmental discussions to this end."[25] King inferred that the wording meant Canadians, for example, would still serve in RAF units, not RCAF ones.

29

Riverdale's position indeed recalled the RFC/RAF Canada training precedent during the First World War, which centralized command and control of all Commonwealth aerial resources in the RAF for convenience, efficiency, and economy. Air training plan graduates were incorporated as individuals into RAF squadrons.

Making yet another statement about Canadian sovereignty, King insisted the document make it clear that Canadian graduates shipped overseas would become part of RCAF units in the critical air battles to come. He described this point as "essential to Canadian participation in the scheme."[26]

Apart from the obvious conflict of national identities, the Canadian and British interpretations posed a whole new set of questions: How many RCAF squadrons might there be? How much would they cost? Would Canadian overseas squadrons consist of both RCAF aircrew and ground grew, or aircrew RCAF and ground crew RAF? And if Canada sent RCAF ground crew overseas, how would that hurt efficient running of the BCATP at home?

* * *

Even as the prime minister and Lord Riverdale haggled over the financing of the scheme and whether BCATP graduates would serve with RAF or RCAF patches on their shoulders, Canadian aircrew were already caught in an RAF public relations exercise in the UK. The British, wanting a display of solidarity between the mother country and the Commonwealth early in the war, were eager to see an RCAF unit at the front right away. And the Canadian government, realizing the massive financial commitment it was making to run the BCATP, made it clear to Britain that "sending an RCAF squadron over-seas should not be contemplated."[27]

Air Ministry came up with what it considered a perfect compromise—assemble Canadian airmen already enlisted and trained in the RAF system overseas into an existing RAF squadron; then assign a Canadian air force officer to lead it, and call it "Canadian." The British didn't even wait for the King government to approve the idea.[28] On paper, the airfield at Church Fenton officially became the home of RAF No. 242 All-Canadian Fighter Squadron on October 30, 1939. Two days later, Squadron Leader (S/L) Fowler M. Gobeil arrived at the base to take command.

Trained at the Royal Military College in 1927, and com-missioned in the RCAF in 1929, Gobeil was likely among the very few RCAF pilots with experience in actual fighter aircraft at that time; he'd flown Siskins as a member of the RCAF's aerobatic team. Promoted to squadron leader in 1939, Gobeil happened to be in Britain on an exchange posting that summer. Air Ministry took advantage of the coincidence and assigned Gobeil to command No. 242 Squadron. He arrived to find an aerodrome, hangars, and barracks, and nothing else. No planes and no aircrew.

In its haste to inaugurate the all-Canadian RAF fighter squadron, Air Ministry had neglected to assign any fighter aircraft and/or qualified Canadian fighter pilots. Gobeil immediately began scouring Britain's home-based squadrons, all thirty-one of them, for any Canadian RAF pilot officers (CAN/RAFs) he could find. He also sought out Canadian trainees in the RAF system to push them through to opera-tional efficiency as quickly as possible. Meanwhile, Air Ministry combed RAF units looking for Canadian aircrew tradesmen to help the new squadron transition from all British to mostly Canadian personnel from the ground up.

Early on, Gobeil welcomed an administrative officer with a unique background to assist him. P/O Peter D. MacDonald, from Halifax, had served with the 85th Battalion of the Canadian Expeditionary Force in the Great War. Postwar, he studied law in Britain and was elected as a member of Parliament representing the Isle of Wight. At No. 242, he became Gobeil's adjutant, responsible for stores, accounting, and records; just as important, MacDonald monitored activity and attitudes around the squadron.

S/L Gobeil's search for Canadian pilots was eased by the fact that as many as 118 Canadians had made their way to Britain and applied for the Direct Entry Scheme in 1938 and 1939. Like Johnny Kent, who'd convinced his parents to pay his way to Britain to apply for a Short Service Commission in the RAF, most of the potential No. 242 Squadron acquisitions had earned their private licences in Canada, before making their way to Britain. They'd had little or no guarantee the RAF would accept them,[29] but they'd arrived in the UK, been interviewed, completed medical exams, and hoped they'd made the grade. Once they'd received RAF probationary pilot officers' commissions, the recruits had been sent to elementary flight training schools; some had gone on to service flight training schools; and the best fliers had moved on to operational training units. But virtually none of those whom Gobeil considered for No. 242 Squadron had fired fighter aircraft guns in anger.

Much like the aircrew in Canada's voluntary non-permanent (auxiliary) squadrons at home, the newly acquired No. 242 airmen tended to be older than most volunteers at that stage of the war, on average twenty-three years old. Five of Canada's nine provinces—Ontario, British Columbia, Alberta, Saskatchewan, and Manitoba—were represented among them. Indeed, their diverse origins spoke volumes about who they were, why they'd enlisted, and how they might perform. They represented nearly every Canadian walk of life. These pilots, the majority of whom arrived at Church Fenton in the first week of November 1939, quickly became Gobeil's primary candidates for secondment to No. 242 Squadron.[30]

Among the earliest to arrive was Flight Lieutenant (F/L) John Sullivan, from Smiths Falls, Ontario, who had served previously in the RCMP. Flying Officer (F/O) John W. Graafstra, of Souris, Manitoba, had come to Britain as a music student. F/O Lorne Chambers, from Vernon, British Columbia, was among the few with actual experience flying Spitfires, which he'd acquired with RAF No. 74 Squadron. P/O Marvin K. Brown, from Kincardine, Ontario, had worked on staff at the University of Toronto, while P/O Noel Stansfeld, born in Edmonton, had worked with Standard Oil and, later, as a stockbroker. F/O James Mitchell, of Kirkfield, Ontario, was following in the footsteps of his father, who'd served in the Royal Flying Corps in the Great War. P/O Roland Dibnah, from Winnipeg, had experience as a printer, while fellow Winnipegger P/O Jack Benzie had served in two different militia regiments before his direct entry to the RAF.

F/L Donald Miller, from Saskatoon, had sailed to England on his own initiative and was literally walking the streets of London when he learned he'd been accepted into the RAF. P/O Arthur Deacon, from Invermay, Saskatchewan, had done it all in civilian life—hardware salesman, hockey player, and band leader. Meanwhile, as a former salmon fisherman based in Victoria, BC, P/O John Latta had worked with retired British mariner Captain (Capt) Henry Seymour-Biggs, who helped Latta prepare his papers and gather enough references to attract S/L Gobeil's attention.

By the end of November, RAF No. 242 All-Canadian Fighter Squadron had its full complement of eighteen pilots and 178 ground crewmen. The Church Fenton aerodrome that Canadian newcomers found when they arrived was only two years old, but hardly leading edge. Its non-commissioned officers' barracks housed thirty men (mostly NCO ground crew) in a room, with each man allocated a steel locker, wooden stand, and three-piece mattress, called a biscuit because it resembled hardtack. Junior officers fared better, two men to a small room with furnishings. Food served at the aircrew messes wasn't memorable; a greasy stew was the staple, so the Canadians generally smothered what was served in Heinz ketchup. Pilot officers made fourteen shillings six pence a day; flying officers eighteen shillings, six pence; flight lieutenants one pound,* one shilling, nine pence a day.[31]

The creation and equipping of the "Canadian" fighter squadron overseas had happened in secret. The press only learned about the existence and makeup of No. 242 Squadron on December 1, 1939. And, even then, the joint Anglo-Canadian press release, intended as a public relations boost for both parties, was misleading. It gave the impression that No. 242's pilots were "about to take [their] place in the first line of air defence" of Britain.[32] Nothing could've been further from the truth.

---

* One pound in 1940 is roughly equivalent to seventy pounds today; that amounts to £490 per week, or £25,480 annually, which is just below the average salary in the UK today.

When training aircraft finally arrived at Church Fenton, they were not Spitfires or Hurricanes but Magisters, Harvards, and Fairey Battles—aircraft the Canadian pilots recognized as service training aircraft, not operational fighters. They commenced training with what they had, but when asked their preference, to a man they said, "Spitfires!" Instead, No. 242 received Blenheim bombers and more Fairey Battles. RAF trainers often chose Fairey Battle aircraft, with their Merlin engines and retractable undercarriages, as a means of preparing their pilots for high-performance Hurricanes and Spitfires.[33]

The miscommunication continued. On December 9, RAF AVM Richard E. Saul, Canadian High Commissioner Vincent Massey, and other dignitaries arrived with Canadian war correspondents to report on the progress of the squadron. Their stories gave the impression that No. 242 pilots had already experienced dogfights and were combat veterans. CBC reporter Matthew Halton queried CAN/RAF P/O Stan Turner about the experience of flying Spitfires—some were actually parked for the day on Church Fenton's flight line. Turner dodged the question.

Percival Stanley Turner was born in England in 1913 and raised in Toronto. Stocky, strong, and with a permanent look of intent on his youthful face, he had worked as a lifeguard, applying his wages to pay for flying lessons. Acquiring his private pilot's licence helped him qualify for RCAF No. 110 ACT Squadron in the 1930s. By October 1938, the RAF had accepted Turner into its Short Service Commission program, and a year later, P/O Turner was sent to operational training; he'd piloted Lysanders, Magisters, Gladiators, Blenheims, and Battles, but not Spitfires. Nevertheless, he expressed to interviewer Halton the impatience that he and many of his comrade pilot officers at No. 242 were feeling: "We are dying for this war to start."

* * *

Not all Canadians serving in the RAF would have to wait to provide meaningful service. Johnny Kent was already decorated and in the training stream for operational combat. Bob Niven, who had entered the RAF on a Short Service Commission and become proficient on every fighter and bomber in its arsenal, had also carved a unique role for himself. Niven was born in Calgary in 1913, one year after the first Calgary Stampede, "the greatest outdoor show on earth." His family lived near the Stampede grounds, but he was more interested in air displays than rodeo. At age fifteen, he quit school to take an aviation course at the Calgary Aero Club and was soon apprenticing there as an aero-engineer. Next, he lobbied the Provincial Institute of Technology in Calgary to teach an aeronautics course. He was among its first graduates in 1931.[34]

Not long after joining the RAF, Niven came to the attention of W/C Fred Winterbotham at Britain's Secret Intelligence Service (SIS), MI6. Winterbotham had realized that "in a war of rapid movement . . . rapid and accurate information about the enemy's intentions might well mean the difference between swift defeat and eventual victory."[35]

In pursuit of visual intelligence in the months before the war began, early in 1939, Winterbotham organized the Air Section of SIS and instructed British Civil Airlines to order a cabin-heated Lockheed 12A Electra aircraft from the United States.[36] SIS seconded Australian flyer W/C Sidney

Cotton and Canadian navigation and engineering specialist F/L Bob Niven to enhance the Electra's features. At Heston Aerodrome outside London, they installed two extra fuel tanks in the cabin to extend the aircraft's range from 700 to 1,600 miles. Technicians fitted two Leica cameras (ironically, manufactured in Germany) behind close-fitting sliding panels, one camera under each wing. The sliding panels were controlled by a switch hidden under the pilot's seat, and a heating system kept the lenses from frosting over at high altitude. Each Leica could take a total of 250 exposures, and together they delivered overlapping images.[37]

In the summer of 1939, Niven and Cotton took off on their first high-altitude spying mission to photograph activity along the German Siegfried Line, a four-hundred-mile-long defensive wall that extended from Nazi Germany's western frontier with the Netherlands, Belgium, and Luxembourg to Switzerland. Flying at 20,000 feet, the Lockheed drew little attention, and its cameras filmed vast stretches of bunkers, tank traps, and reinforced concrete that the Nazis called *Westwall.*

In those final months before war broke out, the team flew the Electra to Paris to share intelligence techniques with French allies. Then, at the invitation of the commandant of Tempelhof Airport in Berlin, the Electra crew attended a flying rally in Frankfurt, Germany. Using cover of the non-existent Aeronautical Research and Sales Corporation of London, they convinced local hosts to guide them over the River Rhine, where most of Germany's munitions factories were located. They enhanced the ruse by bringing two British women, Andrea Johansen and Patricia Martin, as their civilian travelling partners on the flights. As their guests guided them over the Rhine, with Cotton piloting the Electra and

Niven navigating, the women secretly slid back the doors and took photos. "My Lockheed," Winterbotham wrote, "became the forerunner of all spy planes responsible for most of the accurate ground intelligence . . . during the war."[38]

After September 3, 1939, Niven and Cotton modified two "unofficially borrowed"[39] Spitfires, removing their radios, guns, armour, and instruments, and installing camera equipment similar to what had been on the Lockheed so they could take pictures at 30,000 feet. By January 1940, the RAF had given the aviation photo reconnaissance group official status as the Photographic Development Unit. In May 1940, Johnny Kent was one of two more Canadian pilots to join the unit; F/O George Christie, from Westmount, Quebec, followed in June. Christie had flown Hurricane fighters for the first seven months of the war with No. 43 Squadron, so he transitioned perfectly to Spitfires, which by now had also been camouflaged in bright blue, high-gloss paint. The high-altitude Spitfire photos caught the end of the phoney war on film. "It was one of our Spitfire spy planes flying over the French sector," Winterbotham wrote, "which saw the vast armada of German tanks assembling in the Ardennes on May the eighth."[40]

The RAF would later decorate Bob Niven, Sidney Cotton, and George Christie with Distinguished Flying Cross awards for their innovative photo reconnaissance service. All this, and the Battle of Britain hadn't yet begun.

* * *

In the last days of 1939, the two months of to-and-fro exchanges among the four signatories of the British Commonwealth Air Training Plan concluded. Mackenzie King had been pushing to get the plan settled, signed, and announced before the 1st Canadian Division arrived in Britain. It was due around New Year's Day, but the Canadian prime minister didn't want the landing of Canada's expeditionary force to upstage his historic air training announcement. He set a deadline of December 17. Negotiations continued right up to a few minutes before midnight on December 16, when Prime Minister King and Lord Riverdale finally signed the agreement into existence.

King explained the urgency of the BCATP in a speech to Canadians from the House of Commons:

> Tonight, I am speaking particularly of those belonging to the Royal Canadian Air Force. The young men . . . are, I am convinced, fully aware of the appalling nature of the situations facing the world today, and of what it will demand by way of sacrifice ere peace is again restored. . . .
>
> It is not in a spirit of adventure that they are pressing forward in such numbers. Rather are they enlisting in the spirit of the Crusaders of old, prepared, if need be, to give their lives for what, to them and to us, is holy and sacred— the birthright of liberty and happiness in a free land. . . .
>
> In making provision for this vast undertaking, the Government [of Canada] has done so knowing that nothing can be left to haste or to chance. The intricate machine must be perfect. In every phase of their work, the men must be trained by the highest skill, and under the best conditions it is possible for the country to provide. In no other area of the defence services is a man obliged to rely more completely upon his own initiative, his own knowledge, and his own judgment.[41]

Another reason Mackenzie King had been insistent about signing the BCATP into law on December 17, 1939, was that it was
his sixty-fifth birthday. Just before he retired for the night, King
recorded in his diary that "it was certainly a memorable birthday. I suppose no more significant Agreement has ever been
signed by the Government of Canada, or signature placed in
the name of Canada to definitely defined obligation."[42]

In its lifetime, the BCATP would train 72,835 RCAF airmen, 42,110 RAF airmen (including about 2,000 Free French,
900 Czechs, 677 Norwegians, 448 Poles, and 800 Belgian and
Dutch aircrew), 5,296 Royal Navy Fleet Air Arm personnel,
9,606 Royal Australian Air Force personnel, and 7,002 Royal
New Zealand Air Force personnel. Among its graduates were
as many as 6,000 Americans who (until December 7, 1941)
violated the US Neutrality Act of 1937 to join a military air
force at war. The plan would also graduate between 40,000
and 45,000 ground crew tradesmen. Total production of the
BCATP between 1939 and 1945 approached 200,000 personnel.[43] The BCATP would prove to be a major contributor to
the air supremacy the Allies achieved in every theatre of war
by 1944.[44]

* * *

Apart from a few skirmishes, both Germany and the Allies stayed
behind their defences during the phoney war, which lasted until
May 1940. In the British press, it was known as "Sitzkrieg."
Anticipating German advances into the Low Countries, French
forces were entrenching themselves along the Maginot Line, an
array of defences built in the 1930s along the German border
to thwart any future invasion. British Expeditionary Forces, in a

laborious mission, crossed the Channel to reinforce France. At sea, Britain imposed a naval blockade on Germany, losing a number of her aircraft carriers and destroyers in the process. Apart from several bombing raids and reconnaissance missions by both sides, the skies remained relatively quiet. The feared aerial attack on the British home front was yet months away.

Meanwhile, at No. 242, S/L Gobeil kept his Canadian pilots busy with lectures about aircraft recognition, tactics, and battle orders, and plenty of simulator flying in Link Trainers.* The commanding officer ensured that his Canadian aircrew enjoyed Christmas and New Year's treats and entertainment. The station even hosted a wedding. In December, F/O Richard Coe, from Winfield, BC, learned that his Canadian sweetheart, Pauline Browne, had arrived in Britain. The couple hadn't seen each other in two years. Gobeil offered to give the bride away, and No. 242 celebrated the couple's marriage ceremony on December 9.

As 1939 drew to a close, word leaked from Air Ministry that the RAF would assign ten fighter squadrons to provide air support for Royal Navy convoys in waters off the British Isles, as well as for Allied expeditionary forces arriving in France. The RAF had already committed twenty-seven squadrons to France, among them six fighter squadrons.

The Air Ministry memo suggested Britain's war strategists would equip the Canadian squadron with Hawker Hurricanes

---

* Edwin Albert Link grew up in Binghamton, New York, where his father ran an organ and piano manufacturing company. Flying lessons in the 1920s for Link Jr. (at twenty-five dollars an hour) proved expensive. So, in 1929, he patented a cockpit-like device with a simulated instrument panel and control stick floating on a set of organ bellows, simulating an aircraft in flight. The Link Trainer is credited with teaching more than two million military and commercial pilots.

and attach it to Canadian ground troops if and when they were sent to France. But when members of No. 242 returned from New Year's leave in January 1940, Gobeil received orders to proceed to Saint Athan, South Wales, and fly the squadron's first six Hurricanes home to Church Fenton. En route, the pilots encountered a sudden blast of winter weather, more snowfall than forecasters had seen in forty years, requiring all the pilots to come down in forced landings. Gobeil's fighter overturned in his landing; he was unhurt. Pilots John Sullivan, John Graafstra, and Stan Turner landed without mishap, but the recently married F/O Richard Coe crashed and was killed near Warrington, Lancashire. He became the squadron's first fatality.

The blizzard conditions didn't permit a resumption of flying until February 10, when the last of the Hurricanes arrived at Church Fenton. Operational training with the new fighters began immediately. Aircrew worked almost around the clock on formation flying, radio-telephone procedures, night flying, and tactical exercises. They also sorted out remaining issues of identity. There was a question of whether CAN/RAF pilots would be allowed to wear "Canada" shoulder flashes on their RAF uniforms. Initially, only S/L Gobeil had permission to wear one. Other Canadian aircrew at the station, including ground crew, requested the same status. Eventually, it was granted.

Some individual aircrew members were meanwhile working out their own identities. Among No. 242's earliest arrivals was P/O William Lidstone McKnight. He arrived at Church Fenton just shy of his twenty-first birthday, in November 1939. Originally from Edmonton, McKnight was short in stature but handsome, with, according to an acquaintance, "a wonderful

grin."[45] McKnight's grin belied a troubled childhood and ado-
lescence. At twelve, he lost his mother due to complications
in childbirth. He served several years in the militia before
enrolling in medical school at the University of Alberta in
1937. After a year of run-ins with administration over his
behaviour—one night he led a snake dance of partygoers
into downtown Edmonton traffic—he was dismissed from the
medical program. His friend and neighbour, Harry Pegler,
remembered that, almost immediately, McKnight enlisted in
the RAF. By April 1939, he'd earned acting pilot officer rank
and joined RAF No. 242 All-Canadian Fighter Squadron. "He
was having trouble finding himself," Pegler said of McKnight.
"I think he went over there to get the hell out of the way."[46]

McKnight didn't shake his intense nature in the RAF. On
a leave, he wrote a friend at home about his difficulties adapt-
ing to English attitudes. He sensed they disliked the Canadian
airmen overseas, although he acknowledged that "we really
are an ignorant bunch of beggars when it comes to knowing
how to drink or talk."[47]

None of that seemed to matter, however, when pilots such
as Willie McKnight and Stan Turner got into the cockpits of
the recently arrived Hurricanes for combat practice. Each
eagerly followed, and eventually led, flights of three, four, or
six fighters climbing to 20,000 feet or higher and repeating
standard RAF attack procedures. A No. 1 Attack, with the
fighters flying in a line-astern formation, called for the leader
to fire at a towed target, followed by each of the others in
rapid sequence. A No. 2 Attack featured two fighters abreast,
attacking two enemy aircraft (the pattern could also call for two
line-astern strings of Hurricanes delivering a No. 1 Attack).
A No. 3 Attack brought three fighters together to attack an

enemy target from the rear, the side, and the rear quarter (behind and to the side) simultaneously.[48]

"Our machines are all being specially re-equipped with armor plating, self-sealing tanks," McKnight wrote home. "And, by the time they're finished, we'll be the most modernly equipped squadron in the service."[49]

As the winter cold and snow retreated, anticipation grew for No. 242 pilots and ground crew that they'd be thrown into actual operations. The squadron war diarist optimistically wrote of the expected mobilization, "France for Easter."[50] In March, the flyers dodged remaining bad weather to conduct day and night practice sorties. They harmonized their guns, meaning that they set the distance in front of the fighter where bullets would converge. Toward the end of the month, RAF officers from 13 Group Headquarters supervised the Canadians as they launched a scramble interception, formation flight, and Nos. 1, 2, and 3 Attack simulations against a friendly air-borne Blenheim bomber. The supervising officer, sitting in the Blenheim turret, was impressed. The squadron appeared ready for combat in the skies over France, even if the orders to send them there remained in flux. Unfortunately, No. 242 endured another loss as P/O Hugh Niccolls's Hurricane crashed and burned, killing a favourite among the Saskatchewan flyers.

* * *

The phoney war ended the first week of April 1940. A complacent Prime Minister Neville Chamberlain claimed Adolf Hitler had "missed the bus" by delaying his offensive in western Europe by half a year. The führer, in fact, had put his plan, "Sickle," to attack the Netherlands, Belgium, and Luxembourg on hold while he personally took oversight of Plan *Weser*, the invasion of Norway and Denmark. By the beginning of June, the German occupation of Scandinavia was complete. Hitler launched his blitzkrieg into the Low Countries on May 10, committing seven panzer, three motorized, and thirty-four infantry divisions with the support of 2,700 combat aircraft.

That same day, Count Julius von Zech-Burkersroda, the German ambassador to the Netherlands, paid a visit to the Dutch foreign ministry. Acting on Hitler's orders, the ambassador explained to Dutch authorities that German troops had crossed the border into the Netherlands to secure Dutch neutrality against the threat of French and British armies. Simultaneously, the German ambassador to Belgium parroted the same excuse of pre-emptive action in Brussels. In response, Paul-Henri Spaak, the Belgian foreign minister, called out the German mobilization for exactly what it was. "It's the second time in twenty-five years that Germany has committed a criminal aggression against a neutral Belgium," he scolded the German ambassador. "What has just happened is even more odious than in 1914."[51]

As far as Hitler was concerned, the breaches of neutrality meant nothing. Even as his ambassadors delivered their ultimatums, German armies swept across nearly two hundred miles of international border, from Luxembourg to Flanders, and Luftwaffe bombers converged on seventy different Allied airfields. Hermann Göring had dispatched as many as 1,400 Luftwaffe bombers and fighter aircraft to destroy those "neutral" ports and shipping, while also preventing Allied air forces from counterattacking German forces on the ground. The French Armée de l'Air marshalled some 275 day fighters, fifteen day bombers, and fifty-five night bombers, but was overmatched by the Luftwaffe juggernaut.[52] Few, if any, of its pilots had anywhere near the combat experience of the men at the controls of Göring's Me 109s.

Also on May 10, Neville Chamberlain resigned as prime minister in the face of a non-confidence vote. Winston Churchill assembled a national coalition government and at 6:30 p.m. kissed the hand of King George VI to take power in the British House of Commons. That night, he and his new war cabinet ordered RAF Bomber Command to organize whatever attacks they could against targets west of the River Rhine to slow the German advance.

Almost immediately, French prime minister Paul Reynaud appealed to Churchill to send ten more squadrons. With six of the RAF's fifty-two fighter squadrons already in France, Churchill permitted four more to join them, bringing RAF Advanced Air Striking Force strength on the continent to four hundred bombers and fighters. The Luftwaffe outnumbered them roughly four-to-one.

On May 13, Fighter Command ordered four of No. 242's most advanced pilots—John Sullivan, Robert Grassick, Stan Turner, and Willie McKnight—to proceed immediately to France and fly with RAF No. 607 Squadron at Vitry-en-Artois. The next day, all four scrambled into action on a patrol with twenty other Hurricanes over Louvain, Belgium. They immediately tangled with fifteen German reconnaissance aircraft escorted by forty-five Me 109s. The dogfight resulted in ten enemy aircraft downed, but four Hurricanes were lost as well, including the one flown by Sullivan. One report claimed Sullivan bailed out but was fired upon and killed as he descended under his parachute; he was the first airman from No. 242 killed in action during the war.

* * *

It had taken German armies just sixty-two days to overrun and occupy Norway earlier that spring, at a cost of 2,700 German casualties and 7,000 Allied troops. The government of Norway, led by King Haakon, managed to escape to England to form a government-in-exile in London. Among its first decrees was to send to Canada 120 Norwegian naval and army flyers who'd escaped capture by the Nazis. By mid-summer 1940, two Norwegian coastal steamers had delivered the Scandinavian airmen to Toronto Island Airport. There, in "Little Norway," they became among the first international students of Mackenzie King's prized British Commonwealth Air Training Plan. To start, the cadets flew elementary training circuits in Moths and Fleet Finches. As with most Allied nations this early in the war, Canada was short of serviceable aircraft. Eventually, the pilot trainees of the Royal Norwegian Air Force would fly American-built Fairchild PT-19 Cornells.

The RCAF's home-based auxiliary squadrons were meanwhile tasked with the "Defence of Canada,"[53] including army co-operation duties on two coasts, carrying out reconnaissance, air strike, air defence, and coast artillery support. To meet all those requirements, the RCAF's fourteen active service squadrons had at their disposal exactly 252 combat aircraft: twenty-four Hurricanes, eighteen Blenheims, thirty-four Bolingbrokes, twenty Digbys, thirty Stranraers, twenty-four Hudsons, sixty-six Lysanders, and thirty-six Canso flying boats.[54]

Like the CAN/RAF airmen overseas, most auxiliary squadron fighter pilots at home were eager to fly front-line fighter aircraft. So when a shipment of seven used Hawker

Hurricanes arrived from the UK at the RCAF aerodrome in Vancouver early in 1940,[55] everybody wanted to get airborne in the latest and greatest. First, the planes received a once-over from the station's air-engine instructor. When Bill Dunphy uncrated the fighters for a peek, he spotted trouble. It was a teaching opportunity for his young aeromechanic trainees.

"When we took the tops of the engines off, we could see evidence that the engines had been overstrained," Dunphy said. "The damage was pretty obvious. The valves were not only rusted, but they were bent as well. So, we took them all apart and fixed them."[56]

On the very day he and his aeromechanic students finished their overhaul of the Hurricanes' Rolls-Royce Merlin engines, the station received orders to pack the fighter aircraft back in their crates and transport them cross-country by rail to Halifax for transatlantic shipment to the UK. Eager and qualified as P/O Dal Russel and his colleagues may have been to fly Hurricanes at an operational training unit in Canada, they would have to wait to rendezvous with their fighter aircraft overseas.

Events in Europe were now overtaking efforts to get those Hurricane fighter aircraft and their Canadian fighter pilots into skies over the front lines: the German army had rolled into Scandinavia and the Low Countries. When (now) F/O Russel received his graduate wings brevet at Borden air base and was posted to the RCAF Central Flying School at Trenton, Ontario, he had felt certain that the air force would keep him in Canada and assign him flying instructor duties in the fledgling BCATP, teaching the first classes of trainees. He had guessed wrong.

"I was overjoyed to hear that I was going to England with a fighter squadron," Russel said.[57] Air Force strategists had

48

created a composite squadron, combining No. 115 Auxiliary Squadron pilots with other pilots recently graduated from service flight training and a group of seasoned airmen from the peacetime RCAF. The newly christened RCAF No. 1 Fighter Squadron was told to prepare for embarkation to the United Kingdom.

In command of the newborn Canadian squadron was Ernest McNab. Born in 1906, the son of a Rosthern, Saskatchewan grain elevator owner/operator, Ernest was driven and self-confident from the start. One morning, as a child at church, he faced taunts from his Sunday school classmates for dressing in a kilt that his parents insisted he wear. With a single punch, the stocky farm kid levelled one of his loudest critics, and the taunts ended pronto. He later enrolled in engineering at the University of Saskatchewan and stood out in collegiate sports, easily making the Saskatchewan boxing team and first-string football team. Now nicknamed "Pee-Wee," McNab took flying lessons with his friends on weekends. In 1926, at age twenty, he enlisted in the RCAF, but despite being a novice he earned a provisional pilot officers' commission and survived across-the-board air force cuts that had reduced its nearly nine hundred officers and men to fewer than eight hundred.[58]

As the RCAF began to reverse its big-cut mentality of the late 1920s and early 1930s, it received a shipment of nine Armstrong Whitworth Siskins, then the RAF's front-line fighter aircraft, and six Armstrong Whitworth Atlases, their leading-edge army co-operation aircraft. The RCAF had just taken F/O McNab on strength at Trenton, Ontario, where the as-yet-uncrated Siskins became an integral part of an RCAF aerobatics team.

The Canadian National Exhibition (CNE) in Toronto informed Trenton that CNE entertainment organizers had booked a US Air Corps squadron of Curtiss Hawks to perform an air show in the skies over the west-end Toronto summer fair. Would the RCAF like to join in? "Two days before the C.N.E.," said McNab, "[we] decided we had to do something spectacular, so [we] added to our few manoeuvres, spinning in formation."[59]

At the best of times, spinning an aircraft—putting it into an aggravated stall that causes the plane to descend in a corkscrew path—is a dangerous choice. Doing it with three aircraft simultaneously in formation is even more so. Nevertheless, McNab, F/O Dave Harding, and P/O E.A. McGowan practised the stunt at Camp Borden. "It consisted of No. 1 and No. 2 wing men moving out two [wing]spans from the leader. The three [pilots] then picked a point on the horizon, put the aircraft in a right-hand spin, coming out on a picked point on the third turn. It worked!"

The outrageous manoeuvre must have captivated its spectators, because the Canadian Flying Clubs Association invited the Siskin aerobatics team to a full schedule of air displays as part of its 1931 Trans-Canada Air Pageant, designed to stimulate public interest in aviation. McNab and his two aerobatics partners survived their death-defying stunt at air demonstrations from Charlottetown, PEI, to Vancouver throughout 1930 and 1931. "During the years I spent on flight formation flying, I never heard of any unit in the US or UK even contemplating incorporating this manoeuvre in their program. But they didn't have a Dave Harding and two dumb wing men."

McNab rose quickly among other Canadian recruits in RCAF No. 115 Auxiliary Squadron at the Saint-Hubert aerodrome. He was thirty-three in November 1939, when he took command of No. 1 Fighter Squadron. The following spring, he and his charges boarded the Canadian Pacific troopship RMS *Duchess of Atholl*, sailing from Halifax on June 11, all eager to get into the air war. Ten days later, they arrived in Blackpool on the Irish Sea coast of England and proceeded to the temporary home base of RCAF No. 1 at Middle Wallop in Hampshire (it would soon move to Croydon). That's where Russel and his squadron comrades got their hands on the control columns of Hawker Hurricanes for the first time. Six weeks later, on August 17, the RCAF No. 1 Fighter Squadron was declared operational, just in time to join the daily scrambles of the Battle of Britain.

CHAPTER THREE

THE HURRICANE DRAIN

WHEN AVIATION WAS STILL YOUNG, CITIZENS OF SAINT John and its surrounding area flocked every summer to the tiny suburb of Millidgeville, home of the Saint John Flying Club, to see the Trans-Canada Air Pageant. The community at the mouth of New Brunswick's Saint John River witnessed a virtual who's who of civil aviation in the late 1920s and early 1930s. The spectacular RCAF Siskin fighter aerobatics team had visited, as well as such notable aviators and aviatrixes as Al Cheeseman, who'd flown with expeditions to the Antarctic, Amelia Earhart, who'd begun her solo transatlantic flight in Millidgeville in 1932, and decorated Great War ace Captain Wendell Rogers, who had helped establish the Saint John Flying Club in 1928.

In 1931, spectators at the annual air pageant spotted a youngster, dressed in a Boy Scout uniform, ducking under a restraining rope for a closer look at a Gypsy Moth biplane parked on the airshow flight line. Some called out, shooing the boy away from the privately owned plane. That, of course, drew more attention to him. Ignoring the crowd, the boy walked the full length of the Moth, admiring its features. Then, in an instant, he jumped into the cockpit, eliciting a crescendo of concern from the audience.

"Suddenly, the aircraft started with a roar," reported the local newspaper, "[and ran] along the ground with increasing speed, zig-zagging in apparent frantic helplessness and then took off . . ."[1]

The Boy Scout at the controls then dazzled the spectators on the ground with breathtaking rolls and spins in the airborne Moth. Kids hooted and women screamed at the aerobatics demonstration. Not until the boy pilot descended safely, completing his clowning act, did the Saint John audience realize "it was all part of the show."

At the controls was fifteen-year-old Kirkpatrick Sclanders, whom those in-the-know at the flying club called "the youngest pilot in the entire Dominion."[2] Born in Saskatoon, raised in Saint John, Pat (as he was known) grew up overlooking the harbour, with sailboats and motor boats circulating constantly from a holiday camp almost at his front door. None of that interested him. He was hooked on airplane models, aviation pulp magazines, and the periodic takeoffs and landings of Tiger Moths or Gypsy Moths at the Millidgeville airfield. At fourteen, he won a contest, searching out technical mistakes—net and gross tonnage, horsepower, cruising speed, wing area, lifting tension—in a puzzle on the back page of *Flying Aces* magazine. His prize was a leather helmet and goggles, which he used during flying lessons at the local flying club. Both his flight training and his profile with aviation magazines took off. Magazine editor Cyril Caldwell invited young Pat to submit articles to *Aero Digest* in the US, launching his teenage journalism career.

That same year the Saint John Flying Club boasted a new record. "Fifteen-year-old Pat Sclanders, a student at Saint John High School, made his first solo flight yesterday at the civic airport after five hours and forty minutes of instruction," reported the local newspaper in 1931. "He is believed the youngest airman in New Brunswick."[3]

Once the Boy Scout barnstorming novelty wore off, Sclanders acquired his "A" licence, allowing him to take a passenger aloft in a biplane. He then joined businessman Bernard McElwaine in distributing advertising circulars by tossing them from their low-flying Moth, which worked well until the leaflets too often fluttered into the Moth's vertical stabilizer, bunging up the rudder.[4] The young aviator flew at every opportunity, once buzzing McElwaine's girlfriend, Molly Bramley-Moore, as she arrived from New York for a summer holiday in New Brunswick.[5]

When the RAF offered air training and commissions in the mid-1930s, Sclanders dashed aboard a cattle boat to Britain and on arrival began military flight instruction. He whizzed through elementary training at Uxbridge aerodrome and service training at Grantham air base. One of Leading Aircraftman (LAC) Sclanders's classmates, in No. 16 Course, was Bob Stanford Tuck, a former merchant sailor from Catford, England. Tuck would later command RAF No. 257 Fighter Squadron in the Battle of Britain. At Grantham they trained under Flying Officer Alec P.S. Wills, who assessed them both as keen but "quite unsafe."[6]

"We used to have great fun together," recalled Tuck.[7] He and Sclanders would fly solo, each in a Hawker Hart training aircraft, "beating up" the countryside. Once they'd completed their requisite cross-country patterns, they'd fly under bridges, buzz railway stations at low-level, and perform aerobatics a few hundred feet above the ground. On one occasion, instructor Wills found greenery lodged in the Hart's undercarriage.

"How did this happen?" he asked.

"Got lost, sir," Tuck answered. "Had to get down pretty low to read the name of the railway station."

"I know you're hot stuff," said Wills. "But I want you to remember this: nobody ever gets to know everything about flying. Nobody. Understand?"[8]

In June 1936, Sclanders received his Air Force wings and was posted to RAF No. 25 Fighter Squadron at Hawkinge. By then, his former flying buddy Bernard McElwaine had moved to Britain, as had Molly Bramley-Moore and her sister, Catherine. Molly would later marry McElwaine and introduce Pat to her sister. The two Canadians spent any holiday and leave time together with the Bramley-Moores, often taking in the Lovers' Walks in England's Peak District.

"Convivial, clever, and nice looking," was the way Catherine described Sclanders, but, she added, "a little bit wild."[9]

In March 1937, barely into his operational training at Hawkinge, Sclanders suffered a burst ulcer. Forced to leave the air force and return to New Brunswick to recuperate, he survived the last years of the Great Depression writing stories for the Saint John *Telegraph-Journal* and *Times-Globe* newspapers.

Early in 1939, the news he was reading had more consequence than the news he was writing. Soviet premier Joseph Stalin's attack on Finland, in March, inspired Sclanders to apply for service with the Finns' mercenary air force. But by the time he got to New York for passage overseas, the two sides had signed a peace treaty. When Hitler invaded Norway in April 1940, Sclanders's application to fly with the Royal Norwegian

Air Force was also too late; he made it to Britain only to meet Norwegian pilots fleeing their homeland. With the blitzkrieg gobbling up western Europe, Sclanders next determined to join the French Foreign Legion. He arrived on the continent just as Germany prevailed in the Battle of France, and had to run for his life back to England.

* * *

Two other New Brunswick pilots had received their private licences from the same Saint John Flying Club where Pat Sclanders had performed his barnstorming stunts. Born in Toronto in 1919, Duncan Hewitt had moved with his family to Saint John, where his father worked as a hospital superintendent.[10] Harry Hamilton was born in Greenwich, just north of Saint John, in 1917.[11] Both young men excelled at high school sports, hockey in particular, and both jumped at the chance to take flying lessons at the Millidgeville airfield. Hamilton's flying instructor, Fred Hartwick, assessed his knowledge and skill as a pilot as "exceptional." He was flying solo in only a month. Meanwhile, the Rothesay Collegiate High School yearbook applauded Hewitt as "the first boy in the history of the school to obtain a pilot's licence, one of the youngest in Canada."[12] In later years, the three quick-learning Saint John Flying Club graduates—Sclanders, Hamilton, and Hewitt— became known as the Millidgeville Trio.

Hamilton travelled to Britain in 1936, Hewitt in 1937, each emigrating for different reasons. Hamilton wanted to translate his "exceptional" pilot's test assessment at Millidgeville into an RAF Short Service Commission and full training as a fighter pilot. After a year overseas, at age nineteen, he was declared

"fit as pilot," and received an acting pilot officer's commission. He began combat flight training right away. Hewitt had
landed a job in the Brooklands area, southwest of London,
where Vickers-Armstrong was developing the Supermarine
Spitfire and where Hawker was building Hurricane fighters.
He worked in aero-engine design and, in his spare time, joined
the RAF Volunteer Reserve.

On September 3, 1939, the day Britain declared war on
Germany, both New Brunswickers had been posted to active
service: Pilot Officer Hamilton to RAF No. 611 Squadron, flying Hawker Hurricanes and then Spitfires; P/O Hewitt to RAF
No. 501 Squadron, also flying Hurricanes. Both men wrote
home expressing confidence and bravado about the air force,
while also revealing the impact of early setbacks at their units.

"A friend of mine, Peter Fry, was killed yesterday," Hewitt
wrote his parents from RAF Filton base in April 1940. "He
went up first thing this morning. It was such a beautiful one,
that he was filled with over-exuberance . . . and wrote himself
off. That's three who've been killed since I've been here, and
all by their own hand."[13]

In May, as the phoney war ended, Hamilton's No. 611
Squadron lost two experienced pilots in a single day of scraps
with Luftwaffe fighters over the English Channel. Hamilton
reflected on a sudden request from a squadron mate. The pilot
had climbed onto the wing of his fighter aircraft and asked,
"Feed my dog, when you get back from this sortie?"

"Why the hell does he want me to feed his dog?" Hamilton
wondered.[14] But when his comrade failed to return, Hamilton
didn't hesitate to fulfill the man's final request.

The correspondence of Hamilton and Hewitt demonstrated a maturity they hadn't had when they left New

Brunswick four years earlier. They now realized, at age twenty-one or twenty-two, that their missions were more complicated than delivering a three-point landing in a Tiger Moth and pleasing Flying Instructor Fred Hartwick at Millidgeville airfield. Sorties from bases in southern England meant rapid climbs, head-on-a-swivel attention, following orders, staying close to more experienced flight leaders, and almost certainly encounters with enemy fighters. This was about competence at a completely different level: knocking down an enemy, not being knocked down; killing the enemy, not being killed by him. Duncan Hewitt was prepared to accept and share that possibility with his parents back in Saint John.

"Please don't worry if a letter doesn't come for three weeks or more," Hewitt wrote that same spring as the phoney war ended. "If I am killed or taken prisoner of war, you will be notified by the Air Ministry immediately."[15]

The motto of No. 501 Squadron was *Nil time*: "fear nothing."

* * *

Pilots might debate whether fearlessness comes from experience in the cockpit or one's genes. James Smith gained his on the Canadian prairies in the 1920s and 1930s. Born in 1914, he was raised in the working-class North End of Winnipeg. Wages earned by his father, Bill Smith, as an employee of the Canadian Pacific Railway, could barely feed a household of two adults and six children. During the Depression, Jimmy left school to work in a meat plant to supplement the family's income. He showed his ambition by joining the Winnipeg Light Infantry militia, becoming a competitive marksman, learning Morse code and semaphore, and saving enough to take flying lessons. After he soloed and got his licence, he made regular visits to the RCAF recruiting office.

"Apply again," was the steady answer to his repeated enlistment applications.

Rather than go the traditional route most Canadian civilian aviators chose in the 1930s—booking passage on a cattle boat to Britain to apply for the Short Service Commission with the RAF—Smith made a New Year's pact with Norman Lee, a hunting pal, to travel east in search of military flying jobs. By the summer of 1936, Lee and "Smudger" Smith had saved enough for passage aboard SS *Empress of Asia* to Shanghai, China. They made great travelling companions.

"[Smith] knew how to fit in anywhere," Norman Lee said. "If necessary, he could be a bum or a gentleman. And when they served meals on the ship, he could eat with chopsticks better than the Chinese aboard."[16]

Ashore in mainland China, Lee and Smith tried to convince the Nationalist Chinese government to hire them as mercenary pilots. Had it been a year later, when the Japanese invaded, things might have turned out differently, but in 1936 the Chinese Air Force was not interested in recruits. Smith decided to continue west through southern Asia and the Middle East. When he arrived in Britain, he filed an application to serve in the RAF and continued his travels.

"Whenever Jimmy set out to do something," Norman Lee said, "he did it."[17] Indeed, Smith had just completed his circumnavigation of the globe, arriving back in Canada, when the British Air Ministry wired him to report for initial training in the UK as acting pilot officer on probation in November 1937. He received his full commission a year later, and when the war broke out, the RAF posted him to No. 73 Squadron, flying defensive patrols in Hurricanes over France during the last days of the phoney war. Some close calls with German fighters the first week in May did not appear to frighten Smith. It was the overnight promotions caused by a growing number of losses in RAF fighter pilot ranks that unnerved him.

"[Promotion] has been pretty rapid," he wrote his sisters in Winnipeg. "But I'm going to show whoever put me up for it that they didn't make a mistake."[18]

* * *

There was a reason for the sudden upsurge in RAF fatalities. On May 10, the RAF Advanced Air Striking Force supporting British Expeditionary Forces and the French Army suddenly faced the onslaught of more than a thousand Luftwaffe fighters and bombers at once. The day proved chaotic for P/O Duncan Hewitt and his squadron comrades in England. At 8 a.m., RAF No. 501 Fighter Squadron aircrew were wakened by news from their commanding officer that "the Germans have walked into France. . . . We take off at one o'clock sharp for France."[19]

Twelve of their Hurricane pilots, including Hewitt, were ordered to fly across the Channel and join the AASF over French air space. Theirs was one of Churchill's four additional squadrons posted overseas that day. They flew directly to a forward French air base at Bétheniville, not far from the French-Belgian border. The airfield was already home to RAF No. 103 Squadron, comprising Fairey Battle aircraft and their three-man aircrews. No. 501's arrival at the station proved ominous. When they landed, the pilots discovered their only communications link with the outside world was a temporary telegraph line to a headquarters somewhere in north-central France. Adding to the confusion, the Bristol Bombay transport aircraft carrying No. 501's reserve pilots, ground crew, and their gear crashed on landing. Nearly all aboard were killed and the contents destroyed.[20]

When Duncan Hewitt's flight commander, Gus Holden, was sent up over Sedan, inside the French border, to reconnoiter the scene from the air, he discovered a more critical problem: a large concentration of German ground troops. They had spotted him, in turn. Very quickly, Holden found himself chased by several Me 109s. He rolled his Hurricane on its back, dived steeply to the treetops and raced safely home to Bétheniville airfield.

Even enhanced with the additional RAF squadrons in France, the AASF was outnumbered by the Luftwaffe better than four-to-one. The experiences of the aircrews with a sister RAF unit, No. 12 Fairey Battle Squadron, illustrated the lopsided nature of the fight. Each Fairey Battle bomber carried a pilot, a navigator, and a wireless radio operator/air gunner, but the plane once airborne was notoriously slow, vulnerable, and under-armed for combat. Its crews regularly referred to Battles as "flying coffins." The only reason the RAF allowed them into combat was because Bomber Command had so many of them, and too few modern bombers. Consequently, Fairey Battles relied more on the skill of their crews than the technology aboard the aircraft. That was certainly the case with WAG Gordon Patterson, from Woodrow, Saskatchewan.

"I was one of the better shots on our squadron," Patterson said, "possibly due to my training on the prairies shooting gophers."[21] His Vickers gas-operated rear machine gun in the Fairey Battle had a manually operated rocker mount, with ring and bead sights. If he cranked the spring-loaded pans of .303-inch shells to their limit, he might reach as many as 750 shells fired per minute. Still, they were no match for the Messerschmitt's 20-mm cannon shells.

On May 12, Patterson's Battle P5241 and four other volunteer Battle crews took off to destroy the bridges that crossed the Albert Canal defensive line near Maastricht, Belgium. They were told they'd have fighter escort from RAF No. 1 Fighter Squadron, but the bombers and fighters didn't arrive at the targets simultaneously. The first Fairey Battle to dive on a bridge was shot down; the crew was captured. Battle P5241 followed, with Patterson firing all the way in against three buzzing Me 109s. He shot down one and probably another. But by then, the German fighters' shells had set his plane on fire. His pilot ordered his two crewmates to bail out.

"When I bailed out, I hit the tail and smashed up my right forearm," Patterson recorded. "I was knocked out and had a concussion. I landed in the courtyard of the *Hospital des Anglais* in Liege. I [broke] my left foot on landing. The Germans entered the city that evening and I became a POW." He was awarded the Distinguished Flying Medal (DFM), the first of the war given to a Canadian airman. He spent five years in German POW camps.

In just three days of bombing operations against the invading German armies, the Fairey Battle squadrons suffered catastrophic losses: 40 percent on May 10; 100 percent on May 11; and 62 percent on May 12. RAF Bomber Command had shrunk from 135 serviceable aircraft on May 10 to just seventy-two in as many hours. It was the worst rate of loss in Royal Air Force history. Outcomes were slightly better on the fighters' side of the Advanced Air Striking Force. In those first days of the German invasion, numerous CAN/RAF fighter pilots were pressed into action with AASF squadrons against Luftwaffe *Staffeln*, or fighter squadrons.

Among them was Mark Henry Brown, born and raised in Glenboro, west of Winnipeg. He was a stellar athlete as a youth, but his sister Ruby said he loved airplanes more than sport. He started work at a branch of the Bank of Montreal and dedicated his earnings to flying lessons at the Brandon airfield. By 1936, he'd heard about the RAF's Direct Entry Scheme. He scored so high during his initial training (875 out of a possible 1,000) that, in December 1938, he immediately earned a spot in the Royal Air Force and a flying officer's commission. By the time he was assigned to RAF No. 1 Fighter Squadron at Tangmere, he'd already accumulated 150 flying hours.

But Brown had more working for him than skill. Before departing Canada, he packed a prized talisman, the top button of a Royal Flying Corps tunic. "On the eve of my leaving home in Glenboro, a little fellow I knew ran after me," Brown said. "He pleaded with me to take [this button]. It belonged to his father, a veteran pilot of the last war. I've kept it ever since [for] luck."[22] In Britain, Brown explained to a reporter that in memory of his young friend back home and for good luck, he gave the button an extra buffing before every takeoff.

Flying with RAF No. 1 Squadron, Brown was called "Hilly" by his comrades, after the Bruz Fletcher song of the day, "Hilly Brown." He became the first Canadian fighter pilot to fly combat sorties over France. He recalled attacking a Dornier bomber at 25,000 feet when an Me 109 jumped him and shot off part of his propeller. "I had to get back with the engine turned off," he said. "Luckily there were no other

Messerschmitts about and lucky too that my glide just brought me to a French aerodrome."

In his Hurricane, Brown downed two Me 110s on May 11, two Me 109s the next day, a 109 and Junkers 87 (Stuka) on May 14, and another Me 110 on May 15. That day, both Hilly and his Hurricane went missing;[23] he'd crash-landed, but walked back to base already an ace (more than five victories). "F/L Brown had led many flights with great success and determination when consistently outnumbered by enemy aircraft,"[24] his Distinguished Flying Cross (DFC) citation would later state. Credited with destroying at least seven German fighters and six bombers, Brown was asked by reporters about the youngster who'd given him the good-luck RFC button. "He's joined the Royal Medical Service in Kingston, and I wish him luck," Brown said.

Another Canadian in the RAF, flying with No. 3 Fighter Squadron in those early days over France, was John Max Aitken. Unlike Brown and most of his countrymen in the RAF, Aiken had spent most of his youth in England. He had emigrated from Canada as a child with his father, William Maxwell Aitken, later Lord Beaverbrook.

The younger Max distinguished himself at Cambridge with a blue at soccer. For a period after university, he worked at his father's newspapers—the *Daily Express*, *Sunday Express*, and *Evening Standard*—principally on the business side of publishing. His family's position introduced Max to the cream of London society, young men who attended the best schools and spent spare time travelling and skiing. One of "the Millionaires' Mob," Roger Bushell, made Max an offer.

"Why don't you join the Auxiliary Air Force?" suggested Bushell, then a member of RAF No. 601 Auxiliary Squadron.

Aitken had always been curious about flying. He liked the idea.

"I'll arrange for you to meet Philip Sassoon [Britain's undersecretary of state for air] at lunch," said Bushell.

Aitken enlisted and joined a corps of auxiliary fliers that included Bushell and Lord Edward Grosvenor. Life in the pre-war auxiliaries in Britain was akin to belonging to a uniformed flying club. "My companions were a pretty wild and high-spirited gathering," Aitken said, "the sort of young men who had not quite been expelled from their schools, whom mothers warned their daughters against . . . and [who] clustered in unusual density at the headquarters of No. 601 Squadron."[25] But ultimately, Aitken and his comrades would transform No. 601 into a crack fighting unit.

Aitken had received his commission by the outbreak of war, and because of his father's role as Churchill's minister of aircraft production, he was able to help No. 601 shift from Blenheim bombers to Hurricane fighters. Flight Lieutenant Aitken would lead "A" Flight in the squadron during the Battle of France and stack up nearly as many victories as Hilly Brown. On May 18, Aitken attacked and destroyed two Heinkel (He) bombers; the next day a Heinkel, two Junkers (Ju) 87s, and an Me 110; four days later, he damaged an Me 109. In June, he went to Buckingham Palace to receive a DFC from the King.

Brown and Aitken were among the Canadians who thrived and survived in the Battle of France. Some of their country-men did not. Over Maastricht, F/O James Campbell, from Nelson, BC, was killed in combat that first week. So, too, was F/O Albert Ball, from Montreal; he was shot down in a dog-fight and died of his injuries. And from No. 242 All-Canadian

Squadron, P/O Garfield Madore was killed in action in his Hurricane on May 19.

* * *

Having established a bridgehead at Sedan, France, German armies prepared to turn westward from the River Meuse to drive the French and the British Expeditionary Force into the sea. On May 14, French High Command called on Allied bombers for a supreme effort to halt the German break-through. At noon, the remaining French bombers attacked; their losses were nearly total. RAF bombers followed and were annihilated, with forty bombers shot down. It remained up to Fighter Command, the original six squadrons with ninety-six Hurricanes, plus the four additional squadrons with sixty-four Hurricanes sent on May 10, to deliver a miracle.

The telephone at Prime Minister Churchill's bedside rang at 7:30 a.m. on May 15. The emotional voice of the French prime minister filled his ear. "We have been defeated," Reynaud announced. "The front is broken at Sedan. . . . They are pouring through in great numbers with tanks and armored cars."[26] He pleaded with Churchill for another ten fighter squadrons. Churchill convened the war cabinet three times that day, and ultimately chose to meet the French request. There were now twenty-six Fighter Command squadrons across the Channel, leaving the same number at home in Britain. Churchill claimed that his notes from Fighter Command's Hugh Dowding indicated that as long as twenty-five fighter squadrons remained at home, Britain was safe.

In fact, Dowding had earlier pegged the minimum number of squadrons required to adequately defend the UK at fifty-two. That evening, at the fourth war cabinet meeting of the day, with thirty members present, Dowding sat quietly, six seats to the right of Churchill. Cabinet ministers and strategic military chiefs continued to debate Britain's fighter squadron commitment to the defence of France. Remarkably, Dowding did not speak to the cabinet members present that night about his fears that the home strength of Hurricanes was about to be drained beyond the point of no return. Earlier, however, he had shown Churchill, Lord Beaverbrook (minister of aircraft production), Archibald Sinclair (air minister), and Cyril Newall (chief of air staff) a graph in red ink plotting the upward curve of Hurricane fighter aircraft losses. "This red line shows the wastage of Hurricanes in the last ten days," Dowding told them. "If the line goes on at that same rate for the next ten days, there won't be a single Hurricane left, either in France or in England!"[27]

At home and sleepless that night, Dowding felt compelled to emphasize that same point to the undersecretary of state for air. "I remind Air Council that the last estimate [of] the force necessary to defend this country was fifty-two squadrons, and my strength has now been reduced to the equivalent of thirty-six squadrons. . . . If the Home Defence Force is drained away in desperate attempts to remedy the situation in France, defeat in France will involve the final, complete and irremediable defeat of this country."[28]

* * *

Whether they knew it or not, green P/O Duncan Hewitt and his No. 501 squadron comrades were suddenly an integral part of the last line of defence in the Battle of France. They had

experienced their first contact with Luftwaffe adversaries—
Ju 87s and Me 109s—days after their disastrous arrival at
Bétheniville airfield on May 10. One of Hewitt's wingmates
engaged and was shot down, but survived.

By May 27, Hewitt's squadron had moved its Hurricanes,
pilots, and ground crew to Boos airfield just outside Rouen.
The day dawned peacefully enough, with "thin cloud at 5,000
feet, winds light, visibility 10 miles."[29] Two morning patrols
yielded no enemy contact. Then, just before 2 p.m., an alert
and scramble triggered No. 501 Fighter Squadron's single most
successful sortie of the war. Climbing quickly, the squadron
pilots suddenly found themselves amid twelve Heinkel bombers
and an escort formation of Me 110s. The Hurricane fighters
emptied their guns into anything with a German black cross
on it; ten of the thirteen RAF fighter pilots claimed at least
one enemy aircraft shot down. Hewitt claimed one and was
credited with a second.

No. 501's unprecedented victories in the skies over
Normandy were nearly lost in the more significant Allied
news of the day. By May 26, what remained of the British
Expeditionary Force, as well as the French and Belgian armies,
had retreated into a pocket on the northern coast of France,
little more than a hundred miles in circumference around the
town of Dunkirk. They were surrounded and poised to be
crushed by 800,000 German troops of the 4th, 6th, and 18th
Armies. But Field Marshal Karl Rudolf Gerd von Rundstedt
called for the German advance to halt for consolidation and
resupply. Hitler sanctioned the order. He believed air force
commander-in-chief Hermann Göring's promise: "This is just
the job for the Luftwaffe. I guarantee unconditionally that not
a British soldier will escape!"[30]

The romance of flying ignited the imagination of many young Canadians in the 1930s, including Winnipegger Johnny Kent (*right, middle of three*). His first flying instructor, Konrad Johannesson (*bottom right*), a WWI veteran, helped Kent through "Gawd-awful" landings to get his pilot's licence. Then, when the Royal Air Force offered Short Service Commissions for young aviators, Kent jumped at the chance. In Britain by 1934, Kent was learning military aviation on elite fighter trainers, such as the Bristol Bulldog (*top*); then, as pilot officer, he commenced service in the RAF as a test pilot and combat-ready fighter pilot. His early military flying even earned him a trip to Buckingham Palace with Flying Officers Hall (*left of three*) and Rodney (*right of three*) to receive the Air Force Cross from King George VI in 1939.

Anticipating air raids in a second European war with Germany, and amid tight secrecy, British strategists developed RDF, radio direction-finding, to identify incoming enemy aircraft. An early-warning system of Chain Home radar masts (*above*) along Britain's south and east coasts transmitted energy pulses that bounced back from inbound airborne objects. The same towers received the returning pulses, which registered as blips on cathode tubes in receiver huts at the base of the towers. Women's Auxiliary Air Force operators (*below*) monitored the blips and reported them to Fighter Command headquarters, which then scrambled RAF fighters to respond to the threat.

At the outbreak of war, in 1939, Britain looked to members of the Commonwealth to bolster its fighter pilot ranks. The Canadian government had already committed to training nearly a quarter million aircrew in Canada; Prime Minister Mackenzie King had no plans to send an RCAF fighter squadron as well. As a compromise, British Air Ministry assembled Canadian pilots already training in the RAF to form No. 242 All-Canadian Fighter Squadron. By June 1940, they had served in the Battle of France and had Douglas Bader, the legless fighter ace, as their acting squadron leader. In October, No. 242 included (*left to right*) Denis Crowley-Milling, Hugh Tamblyn, Stan Turner, J.E. Saville (*on wing*), Neil Campbell, Willie McKnight, Douglas Bader, G.E. Ball, M.G. Homer, and Marvin Brown.

Given the job of clearing the skies over Britain of RAF fighter aircraft, Reichsmarschall Hermann Göring (*left, in white uniform*), commander of the Luftwaffe, told German Army High Command it would take from two to four weeks to accomplish. He had 250 Stuka dive-bombers, roughly a thousand long-range bombers such as Heinkels (*above, seen over east London during the Blitz*) and Dorniers, and a thousand Messerschmitt fighters (2,250 serviceable aircraft) to fulfill his promise. Over the 113-day campaign, Göring altered the focus of his attacks many times—from British coastal convoys, to radar towers, to fighter bases, to aircraft factories, to population centres such as London. Despite outnumbering RAF fighters, sometimes four and five to one, his air forces failed to crush Fighter Command.

As the Battle of France ended in June 1940, and the Battle of Britain loomed in early July, Air Chief Marshal Hugh Dowding (*top right*), head of RAF Fighter Command, considered the needs of defending the UK from German bombing attacks, or, as he called it, "security of the base." To date in the war, the RAF had lost 959 military aircraft, 477 of them fighters; that left him with 644 fighter aircraft available for operations to defend all of England. Dowding trusted his instincts that the battle would be won only "by science thoughtfully applied to operational requirements," but also by the blood, sweat, and raw courage of 1,259 fighter pilots now available to scramble into Hurricanes (*above*) and Spitfires against a Luftwaffe juggernaut.

Nowhere was Pat Sclanders (*left*) more at home than in the cockpit of an aeroplane. His Saint John flying club claimed he, at fifteen, was "the youngest pilot in the Dominion." He barnstormed, photographed, advertised, showed off to his family, offered his services as a mercenary pilot to Finland and Norway, and flew combat sorties in the Battle of Britain, all in his twenty-four short years of life.

A series of coincidences led brilliant University of Toronto aero-engineer Beverley Shenstone (*left*) from North America to the tin-bashing assembly lines of the Junkers aviation factory in Germany in 1929, and then to the design department of Supermarine in Britain in 1931. There he joined Reginald Mitchell in creating the elliptical wing shape of the Spitfire. In practical terms, the wing design gave the fighter its highly responsive manoeuvrability in combat, while also containing the plane's retractable landing gear, machine guns, and ammunition. No coincidence to Shenstone, however, was that its dynamic shape also "looked nice."

Elsie MacGill (*right*) faced challenges her life through. In the late 1920s and early '30s, she graduated from four different universities in a male-dominated profession, becoming the first woman in North America to earn a master's in aeronautical engineering. She parlayed academic excellence into a career in aircraft production, arriving at Canadian Car and Foundry (Can-Car) in Fort William, ON, when the plant needed her most. As the Luftwaffe launched attacks on Britain, she spearheaded the assembly of Hawker Hurricanes, ensuring their airworthiness (*below*) and delivery overseas in time for service in the Battle of Britain.

In September 1940, when Germany suddenly redirected bombing raids against urban centres, including London (*above*), Dorothy Firth (*below left*) joined the war effort in a variety of capacities. She served meals to soldiers at Waterloo train station downtown and entertained troops near an anti-aircraft battery close to her home in the suburb of Richmond. More vital and certainly more dangerous, when Luftwaffe explosives began falling in her district, she served as a fire-watcher (*below right*), attempting to douse incendiary bombs with a bucket of sand and a stirrup pump.

For seven days prior, the War Office and Admiralty (Royal Navy) had discussed the "possible but unlikely evacuation of a very large force in hazardous circumstances."[31] The operation, code-named "Dynamo,"* was ultimately executed by Vice-Admiral Bertram Ramsay from underground headquarters beneath Dover Castle, directly across the Channel from Dunkirk. Admiralty hoped that with luck the Royal Navy warships, merchant vessels, and civilian boats might manage to pluck as many as 100,000 British, French, and Belgian troops from the Dunkirk beaches.

The German halt order lasted three days and, in that time, 338,000 British, French, and Belgian troops boarded every manner of boat and ship—roughly eight hundred vessels—and escaped to Britain. Credit for the successful evacuation went to hundreds of amateur yachtsmen, the navy sailors, and the merchant crews. Less acknowledged were the RAF fighters trying to keep Luftwaffe dive bombers and their escorts away from the embarkation points.

On the eve of the evacuation, P/O Stan Turner and the No. 242 All-Canadian Squadron were flying daily sorties from their new base of operations at Biggin Hill, England, to Dunkirk and back. On May 25, his improved combat instincts and dead-eye capability on a Hurricane gun sight yielded Turner's first victories. In eight days over the French coast, he shot down five Me 109s, establishing him officially as an ace. Turner noted that finding his targets each sortie that week over Dunkirk wasn't difficult. All he had to do was

---

* Admiral Ramsay directed the evacuation of Allied troops from inside a room deep in the Dover cliffs that had once contained a dynamo, a kind of electrical generator.

look for the plumes of smoke from burning ships, fuel dumps, and abandoned military vehicles along the beach. The entire town of Dunkirk was aflame and could be seen from across the Channel in Britain.

With the port facilities destroyed, the task of coordinating the evacuation of thousands of Allied troops fell to Royal Navy Capt William Tennant. Beginning May 27, he and his beach-masters, including Canadian commander James Clouston, guided tens of thousands of evacuees, four abreast, along the exposed breakwater at the harbour entrance to the embarka-tion point. For five days and nights, Clouston hustled evacuees steadily to narrow wooden walkways and onto boats and ships at the eastern end of the breakwater.*

Forty-eight hours after the Dunkirk exodus began, the Luftwaffe redirected two air fleets to attempt to shut it down. Swarms of Stuka dive bombers screamed down almost ver-tically, raining bombs on the entire scene. By May 28, RAF patrols had doubled in size, eight separate sweeps each day, but their efficacy was hampered by having to fly back to south England to refuel after each sortie. All the while, wave after wave of Stukas attempted to deliver on Göring's promise to annihilate the British evacuation. On June 1, the Royal Air Force lost thirty-one fighter aircraft, while the Luftwaffe saw nineteen of its bombers and another ten fighters destroyed.[32]

During the climax of the Dunkirk air battle, Stan Turner shot down two more enemy fighters. His fellow No. 242 P/Os

---

* On June 2, Commander Clouston returned to Dover to update Vice-Admiral Ramsay; the next day, he boarded a Royal Navy rescue boat to return to Dunkirk and supervise the final night of the evacuation. On his way to France, eight Ju 87 Stukas strafed and sank the boat; Clouston died in the water of hypother-mia. He posthumously received a Mention in Dispatches in July 1940.

Robert Grassick, Willie McKnight, and John Latta also turned in remarkable combat records. Grassick chased and fired at an Me 109 until it crashed, and then claimed a second enemy fighter. At 10,000 feet over Dunkirk, Latta found himself amid twenty-five 109s. He latched onto the tail of one, closed, and fired a twelve-second burst of machine-gun fire and watched it disappear into ground mist. In the mêlée, he'd taken enemy fire into his undercarriage and had to land on one wheel and a wingtip.[33] McKnight shot down an Me 109 over Ostend on May 28, the next day a Dornier 17 bomber and two 109s, and on May 31 two Me 110 fighters. On June 1, he engaged and took out two Stukas. With no ammunition left at the end of that sortie, he made feint attacks on other Luftwaffe raiders, driving them away from the evacuation beaches. McKnight's bold actions and ace status earned him a DFC, the first awarded to a member of the all-Canadian squadron.

Oberleutnant Jocho Helbig, a Ju 88 pilot with Luftwaffe LG 1, bombed Dunkirk numerous times during the Allied evacuation. He noted in his journal that his bombing and strafing runs had reduced the number of British soldiers requiring transport back to England. But on his last low-level attack, three Hurricanes caught him; their combined fire wounded him so badly that he had to fly back to his Luftwaffe base using one arm. "The Hell of Dunkirk," Helbig called it. "We met terrific resistance from the British fighter [aircraft]. It was a turning point. Now we knew what the enemy's mettle was."[34]

While the British Army and Royal Navy repeatedly radioed for non-stop air cover during the week-long withdrawal from Dunkirk, the depleted state of RAF squadrons made answering their pleas nearly impossible. Often, RAF fighters engaged Luftwaffe raiders well away from the beaches, where evacuating troops couldn't see their life-and-death struggles. In addition, Hurricane and Spitfire pilots had to cope with a chronic cross-Channel problem that Luftwaffe crews would soon face: limited range. Flying from bases in Britain to France, RAF fighter pilots could only engage enemy aircraft, at full throttle, for a matter of minutes before racing back to Britain to refuel.[35] Most evacuees on the beaches at Dunkirk complained that they rarely saw RAF aircraft and referred with disdain to Fighter Command pilots as "Brylcreem Boys," or the glamour boys of the forces.

One fighter pilot with No. 54 Squadron, New Zealand ace Al Deere, learned of the forces' contempt for him and his comrades first-hand. Shot down on May 29 during Operation Dynamo, he crash-landed his Spitfire on a beach a dozen miles from Dunkirk. He managed to cycle and hitchhike his way through the long lines of evacuees waiting to board departing ships. An army major stopped him.

"I'm an RAF officer," said the exasperated Deere. "I'm trying to get back to my squadron."

"I don't give a damn who you are," came the major's response.

In the throngs of waiting soldiers, Deere managed to dodge the major and dashed aboard the destroyer, eventually making his way to the wardroom full of unsympathetic army troops. "Why so friendly?" Deere said sarcastically. "What have the RAF done?"

"That's just it," said one soldier in the wardroom. "What have they done?"[36]

* * *

Desperate for any good news in the last week of May 1940, the *Illustrated London News* covered No. 501 Squadron's remarkable victories as part of the air battle above the Dunkirk evacuation. Newsreel cinematographers also shot and edited a propaganda piece entitled "Britain's Fight in the Air." The film featured a photograph of No. 501's victorious pilots, including P/O Duncan Hewitt. The film footage was circulated among theatres in Britain and North America, including a movie house in Saint John, New Brunswick, where Hewitt's family spotted him.[37]

"So, you want to know if I am the P/O from Saint John who shot down the Heinkel 111 bomber and wrecked another?" Hewitt wrote home. "Well, folks, I am. As a matter of fact, our squadron shot down ten in that scrap. The day after, newspapermen and newsreel chaps came along and took our photographs. That scrap was child's play compared to others."[38]

The miracle of deliverance at Dunkirk saved hundreds of thousands of lives. It was nevertheless a retreat, resulting in stunning loss of life: 68,000 Allied soldiers were killed, wounded, or captured during Dynamo. The British and French Armies abandoned 63,000 tanks, trucks, and motorcycles as well as 2,400 field guns in their escape. More than two hundred British and Allied sea craft were sunk, including six British and three French destroyers. Meanwhile, the Battle of France had cost the RAF 453 front-line fighter aircraft, 386 Hurricanes, and sixty-seven Spitfires. Remarkably, only seventy-five of the lost fighters resulted from air-to-air combat; the rest were either bombed by the Luftwaffe on the ground at French airfields, or left behind during the Allied withdrawal from the continent.[39]

In what turned out to be some of the final RAF Fighter Command actions in France that June, several members of

No. 242 Squadron, including Willie McKnight and Stan Turner, joined Duncan Hewitt and No. 501 Squadron in setting up temporary quarters at the famous Le Mans racetrack, southwest of Paris. They too took stock. They'd downed thirty enemy aircraft in France, but the campaign had cost seven of their own pilots killed, two wounded, and their commanding officer, S/L Fowler M. Gobeil, was missing.

"The battle by then was so confused," Turner wrote, "it was often difficult to tell friend from foe."[40] One evening, McKnight and a wingman chased a Dornier bomber in vain. Attempting to return to the Le Mans field, they ran out of fuel. The two pilots brought their Hurricanes down in a wheat field. In the dim light of dusk, they suddenly saw a group of French farm workers emerge from the hedgerows, brandishing scythes and shouting at them. Fortunately, the Canadians convinced the workers they were on the same side. Another night, fifth columnists snuck onto the airfield and turned on the yellow lights in the Hurricane cockpits; this attracted German night-fighters, but their bombs fell wide of the squadron's parked fighter aircraft.

As German armies marched in victory down the Champs-Élysée in Paris on June 14, P/Os McKnight and Turner and their No. 242 Squadron comrades withdrew to Nantes; from there they provided further air cover for Allied troops evacuating through Bordeaux and Brest. Meanwhile, P/O Duncan Hewitt and his fellow pilots in No. 501 moved to Saint-Hélier, on Jersey in the Channel Islands, where they covered BEF troops evacuating via Cherbourg. By this time, however, the ground crews for both fighter squadrons had boarded ships and returned to Britain. The Canadians were left to service their own aircraft, arm their guns, share guard duty sleeping under the Hurricanes' wings, and ultimately prepare for their own evacuation.

At another airfield, just outside Paris, Canadian fighter pilot Howard "Cowboy" Blatchford and his No. 41 Squadron were cut off by French capitulation. With the Germans on the verge of capturing the airfield, P/O Blatchford climbed into the cockpit of the only aircraft serviceable and available, a Tiger Moth trainer. Not since Howard had taken his first flying lessons at Blatchford Airfield—named for his father, Mayor Ken Blatchford of Edmonton—had he flown a trainer aircraft. Howard had built up his hours bush flying in the Canadian North before opting for the RAF's Direct Entry Scheme and enlisting in 1937. Only weeks into the war, in one of the first Spitfires off the production line, he shot down a Heinkel 111 bomber, the first Canadian aerial kill of the war. Now, with No. 41 Squadron short of aircraft, he made his escape in the two-seater Tiger Moth.

Blatchford had enough room to accommodate an "erk," or ground crewman,* in the second seat. "We had no kit, no shaving gear, no food, no anything," he recalled. As they took off, he looked back at the RAF base, littered with charred aircraft and supplies, all of it torched to deprive the Germans of booty. He and his passenger reached another airfield near Saint-Nazaire. "There we found an amazing accumulation of damaged and half-serviceable aircraft of all makes and types. I managed to swap my Moth for a Fairey Battle bomber."[41]

---

* "Erk" evolved from the Royal Air Force short-form term for aircraftman, or "airc"; they were often ground crewmen.

After five days, he landed back at Heston,* near London, ready for the next stage in his RAF career.

After a month in France, P/O Duncan Hewitt and what was left of No. 501 Squadron reassembled at RAF Croydon outside London and were given four days leave. During the French collapse, the other two members of the Millidgeville Trio made their way back to the UK by different means. F/L Harry Hamilton's No. 611 Squadron was so depleted that the unit's few remaining pilots were dispersed to other units; Hamilton joined No. 85 Squadron. For his part, P/O Pat Sclanders, who had hoped to join the French air force, had arrived in France just in time for the capitulation. He was now stranded on the wrong side of the Channel. No stranger to the art of masquerade, he sneaked aboard a ship taking Polish refugees to England. Before long, with a well-travelled flight log and experience under fire on the continent, he and his credentials would come to the attention of the all-Canadian RAF squadron.

P/O Neil Campbell, who joined No. 242 as a reinforcement, described the squadron's last days in France in a letter home: "Up at 3:15 o'clock in the morning. At readiness at 4 a.m., on patrol at 5:30 o'clock until 7 o'clock; then we had to refuel our own aircraft. . . . We finished work about 10 in the evening. . . . a case of rolling into bed and rolling out again in the morning."[42]

In the same letter to his mother, Campbell likely violated all the content rules established by British censors by explicitly

---

* At Heston Aerodrome, on September 30, 1938, then Prime Minister Neville Chamberlain had triumphantly claimed his signed Munich Agreement with Adolf Hitler guaranteed "peace in our time."

describing where his RAF unit was located, in what operations it was flying, and how desperate things had become. The Campbell family in St. Thomas, Ontario, learned their son was "based at Nantes, Le Mans, Chateauduex [*sic*] sometimes operating from a forward base," and that he had "covered the evacuation from Nantes and prevented it from becoming another Dunkirk."

The escape from Nantes was no Dunkirk, but it was difficult. The day France surrendered, French soldiers set up machine guns along No. 242 Squadron's airfield runways and declared, "All aircraft grounded. No more fighting from French soil." Stan Turner wasn't about to take this lying down, and a brawl nearly ensued. A British Army officer intervened, telling Turner, "Go ahead, take off. I'll look after these chaps."[43] He pointed across the field to where his platoon had set up British machine guns trained on the French weapons. The French officer looked, shrugged, and walked away.

At 1 p.m. on June 18, the all-Canadian No. 242 Squadron, one of the last two RAF units left in France, received orders to evacuate the base at Nantes and return with whatever aircraft and belongings they could salvage across the Channel. They destroyed several Hurricanes that didn't have pilots to fly them home. They set fire to their canteen, lamenting the loss of its bar chock-full of liquor. And, finally, they fuelled and armed their aircraft for their exit from France and the last leg home.

The pilots stuffed whatever they could into their Hurricanes. They had no maps, very little fuel, and no indication where they should fly to and land their fighters. Bob Grassick and Neil Campbell chose the beaches of Minehead in Somerset, which was just about where they ran out of fuel. "Landing on the beach tipped up the nose of my plane, breaking the airscrew," wrote Campbell. "[But] the people . . . actually pushed my machine up a 200-foot hill. The last three feet were perpendicular so my machine literally had to be lifted up."[44]

Before leaving Nantes, Stan Turner had paused to look at his motley squadron comrades—unshaven, scruffily dressed, exhausted, grimed with dirt and smoke. "After weeks of fighting, we were all keyed up. Now that the whole shebang was over, there was a tremendous let-down feeling. As we headed for England, we felt not so much relief as anger. We wanted to hit something and there was nothing to hit. The skies were empty—not a German in sight—and the ground below looked deserted, too. It was all very sunny and peaceful, and quite unreal. As if the war didn't exist. But we knew the real war had only just begun . . ."[45]

CHAPTER FOUR

"A TOUGH BUNCH"

BARELY HAD BRITONS ABSORBED THE SHOCK OF DUN-
KIRK in spring 1940 when they learned of the fall of
France. During his one o'clock bulletin on June 17,
BBC announcer Frank Phillips called the news that Marshal
Philippe Pétain had sought an armistice with Hitler "Black
Monday."[1]

On news of the French capitulation, King George VI
wrote candidly to his mother, Queen Mary, "Personally, I feel
happier now that we have no allies to be polite to."[2]

After just a month in office, Prime Minister Winston
Churchill wrote memorably, "We shall go on to the end . . . we
shall defend our island, whatever the cost may be, we shall fight
on the beaches, we shall fight on the landing grounds, we shall
fight in the field and in the streets, we shall fight in the hills; we
shall never surrender."[3]

A few days later, artist David Low captured the moment
in an *Evening Standard* cartoon, showing a British soldier on a
rocky shore facing tempestuous seas and waves of oncoming
bombers overhead; the caption read, "Very well, alone!"[4]

Six-year-old Jill Brown grew up not far from the rock Low depicted in his cartoon, on the south coast of England. Her home was in the town of Freshwater on the Isle of Wight, within walking distance of the shores of the English Channel. She would often walk through the village green, across a small stream, and down to the open water of the Channel. If she got a soaker—water splashed overtop her shoes—her mother might be cross with her, but it was an expected hazard of a walk to the beach.

Suddenly, in spring 1940, Jill's favourite beach was off limits. Volunteers of a local defence force had installed huge concrete obstacles and coils of barbed wire, blocking the way from land to water or, more importantly, from water to land. Jill's hometown, she learned from her parents, could be "the stepping stone the Germans used to invade England, so the beaches were closed."[5]

Life changed almost instantly with Britain standing alone. Churchill bestowed extraordinary powers upon several MPs in his cabinet to mobilize British citizens and thwart any invasion attempt. Labour Minister Ernest Bevin was given the mandate to organize the UK workforce. At his direction, the Emergency Powers Act passed in the British House of Commons in a single day, May 22, 1940. It gave the government the legislated right to control all human and material resources of the country, except the armed forces.

Churchill himself shared responsibility for public safety with Bevin and Lord Beaverbrook, whom the prime minister had also chosen to head the Ministry of Aircraft Production. Beaverbrook, formerly Canadian newspaper magnate Max Aitken, had a proven ability to "cut through red tape and drive ahead with what really mattered,"[6] and much had to be done to move Britain to a greater state of readiness.

Although a vast majority of the British Expeditionary Force had escaped from Dunkirk, its hasty withdrawal had left most of its heavy weaponry behind in France. Any remaining armament had been shipped to British forces in the Middle East, Gibraltar, Malta, Hong Kong, Singapore, India, Burma, and West Africa. That left two-pounder anti-tank guns, some 2,300 Bren guns, and 395 light tanks as a meagre deterrent to armed incursion in the UK.

Even before Dunkirk, War Secretary Anthony Eden had invited men aged seventeen to sixty-five to step forward and offer their services as a kind of "broomstick army"[7] against German invaders. "The new force to be raised is the Local Defence Volunteers (LDV)," Eden announced on radio. "The name describes its duties in three words. . . . When on duty you will form part of the armed forces. You will not be paid, but on duty you will receive a uniform and will be armed."[8]

Within twenty-four hours of the initial call for LDVs, 250,000 civilian men enlisted. By the end of June 1940, their numbers had swollen to 1.5 million. In a subsequent broad-cast, Churchill described the new citizen army as "the Home Guard," and the name stuck. Qualifications were minimal. No medical exam was required. Experience with weapons was not considered essential. Even the age requirement turned out to be flexible: the oldest Home Guard volunteer was well into his eighties, having first seen action in the Egyptian campaign of 1884–85.[9]

Initially, the only hint of a Home Guard uniform was an armband marked "HG." A few fortunate volunteers received Lee-Enfield rifles, the standard infantry equipment left over from the Great War. More were armed in July when the United States government shipped half a million .300 rifles to Britain.

They were embalmed in glutinous oil. It took 250 women volunteers two weeks to clean and release 8,000 of the rifles.

If the tidal wave of Home Guard volunteering didn't illustrate the gung-ho spirit of Britons ready to meet the Nazi challenge, the innovative ways they found to confound and dissuade any potential invader certainly did. Iron posts suddenly appeared in roadways, combined with rusty ploughs, wrecked cars, and piles of concrete and rubble, making passage into and out of towns much slower, if not impossible. At sports playing pitches, treeless fields, and any open spaces, parties of schoolchildren dug anti-tank ditches and erected sharp poles in tripods to keep enemy aircraft or parachutists from landing.[10] Overnight, roadway signposts, mileage markers, and town-limits indicators were uprooted and hidden. "Every sign was taken away, so [the Germans] wouldn't know which direction to go," said Jill Brown.

On the Isle of Wight, Jill and her family managed to maintain some normalcy in their lives. Despite being on the front line of a potential German invasion, at least geographically, the family bus company, owned by her grandfather and managed by her father, Cecil Brown, continued to deliver local passengers across the West Wight part of the island. Jill still went to school each day, but she never left home without a box containing her child-sized gas mask, and a packed lunch in case she got caught in an air raid and had to stay in a shelter until the all-clear siren. Jill's parents encouraged her to listen to the radio, but never to panic. Her grandfather, Joseph Brown, had served in the Royal Army Medical Corps during the Great War, and her mother, Beryl, had lived through bombings by German Zeppelins in the First World War. "Keep calm," Cecil Brown told Jill repeatedly. "You'll be safe. There's nothing to worry about."[11]

Not all British families felt safe, or confident their leaders could fend off a German invasion. Bill Brydon was the youngest of four children living in the town of Hebburn, a few miles up the River Tyne on Britain's northeast coast. Ten years old in spring 1940, Bill considered the war an unexpected thrill. He collected shrapnel after German bombing attacks and mimicked the Home Guard's defence of the British coast. But his father knew too well that Royal Navy shipyards were just a stone's throw from their home on the river and that the neighbouring city of Newcastle upon Tyne was a storehouse for northeast Britain's rich coal deposits. It didn't matter that the city, known as England's northern fortress, had fended off invasions by the Danes in 1080 and the Scots in the twelfth century. After Dunkirk and the fall of France, Bill's father feared for his family's well-being.

"Each family was given an Anderson shelter," Brydon said.[12] Named after Sir John Anderson, the home secretary in charge of wartime Air Raid Precautions (ARP), the Anderson domestic shelter consisted of corrugated steel sheets. The Brydon family, like more than two million others in the UK, received the steel sheets and instructions with diagrams showing how to dig a trench 7.5 feet long, six feet wide, and four feet deep in their backyard. They were then to insert the six arched sheets, bolting them together at the top. At either end of the shelter, they installed flat steel plates, one a doorway, the other an emergency exit, to enclose the occupants. Inside there was room enough for Bill, his brother, Fenwick, their two sisters, and their parents.

Unfortunately, the water table was so high near the River Tyne that the Brydons' Anderson shelter was often flooded. "My father determined that the Anderson shelter was not the place to go in an air raid," said Brydon. "Under the stairs was the place to go. So, every time the siren sounded, he gathered us and shoved us under the stairs."

By summer 1940, after several Luftwaffe attacks on the Newcastle shipyards and collieries, Brydon's father didn't want to tempt fate any longer; he enrolled his two sons with the Children's Overseas Reception Board (CORB) and its program evacuating British children via passenger liners in protected convoys to Canada.

"My father was certain we would lose the war," said Brydon.

* * *

If one hoped to win a war, particularly one moving as rapidly and as menacingly as the Second World War, that person would do well to know what the other side was up to.

Beverley Shenstone grew up in Edwardian Toronto with family connections to the Massey-Harris tractor empire. He learned to sail from his uncles; he also designed, built, and raced model yachts. Shenstone's passion for design led him to study engineering at the University of Toronto. In 1927, while still an undergraduate, he holidayed in Britain, canoeing the waterways of southern England. Before returning home to his studies he worked at an Air Ministry laboratory in the basement of the London Science Museum.

His appetite for aviation whetted by the Air Ministry experience,[13] Shenstone completed his engineering degree at U of T and began post-graduate work with Professor John Parkin, conducting wind tunnel experiments on the Vickers Vedette flying boat; in 1929, he became the first person in

Canada awarded a master's degree in aeronautics. By that time, the RCAF had inaugurated its Provisional Pilot Officers (PPO) program, instructing pilots for potential military service. Shenstone trained for two summers, flying Avro 504s and de Havilland Moth trainers.[14] He was hooked on aviation and wrote about the takeoffs with their "bumps, teeth-rattling bumps, wheels splashing mud, speed, a lurch," and then the airplane's launch into a "perfect smoothness."[15]

Instead of pursuing a career in the RCAF, he chose to further his study of the dynamics of flight. He booked transatlantic passage, arriving in Hamburg, Germany, in October 1929, just days before the crash on the New York Stock Exchange. His Massey-Harris lineage gave Shenstone entrée to an attaché at the British embassy in Berlin, Group Captain Malcolm G. Christie. He opened the doors for Shenstone to take a position in Dessau at the Hugo Junkers *Flugzeugwerk*, or aviation factory. At that time, the company was designing the Junkers G-38, a transport aircraft dominated by its large, delta-shaped swept-back wing.

"[Christie] advised me not to stay for too short a time," Shenstone wrote. "He said if the German government heard of me working there, they would have a fit—a Britisher learning about their sacred aeroplanes.* He suggested that I say I'm an American rather than a Canadian."[16]

Shenstone knew a smattering of German, and having worked at his grandfather's Massey-Harris plant, he was at

---

* Speculation suggests that placing a Canadian aeronautical engineer at the heart of German aviation research in the 1930s made Shenstone a British spy. However, as he diarized, "I just wanted to work in a modern aircraft factory." (Lance Cole, *Secrets of the Spitfire: The Story of Beverley Shenstone, the Man Who Perfected the Elliptical Wing* [Barnsley, UK: Pen & Sword Books, 2012], 42).

home in the Junkers sheet metal department. Observing Hugo Junkers's pioneering work in aircraft design, he was impressed with the factory's use of corrugated metal skin on its aircraft, which allowed the traditional airframe chassis to be lighter at the expense of greater drag. And he was especially awed by the use of swept-back wing aerodynamics. He became skilled at metal cutting, panel beating, riveting duralumin, and relating the drafting table to the actual sheet work.

In July 1930, Shenstone took a leave of absence and travelled to Wasserkuppe, in the Rhön mountains, the home of German gliding. There he learned motorless flight and met Alexander Lippisch, the originator of gliders comprised of virtually nothing but a delta-shaped wing. A fast friendship developed, and Shenstone spent the winter working on an unpaid basis with Lippisch on the design of his swept-winged tailless aeroplane, which he called the Delta.

"Lippisch was nearly always buoyant and talkative," Shenstone wrote. "He did not like to work alone, and had the gift of thinking aloud. So, he would always have with him [other designers] or myself. . . . This turned out to be an education."[17]

When Shenstone returned to Dessau, he learned that Junkers faced competition from an Italian aircraft manufacturer that had created a prototype identical to the Junkers design. Hugo Junkers worried that his non-German employees, such as Shenstone, might be leaking classified designs to competitors or potential enemies. Interviewed by officials at the factory, Shenstone insisted that he'd never shared data with Italian competitors. In fact, he'd written regularly to his mentor, Professor John Parkin in Canada, about his work on tailless aircraft.

Among other visitors to Alexander Lippisch's Wasserkuppe glider school was Air Commodore Sir John Chamier, former

Royal Flying Corps and Royal Air Force pilot. By 1930, Chamier had also gained a position with Vickers-Armstrong aircraft manufacturing in Britain. Upon seeing Lippisch's work, and Shenstone's role in it, Chamier told the Canadian he should work with the British at Vickers, the firm that had recently purchased Supermarine, the British aircraft manufacturing firm that would soon design and build Spitfire fighters.

By 1931, the effects of the Depression on the European workplace and the rise of Nazism in Germany had Shenstone looking to his future elsewhere. He searched for new opportunities in Britain, but didn't start with Vickers. Shenstone wrote to Sydney Camm, chief designer at the Hawker Aircraft company, and gained an interview. When they met, Shenstone noted that Camm was peering at him with considerable scorn.

"If you were told to work out a design to fit a fighter specification," Camm proposed, "what would you do first?"

"I would decide whether it should be a biplane or a monoplane," Shenstone answered.

"No, you would not," Camm snapped back. "It would be a biplane."[18]

Convention dictated that to meet fighter aircraft objectives, wings on monoplane aircraft had to be thick, and therefore too heavy. Working with Hawker's managing director, Fred Sigrist, Camm had developed a distinctive metal construction using cheaper and simpler jointed tubes rather than a welded structure; this led to the successful Hawker Hart biplane. In 1931, Camm unveiled his front-line Hawker Fury, an agile fighter interceptor capable of speeds of two hundred miles per hour. It was a biplane. Well into the decade, support remained strong for the biplane as the dependable design for military aircraft. At that time, early in the 1930s, no fewer than 84 percent of the aircraft in the RAF were of Hawker/Camm design.[19] But the high-performance demands of Air Ministry, particularly with war looming, ultimately positioned the monoplane over the biplane. And Britain's two major military aircraft designers responded.

Camm eventually overcame his reluctance to build monowing fighters and developed the "Interceptor Monoplane," with retractable landing gear, a powerful Rolls-Royce engine, and machine guns (initially four, eventually eight) in the wings. A prototype was tested in 1935. The first production Hurricane flew in October 1937. And by December of that year, Air Ministry had assigned the first four serviceable Hurricanes to RAF No. 111 Fighter Squadron (Treble One Squadron) at Northolt.*

Meantime, Shenstone had left an unimpressed Sydney Camm and called his contact at Vickers, John Chamier, who got him an interview with Reginald Mitchell in the Supermarine division.

Mitchell had achieved success with his high-speed S.6 floatplane, winning the Schneider Trophy race outright in 1931. When the British Air Ministry invited designs of an eight-gun fighter aircraft with a speed not less than 275 miles per hour in 1934, it captured Mitchell's full attention. He'd previously designed the Type 224 monoplane fighter, but its performance had not met the criteria. And because the specs called for eight guns, not four, Mitchell recognized that a modified Type 224 wouldn't do. Supermarine needed a wholly new aircraft. He

* By the summer of 1940, more than 550 Hurricanes were equipping eighteen active Battle of Britain squadrons; together those Hurricanes inflicted 60 percent of the losses sustained by the Luftwaffe.

put Shenstone to work on the aerodynamics of an elliptical wing.

Drawing on his experience at Junkers, Bev Shenstone worked on a wing, elliptical in shape, as thin as possible, and delivering high lift and low induced drag. In addition to wing shape, he proposed altering the taper of the wing. Other contemporary designs used a straight taper from wing root to wingtip; he offered evidence that an elliptical wing, which would taper slowly at first, then more radically toward the wingtip, would create more chord (room inside the wing closer to the aircraft's fuselage) while remaining thin across the span of the wing.

"[Put] simply, the shape . . . allowed us the thinnest possible wing with sufficient room to carry the [retracted landing gear, machine guns, and ammunition magazines] inside," Shenstone said. He had managed to couple an understanding of practical engineering with aerodynamics. "And it looked nice."[20]

Shenstone's view of wing design was broader than his own drafting table and the wind tunnels at Vickers-Armstrong. In 1934, he travelled to the United States to observe the airfoil design created by the National Advisory Committee for Aeronautics. And at an airshow in Paris, he ran his hands over the wing of a new Heinkel aircraft, marvelling at its smoothness; German designer Ernst Heinkel told Shenstone the secret was his technique of sinking rivets flush with the wing's skin. Shenstone's elliptical wing would soon have sunken rivets to deliver the same smooth surface.

By November 1934, the Supermarine design team had taken its original Type 300 aircraft, introduced a Rolls-Royce V12 engine (later known as the Merlin), enclosed the cockpit, and manufactured Shenstone's elliptical wings. On March 5,

1936, test pilot Joseph "Mutt" Summers successfully flew the prototype on an eight-minute test flight at Eastleigh Aerodrome. Within weeks, Air Ministry placed an order for 310 Vickers Supermarine Spitfires, at a final cost of £1,870,242 or £9,500 per Spitfire.[21]

* * *

It didn't take long for production of the initial 310 Spitfires to bog down. Arranging for outside contractors to build and deliver components in large numbers, and finding additional space for production, outside of Supermarine's Woolston plant, dragged into 1937. Meantime, development of the Luftwaffe's front-line fighter, the Messerschmitt 109 (with flush-riveted stressed-skin construction, cantilevered monoplane wings, and retracting undercarriage) had moved from prototype in 1934 to test flight in 1936 to installation of 7.92-mm machine guns and 20-mm cannon fired through the propeller hub in 1936— the same year it was evaluated operationally in the Spanish Civil War.[22] The job of testing the third generation Me 109s fell to Luftwaffe fighter pilot Hannes Trautloft.

"The new [Me] 109 simply looks fabulous," he wrote in his diary at the Seville airfield in December 1936. "A mechanic from Junkers [the 109 then had a Junkers Jumo engine] explains the instruments, levers, undercarriage retraction controls to me, and says, the machine has a tendency to swerve to the left on take-off. . . . In the air, I feel at home in the new bird."[23]

Trautloft had flown much of his adult life, working as an instructor at Schleissheim, the Civil Air Pilots' School near Munich, before the war. When Schleissheim changed over to the Luftwaffe Fighter Pilots' School, he gained a commission and was transferred to the III *Gruppe, Jagdgeschwader* (Fighter Squadron) 134. Arriving for his mission to Spain in August 1936, he'd never flown in an aircraft with an enclosed cockpit, nor with as massive a powerplant, nor with weaponry this lethal. Like most of the military hardware Hitler sent to Spain for experimentation in the war backing dictator Francisco Franco, the Me 109 worked out its mechanical bugs. Problems with its tail wheel, water pump, carburetor, and undercarriage locking mechanism proved to be little more than what Trautloft called "teething troubles."

"Its flight characteristics are fantastic," he wrote. "When I had to land at Caceres [in central Spain] because the weather worsened, the people on the ground seemed like strangely slow-moving inhabitants of a far-away planet. I need time to get used to the earth again."[24]

When Trautloft accompanied the three latest Messerschmitt 109 fighter aircraft to the International Aviation Meeting at Zurich in July 1937, he expected the British entries would be the ones to beat. But the British never appeared. The Me 109s astonished most spectators at the concurrent air show with their qualities of quick acceleration and rapid climb. They consequently won the air speed race.[25]

The Royal Air Force brass had chosen not to bring its fighter aircraft in development, either the Spitfire or the Hurricane, to the International Aviation Meeting. They were both behind schedule. The first operational Hawker Hurricanes would not be put to work at RAF fighter stations until December 1937. And it was a full year after the Zurich show, August 1938, when the first Supermarine Spitfires went into service with RAF No. 19 Squadron at Duxford air base.

There were, however, other cross-Channel meetings of air force leadership in 1937. Both the Luftwaffe and the RAF were curious what the other side was up to, although neither was prepared to reveal too much, nor give the other side any credit. In January of that year, Air Vice-Marshal Christopher Courtney, the RAF's director of operations and intelligence, toured a German aircraft factory at Rostock to see the assembly of the Heinkel 111 high-speed airliner. Luftwaffe representatives meanwhile sought clearance to fly across Britain while delivering aircraft to the Condor Legion in Spain, collecting valuable UK target data with each flight.

In October 1937, Erhard Milch, then state secretary for the Reich Ministry of Aviation, and Luftwaffe pilot Ernst Udet received a guided tour of RAF Mildenhall station. Over refreshments in the RAF Officers' Mess, according to Milch, he asked: "How are you getting on with your experiments in the detection by radio of aircraft approaching your shores?"

RAF officers present laughed nervously in response.

"Come, gentlemen," Milch persisted. "We've known you're developing a system of radio location. So are we, and we think we're a jump ahead of you."[26]

Heinrich Hertz's nineteenth-century discovery of electromagnetic waves ultimately gave pilots the means of speaking to ground control and to each other, on wireless radio, which evolved into high-frequency direction-finding (HF/DF) of aircraft, and ultimately to radar. Initially, German engineers employed HF/DF to prevent ships from colliding in the fog. In the 1930s, the Japanese developed a short-wave direction aerial, while American scientists experimented with radio-detection. The US Navy coined the term "radio detection and ranging," or radar.

In 1934, Rudolf Kühnhold, head of German naval research, pioneered underwater detection (later sonar), showing that a "picture" of the battleship *Hessen* could be beamed across Kiel Harbour. As early as 1937, the Kriegsmarine's battleship *Graf Spee* had gun-ranging radar. And a year later, Freya, the Germans' early-warning radar, was able to detect a Junkers 52 transport aircraft fifty miles away. After the outbreak of the war, Freya detected inbound RAF bombing raids and consequently decimated Bomber Command formations. Following the Dunkirk evacuation, Whitehall intelligence realized that withdrawing British forces had left mobile radar devices behind; the Germans found at least one but considered it primitive by German standards. As illustrated by Milch's remarks in 1937, both the British and the German sides considered their competitors either incompetent or inept at using radar.

If not inept, certainly absurd. In 1935, Oxford scientist Henry Thomas Tizard organized the Aeronautical Research Committee, searching for ways to create an impenetrable air defence system for the UK. He asked Robert Watson-Watt of the National Physical Laboratory if he could invent a kind of "death-ray" to emit damaging radiation to stop aircraft engines, kill or disable aircrews, or weaken the structure of enemy aircraft.

"No," Watson-Watt said unequivocally. But he added, "Attention is being turned to the still difficult but less unpromising problem of radio-detection as opposed to radio-destruction . . . by reflected radio waves."[27]

Watson-Watt elaborated that perhaps radio waves could detect aircraft, that wireless radio-telephone communication could link ground controllers and defending fighters, directing them to hostile aircraft, and, further, that coded signals could be transmitted and received among friendly aircraft. These were exactly the kinds of tools that Britain would need should an unfriendly force of bombers attack. Beginning in 1935, Watson-Watt assembled a team of scientists, later located at a manor house at Bawdsey, on the east coast of Britain. His physicists were dispatched to meet with aviators and wireless radio experts, as well as Fighter Command and Bomber Command strategists, to gather what he called "Operational Research."

First, the Bawdsey innovators developed the technology to discern from a distance which aircraft were British and which were not. The Identification Friend or Foe device transmitted a pulse, such that every friendly aircraft in the system re-radiated a more powerful pulse back than the one it received.

Just as quickly, Tizard organized a reporting network. The research group began construction and testing of twenty-one Chain Home RDF stations (with seventy-foot masts for detecting aircraft), as well as thirty Chain Home Low sets (shorter range direction-finding sets equipped with rotating aerials) to track low-flying aircraft. The towers, facing eastward to the sea, were clearly visible from the French coast. At the base of each twin set of transmitter and receiver towers sat a receiver hut where operators (usually Women's Auxiliary Air Force, or WAAF) monitored cathode tubes. If a pulse issued by the tube was unanswered, there were no incoming aircraft; if the pulse was answered with a returning (echo) pulse on the tube, it represented inbound aircraft.

Equally important, the Bawdsey group developed an integrated air defence system for delivering and interpreting data gathered at the radar stations. The Chain Home operators were trained to estimate strength, altitude, and position of an

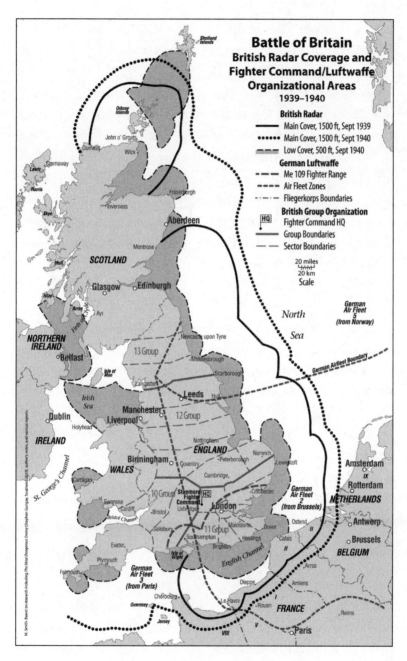

Battle of Britain: British Radar Coverage

inbound force. They telephoned these details into the Filter Room at Fighter Command headquarters at the Bentley Priory on the northern outskirts of London. On the main floor of the Filter Room sat a plotting table, showing Britain, the Channel, and the European coastline. The filtered information was delivered into the headsets of WAAF plotters located around the table; with plotting rods, they moved counters or markers like chess pieces—red for enemy, black for friendly—according to the latest information. Each marker had numbers affixed showing altitude and strength, and an arrow indicating direction and a reference number for that formation of aircraft.

A balcony surrounding the plotting table had tellers and skilled RAF officers who passed the details of these filtered plots to the Operations Room, adjacent to the Filter Room at Fighter Command headquarters. The Ops Room had a wall clock marked to give each five-minute segment a different colour. Every raid's coloured direction arrow was altered to match the clock, and moved with each new report. If the reports kept arriving, all the plots would have the same colour (a lost or neglected raid would be spotted because its colour hadn't changed). Also on the wall of the Ops Room was "The Tote," a board that identified which squadrons were available (within thirty minutes), which were at readiness (within five minutes) or at cockpit readiness (within two minutes), and which were airborne.

For all the cathode tubes, plotting tables, and totes, once enemy aircraft passed over the coast, they were no longer trackable by the seaward-pointing Chain Home radar stations. At that point, members of the Royal Observer Corps, founded by former British Army officer Edward Ashmore, became the eyes of Fighter Command. The Observer Corps had no radar or any detection aids. Its specialty was aircraft recognition, with spotters trained not only to visually locate and identify aircraft but also to recognize the sounds of enemy aircraft engines on days when fog or overcast blocked visual reference.

As Battle of Britain historian Len Deighton observed: "There had never before been a battle in three dimensions, and never a battle moving at such speeds. Yet, for most of the fighting, the coloured counters on the plotting table were no more than four minutes—about fifteen miles—behind events."[28]

* * *

As well-trained as RAF Fighter Command pilots had become by the start of the war, their move from a Miles Master or Fairey Battle aircraft to combat fighters such as Spitfires and Hurricanes proved a challenge.

Unlike piloting a bomber or a two-seat training aircraft for the first time, a pilot taking up a single-seat fighter couldn't do a "circuits and bumps" test flight with an instructor sitting in the same aircraft; in other words, the novice didn't have the advantage of an experienced flyer looking over his shoulder on takeoff, while airborne, or during landing. The first time in a Hurricane or a Spitfire, the pilot was truly flying solo. Most found the transition to the faster, more powerful fighters stirred the blood and sharpened the senses. For Flying Officer Douglas Bader, doubly so.

Bader was the second son of Major Frederick Bader, a Royal Engineer wounded in the Great War. At the age of twelve, in 1922, Douglas lost his father due to war wound complications. His stepfather was a clergyman and Douglas grew up at a rectory in Yorkshire. As a teenager, however, he received very little supervision from either parent and frequently got into trouble. His parents sent him to Temple Grove prep school, with its spartan conditions, then on to St. Edward's secondary school where he thrived on discipline, rugby, and cricket. At age thirteen, he was smitten by aviation when his uncle Cyril Burge, the adjutant at the RAF College at Cranwell, plunked Douglas in the cockpit of an Avro 504 training aircraft. The boy told his uncle he wanted to "come back to Cranwell as a cadet" one day.[29] In 1928, he did.

By 1930, Bader had received his commission as pilot officer posted to the RAF squadron at Kenley, Surrey. His skills as a pilot were only exceeded by his appetite to push them to the limit. In December 1931, while training for the upcoming Hendon Air Show at Woodley Airfield, Bader, on a wager, tried an aerobatic manoeuvre in a Bulldog aircraft too low to the ground and crashed. In emergency surgery, both of Bader's legs were amputated. He later wrote in his flight log: "Crashed slow-rolling near ground. Bad show."[30] In May 1932, he was invalided out of the RAF. As he recovered, he fought to regain full mobility with artificial limbs, driving a car, playing golf, dancing, and flying a plane, hoping to regain his active pilot officer status in the RAF. Accepted initially for ground crew jobs only, Bader campaigned doggedly to have his operational flying status restored by flying solo in an Avro Tutor. He got his wish two months into the war, on November 27, 1939.

"This, then, was the moment," he wrote. "At last I was alone with an aeroplane—almost exactly eight years after my crash. I turned Tutor K3242 into the wind and took off. . . . I recall the feeling of the schoolboy looking at the notice board and seeing his name in the team for Saturday."[31]

His commanding officer rated Bader's flying capability as "exceptional," and he progressed from Tutors to a Fairey Battle fighter-bomber in December, then in January to a Miles Master, the recognized last step before flying Spitfires and Hurricanes. Fortunately for Bader, the phoney war put RAF operations on a temporary hiatus through the winter, giving him time to acclimatize to flying a Hurricane in January. In February, within days of his thirtieth birthday, he was posted to No. 19 Squadron at Duxford and had his first crack flying a Spitfire.

As talented as Bader knew he was, he had to bide his time. For the first while that spring, he flew entirely by the book, following officially approved Attack No. 1, Attack No. 2, and Attack No. 3 tactics, flying line-astern in tight formation behind a flight leader, attacking singly at modest altitudes, and abiding by Fighter Command doctrine that modern fighters were too fast to apply the dogfighting tactics of the First World War against Luftwaffe bombers.

Mindful of his Royal Flying Corps predecessors Billy Bishop, James McCudden, and Albert Ball, Bader repeated their mantra, "Beware the Hun in the sun," since the Germans often initiated attacks out of the sun to blind their opponents. And when it came to formations of German bombers, he recognized that no Heinkel or Dornier pilot under fire would likely fly his bomber in a continuous straight line or at static altitude, allowing enemy fighters to line up one after another and blast away at his aircraft. Even this early in the war, he sensed that Luftwaffe pilots had sufficient experience to "jink all over the place" to escape Spitfires and Hurricanes, and, if possible, to fly "in tight formation to concentrate the fire of their back guns"[32] on incoming RAF fighters.

Training alongside younger fighter pilots, Bader didn't enjoy their ragging about being pre-war vintage. However, it turned out that he needed as much time to learn on the job as his young squadron mates. On his first practice sortie, Bader was so focused on a tight formation landing (his eyes locked on his flight leader's aircraft), that he clipped the top of a hut, shearing off his own Spitfire's tail wheel. Soon after, during a scramble (rapid takeoff), he neglected to switch the black knob of the propeller lever from coarse pitch to fine pitch; he crash-landed the Spitfire in a field at the end of the airstrip. Expecting the worst response from his mistakes, Bader instead learned he'd been promoted to flight lieutenant and posted to an operational unit, No. 222 Squadron, as a flight commander.

Some of his earliest combat sorties had him over Dunkirk during the epic evacuation in May 1940. That week of Operation Dynamo, he shot down two German fighter aircraft and two bombers.[33] His focus now was flying, fighting, and tactics. On June 23, AVM Trafford Leigh-Mallory called Bader to his office at 12 Group Headquarters in Hucknall, Nottinghamshire.

"I've been hearing of your work as a flight commander," Leigh-Mallory began. "I'm giving you a squadron."

Perhaps not fully comprehending this good news, Bader offered apologies for pranging several Spitfires.

"Don't worry," Leigh-Mallory continued. "Your new squadron flies Hurricanes. . . . No. 242 are a Canadian squadron, the only one in the RAF. Nearly all the pilots are Canadians and they're a tough bunch." He added that they too had fought in the Battle of France; they, too, had scored victories over Dunkirk; they, too, had suffered lost pilots and now were short the Hurricanes left behind or destroyed on the continent. The experience in France had left No. 242 "badly mauled" and suffering "low morale." Leigh-Mallory believed they needed better organization and a firm hand.* Bader seemed the best candidate for the job. "The Luftwaffe seems to be gathering across the Channel," said Leigh-Mallory. "We may need every fighter squadron we've got on the top line soon."[34]

With the first phase of the Battle of Britain about to begin, the marriage of Acting Squadron Leader Bader to No. 242 All-Canadian Squadron seemed a reasonable arrangement for the RAF's beleaguered Fighter Command. A squadron created out of political expediency by the governments of Canada and Britain in 1939, and blooded during the withdrawal from France in 1940, probably did need more hands-on leadership. Bader, a squadron leader bent on beating the Luftwaffe with unconventional tactics, needed a tough and talented squadron that he could shape to prove his point.

It was nevertheless a lightning series of promotions for Douglas Bader. Eight weeks previously, he had been an ordinary flying officer in the Royal Air Force. Two squadrons ago, he'd been a reluctant follower, not a leader either by seniority or qualifications. Several damaged Spitfires ago, he'd been dismissed as old-fashioned and pre-war vintage. And nine years after he'd nearly died in a preventable crash, the now "legless fighter pilot" was acting squadron leader of a group of Canadian fighter pilots he'd never met.

* * *

* S/L Fowler M. Gobeil, who had seemed to disappear during No. 242's last patrol out of France, on June 18, 1940, landed safely in England. He was reassigned to instructional duties with the British Commonwealth Air Training Plan in Canada.

By the time he got to the area of eastern Britain known as the Norfolk Broads, it was dark and Acting Squadron Leader Douglas Bader was lost. Even when he asked some of the locals where he could find RAF Coltishall, they couldn't help him. His plight was aggravated by the fact that Britain's Home Guard had done its job; there wasn't a roadside sign in sight to direct him. When he finally stumbled on the barbed-wire entrance to the station, the overnight guard wanted to know the password. Bader had no idea what it was and had to wait until the guardroom contacted the duty officer to give him clearance.

By the next morning, June 24, word had circulated among the pilots: "The new CO? Bit unusual. He's got no legs."[35]

Bader, meantime, had met with No. 242's adjutant, Pilot Officer Peter MacDonald, the man who'd served as former Commanding Officer Gobeil's eyes and ears at the all-Canadian squadron since it was formed the previous October. MacDonald gave Bader a breakdown of the squadron: a few English pilots, but the rest were young Canadians who'd served in the Battle of France but felt discarded by the RAF.

Bader also consulted with Wing Commander Walter Beisiegel, who'd told Bader these "wild Canadians"[36] were the least tractable young officers he'd ever seen. With that bit of intel, Bader entered the "B" Flight dispersal area and got virtually no acknowledgment. Not even when he asked, "Who is in charge here?"

Finally, somebody responded. "I guess I am," said a thickset, wiry-haired pilot with a flying officer's braid on his sleeve.

"What's your name?" Bader asked.

"Turner," Stan said, and paused before he added, "Sir."

Bader told Turner and the rest how dishevelled they

looked, how little they appeared to respect Air Force decorum, and how he'd been sent there to whip them into shape.

"Horseshit," Turner said, and again after a pause, "Sir."[37]

Bader's posting to No. 242 by Leigh-Mallory had only given him command of the squadron; he deduced, now, that the assignment on paper wasn't sufficient to give him their respect in fact. It would take something more to win them over. So, ignoring Turner's last comment and, using his lopsided but quick gait, Bader marched through the door and outside, directly to one of the Hurricanes parked on the flight line. He hoisted himself into the cockpit, donned a helmet, started the fighter's engine, turned the aircraft into the wind, and took off. Bader would assert his authority by exceeding what any of his squadron pilots expected of a legless fighter pilot, and age thirty at that. For half an hour, he threw the fighter around the sky over the station, reminiscent of his days piloting the Bulldog at the Hendon Air Show in 1931, merging one critical aerobatic manoeuvre into the next: loops, rolls, stalls, dives, spins, flicks, and recoveries, all at top speed. When he landed and taxied the Hurricane back to the flight line, all the pilots were standing there watching. He climbed out of the cockpit and disappeared into his office in a hangar.

After that instructive display, it was now Bader's turn to learn. From Warrant Officer (WO) Bernard West, the squadron's engineer officer, Bader found that No. 242 had just received eighteen brand-new Hurricanes, including the one he'd just flown. But West had no means of keeping them in the air. Only one ground crew fitter had managed to salvage a set of tools during the evacuation from France. Everything else was gone. In attempting to replace them, West faced mountains of paperwork. When Bader next addressed his pilots, he discovered why they all looked so scruffy. They'd flown out of France with just the clothes on their backs: no shoes, shirts, ties, no kit, nothing. And any attempts to get those replaced had met with more bureaucracy. Bader realized, despite their respectable combat record in France, they'd seen seven of their comrades killed in action, one go missing, and another have a nervous breakdown. And all the while, it seemed, their air force hadn't the time of day to prepare them for continued active duty.

Bader assembled his pilots again and apologized for his earlier remarks. He told them they'd all visit a tailor shop in Norwich for new clothes, at no expense to them. Next, he sat down to interview every one of his pilots. Then, he confronted P/O MacDonald, WO West, and W/C Beisiegel about breaking the logjam to acquire new tools, spare parts, and station supplies. Over the next couple of days, he took his pilots aloft in twos for flight checks. He knew they'd done more actual fighting than he had, but if he planned to whip them into a fighting force using his combat strategy, he had to know their strengths and weaknesses. Before long, the Bader charm had warmed them to him. The ice was broken.

Almost immediately, to Bader's liking, his pilots looked sharper and seemed tuned back in. He had installed two new flight commanders, experienced British fighter pilots F/L George Eric Ball (to lead "A" Flight) and F/L George Powell-Shedden (to lead "B" Flight). The acting commanding officer managed his men by dropping in to the dispersal halls, maintenance hangar, radio hut, armoury, and instrument section. Then, he led sections of the new Hurricane pilots through tougher formation drills in the air, snapping commands across the R/T (radio), and then, back on the ground, lecturing his pilots on battle strategy. Don't follow an enemy aircraft down.

Never straggle. Use deflection shooting (shooting ahead of a moving target).

When he was satisfied the squadron had begun to gel, he communicated a squadron status report to the powers that be: "242 Squadron now operational as regards pilots, but non-operational, repeat non-operational as regards equipment."[38]

The pronouncement vibrated up the chain of command from RAF Sector HQ, to Group HQ, to the office of Fighter Command's Hugh Dowding. Almost immediately, Bader was at Bentley Priory in front of Air Chief Marshal Dowding himself. Often referred to by his staff as "Stuffy," because he could be, Dowding listened attentively to Bader, just weeks into his role as acting squadron leader.

Dowding reacted just as Bader hoped, although he was still stunned by the lightning response. When Bader laid out the sorry state of No. 242's inventory, Dowding called in the equipment squadron leader and, verifying the failure to deliver equipment, dismissed the man from HQ on the spot. The next day, July 9, lorries rolled into Coltishall with crates of tools, spare parts, and maintenance gear. Bader was on the phone to his engineering officer, Bernard West.

"Have you got enough, West?" Bader asked.

"Enough?" he answered. "Enough here for ten squadrons, sir."

Bader put the phone down and issued a new status signal for Fighter Command HQ: "242 Squadron now fully operational."

CHAPTER FIVE

"TWISTING TURNING MÊLÉE OF FIGHTERS"

T HE BRITISH MILITARY'S PREOCCUPATION WITH PAPERWORK extended beyond just the exigencies of war munitions. In June 1940, Air Ministry notified Hugh Dowding, age fifty-nine, that he was expected to retire on July 14. Remarkably, it took air force bureaucracy until July 5 to recognize the bad timing and invite him to stay until October. Dowding wrote to complain that notifying him ten days before he was supposed to retire was discourteous. A flurry of correspondence followed between Dowding and the government's secretary of state for air, Archibald Sinclair, and between Dowding and the chief of air staff, Cyril Newall, at Air Ministry. Dowding then rendered all this correspondence irrelevant by travelling to Chequers to meet Prime Minister Churchill:

> "He was good enough to tell me that I had secured his confidence," Dowding reported, "and that he wished me to remain on the Active List . . . without any date for my retirement being fixed."[1]

British legend has it that Sir Francis Drake chose to finish his game of bowls before reacting to news of the Spanish Armada entering the English Channel, and that Horatio Nelson, preferring to disregard flag signals ordering him to retreat, looked through his telescope at the signalman with his blind eye. Hugh Dowding's personal assistant during the Battle of Britain, Robert Wright, wrote that his CO had no such bravado, but rather "a more modern temper." He operated with "unostentatious courtesy." Wright claims that even in the most perilous and stressful times in the huge underground block containing the Filter and Operations Rooms at Bentley Priory, Dowding "presented to everybody an outwardly calm, even austere, mien which hid the depths and the sincerity of the emotions that were his."[2] That calm served him well in spring 1940.

In May and June, the Royal Air Force had suffered the loss of 959 military aircraft, 477 of them fighter aircraft (versus the Luftwaffe loss of 1,284 aircraft).[3] That left Dowding's Fighter Command at the end of the Battle of France in a seriously weakened condition, with what Hugh Dowding assessed as his primary task—the defence of Britain against a knock-out blow—still ahead. As of July 7, 1940, Fighter Command's deployment consisted of fifty-two squadrons, nineteen equipped with Spitfires, twenty-five with Hurricanes, two with Defiants, and six with Blenheims. Of 800 aircraft on the books, 644 were available for operations. Of an establishment of 1,456 pilots, 1,259 were ready for active duty.

Dowding at least had the advantage of Britain's wartime intelligence system. On June 12, Reginald Jones, the English physicist and military intelligence expert with Britain's Air Ministry, viewed a message decrypted by the RAF's "Y" Service, which regularly intercepted German radio signals. The

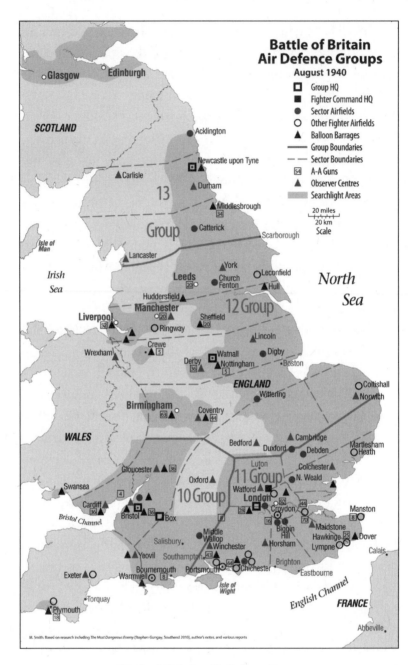

Battle of Britain
Air Defence Groups
August 1940

☐ Group HQ
■ Fighter Command HQ
● Sector Airfields
○ Other Fighter Airfields
▲ Balloon Barrages
━━━ Group Boundaries
– – – Sector Boundaries
54 A-A Guns
▲ Observer Centres
Searchlight Areas

20 miles
20 km
Scale

Glasgow   Edinburgh

SCOTLAND   Acklington

Newcastle upon Tyne

Carlisle   Durham

13   Middlesbrough
34

Group   Catterick   Scarborough

Isle of
Man   Lancaster

Irish   York
Sea   Leeds   Church   Leconfield
20   Fenton
Huddersfield   Hull
Manchester   12 Group
Liverpool   Sheffield
52   20
Ringway

Crewe   Lincoln
Wrexham   5
Watnall   Digby
Derby   Nottingham   Boston
36   5

ENGLAND   Coltishall
Wittering   Norwich

Birmingham   Coventry
63   44

WALES   Cambridge
Bedford   Duxford   Martlesham
Heath
Gloucester   36   Luton   Colchester
Oxford   11 Group   N. Weald
Swansea   Watford   London
4   52
Cardiff   Croydon   Manston
39   Bristol   36   Box   28   16   70   8
Bristol Channel   Biggin   Maidstone
Middle   Hill   Hawkinge   Dover
Salisbury   Wallop   Horsham   25
Winchester   Lympne
Yeovil   43   Calais
Southampton   44   Brighton
Exeter   Bournemouth   Portsmouth   Chichester   Eastbourne
Warmwell   8   Isle of
Torquay   Wight   English Channel   FRANCE
Plymouth
18   Abbeville

10 Group

North
Sea

M. Smith. Based on research including The Most Dangerous Enemy (Stephen Bungay, Southend 2010), author's notes, and various reports

Battle of Britain: Air Defence Groups

message read: "Cleves *Knickebein* is confirmed at position 53°
24' north and 1° west." Jones deduced that the geographical
position (at Retford, in central England) meant the Germans
had an intersecting beam system based in Cleves, Germany,
for bombing England. *Knickebein* ("Crooked Leg") would
guide German bombers via radio-navigation to targets, particularly in bad weather and at night. Four days later, Jones
met Air Chief Marshal Dowding at a meeting of the Night
Interception Committee.

"Well, Commander-in-Chief," committee members asked
Dowding, "what should we do?"

"Jam!" he said.[4]

Now that Britain knew the communication pathways
Germany used to lead bombers to targets in England, the best
response would be to interrupt, block, or scramble beams with
counter-technology. Of limited value to Fighter Command at
first, decrypts such as the *Knickebein* message eventually revealed
Reichsmarschall Göring's full order of battle, including the
organization of the three air fleets allocated to attack Britain.

In the meantime, Dowding quartered the country into
Fighter Group areas, geographically, north to south: 13 Group
defending the north of England and Scotland; 12 Group
responsible for East Anglia, the Midlands, and North Wales;
11 Group covering the expected hottest spots of southeast
England and London; and 10 Group defending southwest
England and South Wales. Each group had its own commander, squadrons, and operations room.

Fighter Command headquarters at Bentley Priory and each
group headquarters decided which forces to commit to which
actions. Airfield control rooms then "scrambled" the squadrons and with coded radio-telephone instructions "vectored"

(directed) their pilots to engage German aircraft formations. All of the operations rooms received updated information about the course of the attackers from coastal radar stations or the Observer Corps centre via the Filter Room at Bentley Priory. Because RAF fighters carried about an hour's worth of· fuel, Fighter Command had to ensure the defensive force had reserves to meet new enemy formations when the first defenders needed to "pancake" (return to base) and refuel. There was always the danger of scrambling too many squadrons too quickly to meet what would turn out to be a feint attack, or conversely, taking a cautious approach and making it impossible for fighters to climb to sufficient altitudes for effective interception. Successful launches of the fighters depended on sound judgment, anticipation, co-operation, and luck.

All that was subtle and reserved about Air Chief Marshal Dowding was the reverse in his opponent, Reichsmarschall Göring. Wounded at age twenty-one in the first year of the Great War, Göring transferred to the Field Aviation Unit as an observer in the German Air Force, rising eventually to command Baron von Richthofen's Flying Circus. In 1922, he joined the Nazi Party, eventually assuming the presidency of the Reichstag, and later organizing the stormtroopers and the Gestapo. He amassed power and political capital to become the second-most powerful official in Nazi Germany; as the war began, Hitler designated him successor "if anything should befall me." As air minister and commander-in-chief of the Luftwaffe, Göring basked in the glory of its quick victories in Poland, Norway, the Netherlands, Belgium, and France.

After Dunkirk, Hitler anticipated a negotiated peace with Britain or, as Italian fascist Galeazzo Ciano wrote in his diary,

"Hitler is now the gambler who has made a big scoop and would like to get up from the table risking nothing more."[5] The führer felt so confident the British would talk armistice that he disbanded fifteen divisions and returned twenty-five more to peacetime readiness. But after the Royal Navy attacked at Oran, in French North Africa, on July 3, destroying the French Navy before the German Kriegsmarine could confiscate French warships, Hitler issued Führer Directive No. 16, his plan for a September landing operation against Britain, called *Seelöwe*, Operation Sea Lion.

The German Army's ambitious invasion plan called for landings along England's south coast, from Ramsgate in the east to the Isle of Wight in the west. In preparation, the army would confiscate car ferries to transport its panzers, trucks, and artillery across the Channel. The first wave of the invasion force, launched from the great ports and harbours of northern Europe (Rotterdam, Antwerp, Le Havre, and Cherbourg), would consist of 260,000 men, 30,000 vehicles, and 60,000 horses.[6] The operation expected to have troops ashore in three days with primary objectives taken between the coast and London in that time.

On July 31, Hitler summoned both Army and Navy chiefs to the Berghof, his chalet in the Bavarian Alps, to discuss Operation Sea Lion. Grossadmiral Erich Raeder explained that the Kriegsmarine was searching all of occupied Europe for enough barges to deliver the invasion force, but getting them to Channel ports any earlier than September 15 would be impossible. Hitler seemed content with that timeline, but asked Göring, in the interim, to rid the skies of the RAF, clearing the way for the invasion. Göring leapt at the opportunity to demonstrate the Luftwaffe's might. "As long as the enemy air

Battle of Britain: Operation Sea Lion

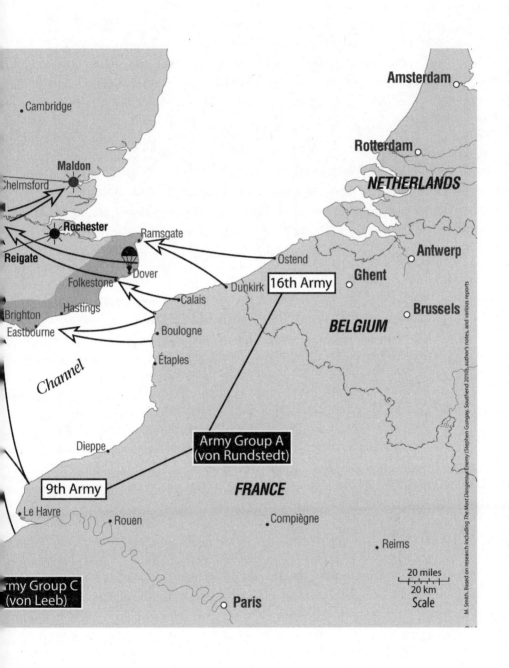

force is not defeated," he announced, "the prime requirement is to attack it by day and night."[7]

Göring's air force had about 2,250 serviceable aircraft, including 250 dive-bombers, 1,000 long-range bombers, and 1,000 fighters, available for the operation to destroy the RAF. The Luftwaffe had organized its bomber and fighter squadrons into *Luftflotten*, or Air Fleets. Since the occupation of Europe, Air Fleets 2 and 3 had moved from bases in Germany to newly occupied or constructed airfields in France and Belgium, most located on the Channel coast. Air Fleets 1 and 4 remained in Germany, and Air Fleet 5 was transferred to airfields in Scandinavia. That gave the Luftwaffe as many as four hundred airfields from which to launch attacks against Britain.[8] Each Air Fleet commander took orders directly from Göring and Generalfeldmarschall Erhard Milch. Luftwaffe bombers and fighters were organized into *Geschwader*, or groups. Every *Geschwader* consisted of three *Gruppen*, or wings, and each *Gruppe* was made up of three *Staffeln*, or squadrons. Bomber groups were known as *Kampfgeschwader* (KG), fighter groups as *Jagdgeschwader* (JG), and dive-bomber groups as *Stukageschwader* (StG). Each Luftwaffe *Geschwader* consisted of 100 to 150 aircraft, each *Gruppe* 30 to 50, and each *Staffel* 10 to 16 aircraft.[9] The *Fliegerkorps*, or air corps, administered all operational matters, including deployment, air traffic, ordnance, and maintenance.[10]

As Hitler's inner circle departed the Berghof in mid-July, its members agreed the grand attack, the invasion, would commence in eight weeks. Until then, the stage belonged to Göring.

* * *

For most of the winter and spring of 1939–40, Jill Brown and her family had soldiered through the disruptions caused by the war on the western end of the Isle of Wight. Her father had readily donated the family's pleasure boat for use in the Dunkirk crisis. Rationing had eliminated access to fresh fruits, fresh meat, and her favourite sweets. In addition to the concrete and wire obstacles the Home Guard had planted on the beach in front of Freshwater, Jill remembered the sudden arrival of barrage balloons, tethered from merchant and military ships to fend off Luftwaffe attacks in the Channel. She continued to attend school, keeping her gas mask handy.

The Browns' home on the island was less than a mile from the south coast of England, with the ancient defences of Hurst Castle clearly visible across the Solent. But it might as well have been a thousand miles. "Once the war started," said Jill, "you couldn't cross from the island to the mainland unless there was a good excuse."

From Freshwater, she could see the ship convoys arriving and delivering cargo and fuel to the busy port of Southampton. Merchant shipping was a lifeline that had to feed forty-one million Britons. As the war began, the country was importing twenty million tons of food per year; about 70 percent of Britons' annual food supply came from foreign nations. Supply experts calculated that one 10,000-ton merchant vessel carried on average enough food and fuel to provide for 225,000 Britons for a week.[11]

While her parents did not speak openly about the war, not wanting to frighten her, Jill joined them listening to Winston Churchill's speeches. "Hitler knows that he will have to break us in this island," the prime minister declared in the House of Commons on June 18, "or lose the war."[12]

Despite her parents' precautions, she would also see plainly the effects of the war in the skies over the Isle of Wight that summer. "The dogfights," she said. "We went out in the streets toward the shore and watched them over the island. Bright blue sky, full of planes zooming all over it. And occasionally seeing one coming down."[13]

* * *

Amid a deluge of senior promotions in July 1940, Hitler had elevated Albert Kesselring to commander of Air Fleet 2. The fifty-five-year-old former army officer had only joined the Luftwaffe in 1933; he was given Air Fleet 2 to keep him from retiring. Well established as commander of Air Fleet 3 was fifty-year-old Hugo Sperrle, Germany's most experienced air force officer, having commanded the Condor Legion in Spain. On July 10, the first day of *Kanalkampf* (Channel Battle), Kesselring and Sperrle launched a large assault on British shipping in the English Channel. Twenty-six Dornier 17 bombers, with fighter escort, were directed to a large Allied convoy, code-named "Bread," leaving the Thames estuary.

Werner Kreipe, a Dornier bomber crewman, was part of that mission. The thirty-six-year-old airman said his battle wing was only airborne half an hour when it sighted the convoy steaming along England's south coast. "As soon as we were observed, the ships of the convoy dispersed, the merchantmen manoeuvring violently, and the escorting warships moving out at full speed," he wrote. "We made our first bomb run and fountains leapt up around the ships."[14]

Anti-aircraft shells from the Royal Navy warships peppered the sky around the Dorniers. Within minutes, twenty-four RAF fighters from 11 Group spotted the puffs of smoke around the bombers and initiated a counterattack, as the Germans had anticipated. Luftwaffe strategy involved bombers attacking convoys to draw out large numbers of RAF fighters. The Luftwaffe fighters, flying above the Dorniers, would then ambush and destroy the British fighters.

"By now the [RAF] fighters had joined in, and the sky was a twisting, turning mêlée of fighters," Kreipe continued. "My wing was in the air for three hours in all. We reported one heavy cruiser and four merchant ships sunk . . . and eleven British fighters shot down. We had lost two bombers, two twin-engined fighters, and three single-engined fighters during this engagement."

Fighter Command, tallying the same action, reported one sloop sunk, one RAF fighter shot down, and eight Luftwaffe aircraft destroyed. Not only was this the opening salvo in the Battle of Britain, it was also the first of hundreds of exaggerated claims made on both sides during the 113-day siege. The problem of overclaiming—when aircrew being debriefed after a combat operation claimed the destruction of more enemy aircraft than were actually shot down—wasn't new. It sometimes resulted when more than one aircraft attacked the same target; often it happened if the aircraft attacked wasn't actually shot down but landed safely. A 1939 Luftwaffe directive required confirmation of the destruction of an enemy aircraft or ship by at least one human witness. So-called shared kills were not accepted. They were, however, accepted in RAF debriefings. Apart from the difficulty of confirmation, overclaiming—inflating kill figures or deflating losses—became a valuable propaganda tool for both British and German military strategists.

* * *

Canadian fighter pilots, including two members of the Millidgeville Trio, flew combat operations in the opening days of the battle. After combat in the skies over France had depleted his first squadron, the RAF had reposted Flight Lieutenant Harry Hamilton to No. 85 Squadron at Debden, northeast of London. Early in their provision of air cover for Channel convoys, Hamilton and his squadron comrades had learned to fly their Hurricanes in the skies between the convoy vessels and the coastline. That way, if they spotted enemy aircraft inbound from France, they could drive them back out to sea and return to their original positions. Also, coming from the land side of the ships, the Hurricanes stood a better chance of avoiding friendly fire from trigger-happy gunners aboard the Royal Navy warships escorting the convoy.

A potentially more lethal problem emerged, however, when the British pilots engaged more experienced Luftwaffe fighters. "On our side," wrote German fighter pilot Hans-Ekkehard Bob, "were people who had already experience of war in Spain, and others like myself who'd seen action in Poland."[15]

By the time the Luftwaffe and RAF first tangled during *Kanalkampf*, fighter pilot Bob, age twenty-three, was already a fighter squadron leader in III *Gruppe* of JG 54. He and his comrades were using tried and true combat tactics. Often the German fighter-bomber squadrons sent one or two Dornier or Junkers bombers adjacent to the convoy to draw the RAF fighters away from their air cover positions. Then the larger attack force would pounce on the less defended convoy.

During one of their convoy patrols in July, F/L Hamilton recorded that he and his wingmate, Flight Sergeant Allard, spotted a Messerschmitt fighter-bomber about ten miles off England's east coast. "E/A [enemy aircraft] put on speed, turned east and endeavoured to escape, and we gave chase in line astern for thirty-five miles. . . . I got abreast of E/A and delivered a stern attack, firing a five-second burst."[16]

The Me 110 returned fire from 1,500 yards, then lurched to the port side, its nose dropping in a death dive. Hamilton watched the 110 plunge into the Channel with one of the two-man crew surviving. He and Allard then pursued another bomber racing for the French coastline, only to lose it in low cloud. Hamilton's combat report doesn't record it, but with two Hurricanes effectively drawn halfway across the Channel, convoy coverage would have been significantly diminished. "The English were good pilots," Hans-Ekkehard Bob wrote, "they simply had not had any previous experience of war."[17]

The second member of the Millidgeville Trio, Duncan Hewitt, whose family had learned about his first victory over Dunkirk watching newsreel footage in Canada, had just completed a move closer to the front line. His No. 501 Squadron was now operating from Middle Wallop aerodrome in 10 Group, just north of Southampton. Prior to the first battles over the Channel convoys, Hewitt had written his parents about his preparations for the sorties to come. "I had my lucky charm put on my aircraft the other day," he wrote home to Saint John. "It consists of a white circle, six inches in diameter, with an Indian head painted in it."[18]

Mid-July proved unseasonably cool and damp along England's south coast. Accommodations not being the best in the dispersal hut at Middle Wallop, the pilots wore added layers—pyjamas, an extra shirt, and underwear—for warmth. There was nothing that could be done about the low cloud and mist over the Channel, however. Visibility was at its worst for both attacker and defender.

Hewitt was in the air on July 12 when the Luftwaffe employed its familiar tactic, sending a lone raider ahead to reconnoiter shipping off the Dorset coast. No. 501's controller scrambled a flight of fighters, with Hewitt and Pilot Officer Gus Holden as wingmen flying in formation with Squadron Leader Harry Hogan. "The weather was absolutely atrocious," Hogan wrote. "Holden saw the bomber and went after it. Hewitt followed. As [the bomber] attempted to disappear into the gloom, Hewitt, pressing home his attack, tried to get underneath it and hit the water. Gus called out, 'We've lost Hewitt.'"[19]

Even if Hewitt had survived the crash, it's not likely that the RAF's air-sea rescue system could have saved him. Fighter Command relied on just eighteen rescue boats along the entire south coast of England. RAF pilots downed in the Channel had a better chance of being rescued by trawlers or merchant ships in the vicinity. To make matters worse, British fighter aircraft carried no dinghies at the time. Pilots, wounded or not, had to inflate their own life vests in the water. The vests were "olive drab" in colour and blended into the sea, making the wearer difficult to spot.

Luftwaffe airmen, on the other hand, stood a good chance of rescue. They all wore highly visible yellow skull caps; they carried flare pistols, sea dye, and one-man dinghies aboard their aircraft. The Kriegsmarine had anchored rescue rafts at intervals in the Channel, and the Luftwaffe's Heinkel 59 floatplanes were capable of locating, landing, and picking up downed aircrew.[20] Only after more than two hundred Allied airmen had died or gone missing in the Channel, some twenty-one days into the battle, did Fighter Command organize more efficient air-sea rescue protocols.[21]

The July afternoon of Hewitt's crash, a rescue boat was dispatched from Weymouth, at Portland Island, to search for him, but neither his aircraft nor his body was ever found. P/O Duncan Hewitt became the first Canadian casualty of the Battle of Britain. His last letter home had reflected the sentiment of Britons and their Allied defenders. "I reckon the next two months will show which way this war will go," Hewitt wrote. "Boy, the things that have happened in this war have the last war all wiped to a frazzle."[22]

Official records of Hewitt's last flight add one final twist to his death. At some point in his pursuit of the enemy aircraft, Hewitt signalled that his target was not a Dornier but a Hurricane with German markings. Since RAF pilots, rapidly pulling out of France in June, had destroyed or abandoned scores of their Hurricanes, it was certainly plausible.

Whether it was Hurricanes with iron crosses or not, Hewitt recognized that his enemy's tactics kept Fighter Command off balance. During one July raid, RAF fighters raced to defend a convoy, while, unopposed, sixty-three Junkers 88s attacked railway yards, anchored ships, and munitions factories at Falmouth and Swansea. The bombing caused eighty-six casualties without any German losses. A similar diversion on July 19 freed Dorniers to deliver a precision bombing raid against the Rolls-Royce plant in Glasgow.

By this time, the Luftwaffe had established new airfields at Brittany on France's westernmost Channel coast. It began sending fighter sweeps as a vanguard to draw out RAF fighters; then, after an interval, the Germans launched bomber streams while Fighter Command aircraft were back on the ground refuelling and replenishing. With pilot losses mounting, Hugh Dowding called on sister commands for support.

"Pilots had to be withdrawn from the Bomber and Coastal Commands," Dowding recorded later, "and flung into the Battle after hasty preparation."[23] Among those pilots hurried into the Channel battle was P/O Dick Howley. Born in 1920 in British Columbia and raised in Newfoundland, Howley had moved with his family to the UK in 1933. He took up flying and applied to the RAF, receiving his Short Service Commission in 1937. Initially trained to pilot Blenheims with Bomber Command, in June 1940, Howley and the rest of No. 141 Squadron were suddenly posted to West Malling to train on two-seater Defiant fighters. Howley teamed up with F/Sgt Albert Curley as gunner in preparation for convoy patrols over the Channel.[24] They'd had barely six weeks of training on the Defiants when, just before 1 p.m. on July 19, Fighter Command scrambled nine of them to cover a convoy off Dover.

German pilot Hannes Trautloft was leading a flight of Me 109s and he spotted the British Defiants flying in formation. "The sun was behind me," he wrote. "My guns fired . . . Pieces of the Defiant broke off and came hurtling toward me. I saw a thin trail of smoke . . . then just a fiery ball."[25] The Me 109s shot down four Defiants on their first pass, another as it sought cloud cover. In a matter of minutes, four pilots and six air gunners from No. 141 Squadron were gone, including P/O Dick Howley and F/Sgt Curley.

P/O Ian MacDougall was piloting one of the surviving Defiants. To him, the tracer bullets from the Messerschmitts looked "like small bright glow-worms"[26] slicing through his fighter formation. He watched in horror as one by one the

Defiants dropped, pouring smoke and flames into the Channel. As German shells ripped through his own Defiant, MacDougall dived for land, calling out to his gunner on the way down. He got no reply. MacDougall crash-landed at Hawkinge base and found that his gunner had been blown from his turret behind the cockpit.

Overall that day, the RAF lost ten fighter aircraft, with five pilots killed and five more wounded. It was Fighter Command's worst defeat of the campaign so far. When Dowding reported on the battle losses to Churchill, the prime minister acknowledged Dowding's doubts about ever using Defiants as fighters again.[27]

* * *

That same evening, July 19, Adolf Hitler arrived at the Kroll Opera House in Berlin to speak to Nazi officials of the Reichstag. On the dais with him sat Hermann Göring and other members of the German high command. Behind them hung massive swastika drop cloths; in front of them was a hall full of party faithful displaying the Nazi salute in unison. Hitler began his speech blaming Jews, the Treaty of Versailles, and "Anglo-French warmongers" for the war. He praised his military commanders, promoting nine of them to the rank of field marshal. Hitler then warned Winston Churchill and the British people of the disasters that would befall them should they continue to fight. "I believe I can do this, as I am not asking for something as the vanquished, but rather as the victor," he said. "I am speaking in the name of reason. I see no compelling reason which could force the continuation of this war."[28]

Churchill chose not to respond publicly, but rather to contrast the führer's dictatorship with "solemn, formal debate . . . and resolutions in both Houses of Parliament" in a democratic Britain. Churchill did, however, chide Hitler's notion that the prime minister "would shortly take refuge in Canada."[29] When Luftwaffe bombers later flew over Britain dropping leaflets of Hitler's July 19 speech, *A Last Appeal to Reason*, copies were auctioned to raise money for local Red Cross and Spitfire Funds.[30] Not to be outdone, Bomber Command dropped leaflets of its own. Why, the British leaflets asked, had Germany chosen "seven years of rearmament and not food distribution?"[31]

In spring 1940, RAF bombers had conducted a series of what were called "nickelling" operations*, dropping propaganda leaflets ("bomphlets") over Germany and occupied Europe. F/L Bill Nelson had flown a number of nickelling ops. Nelson's RAF records had him listed as a Canadian citizen, born in Montreal, and a member of the Church of England. Bill was indeed born in Montreal in 1917, the son of Jewish parents. He was destined to fly from the age of sixteen, when the Montreal Model Aircraft League recognized him as its junior champion model builder; he later won the senior championship, as well. His chums in the league nicknamed him "Orville," after the younger of the two Wright brothers.[32] His family could not finance Bill's post-secondary school education, so he got a job as a draftsman at Fairchild, the aviation

---

* Pulitzer Prize–winning journalist Hubert R. Knickerbocker was deported from Germany for his written criticisms of Adolf Hitler; his views were included in a propaganda leaflet in 1939. The act of dropping those leaflets became known as "nickelling," or nickel raids.

manufacturer in Longueuil, Quebec, which paid for his flying lessons.

In 1936, his application to join the RCAF was turned down, so he boarded a merchant ship for England and applied for an RAF Short Service Commission. Receiving his wings and a commission, Nelson was posted to RAF Dishforth in north Yorkshire where Bomber Command housed No. 10 and No. 78 Squadrons flying Whitley bombers. He was among the earliest Canadian RAF pilots. Both squadrons flew nick-elling operations over northwest Germany; they also bombed munitions factories in the Ruhr River valley.[33]

During the invasion of Norway in April and May 1940, Nelson piloted bombing raids against German-occupied railway yards, floatplane bases, and Luftwaffe airfields. On June 4, 1940, King George VI had personally awarded him the Distinguished Flying Cross. "After an attack on Stavanger, Norway," his citation read, "he encountered a balloon barrage and sent a report to headquarters in time to warn following aircraft"[34] in the bomber stream to avoid them.

Nelson had met and married a civilian woman in Yorkshire and was on leave in June 1940 when the Battle of Britain intensified. By mid-July, when Fighter Command was flying six hundred sorties a day in response to the Luftwaffe day-light attacks,[35] Nelson wrote home to Montreal about the war effort and his faith. "I thank God that I shall be able to help to destroy the regime that persecutes the Jews. I have never had such a great desire to live as I do now; I am happy in the thought that I am helping to crush Hitler."[36]

The Fighter Command losses were rising at such a rapid rate—118 aircraft in July alone—that it was statistically des-tined for extinction in six weeks.[37] With the *Kanalkampf* phase of the Battle of Britain eating up resources and depleting the ranks of qualified pilots, Nelson chose to transfer to Fighter Command, learning to fly Spitfires. By July 27, he had been posted to No. 74 Squadron at RAF Hornchurch, within 11 Group in east London. When attackers set their sights on London's docks or heavy industry, 11 Group fighter stations were inevitably tasked with blocking their path. Thus, on August 1, when Hitler announced his Directive No. 17 "to intensify air and sea warfare against the English homeland," and for "the German Air Force to overpower the English Air Force," Hornchurch and most of 11 Group fighter bases were high on his hit list. The führer ordered the Luftwaffe to destroy all RAF flying units, ground installations, aircraft industry, and anti-aircraft equipment "in the shortest time possible."[38] Nelson would be in the thick of the action.

* * *

Despite the RAF's heavy losses, Canadian fighter pilots flying from 10, 11, and 12 Group stations on the east and south coasts of England managed some successes in defending Allied coastal installations and convoys in the Channel. On July 20, flying from RAF Kenley, F/L Lionel Gaunce, from Lethbridge, Alberta, shot down an Me 109. Four days later, P/O John Bryson, a former RCMP officer from Quebec, scrambled from the base at Croydon and brought down a Messerschmitt fighter. On July 30, New Brunswick pilot Harry Hamilton, flying with No. 85 Squadron from Martlesham Heath, shared in the destruction of an Me 110; then, in August, he would continue his high-scoring sorties and shoot down three more bombers and a fighter. A Canadian graduate of the RAF College at Cranwell,

F/L Peter O'Brian, from Toronto, had served in several squadrons that summer and was recovering from an accident on the ground. But when RAF No. 152 Squadron at Warmwell needed a replacement flight commander, O'Brian stepped up; he would quickly share in the destruction of an He 111 bomber and a Ju 88 bomber. And on August 11, just a few weeks into his Spitfire flying career with No. 74 Squadron from Hornchurch, the newlywed Bill Nelson shot down an Me 109 fighter and an Me 110 fighter-bomber, and damaged another Me 110.[39]

As RAF and CAN/RAF pilots shared their combat experiences, it became clear that Fighter Command's traditional tactics were wanting in the air war over the Channel. Conventional RAF training to fly in close formation, where wingmen focused on staying closely astern of a flight leader, proved inadequate for spotting the enemy. And flying in sections of three aircraft either in "V" formation or line astern, left the section open to attack from above or behind. Meanwhile, the addition of a "tail-end Charlie" moving back and forth behind a flight of fighters (keeping an eye out for enemy aircraft) left him more vulnerable and consuming valuable fuel. As well, the traditional Fighter Command attack practice of peeling off one at a time to dive on an enemy no longer worked. Once they were under attack, enemy aircraft weren't likely to keep flying straight and level; they'd scatter, leaving the rest of the RAF peeling attack with no targets to shoot at. The one long-standing tactic worth keeping, as Douglas Bader, the newly installed squadron leader of No. 242 Squadron, repeatedly told his pilots, was to gain maximum altitude as an advantage over your enemy, and attack with the sun at your back.

Luftwaffe fighters had several years of experience in the skies over Spain, Poland, the Netherlands, and France. They based their combat tactics on the *Schwarm* concept, or the "finger-four" formation. One fighter, A, leads, while a wingman, B, flies on the sun side, lower than the leader. A third fighter, C, slightly back, leads the second pairing with D below and opposite the sun side. In each pair, one fighter leads while the wingman defends. These pairings proved effective. When Fighter Command flyers examined it, they recognized that flying with more space between aircraft also made the formation more difficult for an enemy to spot. Before long, RAF fighter formations copied *Jagdflieger* ones. They flew in pairs, not threes, and remained spaced apart the way Messerschmitt and Junkers fighters did.

Some Fighter Command squadrons adjusted the finger-four formation to more aggressively challenge Luftwaffe opponents. RAF No. 111 (Treble One) Squadron adopted the tactic, on first contact, of flying head-on, line abreast, or side by side at the enemy.

P/O Robert Wilson learned and improved by trial and error as a fighter pilot with Treble One Squadron. Born in 1920 in Moncton, Wilson was a crack shot thanks to boyhood summers spent hunting in New Brunswick's back country. Overseas in 1938, he applied for direct entry into the RAF, and within a year became proficient enough in Hurricanes to fly them in English airshows on a demonstration team. He bragged in letters home that he'd performed aerobatics over the home of an English relative. "I'm uncertain if I ought to be saying so," he wrote, "but I actually buzzed Grandma's house on a training flight. Grandma was thrilled."[40]

During the Battle of France, Wilson flew numerous sweeps over the Dunkirk evacuation. On just his second combat sortie, things seemed uncomfortably quiet. Then he and his wingmen,

F/L Robin Powell and P/O Peter Simpson, were jumped by Messerschmitt fighters. "I looked up to see an Me spitting fire at me," Wilson wrote home to a flying buddy. "It looked like a fireworks display. I was so fascinated it took me about three seconds to realize they were coming for me. I pulled up and shot down another one coming across my path."

Soon Wilson was separated from his wingmen, and the hunter became the hunted. Cannon fire struck his wing. Bullets whizzed between his legs. The Hurricane began smoking from the hits and "I made for dear old England when I started to pass out from the smoke. I turned her over and [bailed) out. . . . I belong to the Caterpillar Club* now."[41]

On July 25, P/O Wilson was back in harness, flying convoy patrols over the Channel. No. 111 Squadron received a scramble call to assist No. 64 Squadron in fending off a formation of fifty Me 109s off the coast of Dover. Wilson's flight of a dozen Hurricanes chose to use its head-on line abreast tactic on the German fighters. Lining up one of the 109s, Wilson pursued it into a steep dive to the Channel; while Wilson pulled up in time, the 109 did not, and the Canadian was credited with the victory. Three weeks later, on an early August day, Wilson's squadron scrambled to thwart thirty inbound Stuka dive-bombers and Dorniers. In the massive dogfight over Margate, Wilson's Hurricane disappeared.

Years later, Robert Wilson's sister Edith recalled the last time she saw her brother: "We all went to Montreal to see [Bob] off," she wrote in 1986, "and watched until the ship

---

* Founded in 1922 by Leslie Irvin of the Irvin Airchute Company of Canada, the Caterpillar Club informally linked all those who successfully used a parachute, originally made of silk threads, to bail out of a disabled aircraft.

became a tiny dot, then disappeared from sight. Quite a lad, and would have been quite a man if he'd survived."[42]

* * *

When the German Army first occupied the French coast of the English Channel, its high-powered photographic equipment captured images of British equipment atop the cliffs of Dover. The photos revealed eight masts of the Dover Chain Home radar system.[43] Some German strategists reached the conclusion that the radar towers were not worth targeting; they theorized that even if the radar masts gave the British early warning of attacks, the RAF was unlikely to use the information to launch stronger forces on short notice. These same strategists wanted the Luftwaffe to concentrate on eliminating RAF fighters and airfields, not radar towers.

Generalmajor Wolfgang Martini of the Luftwaffe Signals Service was nevertheless emphatic that Luftwaffe bombers needed to destroy the radar stations. So, with the next phase of Hitler's assault plan against Britain—*Adlerangriff* (Eagle Attack), scheduled for August 13—the Luftwaffe allocated a single day's raid against British radar installations.

Just before 8 a.m. on August 12, a dozen German fighters made a sweep over Kent to draw RAF fighters away from their intended targets. Sixteen bombers followed to deliver precision attacks on five British radar stations: one at Dover, another to the north at Dunkirk, two more to the south at Pevensey and Rye, and the fifth on the Isle of Wight.

Just after 9 a.m., the spotter watching the cathode tube in the radar shack at Rye identified enemy aircraft. A WAAF aircraftwoman relayed information to Fighter Command headquarters, and British anti-aircraft gunners were alerted. With the WAAF's telephone line open, headquarters heard the whine of German dive-bombers and thud of bombs exploding. In a matter of minutes, every building at Rye radar station except the transmitting shack received direct hits. The station kept on tracking.

Bomb strikes at Pevensey cut off the station's electricity. Those aimed at Dover rocked the towers and wrecked some huts; the same at Dunkirk. But both Kent radar stations continued sending data. Meanwhile, fifteen Junkers bombers dove on Ventnor, the fifth radar station on the Isle of Wight. Word went immediately to the duty Filter Room officer at Fighter Command headquarters. "Ventnor's under attack," Robert Wright was told. He opened the line and called out, "Are you all right?"

"We're being properly beaten up," the corporal at Ventnor said.

Wright asked if the leading aircraftwomen at the radar station were safe, but the din of the bombers and blasts of five-hundred-kilogram bombs interrupted the exchange. The corporal at Ventnor then said, "Blondie's yelling at us from outside. She's trying to count the buggers!" The LAC never completed her count. A bomb struck her vantage point and she was never found.[44]

With a one-hundred-mile gap now opened in Britain's early-warning radar chain, Luftwaffe bombers homed in on RAF Lympne, RAF Hawkinge, and RAF Manston bases, and began dropping bombs and strafing. Of the three targeted stations, Manston suffered the most damage; within five minutes, 150 bombs had demolished most of the airfield's hangars, workshops, and parked aircraft.

August 12 also turned out to be the final day of the Luftwaffe's *Kanalkampf* campaign attacking Allied shipping in the Channel. The RAF and Luftwaffe were destroying each other's resources at about the same rate. From July 10 to August 11, the RAF lost 115 fighters and 64 bombers in combat, a total of 179. The Luftwaffe's combat losses totalled 216 bombers and fighters. The loss of personnel, however, painted a very different picture. The Channel battle had killed or wounded 117 RAF aircrew, and in return had killed or wounded 218 Luftwaffe airmen. Pilot losses were almost two-to-one in Fighter Command's favour.[45] But with plenty of overclaiming, both the Germans and the British thought they were winning the battle. Consequently, spirits remained high on both sides of the Channel.

Nearly lost in the statistics of the air battle was the impact on merchant shipping. From July 10 to August 11, Luftwaffe bombers had sent 40,000 tons of shipping to the bottom of the Channel, but nearly four million tons of freight and fuel had safely run the gauntlet along the British south coast, a major victory for Britain's Merchant Navy.*

Reichsmarschall Göring, receiving exaggerated reports of Luftwaffe combat victories, believed he had destroyed the RAF's ability to strike back. He preferred to believe his pilots' overclaims rather than any suggestion that Britain's defence system could recover or that Fighter Command could bring reserves of aircrew and aircraft stationed elsewhere in the UK into action. He confidently told his audience in a radio broadcast that week: "If an enemy bomber ever succeeds in reaching

---

* In contrast, in the same period, Kriegsmarine U-boats in the North Atlantic sank over 300,000 tons of cargo and more than seventy merchant ships.

the Ruhr, my name is not Hermann Göring. You can call me Meier."*

* * *

The August 12 raid by Junkers dive-bombers against the Isle of Wight's Ventnor radar station had occurred a few miles from the town of Freshwater. It shook the ground where Jill Brown sat in class at school. For her parents, this was the last straw. They had spent the summer watching air battles in the sky over their home and hearing the thunder of bombs crashing into merchant convoys just offshore. They had also noticed advertisements for the UK Ministry of Health Evacuation Scheme. The posters depicted a Home Guard volunteer bending down and offering advice to a British youngster wearing a play soldier's helmet, "Leave this to us, Sonny. You ought to be out of London."[46] Fear of German paratroops landing or Luftwaffe bombings of civilian targets had prompted the government to urge parents, particularly along the south coast of England, to move their children to the north, to the countryside, or even across the Atlantic to Canada.

"My parents figured that the invasion was imminent," Jill Brown said. "They wanted to get us away."[47]

In June 1940, the Children's Overseas Reception Board had received approval to send 24,000 children overseas; more than 1,500 of them arrived in Canada. While Jill, her brother,

---

* While in a forced-labour camp during the war, Polish artist Stanislaw Toegel created a caricature of Hermann Göring dressed in full-dress Reichsmarschall's uniform. In the background, Hitler in lederhosen shouts, "Meier," a recognizable Jewish first name.

Derreck, and her sister, Jacquie, were apprehensive about leaving their parents behind in West Wight, they looked forward to the evacuation as a huge adventure. They felt genuine excitement about sailing off across the Atlantic to a wartime life in faraway Canada, a land without bombs falling on them, where there was no rationing of food and, judging from photographs they'd seen, where endless open spaces awaited.

In the last week of August 1940, Beryl and Cecil Brown painfully but stoically escorted their children to the ferry from the island and said their goodbyes. Their son and daughters were among two hundred Isle of Wight children bound for Liverpool. There, the three Brown children joined 317 other youngsters and 286 other passengers embarking SS *Volendam*, a former Dutch passenger liner now contracted to transport the CORB refugee children to Halifax. The liner steamed out of the Mersey Channel on August 29, part of westbound Convoy OB 205. Two nights later, about 230 miles west of Ireland, the German submarine *U60* spotted the ship and fired two torpedoes into *Volendam*'s forward hold.

"I didn't hear the torpedo hit. I was asleep in our cabin," Jill Brown said. "My sister got us up, told us to get our life jackets on."

Volendam's master, Jan Wepster, gave the order to abandon ship. Amid deafening alarms and with watertight doors closing around them, some of the children panicked, but the crew launched all eighteen lifeboats safely from the stricken liner. The children's voices could be heard singing "Roll Out the Barrel" into the night as rescue ships arrived to pluck them from the lifeboats. All but one of the 606 passengers and all but a few of her 273 crew escaped the *Volendam* onto merchant ships in the convoy. Only one of the two torpedoes exploded;

the other remained lodged in her hull until the ship was successfully beached on the west coast of Scotland.

"All I can remember was being sick. My sister had made
me eat pea soup and I was sick in the lifeboat," Jill recalled.
"It was cold. I just had my night dress on, but I had my teddy
bear, got him into the lifeboat with me." But when the Brown
children were hauled aboard a rescue ship, Jill's teddy bear had
been lost in the confusion.

The Brown children trekked back south to the Isle of
Wight and were immediately booked on the next CORB ship,
SS *City of Benares*. When a child in the Isle of Wight group
contracted chicken pox, however, they were disallowed from
joining *Benares*. She was torpedoed and sunk on September 17.
Eighty-one of the one hundred CORB children died either
in that sinking or from exposure in lifeboats on the North
Atlantic; several of the children lost in the *Benares* sinking had
survived the *Volendam* torpedoing two weeks earlier.

Jill Brown's parents thought better of a third attempt and
hunkered down at home with their three children on the Isle
of Wight through the Battle of Britain and the rest of the war.
"I'm a big believer, when it's your time, it's your time," Jill said.*

---

* Jill Brown eventually did emigrate to Canada eighteen years later, in August
1958, and became a Canadian citizen.

CHAPTER SIX

"OUR NATIONAL DUTY RESTS TERRIBLE AND CLEAR"

G ARFIELD WESTON, EXPATRIATE CANADIAN AND BRITISH member of Parliament for Macclesfield, visited his friend and fellow MP Max Aitken, 1st Baron Beaverbrook, on August 9, 1940, in London. The two influential Canadians met a stone's throw from Buckingham Palace at Beaverbrook's home, Stornoway House, which Beaverbrook used as his cabinet office for the Ministry of Aircraft Production. Neither was a pilot, but Fighter Command losses during the Channel Battle were top of mind for both. Weston asked how many RAF fighter aircraft had been destroyed over the Channel in the first week of August. Beaverbrook told him that Fighter Command had lost sixteen Spitfires and thirteen pilots killed in action.*

"I have a blank cheque here," Weston revealed to his friend.

---

* Actual Fighter Command losses between August 1 and 10, 1940: fifteen Hurricanes, seven Spitfires, three Blenheims; sixteen killed in action, thirteen aircrew missing.

136

Beaverbrook was stunned at the gesture and moved to tears.

"You know, Max," Weston continued, "only God can replace those boys. I'd like to replace the machines."[1] He encouraged his friend to write in an amount that would cover the replacement of the Spitfires.

Beaverbrook wrote the amount £100,000 into the blank space, and recommended that they publicize Weston's gift toward fighter aircraft production.

"I'd rather keep the donation between you and me," Weston said.

Beaverbrook suggested that this wasn't possible, that "there's too [much] power behind this," and that the gift could potentially generate millions of dollars more in donations if made public.

When contacted by the *Daily Express* the next day, Garfield Weston commented, "Lord Beaverbrook is doing a fine job. He's a big man with a big job."

Beaverbrook's job description read, quite simply: pro-duce. When Churchill separated Air Ministry's research and production arms on May 14, 1940, he assigned full respons-ibility for the Ministry of Aircraft Production (MAP) to Lord Beaverbrook. Nothing about the former Canadian newspaper magnate turned British cabinet minister was orthodox. Indeed, from the outset of his appointment, Beaverbrook chose to administer MAP from his home base at Stornoway House. Over a desk in his office, he'd hung a notice: "Organization is the enemy of improvisation."[2]

Though his job was to manufacture whatever aircraft Air Ministry wanted, it was Beaverbrook who decided what types of aircraft would be produced, and also when and in what quantities. Fortunately for those waging the Battle of Britain, Beaverbrook and Hugh Dowding, commander-in-chief of Fighter Command, saw eye to eye. Each of them, it turned out, had a son serving in Fighter Command, but equally important, each realized that MAP, at least in the summer of 1940, needed to manufacture more Spitfires and Hurricanes than bombers. And fast.

There's an axiom in the newspaper business: "efficiency in the existing space." It would have been familiar to Beaverbrook, and applicable to his current task. He knew he had to find innovative ways to deliver fighters using the facilities available. Spitfire production, he discovered, had precious few assembly factories in the country. When Air Ministry gave the green light to build Spitfires in 1938, it had assigned manufacturing of the new fighter to Supermarine's Woolston plant, near Southampton, on England's vulnerable south coast. It also gave Spitfire production rights to the Castle Bromwich car manufacturing plant at Birmingham in the relative safety of England's West Midlands. A multitude of problems had foiled production there, however, including continued modifications to the Spitfire's design, the necessity for dedicated tools to achieve those modifications, a lack of skilled workers, and endless red tape. As a result, by May 1940, when Lord Beaverbrook was appointed minister of aircraft production, Castle Bromwich had not produced a single Spitfire.

Beaverbrook called owner Lord Nuffield. "The government has supplied the financing for the huge production facility," he noted, "so why has nothing been delivered?"

"Perhaps you'd like me to give up control of the Spitfire factory?" Nuffield said, thinking he would call Beaverbrook's bluff.

"Nuffield, that's very generous of you," Beaverbrook responded. "I accept."[3]

Overnight, Beaverbrook gave control of Castle Bromwich Aircraft Factory to Vickers-Armstrong, which installed a skilled staff from Supermarine to run a "shadow factory" producing improved Spitfires. Along with the workers, the Woolston plant shipped to Birmingham finished sets of Spitfire components and completed fuselages for Castle Bromwich to use as templates. Almost immediately, Castle Bromwich was busy building the Spitfire II, with armour built in, cartridge starters, and the high-performance Merlin XII engine.

Before May 1940, planned fighter aircraft production had far exceeded actual fighter aircraft production. For example, in February, 171 were planned and 141 built; in March, 203 versus 177. Beaverbrook's initiatives reversed the trend. Almost right away, actual fighter production exceeded planned fighter production: in May, 325 built versus 261 planned; in June, 446 versus 292; in July, 496 versus 329; and in August, 476 versus 282.[4] Whether Beaverbrook knew it then or not, the Messerschmitt plants in Germany were building only a quarter as many front-line fighters: 140 per month.

Beaverbrook didn't stop there. He found additional efficiencies in what was known as the Civilian Repair Organisation (CRO). Previously a branch of Air Ministry, the CRO coordinated the maintenance and repair of military aircraft that couldn't be repaired at an RAF air station. When Beaverbrook made the CRO directly responsible to his Ministry of Aircraft Production, overnight its highest priority became the delivery of damaged military aircraft or their parts to civilian-run maintenance and repair shops, nearly one hundred of them, all over the country. Defying all precedents, Beaverbrook cleared the way for the CRO to cannibalize two or three damaged fighter aircraft to build a complete one. Just as quickly, the rebuilt fighter was redeployed to Fighter Command.

At No. 1 Civilian Repair Unit, at Morris Motors in Cowley, workers repaired 150 seriously damaged fighters between mid-July and mid-October. They built flight sheds and a small grass airfield where less damaged planes could fly in and out for the "outpatient" service.[5] The CRO even put out a tender for a low-loading trailer to transport damaged fighter aircraft (with wings removed and/or stowed alongside) to civilian repair facilities. A prototype for this "Queen Mary" trailer was designed, built, and tested within ten days. Beaverbrook's initiative ultimately ensured that of all the fighter aircraft struck off squadron strength, more than 60 percent flew again thanks to the work of civilian repair depots.[6]

The RAF fighter production pipeline had yet another shadow factory, even farther from the front lines of the Battle of Britain than Castle Bromwich. At the top of Lake Superior in the northern Ontario city of Fort William, Canadian Car and Foundry (Can-Car) had manufactured railway boxcars, ships, and other all-purpose transportation equipment since 1909. In 1936, Can-Car's managers explored diversifying to produce military aircraft for the first time and won a contract from Hawker to assemble forty Hurricanes. They also made the unique decision to hire a woman to assist the company's chief aeronautical engineer. Elsie MacGill proved a godsend to Can-Car and RAF fortunes in 1940.

Born in Vancouver in 1905, the daughter of Helen MacGill, British Columbia's first woman judge, and James MacGill, a BC lawyer and journalist, Elsie was home-schooled.[7] That facilitated her entry to the University of British Columbia at age sixteen. UBC was the first of four universities where she smashed glass ceilings. She was the first woman to complete an electrical engineering degree at the University of Toronto, in 1927; the first woman in North America to earn a master's in aeronautical engineering from the University of Michigan, in 1929; and, soon after, the first woman pursuing doctoral studies at the Massachusetts Institute of Technology. Just before her graduation from the University of Michigan, MacGill contracted polio. She wrote her final exams for her master's degree while still in hospital and afterward learned to walk with canes while carrying on her studies.[8]

Interviewed for *Chatelaine* magazine in 1931, MacGill made it clear she didn't want her career in aeronautics portrayed as a novelty: "Aviation and women are taking each other seriously. The foggy lighter-than-air mindedness that attended women's first ventures—the glaring headlines, frenzied publicity, and overwhelming popularity of the pioneers—is dissipating."[9]

In 1934, Fairchild Aircraft in Longueuil, Quebec, hired MacGill as an aeronautics engineer, and in 1938 her innovative designs and performance calculations for aircraft earned her membership in the Engineering Institute of Canada. That same year, when Can-Car in Fort William, Ontario, needed an assistant chief aeronautical engineer to assemble those forty Hawker Hurricanes for the RAF, Elsie MacGill got the job. She ran an engineering office of thirty people,[10] familiarized herself with no fewer than 3,600 of the Hurricanes' aeronautical drawings, managed as many as eight hundred distinct operations and parts assemblies, and personally designed de-icing systems for the Hurricanes' wings, winterizing them for war.[11] Her success was rooted in respect for the complexity of industrial aeronautic production. "Aeroplanes are not like

baby carriages," she wrote. "The easy acceptance of the applic-
ability of mass production methods to aeroplane construction
arises from sad ignorance of the problems involved."[12]

Can-Car's retooled workplace and workforce delivered. By
the spring of 1940, Elsie MacGill's team had crated the first
forty RAF Hurricanes in time to transport them to Canada's
eastern seaports and stow them aboard merchant vessels
bound for the UK. Her efforts at Can-Car were rewarded with
additional production contracts. Within two years, and with an
increase of more than 4,000 employees, the Fort William plant
was producing a hundred Hurricanes per month. MacGill was
becoming famous. The American True Comics War Heroes
Series featured her in a 1942 edition entitled *Queen of the
Hurricanes*.[13] Despite the attention her gender and accomplish-
ments garnered, MacGill maintained a clear-eyed view of her
profession. "To our shame, we engineers devote the years of
peace to designing and planning for war," she wrote. "To our
glory, we are the group to which our country turns in time of
war. Heavily upon us, as individuals and as a professional unit,
our national duty rests terrible and clear."[14]

* * *

Of the first forty Hurricane training aircraft that engineer
MacGill and her Can-Car crews had assembled in Fort
William, Ontario, thirty arrived via North Atlantic convoy in
Britain just as spring began in 1940. Their travelling compan-
ions on the transatlantic trip were the first members of RCAF
No. 1 Fighter Squadron, eager to take them into action.

Like most of the Canadian pilots disgorged from RMS
Duchess of Atholl at Blackpool on June 21, Pilot Officer Bev

Christmas hadn't actually flown a Hurricane yet. He and other sprog fighter pilots —Flying Officer Edwin Reyno (an RCAF enlistee from Halifax), F/O Ross Smither (an RCAF enlistee from London, Ontario), as well as F/O Dal Russel, F/O Deane Nesbitt, F/O Arthur Yuile, F/O John Kerwin, and F/O George Hyde from the former No. 115 Auxiliary Squadron in Montreal (along with their flight commander F/L Gordon McGregor)—were all itching to get their Hurricanes uncrated, serviced, and airborne. At their first RAF air base, Middle Wallop, just inland from Southampton, they did.

Not long into his first taste of fighter formation flying and learning standard RAF attack tactics, Bev Christmas and the newly arrived Canadians were paid a courtesy visit by Air Chief Marshal Hugh Dowding. He met the pilots in the officers' mess on June 25, asking them about the Hurricanes they'd brought with them.

"Have you got armour plating in them?" Dowding asked,[15] wanting his pilots to have cockpit protections that were by then standard in Hurricanes built at Hawker's Brooklands assembly outside London.

"Ah, no sir," replied the Canadians.

"Self-sealing tanks?" he asked, referring to a feature in the latest Hurricanes that prevented fuel from a damaged tank spilling into the cockpit.*

"No sir," the Canadian pilots admitted.

---

* Self-sealing fuel tanks were made of neoprene (called Linatex) and designed to mix with escaping fuel to chemically create a seal. Hurricanes had two large fuel tanks in their wings and a reserve tank in front of the pilot, protected by a fuel tank bulkhead.

Christmas remembered Dowding saying, "Well, I'll have you a new lot of aircraft tomorrow!"

With limited experience in RAF supply chains and practices, Christmas and the rest of the No. 1 pilots thought Dowding was talking nonsense. "We're not going to get eighteen new aircraft in a day."

"The next day,"* Christmas recalled, "we got eighteen new Hurricanes with all the latest—armour [plating] behind your back, a piece of glass two inches thick in front of your face, and Rotol airscrews,** which were not on ours."[16]

By July the squadron had moved to new quarters at Croydon airfield. In peacetime, Croydon had served as a London-area hub for air transportation to and from the continent. In summer 1940, it became a front-line air station against Luftwaffe raiders. As soon as the Canadians landed there, Squadron Leader Ernie McNab arranged to have the No. 1 Hurricanes given their squadron markings and camouflaged.[17]

Throughout August, the RCAF pilots followed a daily regimen of operational training that took them from Croydon northwest to RAF Northolt station each morning for instruction supervised by the Air Fighting Development Unit. They flew back to living quarters at Croydon each night. During his ground school instruction, Bev Christmas listened to veterans who'd witnessed Luftwaffe tactics during the *Kanalkampf* phase of the battle and took notes.

---

* In fact, the RCAF No. 1 Fighter Squadron diary shows the Hurricanes arrived five days later, on June 30, 1940.
** The Rotol (short for Rolls-Royce and Bristol) manufacturers took a wooden propeller blade and, using the Schwarz process, pressed a hard metal mesh coating and cellulose sheet over the entire propeller to produce hard composite blades.

Christmas learned from his instructors that the fighter pilots played pivotal roles in both the Luftwaffe's attacks on Britain and the RAF's defence against those attacks. Luftwaffe fighters were charged with protecting Luftwaffe bombers as they approached their UK targets intent on inflicting crippling damage. Allied fighters were tasked with denying the Luftwaffe freedom of action.[18] The job of a Hurricane fighter pilot such as P/O Christmas in this growing battle of attrition was to get through the protective screen of Luftwaffe fighters and destroy as many of the lower-flying enemy bombers as possible. The job of Spitfire pilots was to climb and take on the higher-altitude German fighter aircraft.

At the end of this session, P/O Christmas was given an RAF handout. It listed the "Ten Rules of Air Fighting," according to No. 74 Fighter Squadron flying ace Adolph Sailor Malan:

1. Always keep a sharp lookout.
2. Height gives <u>You</u> the initiative.
3. Always turn and face the attack.
4. Make your decisions promptly.
5. Never fly straight and level for more than thirty seconds.
6. When diving to attack always leave a proportion of your formation above to act as top guard.
7. Fire short bursts of one or two seconds and only when your Sights are definitely 'on.'
8. Whilst shooting, think of nothing else, brace the whole of the body, have both hands on the stick.
9. Go in quickly. Punch hard. Get out.
10. Initiative. Aggression. Air Discipline and Team Work mean something in Air Fighting.[19]

* * *

As P/O Christmas and the newly arrived RCAF fighter pilots were training at Northolt, the Luftwaffe was counting down to August 13, 1940, *Adlertag* (Eagle Day), the first day of *Adlerangriff* (Eagle Attack), the codename for Hermann Göring's operation to destroy the Royal Air Force. On the appointed day, miscommunication on the German side disrupted *Adlerangriff* even as it began. With occupied France experiencing low clouds and light rains, Göring issued an order to postpone the assault. Not all units received the order. Seventy-four Dornier bombers took off for targets along the Thames Estuary while their Me 110 fighter escorts, who'd received the abort order, returned to base.

RAF fighters took full advantage. Canadian F/L Bill Nelson, with No. 74 Squadron, destroyed a Dornier on August 13. And recent arrival P/O Joseph Larichelière of Montreal chalked up two Me 110s and an Me 109 that same day; he would destroy three more enemy aircraft on August 15 but fail to return from a sortie on August 16.

On the first day of *Adlerangriff*, the Luftwaffe lost thirty-four aircraft, while the RAF lost only thirteen fighters in the air and one on the ground. It was a weak start to the Luftwaffe's proposed destruction of Fighter Command, the crucial overture to Operation Sea Lion, Hitler's plan for an amphibious invasion of England, scheduled for mid-September.

By August 15, Göring had retreated to his hunting lodge at Karinhall, outside Berlin, and summoned four of his top Luftwaffe commanders—Kesselring from Air Fleet 2, Sperrle from Air Fleet 3, Generaloberst Hans-Jürgen Stumpff from Air Fleet 5, and General Bruno Loerzer from *Fliegerkorps II*—for a post mortem on *Adlertag*. That left command of the entire *Fliegerkorps II*, who administered *Adlerangriff*, in the hands of chief of staff Oberst Paul Deichmann. The logistics of the Luftwaffe's massive assault on RAF air stations had been distributed to its various Air Fleets, so when Deichmann saw the weather clearing and blue sky to the west, he didn't hesitate. He launched Stuka attacks against RAF stations Hawkinge and Lympne, near the Dover coast. The main Air Fleet 5 force of seventy-two Heinkel bombers and twenty-one Me 110 fighters flew against RAF stations in Scotland; and two more Dornier bombing runs targeted Rochester airfield and RAF Eastchurch. Deichmann had unleashed the full force of the Luftwaffe from occupied Brittany all the way to occupied Norway.

Coincidentally, that day marked marked the RCAF's official entry into the Battle of Britain. While the majority of his No. 1 Fighter Squadron pilots were memorizing air fighting tactics in ground school at Northolt, S/L McNab and F/L Gordon McGregor had been seconded to an operational apprentice-ship with No. 111 Squadron at Croydon. At 3 p.m., the two Canadians were sitting in the dispersal hut at "Readiness," or awaiting a call to action, when a scramble signal came through. Minutes later, McNab was airborne in Blue Section, a formation of three Hurricanes directed against enemy bombers approaching the Thames Estuary.

About 16,000 feet over Beachy Head, McNab spotted two Dornier bombers and closed in. "I did a stern attack on them, firing a short burst with no apparent effect before breaking off," McNab wrote in his combat report. "On my next attack, after the first burst, the rear gunner ceased firing and the enemy aircraft started to lose height. His engines began to smoke and

147

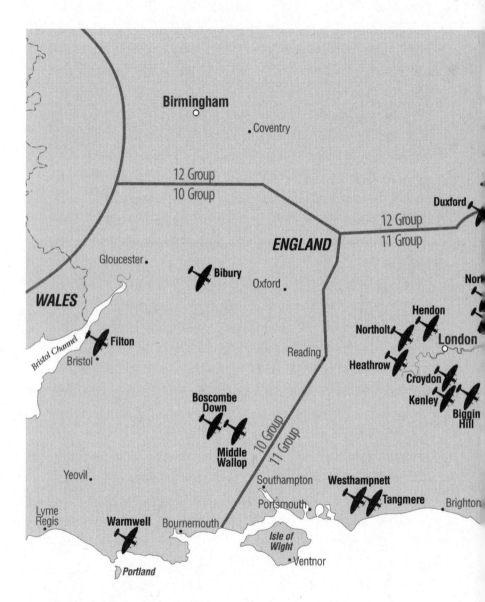

Battle of Britain: Sector Air Fields

Battle of Britain Sector Air Fields
1940

Sector or Fighter Airfield

Group Boundary

20 miles

20 km

Scale

12 Group

11 Group

Norwich

mbridge

Castle Camps

Debden

Martlesham Heath

Weald

Stapleford Tawney

Rochford

Hornchurch

West Malling

Chatham

Detling

Canterbury

Manston

Ramsgate

Tunbridge Wells

Dover

Hawkinge

Lympne

Hastings

bourne

Channel

English

BELGIUM

Dunkirk

Calais

Boulogne

FRANCE

Étaples

M. Smith. Based on research including *The Most Dangerous Enemy* (Stephen Gungay, Southend 2010), author's notes, and various reports he crashed. . . . As my ammunition was used up, I returned to my base and refueled."[20]

McNab's quick turnaround at Croydon was critical. Back in the air, No. 111 fighters dispatched two more Dorniers, and damaged three others and a Messerschmitt besides. While he was airborne on this second sortie, however, fifteen Me 110 fighter-bombers made it past the Chain Home radar stations and completed a low-level bombing run on the Croydon aerodrome. Bombs demolished the station's orderly rooms and set off a massive pyrotechnical display in the armament building. Ground crew suffered injuries. Because McNab and McGregor were in the air and the rest of the squadron had flown to Northolt for ground school and op training, none of RCAF No. 1's fighters were lost.

Canadian Mark "Hilly" Brown meanwhile endured a tougher August 15. Fresh from his visit to Buckingham Palace to receive his DFC for "courage of the highest order . . . and determination when consistently outnumbered by enemy aircraft," Brown led RAF No. 1 Fighter Squadron into battle. Intercepting a low-level raid of German bombers, Brown's Hurricane got hit. His engine began to smoke. He was preparing to bail out when he heard a familiar voice on his radio telephone.

"Getting a little hot in there, Hilly?" radioed Johnny Kent, his old friend from Winnipeg. Kent was leading No. 1's sister squadron, RAF No. 303, but he had separated from his Polish fighters and found Brown just in time to watch him bail from his burning Hurricane. Kent watched Brown parachute into the English Channel and circled so that the downed pilot could be located and rescued quickly.

Kent's comment was typical of the gallows humour fighter pilots sometimes used to break tension. Weeks before Brown's dip in the Channel, Kent's Hurricane engine had suddenly cut out on a patrol. As he struggled to restart the engine, Brown appeared off Kent's wingtip. "Forget to turn on the gas, Johnny?" Kent managed to land safely back at Northolt airfield. Meanwhile, Brown, on August 15, was almost immediately picked up by a trawler in the Channel. He suffered minor injuries to his hands and face, and lamented only that the fire cost him his distinctive moustache.[21]

While Canadian fighter pilots often exchanged friendly jabs as last word on certain missions, sometimes reporters took that opportunity. A Canadian Press correspondent happened to be covering John "Max" Aitken, recently promoted to squadron leader at No. 601 Auxiliary Fighter Squadron, on August 15. Nothing much happened for most of the day. "Max sat in his chair distinctly Micawber-ish," wrote the reporter. "Dressed in his flying clothes and Mae West, [he's] just waiting for something to turn up."

Something turned up when the operational phone rang, "breaking the monotony." Aitken and his fellow pilots dashed for their Hurricanes, their Merlin engines already fired up by ground crew. Interviewing him later, the reporter learned that ground controllers had directed Aitken's flight at an oncoming stream of Heinkel 111 bombers. "He got about a hundred yards behind and below [a] Nazi and . . . adjusting his firing button, he poured bullets into the German. It was point-blank range." The German pilot attempted to evade Aitken's gunfire bursts, manoeuvring into a shallow dive, but the aircraft burst into flame. Aitken, at five hundred feet, broke away to the right and did not see the Heinkel strike the water. He circled the scene, saw no movement, and flew for home. "This alert and courageous young hero of these brilliant exploits comes from Montreal," noted the reporter, finally alluding to Aitken's athletic prowess whether grasping "a mashie niblick or an aircraft joystick."[22]

* * *

As night fell on August 15, both sides counted their dead and exaggerated their victories in what Battle of Britain veteran Peter Townsend called "the biggest air battle yet known in world history."[23] The RAF claimed victory, and so did the Germans. RAF pilots reported 182 planes shot down to their debrief intelligence officers. German diarists claimed 108 RAF fighters downed. Quipped Hugh Dowding, "If the German claims were correct, they'd be in England by now."[24]

In fact, the Luftwaffe had launched five major assaults, 520 bombers, and 1,270 fighters,[25] against a front of over five hundred miles. The Germans had inflicted significant damage, but lost 20 percent of their Air Fleet 5 aircraft in a single day. Most of the Luftwaffe formations, which amounted to 1,790 sorties, had been challenged by Fighter Command Hurricanes and Spitfires, which completed 974 sorties.[26] RAF losses that day had actually totalled thirty-four aircraft, while the Luftwaffe was down seventy-six bombers and fighters.

The Luftwaffe's debilitating losses demoralized even the most capable German aviators. Born in 1912 at Westerholt, Germany, Adolf Galland had struggled in regular school classes, but excelled in the local gliding club courses near his home in Westphalia; as a teenager he was soon instructing others. At age twenty, "the flame of unselfish enthusiasm" earned him an invitation to train at the Lufthansa Commercial Flying School in Berlin, after which he underwent secret military training at Lipetsk, Russia. When the Luftwaffe sent aircrew to support Franco and the fascists in Spain, Galland flew ground attack missions in Heinkel 51 biplane fighter aircraft. [27] On July 24, 1940, during his first action piloting an Me 109 fighter over England, he shot down his first Spitfire (he would score fifty-two victories in the Battle of Britain).[28] Three weeks later, he sensed the Luftwaffe losses were escalating. "We saw one comrade after the other . . . vanish from our ranks," he wrote. "Not a day passed without an empty place remaining at the mess table."[29]

Ultimately, August 15 was given the moniker *der Schwarzen Donnerstag*, or Black Thursday. Luftwaffe strategists had underestimated the importance of Britain's radar network. They had briefly targeted the Chain Home stations on August 12, and punched further holes in the RAF's long-range spotting on August 15—escorted Stukas had cut power to the Rye and Foreness radar stations, blinding Fighter Command over Dover all that day—yet the Luftwaffe otherwise shelved dedicated attacks against British radar. Oberst Paul Deichmann, who'd triggered Black Thursday, arrogantly assumed that any RAF aircraft using radar to find his fighter formations would be destroyed at first sight. In fact, his side suffered far greater losses.[30]

Britain's tactical victories in the south reflected the battle strategy of ACM Dowding and his second-in-command, Air Vice-Marshal Keith Park, the air officer commanding 11 Group fighters. Park's roughly 350 fighter aircraft and 550 pilots, spread across twenty-two fighter squadrons, bore the brunt of Luftwaffe attacks. His aim remained to attack the bombers before they reached their targets, while avoiding costly fighter-on-fighter combat. Similarly, on this occasion,

AVM Trafford Leigh-Mallory, the air officer commanding 12 Group fighters in central England, chose a cautious response to the Luftwaffe, sending up eighteen fighters versus fifty Ju 88 bombers. The raiders destroyed ten Bomber Command Whitleys on the ground, but RAF fighters destroyed or damaged ten Ju 88s in air combat.

AVM Park went further in picking fights that produced tangible results. On August 19, he held a staff conference at which he asked sector commanders and controllers to consider the defence of sector airfields the highest priority.[31] These airfields, he emphasized, delivered the front-line fighter aircraft responsible for blunting the effect of the bombers. Some fighter squadrons needed to be assigned to patrol the airfields instead of rising to meet the raiders. That spelled an end to the tactic of assembling two or more squadrons of fighters—so-called big wings—to overwhelm enemy aircraft. The debate over a big wing approach versus smaller formations (scattering single-squadron attacks over a wider area) was just beginning.

In the north, the RAF got lucky on August 15. Success against Air Fleet 5 attacks in Scotland resulted from a hunch. A 13 Group controller guessed that the Air Fleet 5 attack would be the only thrust in the northern UK that day; he rightly scrambled every squadron from Yorkshire to Edinburgh. Coincidentally, the Me 110s, their range and time-over-target limited by fuel capacity, had left their gunners at home in occupied Norway and Denmark to reduce total aircraft weight and extend their reach. Without air gunners aboard, as a consequence, they were forced to fly in a defensive circle. They still lost fifteen fighter-bombers versus one RAF fighter lost.

At his Karinhall hunting lodge, Göring ranted at his commanders for their incompetence on Black Thursday. The heavy loss of Stuka bombers was outrageous, he claimed, and a direct result of insufficient fighter support. To compensate, commanders would have to assign more single-seat (Messerschmitt) fighters to escort bomber fleets. He also said that aircrew losses were out of control, and demanded that in future only one officer per aircraft be allowed. What he apparently overlooked in his debrief was the haphazard choice of targets: shipping docks, radar towers, civilian and Bomber Command airfields, rather than RAF fighter bases that relentlessly harassed his bomber forces.

"We have entered the decisive phase of the Battle of Britain," Göring told his air fleet commanders. "We have to smash the RAF fighter force . . . attack them on the ground or force them into the air by bombing targets within the range of our fighters." And if necessary, commanders were ordered to launch small-scale night raids to give "enemy defences and population no respite."[32]

For much of August 15, Winston Churchill had watched the ebb and flow of the massive air battle from inside the Fighter Command Operations Room at Bentley Priory in north London. He'd witnessed ACM Dowding's capable delegation of decision-making to his group commanders in the field. The prime minister noted Dowding's foresight, restraint, and calm, applauding him as "an example of genius in the art of war."[33] On his way back to Chequers that night, Churchill was overheard speaking to himself about the prowess and devotion of those fighter pilots. Five days later, he rose in Parliament at Westminster and in a long speech gave special tribute to the airmen: "Never in the field of human conflict was so much owed by so many to so few."[34]

* * *

Without quarters at Croydon, RCAF No. 1 Fighter Squadron picked up its belongings and moved its Hurricanes permanently to Northolt, which had been its operational training airfield since July. Suddenly, in the middle of the summer, Northolt was turned into a "little Canada" by the squadron's fighter pilots and ground crew. Already resident in adjacent quarters at Northolt, RAF No. 303 Fighter Squadron was in the midst of operational training, too. The 303 was made up entirely of Polish pilots, except for one of their flight commanders, F/L Johnny Kent from Winnipeg.

Since late July, Kent had been working with his fighter pilots in Polish and French. They had experience, having flown combat operations against the Germans over Poland and France, but not with English-speaking RAF officers. Communication always seemed forced, confusing, and misunderstood on both sides. Kent went to great lengths to organize a training exercise in which one flight of No. 303 Hurricanes would intercept another in a mock dogfight, yet in the air it nearly ended in disaster.

"I was horrified to see my number three, F/O [Miroslaw] Ferić, pull up into a violent barrel-roll and get right onto the tail of one of the attacking Hurricanes," Kent wrote. "Fortunately, he recognized it just in time as he was on the point of shooting it down. He had completely misunderstood [the] briefing."[35]

Tension caused by repeated readiness and scramble calls and a keenness to get into the fight hadn't only affected the Polish squadron. The Canadians in both the RAF and RCAF fighter squadron ranks felt it, too. They were eager, but to that point, in mid-August, none of the Canadians at Northolt except for Ernie McNab and Gordon McGregor had engaged enemy aircraft over Britain or fired their guns in anger. Then, on August 18, RCAF No. 1 Fighter Squadron had scrambled on its first ever operational sortie, but made no contact with enemy aircraft. F/O Paul Pitcher, who'd combined law studies at McGill with air force training at No. 115 Auxiliary Squadron in Montreal just a year earlier, recalled the front-line tension as physiological. "Apprehension was a constant companion," he wrote, "to the extent that at readiness, when a telephone bell rang in the dispersal hut, twelve pilots automatically drifted outside and peed against the wall of the hut."[36]

Just before 4 p.m. on August 24, Fighter Command issued a scramble call for RCAF No. 1. Pitcher and the rest of his squadron comrades dashed to their Hurricanes and quickly climbed into the misty skies southwest of the station. For Pitcher and the other Canadians in the formation, it was only their second operational sortie, and they had much to learn about aerial combat. Patrolling at 10,000 feet, F/O Dal Russel noted that his squadron leader, Ernie McNab, spotted a formation of five bombers 2,000 feet below them, flying north in line astern toward Portsmouth. McNab led the four sections of Hurricanes in an attacking dive, and then suddenly veered away. Russel realized that the bombers were British Blenheims.

Pitcher radioed, "Friendly Aircraft!"

Several of the other fighter sections in the squadron, diving in formation toward the bombers, didn't receive Pitcher's radio message and continued their attack. F/L Gordon McGregor, as well as F/O Jean-Paul Desloges, claimed to have destroyed a German bomber, while their fellow Canadian pilots—Deane Nesbitt, Arthur Yuile, and Bill Sprenger—all reported hits on other enemy aircraft.

That the Canadians would mistake the Bristol Blenheims on patrol from RAF No. 235 Squadron of Coastal Command for enemy Ju 88 bombers was not farfetched, given the inexperience of the pilots. The profiles of the two twin-engine bombers were eerily similar, except that the Blenheim included an upper gun turret midway back on its fuselage, while the Junkers did not. In his combat report, Bill Sprenger wrote, "The e/a [enemy aircraft] was low-winged, appeared to have radial engines, and no gun turret." He added, "During my attack, tracer bullets spilt past my windshield."[37] The tracers were more likely yellow and red Very pistol flares fired by the Blenheim gunner to signal they were friendly aircraft.

Under attack by the Canadians, one of the Blenheims caught fire and crashed into the Channel. Another crash-landed at Thorney Island. Three RAF aircrewmen were killed in total. Ernie McNab visited No. 235 Squadron immediately to offer his personal apology and condolences, which were accepted. A British Air Ministry investigation chalked the incident up to "inexperience and excitement of [RCAF] No. 1 Squadron's first patrol," and nothing beyond a rebuke was issued. The Canadian squadron leader accurately captured the state of mind of his overeager and overwrought young pilots. "The mental strain experienced by the pilots has been a punishment more severe than any that could be physically given," wrote McNab. "It was some time before these officers settled down."[38]

It turned out that other miscalculations on the same day had greater impact on the direction of the entire battle. Hermann Göring had directed his Luftwaffe commanders to weaken British fighter forces in the air and destroy their ground organization and aircraft industry through concerted bombing operations—by day and by night, if necessary. Luftwaffe bombings subsequently became more concentrated on RAF Sector Stations. And because most of those stations surrounded England's capital city, Air Ministry and the war cabinet expressed concern about the potential for heavy bombing on London itself. Göring had issued instructions that Luftwaffe bombers were not to bomb London except on his orders, meaning a directive from Hitler himself.

Just before 11 p.m. on August 24, British radar stations detected a large aircraft formation of nearly a hundred enemy bombers off the Cherbourg peninsula. Luftwaffe crews had been briefed to target storage tanks at Rochester and Thameshaven (fifty miles east of London). It was well after dark, which meant British forces could not defend airfields, industries, and cities with Spitfires and Hurricanes, but only with searchlights and anti-aircraft artillery. In any event, the German bombers over-shot the storage tank areas along the Thames Estuary and dropped their bombs in the dockland area of East and West Ham, and on North London residential areas.

Anne Elliott, who emigrated to Canada after the war, lived in East Barnet, a suburb of North London, when the bombs fell. She was just short of her eighth birthday in the summer of 1940. Her grandfather had served as a sapper in the British Army and died in the Battle of the Somme in 1916. Her mother had refused to eat rice when rationing was reintroduced in Britain in 1940, since rice was all they'd had as a staple food during the Great War. Now the air war was about to affect the life of a third generation of her family. London was in blackout when the German bombs hit the dockyards that night, and Anne remembered "my dad and I could read the newspaper from the light of the fires in the docks."[39]

It was the first time since the Gotha bomber raids in May 1918 that London had been bombed. In response, Churchill's war cabinet decided "to strike back, to raise the stakes, and to defy the enemy."[40] He sanctioned the war's first air raid on Berlin, a Bomber Command force of eighty-one Hampdens and Wellingtons.[41] Hitler in turn announced *Vergeltungsangriff* (Revenge Attack), declaring, "We shall stop the handiwork of those night pirates, so help us God."[42] Three days later, he would give Göring permission to attack the city of London at will.

The day after Bomber Command's raid on Berlin, all three squadrons resident at Northolt scrambled back in the air against Luftwaffe daylight attacks. The first-sortie jitters and aircraft recognition problems seemed to be behind the pilots. Johnny Kent was leading his Polish Hurricane fighters in another exercise—escort practice with RAF Blenheim bombers—when a stream of German bombers suddenly came into view below their rehearsal. F/O Ludwik Paszkiewicz of No. 303 Squadron reported his sighting by radio telephone to S/L Ronald Kellett, but got no reply. He went with his instincts and attacked immediately.

"I noticed a bomber with twin rudders—probably a Dornier—turning in my direction," Paszkiewicz wrote in his combat report. "I aimed at the fuselage and opened fire from about 200 yards, later transferring it to the port engine, which I set on fire. . . . I have been firing at an enemy aircraft for the first time in my life!"[43]

Kent saw Paszkiewicz attack exactly as he'd been taught, and observed that the pilot then followed the doomed bomber all the way down to make sure that it crashed. Back at Northolt, the Pole was initially reprimanded for breaking away from the exercise, then congratulated.

"This was the Squadron's first victory and the Poles were absolutely cock-a-hoop over it," Kent reported.[44]

The next morning, S/L Kellett asked Fighter Command HQ for permission to declare No. 303 Squadron operational. Permission was granted. The Poles, who'd by now given their flight commander the nickname "Kentowski,"[45] found themselves immediately placed on readiness should Fighter Command need to throw them into combat over London. Sure enough, the following day, August 31, 1940, No. 303 got a scramble call and air controllers directed the Poles toward a formation of Me 109s. In a matter of minutes, the Polish fighters had intercepted and destroyed six German fighters. Their squadron leader suggested that his pilots might have been inspired by an anniversary—it was exactly a year since Nazi Germany had invaded their native Poland.

Meanwhile, after a number of stumbles and setbacks, good fortune also came to RCAF No. 1 Fighter Squadron. On August 26, their Sector Station ordered S/L McNab's fighters to relieve the RAF squadron at North Weald airfield. A first patrol yielded no contact, but a second in the afternoon brought the Canadians over the path of thirty Dorniers escorted by Messerschmitt fighters, all approaching from the northeast at 14,000 feet. An RAF Spitfire squadron drew off the German fighters, leaving the bombers to the Canadian Hurricane fighters.

"We were still outnumbered five to one," McNab noted later.[46]

Apparently, it didn't matter. Leading Red Section, F/L Gordon McGregor managed to overtake a Dornier bomber, fired quick bursts into it, and registered RCAF No. 1's first victory of the war. Then, F/L Vaughan Corbett and

F/O Tom Little destroyed a second, and F/O Hartland Molson and Deane Nesbitt damaged a third. Meanwhile, S/L McNab, leading Blue Section, downed another, but took return fire and had to make a forced landing. F/O Jean-Paul Desloges's Hurricane also had to make a forced landing. The one setback occurred when F/O Bob Edwards chased a Dornier and both the bomber and the Hurricane spun down out of control.[47]

"Edwards finished the attack. He went right in," Bev Christmas said. "It was discovered later—they found a map near the aircraft that he shot down—there was a line drawn on the map to [RAF] Debden. Edwards was the first [RCAF] Canadian shot down in the battle."[48]

Five days later, a patient and studious Bev Christmas was finally able to put all his ground school theory and Sailor Malan's "Air Fighting" tips into action. On the afternoon of August 31, his Blue Section had begun a patrol over the mouth of the Thames, where it intercepted a large formation of bombers with plenty of fighter support above. Accompanied by F/Os Ross Smither and Tom Little, Christmas led the section, climbing to the Hurricanes' maximum altitude and attacking out of the sun.

"When there's a skirmish, there's a general racing around and shooting at one another," Christmas said. Not getting hit in the initial attack, he added, was just as important as scoring a hit.

In the frightening jockeying across the sky, Smither damaged one German fighter, while Christmas and Little eventually gained the upper hand on another Messerschmitt and sent it plunging to earth. Christmas understood from all he'd heard that German fighter pilots had more experience than any of the Canadian fighters, and that their Messerschmitts were superior in performance to the Hurricanes. But Christmas maintained he had one tactical advantage over his adversaries. "During the Battle of Britain, [we] were fighting over [our] own territory," he said. "Everything was very short-range at that stage of the game." The 109s were escorting bombers far up the Thames and operating at the limit of their endurance, with no more than twenty minutes of fuel for combat manoeuvring over London. "So, the Messerschmitts couldn't stay around very long to fight. If you got him really tangled up, he couldn't get back home and he wound up in the Channel. It was always in the back of his mind."

CHAPTER SEVEN

"SAFE IN YOUR HANDS"

HERMANN GÖRING'S ORDERS "TO SMASH THE RAF FIGHTER force" came closest to succeeding in the last week of August. The pilots at Fighter Command who survived this week and the early days of September describe it as "the critical period."[1] The threat began when Luftwaffe Air Fleet commander Albert Kesselring moved his fighter squadrons to the Pas-de-Calais, directly across the Channel from Dover, closer to the German bomber launch point and ultimately a shorter flying time to RAF ground targets. In addition, German fighters began escorting above and below bomber streams, in larger numbers and in tighter formations. In daylight hours, Kesselring sent feint attack groups all along the south coast of England, often confusing the RAF radar controllers and allowing the real raiders to penetrate British air space in larger numbers to attack 11 Group fighter airfields.

For Canadian Flight Lieutenant Harry Hamilton and his No. 85 Squadron comrades at RAF Croydon, the pace was relentless. Each day's sorties—scrambling to beat off the bombers two and three, sometimes four times a day—seemed

In June 1940, members of the RCAF marched from their barracks in Dartmouth, NS, to board the troopship RMS *Duchess of Atholl*, bound for Britain. Formerly auxiliary squadrons, now RCAF No. 1 Fighter Squadron, these trained pilots and ground crewmen were joined by 129 nursing sisters as part of Canada's growing war effort. During the crossing, convoy radios intercepted a German propaganda transmission promising that "these Canadian reinforcements and nurses will not arrive." Nevertheless, the troopship docked safely at Blackpool, England, on June 21.

Among Winston Churchill's secret weapons during the Battle of Britain, ex-pat Canadian, Max Aitken, a.k.a. Lord Beaverbrook (*top left*). In May 1940, Aitken became minister of aircraft production. Meanwhile, Lord Beaverbrook's son, John Max Aitken (*above left*), came up through a corps of auxiliary fliers—sometimes called "the Millionaire's Mob"—that included Lord Edward Grosvenor and Roger Bushell (leader of the Great Escape from Stalag Luft III in 1944), or, as Aitken described them, "the sort of young men whom mothers warned their daughters against." Their RAF No. 601 Squadron claimed one hundred victories in the Battle of Britain.

The first home of RCAF No. 1 Fighter Squadron was Middle Wallop, in Hampshire. Here, for the first time, the Canadian pilots flew the Hurricanes assembled in Canada and transported with them to Britain. Depicted here (*left to right*), Frank Hillock, Frederick Watson, Robert Norris, Norman Richard Johnstone, Joseph A.J. Chevrier, John David Morrison, Ernest A. McNab, Arthur Yuile, Paul Pitcher, Bill Sprenger, and Deane Nesbitt. Later nicknamed "Caribou Squadron," No. 1 first engaged the enemy on August 17, 1940, and over the next fifty-three days, destroyed thirty German planes and damaged thirty-five more. Three Canadian pilots died in action, ten others were wounded. The following year, No. 1 became No. 401 Squadron, which ended the war as the RAF 2nd Tactical Air Force's highest-scoring fighter squadron, with 186.5 victories.

Aircrew in the Battle of Britain spent many hours at dispersal huts (*below*) in a state of waiting. Paul Pitcher (*above right*) said "apprehension was a constant companion." When the pilots finally scrambled their Hurricanes to meet incoming bombers, they looked to the most experienced, like Gordon McGregor (*above middle*), described as "a daring and innovative leader." Pete Lochnan (*above left*) was credited with two enemy aircraft destroyed, Otto Peterson (*left*) with two; neither would survive the war. Indelible images remain from the battle. For Robert "Butcher" Barton (*opposite middle*), it was his fear of taking off; nevertheless, in combat, he shot down four enemy aircraft; Deane Nesbitt (*opposite top*) recalled dogfights over Britain when "the sky rained parachutes" as pilots bailed from their doomed aircraft. Then, for Caribou Squadron's (*opposite bottom, left to right*) Peterson, Russel, Yuile, and Eric Beardmore, it was back to waiting outside the dispersal hut, as if none of this was dangerous or deadly.

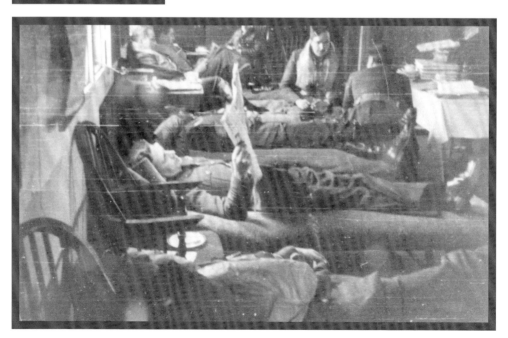

Of the three hundred Canadian airmen who arrived in the UK in June 1940, more than two hundred served in RCAF No. 1 Fighter Squadron's support staff (the headquarters section) and its ground crew (two flight sections). Sometimes called "erks," the maintenance crew on the station kept Hurricane engines running and machine guns fully armed (*opposite*), as well as the aircraft bodies and cockpit instruments repaired and fully functioning. Photographed aboard *Duchess of Atholl* (*above, left to right*), A.L.P. Gagnon, L.G. Saunders, John Burdes, A.C. Wilson, and F. Worrell. Burdes, nicknamed "Slim," coordinated nighttime crews getting damaged Hurricanes airworthy again by morning, even leading them in singsong as they worked through the night. RCAF pilot Ed Reyno said Burdes "had more creative talent in his hands than any man I have ever known."

When the Germans sent bombers to attack London in September 1940, it marked a turning point in the battle; the decision allowed RAF fighters to come back from the brink, but it also doomed more British civilians—over 23,000 killed and over 32,000 injured in the bombings. Anne Elliott (*above right*) experienced the Blitz first at her home in London. But when the bombs fell too close for comfort, her family chose to move to Kent on Britain's southeast coast; they had to smuggle Anne there to do it. Meanwhile, Jill Brown (*above left*) had a front-row seat to the Battle of Britain from her home on the Isle of Wight. When her family chose to send Jill overseas to Canada, they twice nearly lost her (and her teddy bear) at sea to torpedoed passenger liners.

a blinding blur. "Hammy" Hamilton's combat reports each began with similar observations of an overwhelming raider force coming his way.

"I was leading Yellow Section about twenty miles east of Foulness Island when about 200 enemy bombers sighted," Hamilton began his summary on August 18.[2]

A few days later, "I was leading Red Section when at 15,000 feet eighteen [Dornier] 215s and an escort of about thirty Me 109s were sighted."[3] His flight commander, Peter Townsend, leading Blue Section of No. 85 Squadron, ordered a head-on attack against the bombers. Hamilton picked out one bomber and fired a two-second burst into it. "[But] I didn't have time to see the effect of my fire," because he then raced to the assistance of another Hurricane being chased by an Me 109, "doing more than 400 miles an hour." Then, having expended his ammunition, Hamilton returned to base to reload and refuel.

"Action and more action," Townsend wrote later, "was the only antidote against the deadly, crushing fatigue creeping up on us."[4]

When inclement weather, repairs, or refuelling interrupted the action, No. 85 Squadron's Hurricane pilots sought refuge in the dispersal huts along the western boundary of Croydon's airfield. There, Hamilton, Townsend, and the others smoked cigarettes, drank tea (on a good day sweetened with honey), listened to 78 rpm gramophone records, read newspapers, wrote letters home, or catnapped on couches and easy chairs. During one surprise night attack, several German raiders slipped through the Chain Home radar and bombed Croydon airfield, setting two Hurricanes ablaze. Somebody reported seeing light spill from an open door, which probably drew the bomb drop.

That same week, on the morning of August 24, the pilots at Croydon learned that the King's brother, the Duke of Kent, would pay the squadron a visit later that day. Before that could happen, an alarm went off. In the middle of his morning ablutions, Squadron Leader Townsend just had time to tuck his toothbrush in his left breast pocket before dashing to his Hurricane. The scramble was in response to the radar sighting of a hundred-plus bombers from the Luftwaffe's *Fliegerkorps II* heading toward Dover. By the time Townsend's flight had climbed to the scene, the bombers had already hit their targets and were headed back to occupied France. One member of his flight knocked down a Messerschmitt; another was hit by friendly anti-aircraft fire over Dover.

No sooner had the squadron returned, about ten o'clock in the morning, when the base adjutant called out to Townsend. "Get the pilots lined up," he said, noting that the Duke of Kent was waiting. "He wants to meet them."

Townsend escorted the duke to his fighter pilots, who were assembled in a reviewing line, all at attention. First to be introduced was his fellow section leader. "Flight Lieutenant Hamilton from Canada," Townsend announced to the royal guest.[5]

Hamilton could barely keep himself from bursting into laughter. Still visibly protruding from Townsend's tunic breast pocket, beside his Air Force wings and DFC ribbon, was the gleaming white toothbrush he'd deposited there before the morning's scramble. It had gone to battle and back. The duke politely ignored it, but Hamilton made sure his commanding officer got plenty of ridiculing the rest of the day. But the comic relief was short-lived. The number of combat sorties multiplied, and the tension at all fighter stations intensified.

By 3 p.m. on August 29, No. 85 Squadron had already completed three separate sorties. During his third, F/L Hamilton had flown his Hurricane into a formation of Heinkel and Messerschmitt bombers. Catching an Me 109 in his sights, he fired a burst into its engine. The plane caught fire and fell into the sea; it was his fourth overall victory. But there was no time to think on it. Back on the ground, catching his breath, Hamilton waited while his radio telephone was checked, his oxygen tank replaced, windscreen cleaned, machine guns reloaded, and tanks refuelled. Thirty-five minutes later, he joined his squadron leader, Townsend, patrolling in formation at 18,000 feet over Dungeness.

Within a few minutes, Townsend had organized his squadron in formation over the Hastings countryside. With his two wingmates, Hamilton and Pilot Officer William "Ace" Hodgson line astern, Townsend noticed a lone Spitfire join the rear of the flight. "Watch him closely," Townsend radioed his wingmates.

A recurring problem was that Hurricane and Spitfire radios were not compatible. Townsend couldn't talk directly with the Spitfire pilot, who appeared to join the Hurricanes as a tail-end Charlie covering the rear of the section. The sky seemed empty except for Townsend's flight.

"Bandits in our vicinity," came a radio communication from a Fighter Command ground controller. "They're coming from the north."

No sooner had the vectoring signal arrived when Hodgson realized the Spitfire was gone. Three Me 109s were bearing down on the No. 85 formation. "Look out. Messerschmitts," Hodgson called out.[6] Each of the Hurricane sections veered violently to port, as the square wingtip of an Me 109 whizzed past Townsend's canopy. Then, just as quickly, he spotted Hamilton's fighter heeling over. He saw no pilot bail out, no parachute billowing, just the Hurricane descending, wreathed in flame and smoke.

Townsend later researched the incident and speculated that the mystery Spitfire had been flown by celebrated RAF pilot Richard Hillary, and that had Hillary followed protocol and remained in position protecting the rear of the Hurricane formation, the Me 109s would never have surprised the flight, and Hamilton would not have been killed.[7]

August had brought RAF Fighter Command close to the brink. The Luftwaffe sustained the loss of 774 aircraft, about 18 percent of its combat aircraft, but in a month of defending the 11 and 12 Group fighter squadron airfields, aircraft manufacturing plants, and radar installations against bombing raids, Fighter Command had lost 426 fighter aircraft, or 40 percent of the 1,061 available that month. As the Luftwaffe increased the number of attacks and the escort strength of those attacks, during the last weeks of the month, RAF was losing 120 pilots, killed, wounded, or missing, per week.[8] Three more weeks of losses at that pace, the experts projected, would exhaust RAF fighter aircraft and pilot reserves.

On August 31, three days after Harry Hamilton was killed in action, Townsend himself was forced to bail out of a burning fighter over Tunbridge Wells. He survived, received a bar to his Distinguished Flying Cross, and rejoined No. 85 Squadron in September. Eventually, he wrote the Hamilton family in New Brunswick, applauding their son's leadership and heroic death.[9] Composing his memoir, *Duel of Eagles*, a quarter century later, Townsend painted a picture of the mental state of fighter pilots in those critical days of the battle. "Death was always present," he wrote. "We knew if we did die, we would be alone, smashed to pieces, or burnt alive, or drowned. We seemed already to be living in another world, separate and exalted, where the gulf between life and death had closed and was no longer forbidding."[10]

Two members of the Millidgeville Trio, Harry Hamilton and P/O Duncan Hewitt, had now become fatality statistics in the Battle of Britain. Twelve days later, so, too, would the third New Brunswicker.

* * *

As the crow flies, RAF Coltishall, home of RAF No. 242 Fighter Squadron, sat just seventy-five miles from most of the Luftwaffe's key *Adlerangriff* targets in Britain. Within thirty minutes of a scramble, S/L Douglas Bader and his dozen Hurricanes could take off, climb to 15,000 feet, and confront German bombers inbound for London over the Thames Estuary. But as Air Chief Marshal Hugh Dowding had laid out in his defensive alignment, No. 242's first obligation was to defend RAF fighter stations and factories in England's industrial heart north of London in the 12 Group sector. He gave his squadrons in 11 Group sector the responsibility of defending sites from London itself south and east to the English Channel.

Day after day in August, while Bader and his pilots sat in Coltishall's dispersal hut at readiness, burning to get into the fight, the phone never rang. Day after day, German bombers and their fighter escorts seemed to overwhelm the RAF defenders just a few minutes' flying time to the south. Bader even called up Air Vice-Marshal Trafford Leigh-Mallory, the air officer commanding for 12 Group, requesting permission to scramble in order to back up his sister squadrons in 11 Group's air space.

"We can't put all our eggs in one basket," Leigh-Mallory told Bader.[11]

Dowding steadfastly believed that spreading his fifty-two fighter squadrons thinly across 10, 11, 12, and 13 Group sectors implied to the enemy that he could defend more sites. That meant RAF squadrons, with just twelve or so fighters each, would take off and climb to challenge as many as one hundred or two hundred Luftwaffe bombers all at once. Dowding admitted that the impossible odds meant some bombers inevitably would get through, but if his squadrons-spread-thin strategy worked, each enemy bomber formation harassed by RAF fighters would inflict less-concentrated damage.

Bader nevertheless pleaded with Leigh-Mallory to let him bolster 11 Group fighter numbers over its sector, thus giving his No. 242 Hurricanes their baptism of fire and their first crack at the waves of German raiders. "I can't send you in until 11 Group calls for you," Leigh-Mallory answered Bader.[12]

Meanwhile, the downtime at Coltishall was allowing newly arriving Canadians to settle into the station. They familiarized themselves with the new upgraded Hurricanes and adopted Bader's coiled sense of readiness for when an actual scramble call came. P/O Lawrence Cryderman, a former school teacher from Toronto, had joined the RAF in 1939. He had little experience as a fighter pilot but demonstrated his virtuosity on the piano when the squadron pilots gathered in the mess for beer and bawdy singsongs.[13] Also limited in combat experience, P/O Norris Hart, from Montreal, came to RAF Coltishall in mid-July. He'd only been commissioned on July 7, but having been an instructor in civilian aviation,[14] Hart was a quick learner. He was shipped off to an operational training unit and was back on No. 242's flight line within a month.[15]

Late in July, Flying Officer George Christie, from Westmount, Quebec, arrived, fresh from his high-altitude photo reconnaissance experience in Spitfires with RAF No. 212 Squadron (that service would earn him a DFC). P/O Hugh Tamblyn, a former aircraft mechanic from Watrous, Saskatchewan, joined the squadron on August 5; he had combat experience flying Defiants with RAF No. 141 Squadron.[16] And, finally, late in August, the former barnstormer and commercial pilot from Saint John, Flight Lieutenant Pat Sclanders, the third member of the Milledgeville Trio, arrived after having failed in his attempts to serve as a mercenary in both the Finnish and Norwegian Air Forces, and as a volunteer for the French Air Force. Sclanders settled into the routine at No. 242 on August 26, a few days before the idleness and false starts at Coltishall station came to an abrupt end.

On the morning of August 30, the dispersal hut phone rang. No. 242 received orders to scramble and fly to RAF Duxford, on the boundary line between 11 and 12 Group sectors north of London. Whooping and hollering, Bader and his squadron pilots launched in minutes. Halfway there, their sortie was aborted. At midday, however, the squadron was again ordered to Duxford. They'd barely landed and were eating sandwiches next to their Hurricanes when the phone rang in the dispersal hut.

"Angels fifteen," the voice on the other end said, directing No. 242 Squadron to climb to 15,000 feet. "North Weald."[17]

In minutes, fourteen Hurricanes were airborne,[18] headed into 11 Group air space over RAF North Weald station with Bader in the lead. He flicked on his radio telephone switch and spoke to the controller Alfred "Woodie" Woodhall: "Laycock Red Leader," he announced into the radio mouthpiece. "Am airborne."

"Vector one-nine-zero," directed the Duxford controller, punctuating the transmission with the word "Buster," which called for full throttle to get the fighters to their destination as quickly as possible. So that Bader knew what he'd be facing, the controller added, "Seventy-plus bandits approaching North Weald."

As 242's fighters climbed steadily into battle formation, in vics ("V" formations) of three, line astern, Bader splayed a map out on his thigh in the cockpit. He deduced the enemy bombers and fighters would be approaching North Weald from the southwest, right where the sun was situated. Bader ignored the controller's vectoring straight to North Weald and turned the squadron west. He might end up missing the enemy stream completely, but he'd attempt to get his fighters up into an advantageous altitude, coming out of the sun, before the Luftwaffe escorts did the same. Bader sent F/O Christie and Green Section toward North Weald. His hunch was bang on.

There was "a vast number,"[19] Christie radioed back to Bader, of twin-engine Me 110s escorting bombers—seventy or eighty of them at 12,000 to 14,000 feet—heading toward the RAF station. Above them, another swarm up to 20,000 feet.

"Green Section, take the top lot," Bader directed.

Christie climbed up to starboard with his two wingmates toward a swarm of Me 110s. Christie challenged one of them head-on, a risky manoeuvre given that each 110 fighter housed two cannons and four machine guns in its nose section. He must have surprised the German pilot, because the 110 abruptly broke from its formation to escape. With his high-altitude experience flying Spitfires in photo reconnaissance, Christie made sure none of the other 110s was chasing him, and closed to within fifty yards of his quarry. He fired bursts of shells that hit the 110's fuel tank, which exploded. The fighter-bomber fell into a vertical dive and went straight into the ground. Christie's wingmate, P/O Norris Hart, dived at three Heinkel bombers. One veered away, but Hart chased a second, fired, and saw it crash in flames.

Black Section, which had carried out tail-end Charlie duties, keeping German fighters off the back side of the squadron, caught up to the enemy formation under siege. P/O Noel Stansfeld found another Heinkel 111 straggling behind the main stream of bombers. On his first pass, he fired at the rear gun position and watched its response.

"[It] was twinkling like a flashlight on and off," Stansfeld reported later. [20] But none of the German gunner's shells connected with Stansfeld's oncoming Hurricane. On the Canadian's next pass, he started a fire in the port engine. Eventually the bomber lost power and crashed into a civilian airfield.

Meanwhile, S/L Bader had ordered his Red and Yellow Sections to join his formation, line astern on him, and he aimed his Hurricane at the heart of a line of Dornier bombers and their Messerschmitt escorts. The 110s scattered in a fan-like fashion, three to port, three to starboard, and Bader immediately latched onto one of them, firing into its wing roots; the plane burst into flames and heeled over. Above to the right, Bader chased another 110 and got it, too.

As outstanding a day as Bader seemed to be having, his wingmate, F/O Willie McKnight, was outdoing everyone in the squadron. The irascible Edmontonian, whom his friend

Stan Turner had called "absolutely fearless," was proving all of that.

"At [5:05 p.m. spotted] enemy a/c [aircraft] in vic formation and stepped from 12,000–18,000 feet," his combat report read. "Attacked middle section of 110s."[21]

As his fellow fighter pilots had been doing, McKnight pulled in behind one of the fighter-bombers and "opened fire at approximately 100 yards. Enemy a/c burst into flames and dived towards ground." Next, McKnight found a formation of Heinkel bombers, picked one out and, this time firing at right angles into the side of the bomber, struck its port engine from 150 yards away. The bomber burst into flames, rolled on its back, and fell away. Coming under attack from an Me 110, McKnight manoeuvred to get behind him. "Followed him from 10,000 feet to 1,000 feet," he reported. "Enemy a/c used very steep turns for evasive action, but finally straightened out. I opened fire at approximately thirty yards. Enemy's starboard engine stopped and port engine burst into flames. Enemy crashed in flames alongside large reservoir." McKnight had his hat trick for the day.

Within the hour, McKnight and all thirteen of his squadron comrades landed safely back at RAF Duxford. Not a single Hurricane had been damaged in the engagement. Not a single bomb had fallen on North Weald. Between takeoff at 4:23 p.m. and landing at 5:35 p.m., No. 242 Fighter Squadron pilots had accumulated twelve confirmed kills, half at the hands of Canadian pilots: one for Christie, one for Hart, one for Stansfeld, and three for McKnight. The latter was chuffed at the day's scores. "We've either killed all their real good pilots and they're using new young ones, or else they are losing their nerve," he wrote a friend in Edmonton. "They haven't got the same guts they used to have, and except in a few cases try to avoid a real scrap."[22]

Overall that day, August 30, RAF Fighter Command had logged 1,054 sorties, an unprecedented number. Some squadrons got all their fighters airborne four times in daylight, and almost all squadrons in the day's action, including No. 242, flew at least two sorties.[23]

The Canadian pilots of No. 242 were showered with praise by Air Force brass for their performance. AVM Trafford Leigh-Mallory offered applause "on a first-class show." Then, the chief of the air staff, Cyril Newall, added his congratulations for the squadron. "You are well on top of the enemy," Newall applauded, "and obviously the fine Canadian traditions of the last war are safe in your hands."[24]

* * *

Douglas Bader's debriefing with Duxford controller Alfred Woodhall on August 30 sounded more like a pre-flight briefing for August 31. When Woodhall asked Bader why he'd disregarded the controller's vectoring to North Weald, Bader explained his battle tactic—surprising the Germans by flying out of the sun—and pointed out that No. 242's aggressive approach had, in fact, prevented any bombs from falling on North Weald. Bader added that, in future, it would be better if he and the Canadians confronted the bombers before they got to their targets, not while they were bombing them.

"It certainly worked today," Woodhall admitted.

"If the controller will tell us where [enemy aircraft] are in time—direction and height," Bader insisted, "we'll sort out the tactics in the air, get ourselves up-sun and beat the hell out of them before they can bomb."[25]

A few days later, Bader took his argument for new fighter tactics to AVM Leigh-Mallory, explaining that if he'd had more aircraft in the air over North Weald, his fighters could have inflicted heavier losses on the German bomber stream. Bader wondered aloud why No. 242 and other squadrons were regularly forced to stand by at far-flung stations when they could take off and fight the raiders together. When the 12 Group commander asked how he might lead two and three squadrons at a time, Bader said it would be easy. All he needed was an earlier scramble call from the controller, and with more time to gain altitude in larger numbers, his "big wing" approach[*] could destroy more enemy aircraft. Bader got his answer the next day.

"Tomorrow I want you to try this large formation scheme of yours," Leigh-Mallory said. He assigned two of 12 Group's squadrons, No. 19 and No. 310, based at Duxford, to join the experiment.

Beginning on August 31, S/L Bader led his big wing through repeated mass takeoffs from Duxford, the faster Spitfires of No. 19 Squadron climbing quickest and giving cover as the Hurricanes of No. 310, made up largely of Czech pilots, and the Canadians in No. 242 followed. In short order, he reduced the time it took for thirty-six fighters to scramble and assemble in the air in battle-ready formation to just over

---

* A "big wing," sometimes called a "Balbo" (after Italian fascist politician/aviator Italo Balbo, who led an Italian air armada of twenty-four seaplanes to North America and back in 1933), could include as many as three squadrons, forty fighters attacking together.

three minutes. Once airborne, Bader went looking for trouble over North London. That last day of August, his big wing had no contact with enemy aircraft.

Nevertheless, Leigh-Mallory had seen Bader's three squadrons practise. "Next time 11 Group calls on you," he told Bader, "take your whole team."

That same day, the Luftwaffe had enjoyed unexpected and devastating success elsewhere. Kesselring sent 150 bombers into action, escorted by about 1,300 fighters. His bombers hit RAF stations at Eastchurch, Croydon, Detling, and Debden. At Biggin Hill, German bombers scored a direct hit on the operations room. They rained down bombs on Hornchurch, just as Spitfires attempted to get airborne. Likewise, the scramble signal was so late to Northolt that high-flying Messerschmitts unexpectedly pounced on an RCAF No. 1 patrol, shooting down three Hurricanes; F/O Sprenger crash-landed and survived, while F/L Vaughan Corbett and F/O George Hyde received serious burns bailing out of their fighters. During a second scramble the same day, F/O Jean-Paul Desloges's Hurricane took a direct hit in the cockpit. He, too, bailed out, suffering severe burns and lacerations. The RAF lost thirty-nine fighter aircraft and fourteen pilots killed that day, while the Luftwaffe lost forty-one aircraft.

ACM Dowding did not see attrition as a path to victory, and he wrote in a dispatch, "Fighter pilots [are] no longer being produced in numbers sufficient to fill the gaps in the fighting ranks."[26] Worse, the gaps were widening dangerously. Since July 1, 1940, Fighter Command had lost eleven of its forty-six squadron commanders, and thirty-nine of its ninety-seven flight commanders killed or wounded. Sprog pilots (rookies) arrived at operational squadrons with fewer than twenty hours logged in the cockpits of Spitfires and Hurricanes; many of those green pilots didn't make it back from their first combat sorties.[27]

The ranks of Canadian fighter pilots in the battle reflected these deadly trends. As September began, RCAF No. 1 Fighter Squadron had been operational since August 13, for exactly eighteen days. Its pilots had mistakenly shot down friendly Blenheims on the 24th before righting things through the early days of the German *Adlerangriff* offensive. Still, F/O Bob Edwards had died in action on August 26 and, five days later, the squadron had three more Hurricanes downed with serious wounds to their pilots. On September 1, during a head-on attack against twenty bombers with escorts, the relative inexperience of the squadron again brought casualties. F/Os Yuile and Kerwin bailed out of their disabled fighters, both suffering burn wounds, while F/O Beardmore took heavy cannon fire and barely made it back to base. In seven days, mostly as a result of insufficient combat experience, RCAF No. 1 had fought four engagements, destroyed eight German aircraft, and lost one pilot killed, four injured, and seven aircraft destroyed.[28]

At age twenty-one, Camille Bon Seigneur had plenty of life experience when he arrived in the UK in 1939 to train in the RAF. Born in Gull Lake, Saskatchewan, in 1918, Bon Seigneur was still an infant when his father, a doctor, died in the flu epidemic. He tried school, then selling cars in Regina, and eventually enlistment in the Royal Canadian Corps of Signals. But when war broke out, he wanted nothing more than a chance for that Short Service Commission in the RAF. He sailed to the UK in a cattle boat, got his commission, and trained to become a fighter pilot.

By May 1940, he'd been posted to RAF No. 257 Fighter Squadron, at Hendon, flying Hurricanes on sorties against Luftwaffe bombers and fighters. In July, he shared in the destruction of a Dornier 17, but with relatively few hours of combat experience, his Hurricane was bounced—attacked unexpectedly—by "an avalanche of German fighters" during a sortie on September 3 over Ingatestone. [29]

Roy Sweeting, a resident in the town, watched the stricken Hurricane spiralling down to earth, its engine "making an awful howl before the plane crashed and burned."[30] Then he spotted a bundle hurtling down and a parachute partially opened. At the crash scene, Sweeting and other civilians found Bon Seigneur and carried him in a blanket stretcher to a town taxi that rushed him to hospital. Bon Seigneur was already dead. The idiosyncrasies of Air Ministry bureaucracy delayed notifying his parents until January 1941.

P/O Alec Trueman had plenty of flying experience, just not on fighters. Born in 1914, the son of Mount Allison University president George Trueman, Alec chose post-secondary education at Parks Air College, America's first federally certified school of aviation. While studying engin-eering, he accumulated 115 hours of flying time and a private pilot's licence. He then moved to Boston for courses on aero-engines.[31] By 1938, like so many others, he'd been accepted by the RAF's Direct Entry Scheme and was streamed into Bomber Command flying Hampdens. During his active service in Lincolnshire, he married Patricia Lord; when the RAF trans-ferred Trueman to fighters in July 1940, his wife was pregnant. By September 4, with only a month's worth of Hurricane time, he'd joined RAF No. 253 Fighter Squadron, led by legend-ary commanding officer Tom Gleave, who days earlier had shot down four Me 109s in one afternoon's dogfighting over Maidstone.

On September 4, the communication pipeline at Fighter Command was dangerously backed up. Plotting tables in the Operations Room were so saturated with bomber sightings that somehow an inbound stream of enemy bombers over southwest London was reported only at the last minute. P/O Trueman and the rest of his No. 253 comrades had been sitting in their dispersal hut at continuous readiness. Suddenly, they got a scramble call and managed to intercept Me 110 fighter-bombers as they attacked the Vickers aircraft factories in Weybridge. At the time, the facility was responsible for manufacturing two-thirds of Bomber Command's Wellington bombers. Thanks to the fighters, only six bombs hit the works, but when the intercept was over, Trueman had disappeared.

Squadron mate F/O John Greenwood thought Trueman had just been separated from his section during the sortie. "I recall he went missing," Greenwood wrote, "and the whole squadron returned intact. We were all waiting to hear that he had landed on some other airfield, but his plane was found with him still in the cockpit. He'd gone in vertically near Banstead in Surrey."[32] Trueman was the first native son of Sackville, New Brunswick, killed in the war.*

The Canadian fighters with RCAF No. 1 encountered some of that same formation of Me 110s. The initiative of one of their more experienced flight commanders proved the

---

* Trueman's twin sons, Alec and Michael, were born two months later in Lincoln, England. Only when they travelled to Canada after the war did the boys learn about their father's lifelong commitment to aviation and his deep connection to the Maritimes ("Enjoying First Visit to Canada," *Sackville Tribune*, August 17, 1951).

difference in the outcome. "[Gordon] McGregor was a daring and innovative leader," said Paul Pitcher, who often flew as McGregor's wingmate in the section. "He was always drawing up new types of operations designed to get at the enemy."[33]

When McGregor and the rest of the squadron spotted the Me 110s over East Grinstead, the Hurricanes had reached an altitude of 18,000 feet with the enemy aircraft 3,000 feet below them. The Canadians had the midday sun at their backs, but the Germans had configured their fifteen aircraft in a previously unseen formation. They were flying in a defensive circle, rotating counter-clockwise. And while their tight prop-to-tail formation offered overall security, the trajectory of their nose and rear guns was limited by the close proximity of the next Me 110 in the circle.

McGregor ordered his pilots to prepare to attack individually in a line, then led the entire squadron into the centre of the defensive circle.

"We formed in line astern—or follow the leader—and dove down," Ernie McNab said. "We cut into the inside of the circle, only in the opposite direction and had a shot at each [Me 110] as it passed."[34]

As each Hurricane sliced through the middle of the circle, it could deliver a nearly head-on attack against each Messerschmitt, whose gunners had too little time to line up a shot without striking another Me 110. In just two minutes of diving and shooting, the sweeping scythe of fire by the Hurricanes resulted in two destroyed Me 110s, one more likely destroyed, and five more damaged. The Canadians suffered no losses using McGregor's manoeuvre. Dal Russel, who completed the sortie with two probable bombers destroyed, called the action "a hellish game of ring 'round the rosie."[35]

* * *

During those last days of August and first days of September, any advantage one side seemed to have over the other, either by way of tactics or victories-versus-losses, was disappearing. On August 30, the RAF lost twenty aircraft to the Luftwaffe's twenty-four. The next day, thirty-nine to forty-one. On September 2, twenty-three to twenty-six; the next day, fifteen to twelve; the next, eighteen to twenty-one; and the next dead even at twenty-one. The margin of one side over the other had dwindled to nothing.[36]

A Hurricane with No. 249 Squadron was among the fifteen RAF fighter aircraft the Germans shot down on September 3. Canadian fighter pilot Robert "Butcher" Barton had flown from North Weald to deflect Luftwaffe attacks on RAF bases on the London periphery. Raised in Vernon, BC, the diminutive Barton had gone to school in the 1930s by taking a Lake Okanagan steamboat to Penticton each day. Aged nineteen, in 1936, Barton got the nod for an RAF Short Service Commission and arrived at No. 249 Squadron as the Battle of Britain began. During this early September 1940 sortie, a Dornier rear gunner had hit Barton's Hurricane, and he was forced to bail out.

"As I fell through the sky," Barton recalled, "I thought, 'You'd better find the ripcord on the parachute at your chest.' And when I finally landed, I just stripped a pear tree and ended up in somebody's backyard."[37]

The disappointment of losing his Hurricane in one of his first combat flights was only exceeded by the ribbing he took back at the station for allowing himself to be shot down by the gunner in a bomber. Barton would eventually redeem himself, assume command of No. 249 Squadron, score eight victories in the skies over Britain, and earn a DFC and bar. In the meantime, his forced exit from a Hurricane was indicative of RAF attrition. On September 2, Air Commodore Douglas Evill, senior air officer at Fighter Command, provided Dowding with analysis that showed Fighter Command's pilot loss rate was 125 per week; at best, RAF training units would provide 150 new pilots by September 21.[38] Bottom line: the RAF was losing the battle.[39]

Dowding sensed exhaustion was setting in. He felt he needed to classify his squadrons not based on proximity to the targets anymore but on ability to carry on. In a meeting at Bentley Priory on September 7, he presented Air Ministry with the means for Fighter Command to "go downhill" in the most economical fashion, and subsequently go back uphill as easily as possible. His plan categorized squadrons as "A" squadrons, those likely to find themselves in the front line; "B" squadrons, those not at the front line but able to fight; and "C" squadrons, those with too few machines or too little experience to face combat.[40]

At the same time, RAF intelligence noticed a shift in the nature of Luftwaffe attacks. Intelligence Summary No. 166 observed that German bombers and fighters generally were flying at higher altitudes than previously, delivering bombs from 20,000 feet. And when a lead aircraft bombed, so did they all. RAF intelligence read this to mean that, like the RAF, the Luftwaffe was growing short of experienced aircrew.[41] Fighter Command's priority, then, had to be to scatter the Luftwaffe formations before they reached their targets.

For Göring, in the eighteen days since Eagle Day (August 13), the massive assaults across the UK had evolved to specific sorties against the sector airfields protecting London. And while German aircrewmen were assured again and again that victory was at hand, the truth was the Luftwaffe had lost eight hundred aircraft in the prior two months of battle. And RAF Fighter Command, despite being horribly depleted, had still managed to muster more sorties than the German bomber and fighter forces combined.

More alarming for the reichsmarschall was a fast-approaching deadline. Göring had promised to rid the skies of the RAF before the launch of Hitler's Operation Sea Lion, the amphibious invasion of Britain scheduled for mid-September. Oberkommando der Wehrmacht, or German High Command, considered the coming operation to transport and land 260,000 troops and 30,000 vehicles along 230 miles of the English coast the *coup de grâce*. And as far as it was concerned, the order to embark was imminent. The Germans had assembled 1,910 barges, 1,600 escort vessels, 419 tugboats, and 168 requisitioned transports[42] in the Channel ports and in the Scheldt Estuary. The moon and tide would be right for the invasion between September 8 and 10.

An impending invasion was no secret to many Britons. Indeed, at 8 p.m. on September 7, the British armed forces headquarters issued the code word "Cromwell" to its eastern and southern commands. Translated, it meant all branches of Britain's military at home had eight hours' notice that they could be brought to "readiness for immediate action" to combat an actual invasion.[43] In response to the "Cromwell" signal, some communities erected roadblocks and set church bells ringing an alarm. In East Anglia, overanxious engineers blew up bridges and laid landmines (that later killed Home Guards).[44] At training barracks in Sussex, commanders of the

2nd Canadian Infantry Division were alerted to bring troops to "standby at immediate notice."[45] Acknowledging the false alarm, Winston Churchill eventually called off the readiness order; in future, he instructed, only if Home Guard members spotted large numbers of parachutists would "Cromwell" be issued again.

More tangibly, the high-altitude Spitfires of the RAF's Photographic Development Unit had recorded evidence of a large number of barges assembling across the Channel. That brought RAF Bomber and Coastal Command into the picture. The prospect of raids across the Channel to attack inland ports full of German invasion barges forced RAF bomber crews to confront the realities of repeated night operations. Starting in early September, streams of RAF Blenheims, Hampdens, Wellingtons, and Whitleys were launched against German-occupied ports from Dunkirk to Calais, known as the "Blackpool Front." In blackout conditions and without sophisticated navigational equipment, aircrews spent long hours flying on penetratingly cold nights, searching out flotillas of barges by dead reckoning and dropping their payloads.

"Calais docks were on fire. So was the waterfront of Boulogne," wrote F/O R.S. Gilmour about his bombing run. "The whole French coast seemed to be a barrier of flame broken only by intense white flashes of exploding bombs and vari-coloured incendiary tracers soaring and circling skywards."[46]

Suddenly, the entire focus of the Battle of Britain shifted yet again. Göring had promised a four-day war to eliminate the RAF, but after four weeks the job remained unfinished. He decided that his death-blow strategy would be to bomb London into chaos. Hitler gave him the green light.

Oberst Paul Deichmann believed the RAF would surely launch all their fighters to defend the capital. Kesselring agreed. Only Sperrle believed the bombers should stay focused on attacking RAF airfields, and recommended bombing the air installations by day and London by night. Kesselring won the argument. London became the new primary target to draw the RAF into a doomsday dogfight. And Hitler made *Zielwechsel* (Target Switch) official during a speech to women nurses and social workers at the Berlin Sportspalast on September 4.

"When they declare that they will increase their attacks on our cities," Hitler warned the British, "then we will raze their cities to the ground."[47] He issued the code word *Loge*, after the god in German mythology who forged the sword of Siegfried the dragon-killer.

The decision to switch from the Luftwaffe's targeted attacks against the RAF to massive bombings of London was a pivotal moment. It made certain that many thousands of British civilians would die in the continuing siege. It also allowed Fighter Command time to get off the mat. As painful as he knew the Germans' decision to bomb London would be for average Britons, ACM Hugh Dowding admitted feelings of "intense relief" to his personal assistant. "I could hardly believe that the Germans would have made such a mistake," Dowding told Robert Wright, and went on to describe this turning point as "a supernatural intervention . . . really the crucial day."[48]

On Saturday, September 7, with RAF fighters still licking their wounds, the great London air attack known as the Blitz was underway. Late that afternoon, the first wave of 320 bombers, protected by every fighter the Germans had, nearly 1,000 aircraft in all, departed occupied France. Once organized over the Channel, enemy aircraft formations were stacked up one and a half miles high and spread over eight hundred square miles of sky.[49] London would be bombed for fifty-seven straight days and nights. About 19,000 tons of explosives would fall on the city, killing 30,000 civilians, injuring another 50,000, and destroying more than a million homes. Göring, having announced, "I myself have taken command of the Luftwaffe's battle for Britain,"[50] stood on the cliffs at Cap Blanc-Nez to watch the armada depart to attack London.

At one time, all Luftwaffe airmen had supported Hermann Göring, the hero of the Great War. But a month of pounding since the start of *Adlerangriff*—harassment from RAF fighters in the air and severe criticism from the reichsmarschall on the ground—had depleted morale in the ranks. Even Adolf Galland, now commander of *Jagdgeschwader* (Fighter Squadron) 26,[51] harboured doubts about Göring's insistence that Me 109s protect attacking bombers closely at all cost. "The [109s] were bound to the bombers and could not leave until attacked," Galland wrote, "thus giving their opponent the advantage of surprise, initiative, superior altitude, greater speed, and above all fighting spirit, the aggressive attitude which marks all successful fighter pilots."[52]

In contrast, the mutual respect between Douglas Bader and his commanding officer, Leigh-Mallory, had grown. The maverick squadron leader and his No. 242 All-Canadian Squadron had scored so many victories in late August and received such glowing praise from Fighter Command that Leigh-Mallory designated Bader's three-squadron combat experiment "the Duxford Wing." Bader couldn't wait for the next chance to prove himself and his charges. He got it the same afternoon that the Luftwaffe threw the works at London.

At 4:17 p.m. on September 7, AVM Keith Park, commanding 11 Group, realized the peril his sector faced and scrambled every fighter in the path of the bomber striking force. Park's call was relayed north to 12 Group. Forty-five minutes later, Bader's Duxford Wing was scrambled to meet the German armada headed for London.

"Hallo, Douglas. Orbit North Weald. Angels ten,"[53] came the familiar voice of Controller Woodhall, instructing Bader to fly to North Weald and circle at an altitude of 10,000 feet.

Bader, predictably, took his own bead on the altitude and direction of the specks he saw to the southeast, heading west toward London. He directed the wing to climb to 15,000 feet.

"Seventy plus crossing the Thames east of London," continued Woodhall. "They're heading north."

All the Dornier bombers and Me 110 fighter-bombers were crossing the Duxford Wing's path, but still 5,000 feet higher than the Hurricanes. Higher still, above the German bombers, flew the Me 109 escorts surveying the entire scene. The Hurricane section leaders had only one option: to climb at full throttle and maximum boost to overtake, attack, and break up the box formation of bombers before it got any closer to London.

As the Hurricanes raced upward astern of the bombers, tracer bullets came streaking toward them from the German rear gunners. P/O Noel Stansfeld, with two bomber kills to his credit, flew straight at a Dornier and fired his machine guns continuously from three hundred yards away to fifty yards away; the bomber rolled over and dove straight into the ground. Bader fired bursts of shells into an Me 110 and set it ablaze. In response, an Me 109's shells ripped through Bader's left aileron and his cockpit, tearing open his flying suit, but no deeper.

The pattern of closing to attack and being bounced in return repeated itself across No. 242 Squadron that afternoon. P/O Stan Turner zeroed in on an Me 110, but before he could complete the attack, his Hurricane came under fire from an Me 109 fighter. No sooner had he outmanoeuvred his pursuer than another 109 jumped him. Turner got off several bursts of machine-gun fire before taking evasive action and descending out of the fight.

Similarly, P/O Hugh Tamblyn closed his Hurricane to within two hundred yards of an Me 110, fired into it for five seconds, saw it burst into flames, and then had to whip his aircraft into a steep-right turn to elude shells fired from another 109. His quick manoeuvre put him into an ideal attack position against another enemy aircraft, and he immediately shot it down.

On this first day of the Blitz, S/L Bader's Duxford Wing had delivered what he'd promised. His combined three squadrons were credited with putting more than twenty enemy aircraft out of action: No. 19 (Spitfire) Squadron chalked up five destroyed and one damaged; No. 310 Squadron had confirmed five destroyed, five more probables, and four damaged; while No. 242's Canadians had destroyed two, probably a third, and damaged one more.

The moment Bader touched down at Coltishall, he brought his Hurricane to a stop in front of the maintenance hangar and leapt out, shouting to his ground crew chief, "I want this aircraft ready again in half an hour."

Warrant Officer Bernard West and his riggers and fitters surveyed the Hurricane's shattered left aileron and bullet-riddled cockpit. They informed Bader that enemy shells had smashed his turn-and-bank indicator, his prop revolution counter, and his undercart quadrant. They estimated the plane would more likely be grounded for a week.

"That's no damn good," Bader snapped back.

Biding his time, West looked more closely at the bullet trail through the Hurricane's fuselage. He smelled the stink of fuel in the cockpit and added, "You've got four bullets that I can see through the petrol tank. You're lucky it's self-sealing."[54]

Perhaps more sobering for Bader was the news he received at the base that P/O Jack Benzie's Hurricane had gone down with no sign of pilot or plane. Just twenty-five, Benzie had given wartime service to the Queen's Own Cameron Highlanders and Princess Patricia's Canadian Light Infantry in Canada, and was one of the originals at No. 242 when the RAF designated it the All-Canadian Squadron in November 1939. Bader would have to write Benzie's parents and brother back on Polson Avenue in Winnipeg about their loss and the lack of known remains.*

Despite the best efforts of Fighter Command, the first day of enemy raids on London, between 8 p.m. and dawn, saw 330 tons of high explosives and thousands of incendiaries fall on the city's east-end industrial docks.[55] Some of the bombs fell as far west as Kensington, killing 448 civilians downtown and in the city suburbs.

While 12 Group's Duxford Wing had fared well, No. 249 Squadron flew up to meet the waves of bombers and lost six Hurricanes without taking down a single enemy aircraft. The day's setbacks included twenty-eight RAF fighter aircraft

---

* P/O Jack Benzie's name would eventually join those of 20,450 other Commonwealth aircrew (3,050 of them Canadians) lost during the war with no known graves and inscribed on the Runnymede Memorial, west of London.

lost, along with nineteen pilots.[56] The Luftwaffe was down thirty-nine planes. September 7 earned its moniker of "Black Saturday."

S/L Bader, feeling that his Canadians had not yet begun to fight, held another beef session with Leigh-Mallory on Sunday morning. Bader complained that his Duxford Wing had not received a scramble signal early enough for it to climb to sufficient altitude for the No. 19 Spitfires to take on the German fighters and for his No. 242 and No. 310 Hurricanes to scatter and disable the bombers. Leigh-Mallory promised he'd look into improved timing. He delivered the next afternoon, Monday, September 9, when Bader's Duxford Wing scrambled all three squadrons to patrol North Weald and Hornchurch. As he'd done on previous outings, Bader ignored the patrolling order. He began stalking two box formations of enemy aircraft, the first of sixty bombers and fighters at 22,000 feet, the second a quarter of a mile behind at a slightly higher altitude, both flying toward London. He directed the Spitfires to climb and strike the latter formation, which included Me 109s, while Bader would lead the Hurricanes out of the sun, line astern, heading right for the middle of the lead box of bombers.

As the engagement began, some Me 110s detached themselves from the lead bomber formation, and P/O Hugh Tamblyn followed them in a right-hand circle.

"I turned into a stern attack," his combat report stated.[57] And he was about to fire at the closest bomber when he spotted an Me 110 firing at another Hurricane in his section. Altering course, he fired into the enemy aircraft, setting both its engines on fire. He saw two more Hurricanes under attack, their wings folding up and falling out of the sky.

"I went to the far side of the formation and climbed again," Tamblyn continued. "I saw a 110 making across me in a steep turn. I gave a short burst and went into dead astern where after a burst of about seven seconds the port engine caught fire. . . . I followed him down and watched him crash in front of a cricket clubhouse."

About the same time, Bader called for the sections of Hurricanes following him to join in formation, line astern, and attack the second box formation. Bader homed on a Dornier, fired for two seconds, and watched it fall away with smoke pouring from both engines.

Behind Bader, the next Hurricane section, with Royal Navy Sergeant Pilot Robert Lonsdale and Canadian F/L Pat Sclanders, entered the fray, as did a number of Me 109s, which had the altitude advantage. One of the Me 109s bounced Sclanders's Hurricane as he was dodging fire from a Dornier rear gunner. Clearly overpowered, Sclanders tried evading the crossfire. It was too late. His Hurricane was ablaze and out of control. Sclanders's plane was last seen falling toward Thames Haven oil refineries.

Meanwhile, P/O John Latta chased a single-seat Messerschmitt from behind and, from a distance of three hundred yards, fired into its cockpit area. He must have struck the plane's fuel tank, because it lit up like a torch and spun away out of control. Latta also took hits across his Hurricane's wing. His aileron jammed and he dove away for home.

In another part of the whirling dogfight, P/O McKnight closed and fired on an Me 109 but was promptly bounced by two more enemy fighters. Outnumbered, he still managed to dispatch two German aircraft. His fighter took hits in one wing, but he managed to cut away and descend to a safe landing. With his Distinguished Flying Cross and so many combat victories to his credit, McKnight had recently been offered an instructor's position with the BCATP back in Canada; he admitted in a letter home that he preferred the excitement of the fight. "I suppose I shall remain here until the end or the *other* end," he wrote. "I've got so used to the thrill and the . . . final feeling of victory that I'd feel lost and bored by a quiet life again."[58]

As he'd promised it would, Douglas Bader's Duxford Wing used its pre-emptive scramble, greater strength in numbers, and the wing leader's aggressive tactics to rack up remarkable totals: the No. 19 Spitfires had shot down three enemy aircraft, the No. 310 Czech Squadron four more, and the No. 242 Canadian Squadron eleven enemy machines. But, once again, the wing had sustained a tough loss. F/L Pat Sclanders, the only surviving member of the Milledgeville Trio from New Brunswick, had died on just his fourth sortie with No. 242 Squadron. When news of the young Sclanders's death reached Saint John, the meeting of the local Board of Trade was postponed, respecting the memory of the president's son.[59]

The third day of the Blitz had cost RAF Fighter Command twenty-one aircraft, the Luftwaffe Air Fleets twenty-seven; and it had killed another 370 civilians in London. The Battle of Britain was now not only a siege against the Royal Air Force but against the British people. Hoping he could make the British people turn on their leadership, Hitler had instead united them.[60]

CHAPTER EIGHT

"JUST SORT OF GOT USED TO IT"

THERE WERE LITERALLY THOUSANDS OF REASONS FOR Dorothy Elizabeth Firth to be on alert during the first days of the Blitz, but almost none of them within her control. The first night of the German bombing of London, September 7, 1940, Luftwaffe aircraft dropped 13,000 explosives containing thermite (a mixture of aluminum powder and iron oxide) inside magnesium casings. When these incendiary bombs hit warehouses, fuel tanks, chemical plants, and railway yards in London's industrial areas or hospitals, churches, hotels, theatres, and schools along residential streets, they ignited fires that burned at temperatures up to 4,500 degrees Fahrenheit; they generated enough heat to melt metal and even rock.

By 6 p.m., about ninety minutes after the first air raid sirens had sounded across London, thousands of incendiaries had fallen on the east-end waterfront and the densely populated residences of Greenwich, Poplar, Stepney, and Bermondsey— the riverside boroughs on either side of the Thames's double meander, where the great Victoria and Albert Docks, the West

India Docks, and the Surrey Commercial Docks were concentrated. Entire streets of two-up-two-down row houses, thrown together cheaply by nineteenth-century speculative builders, burned like matchsticks.[1]

It wasn't the residences the bombers were targeting, but the docks and warehouses crammed with war munitions, raw materials, fuel, and food—London's wartime inventory. Every warehouse fire threw a different hazard at the firefighters sent to douse the flames. Fire in a rubber storage facility belched clouds of asphyxiating smoke. Buildings with burning pepper filled the firefighters' lungs with stinging particles.[2] Fire in a rum warehouse spilled flaming liquid into the river; there was a 1,000-metre wall of flame below Tower Bridge, and the Thames was ablaze "like a Christmas pudding."[3]

"The whole bloody world's on fire!" reported the fire officer at the Surrey Docks. He and his fire brigade faced 250 acres of piled timber all ablaze. Before the war, any fire requiring thirty pumps was considered a major incident. By midnight on September 7, London fire brigades were fighting nine fires, each out of control, each requiring over one hundred pumps. Two fires at the Surrey Docks brought 430 pumps and thousands of firefighters from across southern England to battle them. The heat was so intense that it blistered the paint on fireboats on the Thames. Foot-long fire embers were catapulted from the Quebec Yard onto distant streets, igniting new fires in residential neighbourhoods. Stacks of flaming timber that the fire brigades had doused smouldered until dry and then burst into flames again.[4]

At the start of the war, London's fleet of fire trucks numbered 120, augmented by 2,000 motorized pumps. With the city's firefighters facing a new fire wherever an incendiary landed, it fell to a citizen army of professional and volunteer firefighters to respond in the first moments after the bombs hit the ground and ignited. Eventually, six million civilians in Britain would volunteer to augment the fire brigades.

Dorothy Firth joined the volunteer fire-watchers' force at the Richmond Fire Station in west London. Station firefighters taught her how to smother incendiaries with stirrup pumps and water, or buckets of sand. For her service, Firth received stockings, blouse, boots, a tin helmet, and a serge skirt and jacket.

"The blue serge uniform was dreadful to wear," she said. "It was rough like contract carpeting."[5]

Dorothy Firth chafed at whatever seemed impractical or out of character, no less so during the Blitz. Her father was Irish, her mother Scottish. In 1922, they had moved with Dorothy, age two at the time, and her older brother to London in search of better work. As a teenager at the Richmond County School for Girls, Dorothy was tall. They wanted her to be a gymnast, but she preferred basketball. She also wanted to go to university, but when the war began, she felt a tug to volunteer. The ARP Act of 1937 laid out plans for county councils to recruit volunteers as air raid wardens, ambulance divers, auxiliary police, and (in 1938) auxiliary firefighters. Dorothy juggled work as a clerk in downtown London during the day with volunteer fire watching after hours. "Everybody was trying pull their weight," she said.[6]

Londoners quickly recognized that the sheer number of incendiaries dropped by the Luftwaffe every night over-whelmed the city's fire service, and that suitably trained and outfitted volunteer householders could tackle the smaller fires caused by the bombs.[7] Peering into the blacked-out streets or positioned near buildings not occupied at night, Dorothy and her fellow volunteers were trained to spot incendiaries the moment they hit the ground and ignited. If they could arrive soon enough, the fire-watchers attempted to smother the initial blaze with buckets of loose sand or, working in tandem with buckets of water and hand-manipulated stirrup pumps, tried dousing the flames before they spread.

Richmond had no high-priority targets for the Luftwaffe, but on the second night of the Blitz, high explosives and incendiaries rained down near Dorothy's home on Mount Ararat Road. The intended target was nearby Richmond Park, where anti-aircraft guns and troops were positioned to defend London. It was the first of 450 bombings registered in Richmond during the fifty-seven nights of the Blitz. Incendiaries set the Richmond Town Hall ablaze and all but destroyed the community's public library. Ninety-eight residents of Richmond died in the attacks and another four hundred suffered serious injuries; eight hundred were left homeless.[8] On those occasions when she wasn't serving soldiers meals and tea at a canteen inside London's main Waterloo Station, Dorothy reported to the fire station to take on the incendiaries.

"Our job was to stay alert, be aware of anything unusual," she said. "It was stressful, but they looked after us pretty well with a short tea break and then back on shift until 10 p.m."[9]

As if her days weren't busy enough, with her day job in the city and fire-watching many evenings, Dorothy Firth joined a troupe of entertainers performing for soldiers stationed around London, often those posted to the Richmond Park gun emplacements. With orchestra leader Bill Nightingale, the group of half a dozen amateurs choreographed dance numbers, sang wartime favourites, and prepared skits with corny jokes. One night as Dorothy and her dance partner in the show walked to a rehearsal at Nightingale's home, a Luftwaffe raid started. Bombs began falling on Richmond.

"I think we should take shelter," Dorothy told her friend.

"Let's keep walking," the other said.

"We could go into that garage," Dorothy said, feeling more threatened by the explosions nearby. But her friend insisted they continue. They arrived at the rehearsal and waited out the bombing in a shelter. On their return, they came across the garage Dorothy thought would have provided refuge. A bomb had demolished it. "We would never have survived," she said.[10] Dorothy would never have met Canadian tank commander George Marshall. She wouldn't have lived to marry him and emigrate to Canada as a war bride. She'd have become one of more than 20,000 Londoners killed during eight months of the Blitz.

Dorothy's wasn't the only show that went on despite the bombing. On the first night of the Blitz, even as the city's docklands blazed out of control, Londoners listening to the British Broadcasting Corporation's Home Service heard a concert by the WAAF choir, a variety show hosted by comedian Cyril Fletcher, a lecture on "Picture Postcard Beauties," as well as the news in Gaelic and Norwegian.

Unfazed by the threat of bombs falling on the city, Myra Hess remained seated at a piano in the National Gallery at lunchtimes, offering morale-raising concert music. And with the original wartime entertainment curfew lifted in 1940, the Entertainments National Service Association organized shows at military bases and even sponsored George Formby to entertain thousands of displaced civilians sheltering in London's Underground.

"In wartime, music fills an important niche in national life," wrote Vera Lynn, the sweetheart of the British Armed Forces. "In the Second World War [music] was not used as a war drum . . . but to stimulate workers in the war factories, to hearten people in their homes . . . to provide good cheer for the forces."[11]

* * *

The afternoon Dorothy Firth was introduced to incendiary bombs falling on Richmond also proved significant for one Canadian Spitfire fighter pilot. After thirteen months in Britain, mostly training on his short service commission with the RAF, Pilot Officer Alfred Keith Ogilvie would fire his first shots in anger on September 7. Posted to RAF No. 609 "White Rose" Fighter Squadron only two weeks earlier, Ogilvie sat in the dispersal hut that Saturday with other members of his fighter squadron based at Middle Wallop in 10 Group sector, northwest of Portsmouth. Skies were mostly clear, and so was visibility. The temperature was a warm seventy degrees Fahrenheit. Ideal flying conditions for friend and foe.

Just after 1 p.m., the ops phone rang with a scramble order and everything heated up fast. By the time Ogilvie reached his fighter, the station's fitters and riggers had the engines ticking over sufficiently for takeoff. The prop slipstreams from a dozen Spitfires were blowing grass on the airfield flat, and an erk helped harness him into the cockpit.

"London. 20,000 feet," was all the order said.

Ogilvie recorded in his journal how excited he felt, and noted he "was not frightened."[12] There was too much to prepare as he climbed at several thousand feet per minute toward the designated altitude. He checked his instruments, turned on his gunsights, and switched the gun button to "fire," all while maintaining his formation position, third behind Squadron Leader Horace Darley and P/O Mike Staples. Then he saw "what seemed to be a cloud of little black beetles crawling towards us, and there was no doubt but that they were headed our way."

Darley led the section into a half-roll out of the sun, lining the Spitfires up for a beam approach toward the enemy aircraft. Both his classroom lectures and mock dogfighting instruction had taught Ogilvie to attack the German bombers from the side, where they were least defended and most vulnerable.

"I must have hit one because he pulled up and over, giving me a clean shot at his belly," Ogilvie continued. "I opened fire and hit it for a few seconds and he fell away."

Just as quickly, he found himself approaching two Me 109s. As they passed in front of him, he realized he'd never actually seen their distinctive yellow-painted noses before. More important, since he'd descended out of the sun, they hadn't seen him.

"I opened fire on the second one . . . and connected as he rolled over and dove, turning on his back," wrote Ogilvie of the attack. "I got very close and emptied my guns as he streamed glycol, then smoke, and finally a sheet of flame."[13] Ogilvie had definitely destroyed one Me 109 and probably an Me 110, but he considered the kills more luck than skill.

Adding to the suspense of the day, Ogilvie had landed to refuel at Worthy Down airfield. That left him late on his return to Middle Wallop, so for a short while he was considered missing in action. In fact, the squadron had suffered no casualties. With Ogilvie's victories, No. 609 had upped its score to sixty-two enemy aircraft destroyed. When he did make it back to his home station, the squadron's fighter pilots gathered to celebrate Ogilvie's success over cocktails. Later, "Skeets" (a nickname he'd acquired for fleet-footed football play back at high school in Ottawa) wrote in his journal that he was feeling "nothing except my insides were frozen and my heart was beating up where my tonsils should be."[14]

What appeared even more remarkable to Skeets's son and biographer, Keith C. Ogilvie, was his ability to adapt to the task at hand. He'd arrived at No. 609 Fighter Squadron in mid-August with about 155 hours of solo flying behind him and little more than twenty hours in high-performance fighters.[15] When he shot down the Me 109 on September 7, he'd not yet studied or practised combat aerobatics, let alone such gunnery techniques as deflection shooting (leading a target). His ops instructors had taught him that his Spitfire (like the Hurricane) was equipped with eight Browning recoil-operated machine guns of .303-inch calibre. Each gun had a muzzle velocity of 2,440 feet per second, firing 1,200 rounds per minute. Perhaps most important, the eight guns were harmonized to converge at four hundred yards' range. Fighter pilots such as Ogilvie eventually directed fighter squadron armourers to modify the convergence to 250 yards for greater destructive impact on a target.[16]

Bombing and fighter tactics in the air over London were also changing. From a sequence of separate attacks, the Luftwaffe began organizing a configuration of three hundred to four hundred bombers in several consecutive waves against London. In response, Air Vice-Marshal Keith Park, commanding 11 Group, ordered his controllers to scramble his squadrons in pairs and for his squadron commanders to line fighters up in a strike formation of four aircraft not line astern, as had been the practice since the Great War, but line abreast. As before, the Spitfires attacked the high-altitude German fighters while the Hurricanes went after the bombers and escorts in the lower-altitude formations.

In the two weeks before September 7, when the sector airfields were under attack, Fighter Command lost 277 aircraft against 378 lost by the Luftwaffe—five British aircraft for every seven of the enemy. In the fortnight from September 7 to 21, when the German objective was London, Fighter Command lost 144 aircraft versus 262 lost by the Luftwaffe, or five British aircraft for every nine of the enemy.[17] The ratio was improving. Nevertheless, losing a brother fighter pilot in combat always left emotional scars. Through 1939 and most of 1940, P/O Ogilvie included notes about his roommates in his diary; he made it clear that No. 609 Squadron was close-knit. Its pilots fought together, played together, got drunk together, and carried each other home. But when his roommate P/O Geoff Gaunt was killed at the height of the Battle of Britain, Ogilvie's diary suddenly stopped referring to any roommates at all. "People came and went," he wrote matter-of-factly. "You'd get to know a guy pretty well, then all of a sudden he wasn't there anymore. You just sort of got used to it."[18]

* * *

Flight Lieutenant Johnny Kent's lengthy RAF record and his Air Force Cross were indicative of his experience, yet after a month leading "A" Flight of No. 303 Polish Squadron, the twenty-six-year-old Winnipegger was still learning about the untapped skill and courage of the men in his outfit. Most were older than Kent and had seen combat in the earliest days of the Nazi invasion of Poland in September 1939. Outgunned by the Luftwaffe, they had evacuated to the UK, where the RAF assembled them in No. 303.

Among those in Kent's "A" Flight, it turned out, was the cream of the former Polish Air Force: twenty-nine-year-old F/L Zdzislaw Henneberg, whose pre-war experience had elevated him to flying instructor in the Polish Air Force; Sergeant Stefan Wójtowicz, twenty-nine, and P/O Mirosław Ferić, twenty-five, had both served in the Polish Pursuit Brigade defending Warsaw in 1939; P/O Jan Zumbach, twenty-five, had flown with the 111th Fighter Escadrille in Poland; and twenty-eight-year-old Flying Officer Arsen Cebrzyński, who in the first three days of the war had shot down or destroyed three German fighter aircraft over Poland and three more in the Battle of France. It was only when the Blitz began in early September and when he witnessed London ablaze for the first time that Kent felt truly connected to his Polish pilots.

"I could see the fires in London that the Luftwaffe had started," he wrote. "I found myself beating my fists against the sides of the cockpit in a fury. I was beginning to understand the attitude of the Poles."[19]

Not to mention their skill. Two days into the Blitz, late on the afternoon of September 9, "A" Flight had scrambled, making no enemy contact. But just as Kent was turning for home, he spotted a formation of about forty bombers with Me 109 escort in a shallow dive dashing back to occupied France. To accelerate his Hurricane so that he could catch them, Kent pulled the boost override plug and opened the throttle of his Merlin engine wide. Closing on a Ju 88 bomber, he was about to attack when one of the German escorts dove at him from above. He nearly broke off his attack when, unannounced, a

Hurricane flashed in front of the German fighter, drawing him away from Kent. It was Henneberg's Hurricane. Kent lost sight of the Junkers bomber, but, just as quickly, a Messerschmidt 110 crossed into his sight line. It was a textbook example of aim and fire, and he did. Kent followed the fighter-bomber until it crashed into the sea; he saw no survivors.

"It was my first confirmed victory," Kent said. "And I flew home beside myself with excitement and a sense of achievement."

Back on the grass field at Northolt, he taxied his Hurricane in front of the dispersal hut, indicating his victory. He glanced to one side to see his commander-in-chief, Air Chief Marshal Dowding, and the station commander, Ronald Kellett, ducking wildly to avoid his passing wingtip. Given the reason for Kent's exuberance, nothing more was said. More startling to Kent than almost decapitating an air marshal, however, was a short conversation with his wingmate, Henneberg, on the success of the day.

"Thanks for keeping that Hun off my tail," Kent said.

"Not *one* Messerschmitt," explained Henneberg. "It was *six*!"

Not only had Henneberg fended off half a squadron of enemy fighters, the rest of No. 303 Squadron had damaged or destroyed three more enemy aircraft during that late-day sortie.

The exhilaration was short-lived. On its next major operation, the Polish squadron suffered its first fatalities of the Blitz and the entire Battle of Britain campaign. F/O Cebrzyński, who'd eerily told Kent he would not make it to the end of the month,[20] single-handedly attacked a Dornier 17 bomber in formation and shot it down. His Hurricane was badly damaged, however, and crashed near Pembury, England.

Meanwhile, Sgt Wójtowicz was shot down in a fierce combat exchange with six Me 109 fighters. "It was a fearful jumble of roundels and black crosses," Wójtowicz's wingmate P/O Zumbach wrote later, referring to the aircraft insignia.[21] Despite being outnumbered, Wójtowicz had managed to shoot down two enemy fighters before one of the Germans fired cannon shells into his cockpit. "The roar of explosions and whining engines almost drowned the shouts coming over the earphones in a medley of Polish and English," Zumbach wrote. Because the dogfight occurred so close to the ground, F.C. Paige, chief of the Westerham Fire Brigade, south of London, witnessed the battle and wrote to the squadron commanding officer to say that Wójtowicz "fought magnificently [and that he'd] brought down two Me 109s."*

The fact that Kent's flight mate had predicted his own demise tugged uncomfortably at the Canadian flight commander's sense of responsibility. His job was to lead as much as to fight; to bring the greatest number of guns to bear against the enemy in the shortest possible time; to control progress of the engagement and keep the flight together as a fighting force and not get split up into isolated, ineffective packets; to avoid being caught off guard and overwhelmed by the enemy; and to keep losses to a minimum.[22] His wingman, Cebrzyński had dispassionately stated that he would not survive long, and he hadn't.

Johnny Kent learned one other thing about the Poles early in the Blitz. They took no prisoners. During a stretch of clear

---

* Because Sgt. Stefan Wójtowicz was neither British nor a British subject, his RAF commanders could not recommend him for the Victoria Cross; later, the Polish government awarded him the equivalent, the *Virtuti Militari*.

weather, Northolt dispatched all three squadrons on a patrol, with Kent leading. They had moved under a line of Me 109s when one of them suddenly dived right across Kent's nose. The Canadian fired a short burst, then followed the German pilot into a vertical dive. His pursuit brought the 109 down, but the pilot managed to level off and bail out before the plane crashed into the sea. When Kent returned to base, he informed his Polish pilots that he'd circled round the German drifting down in his parachute, but couldn't bring himself to shoot the man.

The Poles challenged Kent's hesitation and reminded their flight commander of an incident reported earlier in the month. Was it true that German fighter pilots had machine-gunned RAF pilots after they'd bailed out of their crashing aircraft? Kent said it was true, and then tried to rationalize that the Germans were within their rights to shoot Allied pilots over the UK. And that if a Polish squadron pilot shot down a German over France and he bailed out, the Poles were entitled to shoot him. Kent pointed out, however, that shooting a German pilot parachuting into Britain wasn't wise; the man would be out of the war anyway and might provide useful information. But there was one other scenario Kent hadn't addressed.

"What if he is over the Channel?" the Poles wondered.

"Well, you can't let the poor bugger drown, can you?" Kent joked.

Kent's charges got the joke, but they couldn't swallow their commander's clemency, choosing not to machine-gun the Me 109 pilot that day as he watched him parachute into the sea. "There was no doubt about it," Kent wrote later. "The Poles were playing the game for keeps far more than we were."[23]

* * *

The same day of Kent's first victory, September 9, his country-men scrambled from another corner of the Northolt airfield. The Canadian pilots of RCAF No. 1 Fighter Squadron were about to get their first crack at Luftwaffe bombers attacking London. Each of the squadron's dozen pilots had been up since 3:30 a.m., getting breakfast, picking up his Mae West, parachute, and helmet, and making his way to the dispersal hut to await Fighter Command's call to scramble. Up even earlier than the pilots, sometimes most of the night, were members of RCAF No. 1's ground crew.

Of the three hundred Canadian airmen who'd arrived in the UK in June 1940 aboard RMS *Duchess of Atholl*, more than two hundred served in the squadron's support staff (the head-quarters section) and its ground crew (two flight sections).[24] The latter, the maintainers, or "erks," were responsible for ready-ing the Hurricanes for as many sorties as Fighter Command demanded of them every day. They consisted of airframe and aero-engine mechanics (riggers and fitters), instrument techni-cians, wireless and electrical mechanics, as well as armourers, and the repair trades of carpenters, fabric workers, and metal workers.

One of the squadron's leading erks brought rugged work experience from Canada to the flight lines of the Battle of Britain. As a child, before the Great War, Arthur Warner immigrated from Michigan with his family in search of more fertile farmland in Alberta.[25] He married in the early 1920s and with his wife, Winnie, raised four children. He enlisted part-time just as the RCAF became official in April 1924, and in 1927 joined a year-long Air Force expedition flying Fokker

Universals over the Hudson Strait; their visual and photo reconnaissance would determine the feasibility of shipping Canadian grain from Churchill, Manitoba, on Hudson Bay, to Europe. The expedition flew 227 patrols and took 2,000 aerial photographs. At Wakeham Bay, in northern Quebec, mechanic Warner kept the Fokker Universal aircraft functioning in minus-thirty-degree winter conditions.

"Mechanics drained the oil from the [Fokker] engine after every flight and heated the engines with blow torches before the next one," explained S/L Thomas Lawrence, leader of the expedition. "Meanwhile, the mechanics also turned the prop periodically to keep the engine from seizing."[26]

At Northolt with RCAF No. 1 Fighter Squadron in the summer of 1940, Warrant Officer Warner didn't have to keep Merlin engines warm; the Blitz kept things hot enough. For fifty-three days, from August 17 to October 7, the Canadian squadron—air and ground crew—answered two and three scrambles a day, while ducking into shelters during periodic German bombings at night. As head mechanic, WO Warner oversaw the replacement of worn or nearly expired Merlin engines; he also trained newly arriving Canadian erks.[27]

Another Canadian erk, John Burdes, had worked as a tradesman in a lumber camp in British Columbia during the 1930s. When war broke out, he was persuaded to join the RCAF as an airframe mechanic; he led one of the Canadian fighter squadron's two flight sections. Tall, raw-boned, and muscular, Burdes was recognized by all the tradesmen and officers of the squadron not just for his skill as an aircraft rigger and fitter, but even more for his leadership. Any downtime activities at the station were organized by "Slim" Burdes, who led Rabelaisian singsongs that included his show-stopping impersonation of Cab Calloway singing "Minnie the Moocher."

"He had more creative talent in his hands than any man I have ever known," fighter pilot Edwin Reyno said.[28]

In the pre-dawn hours, before the pilots were awake, Warner and Burdes and their maintainer crews fine-tuned all the Hurricanes' engines and checked their radios, batteries, and gun ports. Then, like the pilots, they waited. When the phone rang in the crew room of the dispersal hut announcing a scramble, the flight section's aeromechanics fired starter cartridges, bringing the Merlins to life. Most often, the pilot arrived on the run. A maintainer usually helped his pilot into the cockpit and secured his harness, then jumped down off the wing to pull the chocks from in front of the landing gear for the Hurricane's quick getaway.

Burdes's admirer, F/O Edwin Reyno, was twenty-three, just four years out of Saint Mary's University in Halifax. Now all the operational training he'd logged since arriving in England in June 1940 was about to be put to the test. On the afternoon of September 9, Reyno recalled hearing a "mighty roar as twelve Hurricanes climbed into the sun."[29] S/L Ernie McNab led the four sections of Hurricanes climbing to 20,000 feet up toward black specks over the Guildford-Redhill area southwest of London. Reyno counted fifteen Dorniers with their long, tapered fuselages, and about the same number of Messerschmitt 110s nearby. Before long, from a higher altitude, a section of Me 109s descended on the RCAF attack group and engaged. McNab pursued one of the enemy fighters, closing to within firing distance.

"There is nothing to compare with the excitement of plunging into an air battle like that," McNab wrote. "Your mouth dries up like cotton wood. F/O Dal Russel . . . was chewing gum when he went into his first scramble. He had to pick bits of gum from the roof of his mouth afterwards."[30]

So focused was McNab on chasing the Messerschmitt ahead of him, he didn't realize that two enemy Me 109s had slipped in behind him and were closing fast. The moment McNab spotted the fighters, two of his flight mates pounced on them. Reyno took one and P/O Otto Peterson caught up with the other and fired from closer than fifty feet. "[The fighter] just seemed to disintegrate in the air," Peterson wrote later.[31] What's more, Peterson's Hurricane flew right through the wreckage, which in turn damaged his propeller and smashed his windscreen. In seconds, the debris and bits of his Perspex had cut his face and obscured his vision. His Hurricane plummeted 11,000 feet before he could see his instruments again; he was a bit more than a thousand feet off the ground when he regained control of his aircraft and managed to return to the station.

"He crawled from the cockpit with his face a red mask. His eyes were streaming with water," McNab said. "The medical officer grabbed his hands so that he could not rub his eyes [and] said later he had taken a couple of teaspoonfuls of glass fragments from Pete's eyes."[32]

Medical staff at Northolt weren't the only ones at the ready when fighter pilots brought their aircraft home from operations. Members of the ground crew experienced nearly as much tension waiting for the pilots to return as the pilots themselves felt in aerial combat. Hurricanes returning individually, or sometimes in their flight sections of three, brought much relief. Not that the ground crew had time to dwell on it in this "firehouse" atmosphere.[33] Armourers had to replenish the Browning machine-gun ammunition boxes with belts of bullets—338 rounds for each inner gun, 324 rounds for the next gun, and 338 each for the two outer guns, or the equivalent of 1,100 rounds per minute. Fitters brought oxygen bottles to replace expended ones and fuellers drove up a bowser (truck) to refill as many as three Hurricanes' tanks at a time.

Meanwhile, aeromechanics checked engine oil and radio batteries. Ticking off every item on the checklist, the crew inspected wheels, brakes, and oleos (struts cushioning the landing gear). If there wasn't time to jack up the plane to change a wheel, ten men under the mainplane lifted the wing while it was replaced. Ideally, the Canadian ground crew could get a Hurricane back in the air twelve minutes after landing.

Normal days consisted of at least one scramble. Even if the scramble yielded no contact with enemy aircraft, though, squadrons carried out regular patrols to protect airfields around London. In addition, most RAF bases conducted meteorological flights. But it was the scrambles that resulted in aerial dogfights that generated the most work for the ground crews. Fighter aircraft frequently sustained damage. Category 2 damage meant an aircraft came off the flight line; Category 3 usually meant the aeroplane was a write-off. When damaged fighters were desperately needed for service the next day, F/Sgt Burdes and his erks performed miracles getting them battle ready overnight.

Reyno described Burdes as a "water walker," a Superman. "In the midst of the Blitz, at Northolt, the crews worked all night," he said. "Along the flight line, Burdes had his boys changing [spark] plugs in the Merlins by flashlight because of the blackout. He even had them singing at the tops of their voices while doing it."[34] No doubt including a few "Hi-de-hi-de-hi-de-hi's" from "Minnie the Moocher."

* * *

Although Winston Churchill had nipped the "Cromwell" code in the bud on September 7, civilians still experienced frayed nerves and high expectancy of a German invasion in the early days of the Blitz. S/L Ernie McNab catalogued a number of close calls for Canadian fighter aircrew who happened to parachute into the English countryside. In one instance, a pilot managed to set his damaged aircraft down in a grain field only to be met by a farmer rushing at him with a shotgun. A Home Guard soldier had also spotted the crash and came running.

"I'm an air force officer," the pilot called out, putting his hands in the air.

Unmoved, the farmer pointed the gun at the pilot's head.

"Get my papers out of my pocket," the pilot appealed to the arriving Home Guard soldier. "Tell him to put that thing down."

"Just stand aside, lad," the farmer said to the Guard, "and I'll blow his blooming head off."

The pilot's papers verified his story, S/L McNab explained, and nobody got hurt.[35]

Other Canadian flyers received warmer welcomes in similar circumstances. The family of Spitfire pilot Harry Edwards, who served in No. 92 Squadron at RAF Tangmere, received a letter from W.P. Coward, who ran a small brush factory in a village in southwest England.

"Last Thursday afternoon [July 4] I was working in my factory when suddenly there was a terrific burst of machine-gun fire," Coward wrote. "Everybody dashed out and quite low overhead there was a large German bomber being attacked by two of our Spitfires."

Coward watched dispassionately as the German bomber crashed and burned, and was surprised when both Spitfires landed nearby. Thrilled at the opportunity to meet fighter pilots, the Cowards invited them for tea. They must have exchanged home addresses, and the Cowards wrote Edwards's family to say they "surely have a son to be proud of. The British Empire depends on lads like these and I'm sure they will not let us down."[36]

In much the same way as W.P. Coward recognized the importance of RAF fighter pilots in the Battle for Britain, so too did Winston Churchill have a sense of the bigger picture.[37] In a September 11 broadcast to the nation, he summarized Hitler's attempt "to secure mastery of the air." Most days, the Luftwaffe waited for fair weather to send waves of bombers and fighters at London, said the prime minister, and the RAF fighter squadrons routinely broke up their attacks. Churchill claimed optimistically that the clashes cost the Germans three machines to each British one, and six Air Fleet pilots to every Fighter Command pilot. For the Germans to attempt an invasion of Britain without achieving such mastery of the air, Churchill concluded, would be hazardous. He considered this "the crux of the whole war.

"We must regard the next week," he concluded in his BBC speech, "as . . . when the Spanish Armada approached the Channel, and Drake finished his game of bowls, or when Nelson stood between us and Napoleon's Grand Army at Boulogne. . . . But what is happening now is . . . of far more consequence to the life and future of the world and its civilization than those brave old days."[38]

That very afternoon, Luftwaffe Air Fleet commanders Albert Kesselring and Hugo Sperrle launched coordinated attacks on London, first in feint sorties against the capital, and then later with two waves of about one hundred bombers each. The bomber stream was so elongated, however, that many of the Me 109 fighters flying in its support ran low on fuel and had to return to their bases at Calais. RCAF No. 1 Fighter Squadron, by now dubbed "Caribou Squadron," received its scramble call just after 4 p.m. S/L McNab led four sections of Hurricanes, climbing to the ceiling of their capability, between 25,000 and 30,000 feet. He described the mandatory nature of oxygen supply to dogfight at such altitudes. "We wore an oxygen mask over our nose and mouth," he said. "The mask and the wireless microphone were part of a flap of our leather helmet. It covered our face from the nose to the chin just beneath the goggles."

Even as he climbed to the required altitude, each Hurricane pilot had to ensure his mask was working properly. Every 5,000 feet, he made an additional adjustment for the delivery of sufficient oxygen "to maintain your mind and body at normal." Meanwhile, the Hurricane pilot also had to ensure that his aircraft's air blowers were delivering maximum air flow to supercharge the plane's Merlin engine in the thinner atmosphere. McNab called fighting at such great altitudes "a world of freezing cold, of limitless space, traced with trails of condensed exhaust—like sky-writing gone mad."[39]

On September 11, McNab's sections, adjusting their oxygen intake as they climbed, topped 18,000 feet when they located a formation of twenty Heinkels below. McNab ordered the squadron into port echelon, each section stepped back in tiers to the left, and led the attack into the midst of the bombers at 14,000 feet. The German raiders scattered in self-defence and, with diminished Me 109 fighter escort to protect them, were easier prey for the Canadians.

McNab led his numbers two and three wingmates, P/O Pete Lochnan and P/O Bev Christmas, in a right-hand beam attack on the top group of Heinkels. McNab hit a bomber's starboard engine. Lochnan followed, but the Heinkel's rear-gunner landed shots into his engine and Lochnan had to descend and force-land. Christmas retaliated from the opposite side and knocked out the Heinkel's rear-gun. He and McNab claimed a damaged bomber between them.

Red Section, with F/L Gordon McGregor leading and P/O Deane Nesbitt and F/O Hartland Molson as his numbers two and three, respectively, came at the formation line astern from the right. On the follow-through, McGregor levelled off and was suddenly racing at another Heinkel coming at him head-on. He fired, but had to stop momentarily when another Hurricane cut in front of him to attack. McGregor quickly resumed, using short bursts from one hundred yards and the Heinkel went into a spiral dive and crashed. Molson joined another Hurricane chasing a bomber and fired shots on a beam attack; the aircraft burst into flames and fell from the sky.

In Yellow Section, F/O Arthur Yuile lost contact with the Heinkels but found a German transport and made separate attacks, one head-on from above, another from behind, until the Junkers's undercarriage dropped down. Yuile saw several people jump and parachutes pop open until the burning aircraft rolled over and exploded on contact with the ground. All of Caribou Squadron returned safely, including Lochnan, who made a dead-stick landing, and Tom Little, who bailed out safely from his disabled Hurricane. RCAF No. 1's totals for the day were three enemy aircraft destroyed and two damaged, a high-water mark for the squadron.

Elsewhere across the aerial battlefield above London, on September 11, RAF sorties went poorly. Fighter Command lost thirty-one aircraft in combat to the Luftwaffe's twenty-two lost bombers and fighters.[40] Among those RAF fighter pilots killed in action, P/O Harry Edwards from No. 92 Squadron; in the process of shooting the tail off a German bomber, he took return fire and the hunter fell with the hunted.[41] His family had only just received W.P. Coward's laudatory letter about sharing afternoon tea with their son when an RCAF telegram arrived in Winnipeg informing his parents that P/O Edwards had died in action on September 11. He was the thirteenth Canadian pilot to die in the Battle of Britain.

The next day, September 12, inclement autumn weather moved into the British Isles. The air space over London and the south coast went quiet. Meanwhile, the atmosphere at Adolf Hitler's living quarters, the New Reich Chancellery in Berlin, was decidedly upbeat. The führer had read the Nazi Party newspaper, *Völkischer Beobachter*, and its propaganda that on September 10, London had witnessed "a morning of terror after nine and a half hours of air raid."[42] With Reichsmarschall Hermann Göring on hand at the Chancellery, on September 13, Hitler was confident London was cracking under the strain of the Blitz and might surrender without the Germans ever having to launch an invasion. So, that day, Hitler chose to postpone a decision on Operation Sea Lion, feeling confident that Göring could finish off the RAF with the return of good weather over the UK.

But the next day, September 14, with Göring absent and Erich Raeder, grossadmiral of the Kriegsmarine, on hand at the Chancellery, all the promise of Göring's optimism seemed to evaporate. Raeder had little respect for the Luftwaffe chief or the air supremacy Göring continued to guarantee. Raeder told Hitler, "the present air situation does not allow the undertaking of Operation Sea Lion [but] it is indispensable that Sea Lion should not be abandoned." Now the führer was again conflicted. On one hand, he contemplated that "a successful landing followed by occupation would end the war," so a decision on Sea Lion could wait a few more days until Göring had finally delivered the *coup de grâce* on the RAF. On the other hand, "a long war [was] not desirable," so a rapid landing and conquest of Britain was the better scenario. "Four or five days of clear weather," Hitler said, "and we have a good chance of forcing England to her knees."[43]

As Hitler considered his next step, his Reich Central Security Office (RSHA) under Heinrich Himmler, reichsführer of the *Schutzstaffel* (SS), had already mapped out the subjugation of Britain. Archives captured later show that once the 9th and 16th Germany Armies had completed landing and occupation of Britain, they were to carry out RSHA orders drawn up during the summer of 1940. All able-bodied British men from age seventeen to forty-five would be interned and dispatched to the Continent. In the process, everything of value would be confiscated, hostages taken, and any who resisted executed.[44]

In the meantime, SS Colonel Dr. Franz Six was appointed head of British occupation. His orders from Reinhard Heydrich, head of the *Sicherheitsdienst* (Security Service) read: "To combat with the requisite means, all anti-German organizations, institutions, and opposition groups seized in England, to prevent the removal of all available material and to centralize and safeguard it for future exploitation,"[45] with his headquarters in London still to be determined.*

The "four or five days of clear weather" that Hitler had hoped for arrived on Sunday, September 15.

---

* The fate Britons avoided under Dr. Six was meted out in Russia, where his SS *Einsatzgruppen* (Nazi death squads) carried out wholesale massacres and executions of political prisoners.

CHAPTER NINE

"A SINGLE SAVAGE PURPOSE"

B Y MID-SEPTEMBER 1940, THE BLITZ WAS A WAY OF LIFE for many Britons. Watching the aerial war from the streets of London became a necessary evil for adults, and an adventure for those youngsters not evacuated to the countryside or overseas.

Living in a suburb of North London, eight-year-old Anne Elliott and her family had no choice but to keep an eye on the sky in daytime and spend their nights in some form of shelter. Without access to an actual air-raid shelter early in the Blitz, Anne huddled with her mom under a piano. During one raid, Anne heard a repeated banging on the family's front porch letter box.

"Oh, my God," her mom said. "There's someone out in the raid." She ran to the door and opened it.

"Who's there?" Anne called out.

"No one there at all," her mom answered as she crawled back under the piano. The following morning, Anne found her front driveway littered with shrapnel from bombs dropped nearby the night before.

Bombs fell all along Anne's street, uprooting and cata-
pulting a tree into the house next door. She and her friends
thought it was hilarious that a fire crew had to rescue their
neighbour from his second-floor bathroom. However, a daytime raid proved even more serious. Bombs began falling close
to a train on which Anne and her mother were travelling in the
city. Fearing for her daughter's safety, Ethel Elliott had Anne
stay under the train's carriage seat. When the train stopped at
a station and they disembarked, "There was a terrific roar,"
Anne said. "Mother thought they were going to bomb the train
station. She threw me to the ground and laid on top of me."[1]

Along with many other young Londoners, Anne collected
shrapnel like trophies after each raid. Meanwhile, her father
drove food trucks in and out of London for a living. One day
when bombs struck the vehicle in front of and behind him, he
decided the war was getting too close for comfort. His company
agreed to transfer him to a food depot away from London in the
county of Kent. There was one problem: the threat of German
invasion in southeast England meant bringing children into the
region was forbidden. Nevertheless, Ernest and Ethel Elliott
chose to sneak their daughter into Kent so they could all live
together. They travelled from London in a car and, on arrival
at a checkpoint at the entrance to the county, hid Anne amid
meats and vegetables in an accompanying food van.

"When they open the doors to the van, don't move, don't
sneeze, don't even breathe!" her parents implored Anne.

As expected, a police officer at the Kent checkpoint opened
the van doors to inspect contents. "I could hear the driver
talking to the policeman," said Anne. "Finally, they closed the
door and we drove off. I was smuggled into Kent between two
sides of bacon."

Away from the threat of being bombed in the Blitz and relocated to the hilly North Downs of southeast England, Anne Elliott watched the life-and-death struggle in the skies above her as the Battle of Britain came to a climax.

* * *

When he first piloted a Hurricane fighter aircraft in July 1940, Flying Officer Paul Pitcher described the experience as being "thrown" into its cockpit. In the race to get the RCAF No. 1 Fighter Squadron battle-ready that summer at Northolt station, none of the Canadians had received any operational (combat) training. Instead, Pitcher and his comrades learned about formation flying, tactics, and air firing by reading what he called "antediluvian Air Ministry manuals"[2] and by practising in outdated Fairey Battle trainers. But with Air Chief Marshal Hugh Dowding's promised delivery of fully equipped Hurricanes, the Canadians moved up to leading-edge technology. By July, thirty-one of Fighter Command's sixty-one fighter squadrons were equipped with Hurricanes. During the Battle of Britain, the "workhorse" Hurricanes accounted for 55 percent of the 2,739 German aircraft lost.[3]

F/O Pitcher considered his Hurricane "the ideal aircraft,"[4] sturdy and easy to fly. Once he got used to it, he learned to "wear" the aircraft in the same way he'd put on a flight suit. He claimed the Hurricane had very few vices. It took off without swinging madly. It answered every call of its pilot. Pitcher recognized the Hurricane's shortcomings regarding speed— 30 miles per hour slower than a Spitfire, and 33 miles per hour slower than an Me 109. And he knew that its performance above 20,000 feet diminished rapidly, but below that altitude it was more manoeuvrable than a Spitfire, and outstandingly so against an Me 109. In a dogfight, Pitcher's Hurricane could "turn on her tail" to evade, and then cut corners in pursuit to greater advantage than any Me 109; only when the superior climb or dive capabilities of the Messerschmitt took the German fighter out of danger did the Hurricane pilot have "to look for other game."[5]

Unlike the Spitfire and Me 109, the Hurricane had a wide undercarriage, able to withstand rough treatment on takeoffs and landings, while its fabric-covered fuselage proved easier to repair than the metal-covered Spitfire and Messerschmitt. Pitcher described his Hurricane's gun platform as "steady," meaning it could absorb enormous punishment. Even when badly chewed up by Messerschmitt bullets and cannon shells from the cockpit to the tail plane, a damaged Hurricane could still bring its pilot home safely, so that both could live to fight another day. In a phrase, Pitcher said the Hurricane was "a great fighting lady."[6]

If Canadian pilots gave their Hurricanes the highest of praise in a dogfight, opposing German pilots boasted just as often that their Messerschmitt fighters were unbeatable. Conceived as an interceptor by designer Willy Messerschmitt and Robert Lusser in the early 1930s, the idea of an all-metal, mono-wing aircraft with retractable landing gear, closed canopy, and high-speed capacity was born at Bayerische Flugzeugwerke in 1933. With Germany still technically forbidden by the Treaty of Versailles (1919) to manufacture war munitions, Hermann Göring gave his secret blessing for "the development of a lightning-fast courier aircraft,"[7]; that is, a military fighter. Eventually, the light-weight fighter was armed with two machine guns (mounted in the cowling) firing over top of the engine and through the propeller arc. When the Luftwaffe discovered that the British were building fighters with eight guns, Messerschmitt increased the 109's armament with two more machine guns and/or 20-mm cannons in its wings. By the outbreak of the Spanish Civil War in 1936, German support of Franco's fascists introduced the Me 109 with its high-performance Daimler-Benz engine.

Indeed, it was the Messerschmitt's power plant that gave Hans-Ekkehard Bob such confidence one-on-one against RAF opponents. He described his Me 109 as "a handsome, racy machine," and "very impressive" in the air. "When the Spitfire's [or Hurricane's] engine carburetor went into a dive, the flow of fuel stopped [because of gravity force] and the engine ceased to produce power." Bob wrote: "The 109's fuel-injected engines could run at full power in any situation. So, if there was a Spitfire [or Hurricane] attacking me . . . I would simply go into a nose-dive at full speed. The English fighter couldn't do that."[8]

Bob knew from the moment he discovered the flying Hitler Youth organization in the early 1930s that he would become a fighter pilot. He'd enlisted in the Luftwaffe in 1936 as an officer candidate, fought in the skies over Poland and France, and by the middle of the summer of 1940 had served with III *Gruppe* of the Luftwaffe flying daily operations against the RAF. Bob had taken over leadership of a Luftwaffe *Staffel* unit just ten days before the squadron, based near Calais, received

---

* To correct the problem, Beatrice "Tilly" Shilling, an aero-engineer in the Royal Aircraft Establishment at Farnborough, soldered a metal disc, the size of a three-penny bit with a small hole in the middle, into the Merlin fuel line; when a Hurricane or Spitfire pilot accelerated in a dive, the disc prevented even momentary fuel starvation in the engine. The device was nicknamed "Miss Shilling's Orifice."

its phone call to launch on Sunday morning, September 15. In as few as three minutes, his twelve Me 109s were racing across the grass airfield at Guînes and climbing into clear skies to rendezvous over Cap Gris-Nez with the Luftwaffe's largest bomber strike force of the war.

Air Fleet commander Albert Kesselring would dispatch nearly his entire fighter arsenal, about 620 Me 109s and 100 Me 110s, to escort two successive daylight waves totalling five hundred bombers. The first smaller wave consisted of twenty-five bombers, twenty-one fighter-bombers, and 150 fighters all aimed directly at the railway lines between Clapham Junction and Battersea Power Station in the heart of London.[9] But they would be the bait to draw up RAF fighters and exhaust them before the larger wave, headed toward the West Ham Docks, early in the afternoon.

In each wave, the Luftwaffe formation was led by freelance fighters to engage RAF fighters and entice them away from the main stream of bombers behind. Also, in advance of the bombers, indirect escorts flew at about 24,000 feet, again to deflect RAF fighters. The main body of bombers, 8,000 feet lower, flew line astern in waves staggered in altitude, but they were protected by direct escorts flying above and below in close formation.[10] Finally, another indirect escort flew at the tail end of the bomber stream, repulsing any RAF attacks from the rear. The first volley of this September 15 double-barrelled assault on London would reach the Thames Estuary just before noon. And because German intelligence estimated that the RAF was on the verge of collapse, "the feeling of success was very strong," Hans-Ekkehard Bob said.[11]

* * *

Winston Churchill had several times visited the headquarters of 11 Group of Fighter Command at Uxbridge (a suburb of London) to witness the conduct of the air battle. On most of those occasions, not much had happened. However, on this Sunday morning, with the weather clearly favouring the enemy, the prime minister decided to travel from his residence at Chequers to Uxbridge, where Air Vice-Marshal Keith Park had directed the defence of London and the south of England for the better part of six months. RAF staff led Winston and his wife, Clementine, into the bomb-proof Operations Room, about fifty feet below ground. While supreme command of the overall battle was exercised by ACM Dowding from Fighter Command Headquarters at Stanmore, about ten miles away, the actual direction of the squadrons in the hottest sector of the battle around London came from this facility at Uxbridge.

On all his visits, Churchill had sat in what he called "the dress circle," observing activity in the theatre-like setting in front of him. Two stories high and about sixty feet long, the room featured a large map table surrounded by twenty staff and their telephone assistants. A vast tote board stood where the theatre curtain would have hung. It was divided into seven columns, one for each of seven squadrons in this sector of 11 Group. Each column bore a series of electric light bulbs ascending the column. The lowest row of bulbs signified that the squadron was "Landed and Refuelling" or "At Readiness." Lights higher up the board indicated stages of enemy engagement: "In Position" or "Enemy Sighted" or "Detailed to Raid," and, eventually, "Released."

To the left of the tote board stood a glass stage-box where a handful of officers received and weighed the information coming from the Filter Room and the thousands of men and women of the Observer Corps scanning the skies across England's frontiers. Once this information was assessed by these officers, the movement of both enemy forces and Fighter Command squadrons was transmitted directly to plotters and displayed by moving pieces on the map table. To the right of the tote board stood another glass stage-box where army officers received reports on the actions of British anti-aircraft batteries.

AVM Park and the Churchills chatted on their arrival and expressed their different expectations of the day. "I don't know whether anything will happen today," said Park. "At present all quiet." For his part, Churchill had in mind an illustrious precedent. "Like the Battle of Waterloo," he noted, "it is a Sunday."[12]

A quarter hour later, about 10:30 a.m., the raid plotters in the room at Uxbridge began moving about. The Chain Home radar station at Dover had picked up intense radio activity from the French side of the Channel. The Filter Room at Stanmore determined the formation as enemy aircraft and sector commanders across the south received readiness calls; they estimated forty-plus enemy aircraft would soon enter airspace over Kent.

Park's response to the threat was critical to success or failure this day. He needed to apportion and time the defence so that his fighter squadrons could climb to favourable attack positions, but not so early that they might run short of fuel before confronting the bomber formations. Timing meant everything.

By 11:15 a.m., the Stanmore Filter Room had increased the estimate of the size of the attack, determining that as many as 150 enemy aircraft were heading for London. To bolster his defensive presence, Park scrambled four pairs of fighter squadrons, nearly one hundred Spitfires and Hurricanes, to intercept the Luftwaffe. There were Canadian pilots serving among these first responders. By 11:30, Pilot Officer Johnny Bryson, flying a Spitfire with his No. 92 Squadron from Biggin Hill, was airborne. Almost simultaneously, Flight Lieutenant Johnny Kent's No. 303 Squadron and RCAF No. 1 Squadron Hurricanes had all taken off from Northolt, and P/O Keith Ogilvie with No. 609 Squadron was aloft from Middle Wallop, in 10 Group's sector.

"Over London and the Jerries are really throwing everything in now," Ogilvie wrote. "We're ordered to intercept a heavy bomber formation . . . Dornier 215s [with] an armoured shield of Me 110s in front as a spearhead."[13]

Spotting the Spitfires from Middle Wallop racing toward them, German 110s fired cannon shells head-on at Ogilvie and his section. The Spitfires dove down and away, but not before a shell struck the fighter beside Ogilvie; the flaming Spitfire was piloted by Ogilvie's roommate, Geoff Gaunt, among the first killed in action that morning.

As Ogilvie tried to regain altitude to pursue the Dornier bombers, several formations of Me 109s roared overhead, but none veered from their course; their orders were to maintain a close escort around the attacking bombers all the way to the target. "Damn good thing for me that they didn't come down," Ogilvie noted. He continued to chase the Dornier formation.

Also at that hour, Spitfires from No. 92 Squadron and Hurricanes from RCAF No. 1 Squadron had arrived over Canterbury to the east. Flying 3,000 feet above the German escorts, the Spitfires dove and engaged them at 22,000 feet. Making his way through the fighters, P/O Bryson in his Spitfire from No. 92 Squadron caught up to a Junkers 88 and began firing at the rear of the bomber as he closed to within feet of it; he'd come so close to the bomber that its slipstream knocked his aircraft into a violent spin.

The German escorts tried driving the RAF fighters away from the bombers and were soon embroiled in dogfights all over the skies above Kent. In the mêlée, a Hurricane from No. 229 Squadron collided with a 109 and both went down.[14]

At a lower altitude, the RCAF Hurricanes charged at the German bomber stream head-on. They, in turn, were bounced by Me 109s diving on them with the sun at their backs. The Canadian formation scattered, and only two of the RCAF pilots managed to engage German fighters. As number three in Red Section, F/O Deane Nesbitt directed machine-gun fire into one Me 109 and it fell in flames, but his Hurricane was attacked immediately and it caught fire. Nesbitt managed to bail out safely but sustained head injuries. "The sky rained parachutes" of aircrew from both sides, he reported.[15]

Meanwhile, Nesbitt's squadron mate, the former ground crew fitter F/O Ross Smither, who had only just registered his first air combat credits—an Me 109 on August 31 and an Me 110 on September 4—was bounced by a German escort diving out of the sun. Smither was killed in the resulting dog-fight, the fourteenth Canadian to die in the battle.

His countryman, F/O James "Smudger" Smith, had also scrambled to meet the German bomber stream. Members of his No. 73 Squadron from RAF Debden raced to gain altitude in their Hurricanes and engage the raider force over Margate, at the far east end of the Thames Estuary. As his RCAF comrades had learned a week before, the Me 110 fighter-bombers under attack quickly formed a defensive circle and looked to the Me 109 fighters to give support.

"At 12:05 sighted approximately twelve enemy aircraft [Me 109] below and another eight or ten above flying in pairs," Smith's combat report read.[16] He noted that these Messerschmitt fighters sported camouflaged top surfaces. Viewed from above, they disappeared into the ground, while their blue-white bellies when viewed from below made them blend into the sky. Smith's Blue Section broke formation and singled out an Me 109. "Noticed another Me 109 roll onto the tail of a Hurricane [so] I immediately dived delivering a two-second burst into that enemy aircraft."

A pattern of attackers being attacked played out across the sky. When Smith in turn was chased by another Me 109, he had to throw his Hurricane into violent evasive manoeuvres. The two fighters engaged in flick rolls, spins, and climbs, each trying to gain the advantage to fire at close range. Eventually, Smith managed to close and fire a burst of shells into his prey from astern. "I was eventually fifty-to-twenty-five yards behind E/A, which continued in dive with thick black smoke pouring from it. I was forced to break away to avoid colliding." The Royal Observer Corps credited F/O Smith with one Me 109 destroyed.

Despite the apparent chaos in the sky, AVM Keith Park's strategy was paying off. He spent the morning scrambling squadron pairings from 11 Group to attack the bombers in sequence all along the route to their targets. The German escorts were burning up extra fuel driving off Hurricanes and Spitfires. Consequently, as the bombers reached the city limits over London just after noon, their fighter escorts, with low-fuel cockpit warning lights flashing, were forced to vacate the battlefield. That left the German bomber formations relatively intact, but now alone for the final minutes of their bombing runs against London targets.

At that moment, Squadron Leader Douglas Bader's Duxford Wing approached the scene, bigger than ever. Not only did he have his original thirty-six fighters—Spitfires from No. 19 and Hurricanes from Nos. 242 and 310—but the additional strength of Hurricanes from No. 302 and Spitfires from No. 611. Fifty-six fighters in all.

Bader aligned his three Hurricane squadrons climbing in vic formations astern with his two Spitfire squadrons off to his left. In minutes, he had the Hurricanes flying line-abreast at 23,000 feet with the Spitfires stepped up to 27,000 feet, all of them closing on the bomber stream out of the sun from the southeast. Through his windscreen, Bader could see Ju 88s and Dorniers, maybe forty of them, and black puffs of anti-aircraft flak dotting the sky around them. There wasn't a German fighter in sight. Moreover, by that time, four additional RAF squadrons had arrived. The unescorted bomber formation was in disarray. Bader called it "the finest shambles I've ever been in,"[17] as No. 242 pilots brought down no fewer than six enemy machines. Canadians Noel Stansfeld and Stan Turner each shot down a Dornier 215, and Neil Campbell damaged another. Hugh Tamblyn had to find a gap in the lineup of Hurricanes firing bursts of shells into the bomber formation; he shared in the destruction of one aircraft. Meanwhile, the rest of the Duxford Wing claimed twenty-three destroyed, eight probably destroyed, and several more damaged.[18]

Bader himself brought down a Dornier. As the sky emptied of combatants, he followed the burning, plummeting bomber long enough to see one of its crewmen bail out and be consumed "to nothingness in a sheet of flame."[19] Gone at this stage was any feeling of having killed a man, any remorse. In the frenzy of battle, when hearts beat faster and efforts became more frantic, life and death lost their importance. "Desire sharpened to a single savage purpose," one pilot said, "to grab the enemy and claw him down from the sky."[20]

During his escort of German bombers toward London that day, Staffelkapitän Hans-Ekkehard Bob recognized his fighters were at a disadvantage. Flying close escort meant either lowering flaps on their Me 109s to reduce speed and maintain contact with the bomber formation, or weaving back and forth over the bombers, burning up plenty of fuel. It would also take precious time to get back to combat speed. On first contact with RAF fighters, Bob's Messerschmitt fighter took cannon fire in its engine radiator, and he was forced to return to France before his engine overheated. Bob would eventually claim nineteen victories in the Battle of Britain,[21] victories he described as dispassionately as did the RAF pilots. "I wasn't thinking that I had injured or harmed a human being," he wrote. "I was only thinking about the plane I had destroyed . . . about gaining an advantage for the Fatherland."[22]

Another raider to escape the sequential attacks by Keith Park's RAF fighters, initially, was German bomber pilot Robert Zehbe. He and his Dornier 215 crew (observer, mechanic, wireless operator/gunner, and a second gunner) had broken away from the original bomber formation and carried on in search of their target. They caught the eye of P/O Keith Ogilvie, still in the air chasing bombers from his No. 609 Squadron base at Middle Wallop. He descended quickly in hopes that he could drive the bomber down, or at least away from the populated areas of the city. "I attacked him from the beam," Ogilvie wrote in his journal.[23]

The rear gunner fired back, but Ogilvie silenced the return fire on his second pass. Because the tangle between Ogilvie's

Spitfire and the Dornier bomber now unfolded at low altitude over the city during lunch hour, many London citizens and newspaper reporters witnessed the entire dogfight. On Ogilvie's third run at the bomber, he saw fire inside the cockpit of the aircraft and two of the crew bailing, one narrowly missing a propeller as he jumped. "It was an incredible and terrifying sight to see the bomber spin slowly," Ogilvie continued. He saw a third German crewman bail out. It was Oberstleutnant (Oblt) Zehbe, the pilot; he had set the Dornier on autopilot and leapt from the disintegrating Dornier. "Suddenly, the tail snapped off and then the wings and the wreckage plunged into the heart of London."[24]

Photographers and reporters from the *Daily Mirror* recorded the entire episode, including the Dornier parts tumbling to earth. The main portion of the bomber crashed into the fore-court of Victoria Station, while two 110-pound bombs and a container of incendiary bombs came down on Buckingham Palace—one penetrated the roof and smashed through several floors, coming to rest in the royal apartments; the rest landed in the palace grounds—but since fuses in the large bombs had not been made "live," neither detonated. The royal family wasn't in residence that day. Two German crew died in the crash of the bomber; the pilot later died of his injuries; and the remaining two Luftwaffe airmen were captured. Ogilvie was interviewed, and modestly pointed out that two other Spitfires had joined in the attack on the bomber.*

---

* Sgt Pilot Ray Holmes claimed he ran out of ammunition, lined up his Hurricane to ram a bomber, and then bailed out over Chelsea; Sgt Pilot Ginger Lacey shared credit for downing Zehbe's Dornier, the only aircraft to drop bombs on Buckingham Palace.

The fact that the Dornier's bombs fell in the courtyard of Buckingham Palace drew much more attention, however, as did the response of one unexpected witness to the incident. Since the invasion of the Netherlands earlier in 1940, members of the Dutch royal family had been given refuge at Buckingham Palace. That midday, Queen Wilhelmina stood on a balcony watching the dogfight between the fighter and bomber, and then instructed her aide-de-camp to forward her reaction.

"Her Majesty was most gratified to see from her London House a German bomber shot down by an eight-gun fighter," the Queen's note read, "and would be very pleased if Her congratulations should be conveyed to the Squadron concerned . . . and to the pilot who shot down the German aircraft."[25]

Accounts of gains and losses in the air over Britain that morning varied widely. The attackers admitted six lost bombers and a dozen Me 109s. Fighter Command pilots claimed as many as eighty-one German aircraft destroyed or damaged; Oblt Zehbe's Dornier alone was claimed by nine different pilots. In fact, only fifteen first-wave Dorniers had reached their London targets; in addition, the attacking force had lost twelve fighters. Fighter Command lost thirteen. The defenders had destroyed a quarter of the first-wave bombers. But as Dowding and the rest of Fighter Command quickly deduced, that meant three-quarters of the raiders had made it through to London.

Some of the September Luftwaffe raids came closest to undermining civilian morale in the city. Harold Nicolson, the parliamentary secretary to the minister of information, wrote in his diary that there was much bitterness among survivors of the shattered tenements in London's East End. "It is said that even the King and Queen were booed when they vis-ited the devastated areas," he wrote. But when bombs fell on Buckingham Palace, the Luftwaffe seemed to have struck an unintentional blow for democracy. Queen Elizabeth remarked, "I'm glad that we've been bombed. It makes me feel that I can look the East End in the face."[26]

The 224 tons of high explosives and 279 incendiary canis-ters German bombers had dropped on London that day may have inspired a feeling of solidarity among all classes of people in the capital, but the wounds went deep. One woman recalled rushing to where bombs had struck a school. She joined those digging through the debris, hoping to find survivors. Instead, she spotted a small pink purse and held it up. "The mother of the child to whom it belonged held out her hand, her face so anguished, it was frightful to behold. She took it and was led wordlessly away."[27]

That dead child was one of 60,595 civilians killed by enemy action in Great Britain during the war; 86,182 others were seriously injured. Londoners accounted for the largest single group of these casualties; between September 7 and December 31, 1940, 13,339 citizens of the capital died in the bombings and another 17,937 were seriously injured. The epitaph of one little girl found in the ruins of her home read simply: "Age about two years; hair, fair; eyes blue grey; division between top row of teeth; no other distinguishing features."[28]

* * *

At 11 Group headquarters of Fighter Command in Uxbridge, most of the markers on the big table map were retreating, indi-cating German bomber groups were headed back to occupied

France, and Fighter Command aircraft to their home stations to prepare for the next scramble call. From his perch at the dress circle in the Operations Room, Churchill saw no panic and little concern in the faces of the Fighter Command staff, but he recognized this was only the first action of what would likely be a long day. Just after one o'clock, ten RCAF No. 1 fighters landed back at Northolt (minus the Nesbitt and Smither Hurricanes forced down at Tunbridge Wells).

Ready and waiting for their returning comrades were nearly two dozen ground crewmen. They swarmed the surviving aircraft to help the pilots climb free of their cockpits. Then the erks began the vital process of damage checks, engine checks, and the refuelling and rearming of the aircraft. No sortie passed in which most of the fighters hadn't expended an entire supply of ammunition.

Armorer George Levesque attended to F/L Gordon McGregor's Hurricane, replenishing its Browning machine-gun ammo boxes, giving him enough ammunition for seventeen seconds of continuous firing during his next aerial attack. No matter how difficult the sortie, said Levesque, "the pilots were always pleasant. They always had time to exchange a joke, although sometimes they were pretty bum jokes."[29]

Since most RCAF No. 1 pilots had been up since 4 a.m., they'd pulled their flying suits on over their pyjamas. On their return, some simply pulled off their flying gear and fell into chairs or bunks to catch a few winks. McGregor, fearful of falling into a deep sleep, had a batman put a cup of hot tea in his hands so that if he accidentally dozed off, he would burn himself and wake up immediately, ready to scramble.

"Every time that phone rang," F/O Paul Pitcher said, "your stomach rolled over. All of us would scramble off the bunks and stroll about, trying to look nonchalant. This was the worst moment. We were all fearful waiting for action."[30] The pace had made the thirty-one days since the Canadian squadron's first action, on August 15, seem relentless.

Across the Channel, the Luftwaffe had already begun a hand-off from the first German bomber wave to the second, much larger one of the day. Just before 2 p.m., forty-plus Dornier 17s took off from Cambrai, twenty-plus Heinkel 111s lifted off from Lille, nearly twenty Dornier 17s departed Antwerp, and nearly thirty Heinkels took to the air from the occupied Netherlands—114 bombers and twenty heavy fighters in total—headed for London's docks on the north side of the Thames and warehouses in Surrey on the south bank. As the bombers formed up over Calais, the 340 fighter aircraft under the command of Adolf Galland rose to escort them; again, their orders were to stay in close formation with the bomber stream. Only this time there were three fighters launched to escort every bomber, close to 450 aircraft in all.

Once assembled that afternoon, the Luftwaffe faced a strong westerly headwind, and the close escort of so many fighters made progress even slower. Soon after two o'clock, Chain Home radar registered the German raiders, but underestimated their strength at 225 aircraft. At 11 Group's Operations Room, AVM Keith Park chose the same tactic he'd used earlier in the day. He ordered four pairs of squadrons, nearly one hundred fighters, to patrol the airspace between Sheerness on the Thames Estuary and RAF Kenley, south of London, all of them flying at advantageous altitudes in the afternoon sun.

Over the Channel, the German bomber groups had begun separating into three distinct streams, all still headed for London's docks and warehouses; at the same time, concentrations of freelance fighters, Me 109s, roared straight toward London in hunting patrols. As they neared, Park launched his second defensive force, another eleven fighter squadrons, including the Canadians in RCAF No. 1 Squadron and Douglas Bader's Duxford Wing, with his No. 242 All-Canadian Squadron. Minutes later, Park scrambled a third defensive force, four more squadrons, including Winnipegger Johnny Kent leading his No. 303 Polish Squadron. In thirty minutes, AVM Keith Park had committed thirty-one squadrons, more than three hundred British fighters, to the looming battle.[31] He didn't know it, but at that hour there were three Me 109 fighters in the air for every two Spitfires or Hurricanes.[32]

First contact between opposing forces occurred over Romney Marsh, wetlands in Kent situated closest to Pas-de-Calais. RAF fighters of Keith Park's first and second defence scrambled and initiated head-on attacks against Adolf Galland's Me 109 fighters. Bound by their orders to remain in tight formation around the bombers "like a dog on a chain,"[33] the German fighters had to break off their counterattacks, allowing the RAF fighters to attack the bomber streams again and again. As the battle intensified, one Hurricane was hit so severely that the pilot aimed his aircraft at a bomber and bailed out; the collision destroyed the bomber, but left the impression on German aircrews that the ramming tactic was premeditated and that the British were desperate.

The Dornier and Heinkel bombers ploughed on at 22,000 feet, directly into the path of six oncoming RAF squadrons over Gravesend, where the Thames Estuary narrows at the east end of London's city limits. By that time, about fifty Heinkel 111s led one bomber stream, followed by Dornier 17s and 215s. Beyond them, a solid phalanx of forty fast and formidable

Junkers 88s. Above them flew a squadron of Me 110 escorts and another of 109s—in all, perhaps 250 "bandits" headed directly for London's populous city centre.[34]

Canadian F/L Robert "Butcher" Barton led the first section of No. 249 Squadron Hurricanes against the formation of Dornier 17s. This was his first sortie substituting for S/L John Grandy, who'd been wounded the week before. He admitted to some jitters until he spotted his prey.

"I was very much afraid on takeoffs," Barton said. "But when we got to altitude and sighted the enemy, the fear disappeared. 'God. There they are!' I'm saying. 'You've had it, boy.'"[35]

Fortunately, Barton and the vanguard fighters had chosen to attack the Dorniers. The Me 109s were accompanying the Heinkels some distance away, and under strict orders not to abandon them. The Dorniers were therefore left exposed. "The first aircraft I shot at, didn't do anything. Then, I tried another one. And as we went down, I followed him . . . I said to myself, 'This one I'm going to make sure he's bloody well down.'" On that first pass, the No. 249 Hurricanes shot down three enemy aircraft.

Back in the air for their second sortie of the day, the Hurricanes from RCAF No. 1 Squadron at Northolt began a patrol across south London. About thirty minutes later, S/L Ernie McNab, leading three sections of fighters, intercepted twenty Heinkel bombers south of Biggin Hill. The first bomber targeted by McNab immediately dropped its bombs and broke from the formation to seek refuge in cloud cover. One of the German escorts temporarily drove McNab off, but he persisted and forced the bomber to a controlled landing near Southend.

Second in Blue Section, Dal Russel began a steep dive to attack another Heinkel from the rear, but his Hurricane stalled and he was forced to climb and repeat his attack approach, this time laterally from right to left. "Experienced rear gunfire and after a short burst [enemy aircraft] did wing over and went into tight vertical spiral straight for the ground." Then, emphasizing the certainty of his kill, he added, "I would say its remains could be found around East or South East London suburbs."[36] He was only credited with a "probable."

Leading Red Section, F/L Gordon McGregor latched onto a Heinkel and fired nearly his entire ammunition allotment into it. Both engines of the enemy aircraft began smoking and the plane began falling earthward. When he looked around, all McGregor could see were two other fighters above him. He thought they were RAF Hurricanes. He waggled his wings in greeting, and then saw them dive and open fire at him. They were Me 109s bent on blowing him out of the sky. Large pieces of debris cascaded off his Hurricane's wings, and bullets tracked across his fuselage. Diving away violently, McGregor managed to elude further fire and limp back to Northolt. On inspection, a 20-mm cannon shell had almost shattered his left-wing spar, and machine-gun bullets had ripped gaping holes in his right wing.[37] His Hurricane had miraculously held together to get him home.

"Blue and Red Sections attacked," cited F/O Paul Pitcher in his combat report, "while I stayed behind to reform my [Yellow] section for its attack. I attacked a He 111 which was lagging about fifty yards behind . . . in a quarter astern attack. . . . I fired all my rounds. When I broke off, smoke was belching from the tail and starboard engine of the e/a."[38]

On this occasion, Pitcher's wingmate was F/O Bob Norris, who found what looked like a German fighter flying way off the beaten path. The enemy aircraft disappeared into cloud in the midst of a left-hand turn. Norris used his increasing descent speed, better than three hundred miles per hour, and estimated the Messerschmitt's rate of turn cutting inside his flight path. "I saw a yellow-nosed Me 109 appear about 100 feet below and in front," Norris wrote in his combat report. "I fired from rear quarter beam at about 200 yards."

The German fighter tried to inside-turn Norris's Hurricane. "Instead, I turned inside him and fired two more good bursts from about fifty yards. Smoke emerged after the second burst and flame from the cockpit section after the last burst. The Me 109 fell off on one wing through the clouds and when I straightened out, I was almost in them."[39]

The increasing cloud cover over south England at this hour began to influence the direction of the battle. The cloud density made it more difficult for RAF flight controllers to direct squadrons accurately to the bomber formations once they were over land and well beyond the coastal Chain Home radar towers. At the same time, clouds began to obscure the target areas and hampered bomber accuracy too.

In F/O Norris's case, a combination of the dense cloud and the intensity of the dogfight he'd just survived left him disoriented. Unable to find his way to Northolt, he landed at Biggin Hill to get his bearings.

Perhaps the most exceptional engagement that afternoon involved the youngest member of RCAF No. 1 Fighter Squadron. Following midday refuelling and rearming at Northolt, P/O Pete Lochnan took off later than the rest of the squadron, but caught up to Green Section in time to carry out three direct attacks on a Heinkel bomber—once head-on, a second time from the beam, and a third run astern. The enemy aircraft engines began smoking and failing. Several other RAF fighters joined Lochnan in driving the bomber down. Incredibly, the bomber pilot managed a controlled crash landing of the burning Heinkel near West Malling. Lochnan must have recognized there were aircrew still alive in the burning bomber, and chose to investigate.

"The burly Ottawan set his plane down beside [the bomber,]" cited a Canadian Press report that went on to describe Lochnan's selfless efforts to remove wounded German aircrew from the crumpled bomber. "[Lochnan found that] the German pilot [Feldwebel K. Behrendt] was able to walk, although half a bullet was protruding from his back. When the Canadian removed it, the Nazi asked for it for a souvenir. In exchange, the German handed the Canadian his field glasses."[40]

Caribou Squadron pilots scored well on their second sorties of the day: Lochnan had shared destruction of the downed Heinkel with a pilot from No. 222; and Norris had shot down the Me 109. Meanwhile, F/O Arthur Yuile had taken bullets in the shoulder but managed to land his Hurricane safely at the base. And S/L McNab had destroyed a bomber and shared two damaged enemy aircraft with F/O Pitcher.

"There were more than 1,000 planes in the sky south of London that day," S/L McNab wrote. "I counted nine aircraft falling at one time, and there were parachutes everywhere."[41]

By this time, the prime minister had a knowledgeable eye fixed on the tote board in the Operations Room at Uxbridge. All six squadrons in that sector of 11 Group had reached "red light" status of action. So, too, had the remaining seventeen squadrons of 11 Group, and the big wing of five squadrons from 12 Group, as well as the closest three squadrons from

10 Group. Churchill sensed the anxiety of the officer commanding, AVM Keith Park.

"What other reserves have we?" the prime minister asked.

"There are none," replied Park.[42]

Churchill said nothing. He looked grave.

* * *

Meanwhile, at 12 Group, Douglas Bader's five squadrons had rearmed and refuelled at their stations north of London through the midday. AVM Park scrambled them again just after 2 p.m. to patrol between Kenley and Maidstone. Park thought their morning claim of twenty-nine enemy aircraft destroyed or damaged was impressive, even if exaggerated. But with enemy bombers still managing to navigate through Chain Home radar and airborne fighter squadrons, Park needed a convincing backup performance from Bader's wing with enemy aircraft closing fast on their London targets.

Unlike during the morning ascent, the wing of five squadrons headed straight south from Duxford, working its way through the increasing cloud cover. If nothing else, S/L Bader wanted altitude and whatever blinding sun he could find in the eyes of his enemy. When he spotted puffs of anti-aircraft shells ahead, indicating ground batteries firing at the bomber stream, his Hurricanes had reached 16,000 feet, with the Spitfires slightly higher. Bader made a beeline for the bombers.

At that moment, the entire Duxford Wing was at a 4,000-foot disadvantage, because German fighter escorts were flying higher still. They announced that advantage by diving straight into the British fighters. Bader made the reflex decision to break his formation of Hurricanes to face the Me 109s, while sending his Spitfires after the bomber formation.

In seconds, the German fighters had pounced on the Hurricanes. Bader ordered his section to "Break up!" A 109 roared over him and Bader got caught in its slipstream, which stalled his Hurricane and sent it spinning downward 5,000 feet. As he regained control, his section mate P/O Stan Turner homed on another German fighter. Turner fired into the 109's cockpit, and thought he'd killed the pilot, but just as quickly a cannon shell exploded near Turner's tailplane, throwing him into a wild spin. When he regained control, a Dornier 17 lay directly ahead. Anticipating the bomber's flight path, he lined up a deflection shot and fired; the bomber's right engine began burning right away and the aircraft slipped into a dive and crashed into a residential area on the north side of the Thames. After all of that, Turner managed to land his damaged Hurricane.

Above the Kentish hills, a whirling dogfight unfolded as Duxford Wing Hurricanes and Spitfires chased Heinkels, Dorniers, and Messerschmitt fighters every which way, writing script of a life-and-death struggle in contrails across the sky. During the same Messerschmitt diving attack on the No. 242 fighters, a German fighter pilot bounced P/O John Latta's Hurricane. But the German pilot overshot his attack and just as quickly was in Latta's gunsight; the twenty-five-year-old Canadian, with six victories to his credit to date, fired a machine-gun burst into the Me 109. It quickly burst into flames and vanished in the broken cloud below. He was credited with a seventh "destroyed" enemy aircraft.[43] At a lower altitude, P/O Stansfeld sighted a Heinkel at about 1,000 feet; he joined other Hurricanes that together knocked out the bomber's engines, forcing it to pancake on an aerodrome field, where its crew became prisoners of war.

* * *

As reports of victories and defeats streamed into Fighter Command operations rooms, the battle in the sky became a battle of statistics or, more specifically, claims. In a state of euphoria toward the end of the afternoon, based largely on pilot debriefings, Air Ministry claimed that 185 German aircraft had been destroyed, or about 20 percent of the German raiders, versus a loss of only twenty-five RAF aircraft. Bader's Duxford Wing alone claimed it had destroyed fifty-two enemy aircraft.

More accurate data has since placed the number at sixty-one German aircraft downed, and twenty-nine British.[44] In terms of aircrew lost, on the German side, eighty-one aircrew were killed or missing, with sixty-three taken prisoner. That represented not 20 percent of the German force lost, but 5.5 percent. But so too did the German side overclaim. They reported seventy-nine British aircraft destroyed on September 15. Once again, more accurate information later showed that twelve RAF pilots were killed, another dozen wounded, and one taken prisoner. The actual ratio of losses showed that for each RAF pilot casualty that day there were seven Luftwaffe casualties.[45]

"No one will know the correct assessment," Douglas Bader said unrepentantly, "unless the English Channel and the Thames Estuary are drained."[46]

Neither ACM Dowding nor 11 Group commander Park was convinced that Bader's big wing tactics had proved overwhelming. While the Duxford Wing Hurricanes had drawn German escorts and those freelance Luftwaffe fighters away from their bomber formations, making it easier for the Spitfires to knock down bombers, a substantial number of bombers had still reached their intended targets; one estimate claimed one hundred bombers reached London and dropped 120 tons of explosives on the city.[47]

As much as the Canadian pilots of Bader's home squadron, No. 242, followed and endorsed their squadron leader's dictums—gain altitude to gain advantage, dive on the enemy out of the sun, and attack en masse—some Canadians had misgivings. F/L Johnny Kent, who led "A" Flight with No. 303 Polish Squadron, was dead against Bader's relentless campaign to use the big wing. What's more, he claimed his experience on Sunday, September 15 revealed some of its weaknesses.

That afternoon, AVM Park had scrambled both No. 303 Squadron and No. 229 Squadron together, about a dozen fighters in each. While both squadrons' aircraft flew with radio communication equipment aboard, allowing each squadron to speak to the controller in the Operations Room, neither squadron could speak to the other.

Departing Northolt, the two squadrons used visual sighting to assemble in formation and fly southward. Patrolling over Croydon, Kent spotted a large number of enemy aircraft, approaching from the south. Their flight path put the fighters in perfect line for a head-on attack. Kent waited and waited for the No. 229 wing leader, John Banham, to commence the attack. Instead, No. 229 banked away from the oncoming bombers.

"It suddenly dawned on me that he had not seen the enemy as he continued his turn away," Kent wrote. "We experienced . . . just how impractical the wing theory was."[48] The

Canadian flight leader relayed a message via the controller to Banham, but by that time both squadrons had arrived at the extreme edge of audible radio communication. Kent's message was garbled. Instead of a wing-sized attack on the bombers, Kent and his Polish pilots threw themselves at the bombers and fighters: nine Hurricanes against an escort screen of fifty Me 109s. As a consequence, the German fighters delayed Kent's attempt to destroy or damage the bomber stream.

"By this time," Kent reported, "we were [in] nowhere near as good a position and the bombers were already dropping their bombs [and soon] the only enemy machines to be seen were away in the distance heading to France."[49]

While the dogfight had kept them away from the bombers, Kent's section of three Hurricanes stalked a pair of German fighters heading eastward over Rye. When they closed in, Kent fired at one of the 109s. It rolled and Kent saw what he thought was a large piece of the enemy aircraft spin away over top of his Hurricane. The 109 then dove straight into the Channel. An intelligence officer later verified the victory, telling Kent the object from the enemy plane was the pilot, whose body was later found on the coast.

Emblematic of No. 303's tenacity, Kent and the Poles did not allow any sortie to be wasted. Over the course of forty-two days in the Battle of Britain, No. 303 Squadron shot down 126 German warplanes. Nine of the squadron's pilots qualified as aces (shooting down five or more enemy aircraft). Group Captain Stanley Vincent, commanding officer of RAF Northolt station, verified the Poles' victory claims. "They fight with near suicidal impetus," he said.[50]

The All-Canadian Squadron completed its second intelligence debrief of the day to determine the number of destroyed, damaged, or probables of German aircraft losses. All pilots but one had returned safely to Coltishall. Before long, the one missing pilot, a British flight commander, called in to say he'd been shot down and wounded, but would survive. S/L Bader approached P/O Turner, who'd been the top-scoring Canadian that day and whose seniority dated back to Dunkirk in May.

"Stan, how'd you feel about taking over 'B' Flight?" he asked.

"Swell, sir," Turner replied, and with the assignment came a rank promotion to flight lieutenant.

AVM Leigh-Mallory meanwhile phoned Bader to congratulate him on being awarded the Distinguished Service Order the day before, and to applaud actions by the Duxford Wing. As usual, the very direct squadron leader claimed the second sortie had been "a sticky time" because headquarters had "scrambled us too late again."[51] Still, all of No. 242 Fighter Squadron was allowed to stand down. Aircrew gathered in the mess, hoisted plenty of beer and, accompanied by P/O Lawrence Cryderman on the piano, sang such satirical ditties as "Our Flight Sergeant Ain't Going to Fly No More," "An Aircrew Cadets' Lament," and "Hitler Has Only Got One Ball," well into the night.[52] The All-Canadian Squadron basked in the afterglow of credits and near credits and the good fortune that they had all come home in one piece that day.

The last phase of the Luftwaffe's second-wave offensive that Sunday afternoon arrived almost unnoticed by the controllers at Fighter Command. Just after 3 p.m., Chain Home observers spotted what appeared as a half dozen enemy aircraft approaching the southwest coast of England from Cherbourg. On the premise that the RAF had sent all of its fighters to defend the London area, Air Fleet commander Kesselring had dispatched Heinkel bombers, without fighter escort, to attack Portland's Royal Navy base.

But the six Heinkel 111s turned out to be thirty, and Canadian fighter pilot Peter O'Brian led a flight of six Spitfires from RAF No. 152 Squadron to intercept the raid. Only three weeks before, he had been promoted to temporary flight commander at the Warmwell base. By the time F/L O'Brian spotted the Heinkel bombers, they had already attacked the naval yards. However, just five bombs landed among naval installations. O'Brian and his two wingmates gave chase over the Channel and overtook one of the straggling bombers.

"I concentrated fire on the starboard engine," he noted in his combat report. "I carried out another astern attack from slightly underneath the enemy aircraft." O'Brian's two section mates joined the attack. In two bursts, O'Brian had fired eight hundred rounds of shells into the Heinkel, after which, "I saw enemy aircraft losing height, with its undercarriage down and considerable smoke pouring from its starboard engine."[53] The bomber fell into a steep dive and plunged into the sea. One of the four crew survived and was rescued by a British rescue boat.

O'Brian's shared victory was his first. It was also the last action of September 15 involving a Canadian pilot.[54]

German daylight operations of the Luftwaffe on September 15, the sixty-seventh day of the battle, had nevertheless delivered deadly results. At the climax of the assault in the late afternoon, major downtown London railway lines had been demolished, gasworks and electrical substations were still ablaze, and high explosives killed or wounded 150 civilians in West Ham. Evening attacks launched from Luftwaffe bases at Cherbourg targeted the Spitfire factory in Woolston; the bombs inflicted thirty-three human casualties but missed the assembly plant. Although RAF fighters operating in the diminishing light brought down a few more raiders, the German bombers still managed to penetrate British airspace and strike populous targets.

The earliest days of the Blitz registered some of the highest fatality statistics. Air raid casualties in London climbed to their highest in September, with 6,954 killed and 10,615 injured. British songstress Vera Lynn, who wrote about her own experiences in London during the Blitz, captured the aftermath of the daily bombings. She noted that "underfoot, the streets were frosted with millions of fragments of broken glass. . . . After a raid the nostrils were assailed by the acrid smell of a bombed out street, an unforgettable mixture of dust, smoke, charred timber, and escaping gas the smell of violent death itself." She added that bomb blasts could mangle the bodies of victims or capriciously leave a human being unhurt but stripped naked.[55]

By mid-September, the worst-hit boroughs of London had lost a quarter of their populations, and up to 25,000 residents had been left homeless. Contrary to popular myth, however, at the height of the Blitz, relatively few Londoners retreated to shelters in the city's Underground rail system—only 177,000 people, or roughly 4 percent of the capital's population.[56] It seemed that if buildings remained standing or public rest centres were available in their neighbourhoods, most Londoners would stick it out at or near home.

* * *

Aboard *Asia*, Hermann Göring's personal war train, parked at his Cap Blanc-Nez headquarters in occupied France, the reichsmarschall absorbed the grim statistical scoresheet for September 15. The more bombers Albert Kesselring had sent over Britain with each offensive wave that day, the more he had lost to Keith Park's aggressive defence.[57] Unescorted Luftwaffe bombers were straggling back to bases at Calais in twos and threes. At least a dozen of Göring's prized Messerschmitt fighters, out of fuel, had ditched in the Channel or short of their airfields along the French coast.[58] The bomber commanders blamed the fighter commanders; the fighter commanders blamed the orders; Göring blamed everybody but himself. The Nazi Party newspaper, *Völkischer Beobachter*, raced to publish stories of destruction at the heart of London, claiming seventy-nine RAF fighters had been downed, while the Luftwaffe had lost just forty-three.

Albert Kesselring told Göring the truth: "We cannot keep this up at this rate."[59]

Hitler's imminent invasion plan had taken a further body blow that same day. Bomber Command had enjoyed a successful outing of its own: 155 RAF Hampden bombers from No. 83 Squadron attacked the docks at Antwerp, targeting a stockpile of six hundred barges ready to transport German troops as part of the invasion, Operation Sea Lion. The Kriegsmarine reported "powerful enemy air attacks along the entire coastal zone between Le Havre and Antwerp,"[60] and sent an SOS for more anti-aircraft installations. In a fortnight, from September 1 to 15, Bomber Command had destroyed 12 percent of Germany's invasion shipping.[61]

Hitler's patience with Göring's promises to rid the skies over Britain of RAF fighters had reached its limit. It was now two months since Führer Directive No. 16 had called for the invasion of Britain to begin. Operation Sea Lion should have been ready to deliver a quarter million German soldiers to British shores. It seemed, however, that his elaborate plan for invasion was inoperative. On September 17, Hitler ordered Göring to the Berghof to account for his failure to fulfill the directive "to eliminate the English homeland as a base for the prosecution of the war against Germany."[62] Following an exchange between the two Nazi leaders, Göring would transfer from daily command of Luftwaffe operations over Britain to planning for the invasion of Russia.

On that same Tuesday, September 17, British decoders at Ultra learned that the German general staff had issued orders to their occupation authorities in the Netherlands. The message called for the dismantling of air-loading equipment at Dutch aerodromes; without such transport, Germany could not launch an invasion.[63] Whether officially announced by Hitler or not, Sea Lion was postponed indefinitely. Chief of Air Staff Cyril Newall passed the Ultra message to Winston Churchill, suggesting the invasion was at least unlikely in 1940. Also in the room was Wing Commander Fred Winterbotham, of Britain's Secret Intelligence Service, who noted: "There was a very broad smile on Churchill's face now as he lit up his massive cigar and suggested that we should all take a little fresh air."[64]

F/L William Ewart Cockram travelled in an RCAF vehicle to Tunbridge Wells on September 17 to retrieve the body of F/O Ross Smither, shot down and killed two days before. The squadron padre then took Smither's casket to Woking, Surrey, for a funeral and burial at Brookwood Military Cemetery.

"During the morning the sun shone brightly," Padre Cockram wrote Smither's parents. "But as we entered the funeral service, it seemed that the heavens over England could not contain their weeping, and the rain came.

"You have every right to be proud of your boy—all Canada ought to be proud and thankful to you for giving him to help save humanity's cause."[65]

CHAPTER TEN

"GREAT AND GLORIOUS DAY"

KEITH OGILVIE, THE CANADIAN SPITFIRE PILOT WHOM Queen Wilhelmina had credited with shooting down the German bomber over Buckingham Palace on September 15, did a second sortie over Kent that afternoon. He and other members of his flight from No. 609 Squadron were too late to catch a formation of twenty Dorniers before they dropped their bombs on south London. But Ogilvie caught up with one of them and shot it down along the coast. One parachutist emerged from the stricken bomber and Ogilvie shot some film of the German's descent. The airman waved wildly at Ogilvie as if pleading not to be machine-gunned. Ogilvie had no such intention.

"He landed about ten miles out," Ogilvie wrote in his diary, "and I doubt if he was picked up at all as there was nothing in sight."[1]

Ogilvie's next diary entry sums up much of the week that followed the climactic aerial clashes of that historic Sunday for his squadron and the rest of Fighter Command. It was a period "conspicuous for its lack of action," he wrote, largely because the cloud cover that blanketed southern England that week brought a "good old English fall, with lots of rain." Inclement weather reduced German bombing activity, so Ogilvie, who had just turned twenty-five on September 14, finally got some leave in London to celebrate with his aircrew comrades. He wrote to his brother, Jim Ogilvie, in Ottawa: "Eleven o'clock at night and a fine rest I'm getting," he wrote, pointing out that German bombing outside London had painted the sky red with explosions and triggered loud anti-aircraft fire, "and at home you are probably cursing at the mosquitoes."[2]

Leave in London offered aircrew an array of escapes. But when the fighter pilots of RCAF No. 1 got a twenty-four-hour or forty-eight-hour leave, they enjoyed an added benefit: a dedicated chauffeur. Bev Christmas had no idea how the RCAF No. 1 pilots found him, but "we had a taxi driver named Sebastien, who had a [Rolls-Royce] limousine. He used to pick us up when we got leave and drive us into London."[3]

Sebastien's comings and goings were so routine that the RAF guards at Northolt seldom bothered to stop his limo when it arrived at the station gate. The car had enough room to carry six or eight pilots into the city, and its driver knew exactly where to deposit his fares as they began an overnight or two-night bender. Despite the Blitz, Piccadilly and Soho hummed with barroom conversation, sometimes singing and swing dancing, and plenty of companionship, all behind war-time blackout curtains. Many fighter pilots made their way to the Regent Palace Hotel near Piccadilly Circus; when the Canadians invaded London in 1940, the hotel became known as "the Canadian Riding School."[4] Londoners took a fancy to fighter pilots, and so the Canadian Riding School, where a double room (with communal bath) cost seventeen shillings a night, drew the admirers and the admired to its nightlife. Then, on the morning after, the Canadians' guardian angel arrived like clockwork. "Somehow, Sebastien managed to gather us all up from various places around London, and get us back to base. How he did it, I'll never know. He never missed."[5]

The Canadians acquired a trick that helped those on leave recover and refocus on the job at hand. Either by accident or experiment, fighter pilots discovered that taking a couple of whiffs of pure oxygen—available when testing their cockpit gear before takeoff—had a magical, remedial effect. Not only did the pure oxygen keep a man functioning at high altitudes where the air was thin, but it also helped get him off the ground "on those mornings when a London celebration was a dark, brown taste on the tongue."[6]

For fighter pilot Hartland Molson, trips into London on leave left a different impression. On one September night, he accepted an invitation to meet W.A. "Billy" Bishop, the RCAF air marshal and Victoria Cross winner, who was visiting from Canada. The two officers and family friends met for dinner at Claridge's Hotel in Mayfair. After their meal, Bishop arranged for chairs, ice, and whisky on the hotel rooftop to witness the bombings in the distance with a pair of binoculars. Coincidentally, while Molson was away from the station that night, German bombers dropped explosives on Northolt's RCAF barracks. While no one was hurt, it seemed to him there was no place to hide.[7]

More instructive for Flying Officer Molson was his transit into and out of London. In areas that had sustained heavy damage from the bombing, he saw burst watermains, ruptured and burning gas lines, and civilians crowded into shelters. He described the impressive calm among Londoners, each doing his job, none ever able to fully escape the effects of the Blitz. "Every person in London or in a factory or in a big town is in the lines, because the war is here," Molson wrote his wife. "The police, the fire services, and thousands of volunteers in the auxiliary services are on the job at all times, doing their work with an earnest will, coolness and cheerful bravery that makes your heart ache."[8]

During the respite afforded Londoners and Fighter Command by Britain's autumn weather, Squadron Leader Douglas Bader became impatient, if not cocky, if not blood-thirsty. Buoyed by praise from Air Vice-Marshal Leigh-Mallory for his big wing's actions on September 15, and anxious to run up the scores for his Duxford Wing, Bader admitted to his superior that he'd like to shoot down a complete German raid, not allowing a single fighter or bomber to escape back to its French base. His Duxford Wing got their chance on Wednesday, September 18.

That morning, the Luftwaffe sent some Me 109s to conduct high-altitude sweeps over the British coast, but it wasn't until mid-afternoon that AVM Park scrambled the Duxford Wing to meet a strong force of Ju 88s that Fighter Command expected would be escorted by the usual swarm of Me 109 fighters. Airborne, Bader immediately homed on the anti-aircraft fire appearing ahead of him at an altitude of 16,000 feet. The leader of the big wing saw what he thought were two formations of twenty bombers and escorts. Inexplicably, by the time Bader's wing began its attack, any German fighter protection had disappeared. Bomber crews realized how vulnerable they were. Their formations disintegrated and Bader's wing picked out individual enemy aircraft, destroying, damaging, or chasing them back to the Channel. The engagement turned into a slaughter.

Flying alongside S/L Bader, Flight Lieutenant Willie McKnight joined a Spitfire and together they knocked out both engines on one Junkers bomber and saw the entire crew bail out. In the free-for-all, Pilot Officer Neil Campbell took on one Junkers by himself and sent it crashing to earth. Then he damaged one engine on a second bomber and teamed up with a Spitfire to knock down a third. P/O Hugh Tamblyn fired bursts into a bomber and evaded crossfire from Junkers gunners; McKnight saw Tamblyn's victim go down, too. Elsewhere, P/O Norris Hart fired on a bomber and watched it crash into a railway line; then, climbing back to altitude, he fired into the belly of another and it also went down. The Canadians said they had never seen so many parachutes in the sky.

Bader attacked one victim at such close range, he was able to watch the individual German aircrew leap from the stricken bomber. The final crewman's parachute got tangled on the tailplane. Bader followed the bomber down to the end. McKnight saw a similar drama, as another German crewman's chute snagged on the hatch of a crashing bomber; fellow crewmen struggled to get the last man free; they succeeded and jumped clear just as the bomber ploughed into the sea.

Bader noted immodestly in his logbook that the wing had "destroyed thirty . . . 242 got eleven . . . No casualties in squadron or wing." The truth was likely about a third of that total destroyed, or about ten enemy aircraft. "There seemed to be about three British fighters for every German," Bader added, "a most satisfactory state of affairs, if a little dangerous from the collision point of view."[9]

RCAF No. 1 Caribou Squadron was called to action slightly earlier that day. Their Hurricanes scrambled and climbed to intercept mostly German fighters. In the ensuing dogfights, Eric Beardmore got separated from his section and his fighter was hit; he parachuted safely into the Thames, near its riverbank.

P/O Otto Peterson led a section against the Me 109s. He climbed into the sun to get some altitude advantage over a second formation of German fighters. He attacked the tail-end 109 and fired a burst, and white smoke emerged; the plane fell away in a vertical dive. He then tracked on a second fighter and saw white smoke streaming from it. Peterson was credited with one enemy aircraft destroyed and another damaged that sortie.

RCAF No. 1 pilots returned to Northolt just in time to receive an urgent message from RAF headquarters in London. No congratulations. No tribute for service above and beyond. Just a regulation announcement that "scarves and sweaters will not be tolerated in future, in place of collars and ties." One wondered how much consideration had gone into issuing such a directive when Caribou Squadron, like most units of Fighter Command, had served in the front lines of the battle with distinction since July 10. Now, seventy days later, Air Ministry was suddenly worried about dress code. S/L Ernie McNab was not amused. In response, and with remarkable restraint, the squadron diarist noted: "Apparently when called from 'thirty minutes available' to 'immediate readiness' and expected to be airborne in no time at all, the pilots have to be inspected and passed as neat and tidy to go up and engage the King's enemies."[10]

* * *

While RAF brass hats may have had cause to question fighter pilots' adherence to official dress code, nobody at Fighter Command doubted their cockpit skills nor their commitment to defeating the Luftwaffe. Front-line pilots regularly debated combat tactics. Some had even chimed in on the issue of big wing versus smaller squadron-sized attacks. But when the dispersal hut call moved from "At Readiness" to "Scramble," by now most squadrons moved like synchronized machinery to get a flight of fighters or a squadron airborne. At most RAF stations, that meant launching a dozen aircraft or sometimes twice that many simultaneously. On September 21, at Northolt, a still more ambitious scramble occurred unexpectedly.[11]

Northolt had a storied history. Built in 1915, it predated the launching of the Royal Air Force itself in 1918. The station had received delivery of the first advanced fighter Hawker Hurricanes in 1937. Active from the very moment the Battle of Britain began in July 1940, RAF Northolt had become home to three respected fighter squadrons. Each with its own barracks, mess hall, and dispersal hut: RCAF No. 1 Squadron, RAF No. 303 Polish Squadron, and RAF No. 229 Squadron all resided at different corners of the grass airfield. However, with Fighter Command considering larger RAF fighter formations more often, Northolt became a candidate to fly all three of its squadrons as a single unit, a big wing.

On September 21, the station commander, Group Captain Stanley Vincent, called a meeting of squadron leaders Ernie McNab (RCAF), Ronald Kellett (No. 303), and Frederick Rosier (No. 229) at his office. The four senior officers worked out protocols for all three squadrons to launch in sequence. Vincent, recalled F/O Bev Christmas, had "decided that the three squadron commanders would lead [the wing] in rotation."[12]

That very day, recalled F/L Gordon McGregor, an order came to all Northolt squadrons to attack as a wing: "Scramble. Angels 18!"[13] All three dispersal huts cleared of their pilots, and within minutes the Merlin engines of thirty-six Hurricanes were humming at the corners of the base.

"The airfield had a slight mound in the middle," Christmas said, "so you couldn't really see from one end of the field to the other. But we all jumped into our fighters waiting for somebody to start us off."

By this time, all three squadron commanders were racing in cars to their respective corners of Northolt station. Since the sequence had been discussed only minutes before, said RCAF F/O Molson, "the inevitable result was that thirty-six pilots opened their throttles simultaneously, all with their aircraft pointed to the centre of the field."[14]

"Just as the undercarriages of the twelve [Canadian] Hurricanes lifted off," McGregor said, "the noses of the dozen No. 303 Polish squadron Hurricanes appeared dead ahead."

Christmas recalled the horrific moment with so many Hurricanes meeting in the middle of the airfield. "There were airplanes everywhere," he said. "Some over top. Others under each other. Somebody went over top of me. It was such a big conglomeration of aircraft," and, he added figuratively, "I remember going in the front door of the officers' mess and out the back!"

The only casualty, Molson said, was the station commander. Vincent was helped to his staff car and driven to the mess for a stiff drink.

Pilot Officer Keith "Skeets" Ogilvie (*above left*) remembered his first scramble, racing at-the-double to his Spitfire in time for fitters and riggers to strap him into the cockpit; he remembered that checking his instruments and turning on his gunsights and gun buttons "were all calming and reassuring factors." Flight Lieutenant Johnny Kent, in the middle of his first dogfight, recalled a general mêlée: aircraft—some with black crosses, others the brown/green of Hurricanes; pilots having difficulty keeping a steady aim; snap-shooting being the order of the day; a confused fight; and, just as suddenly as it began, "it was over and the sky was empty."

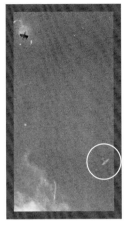

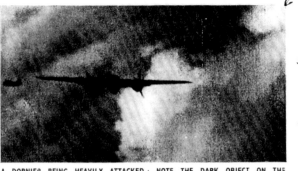

A DORNIER BEING HEAVILY ATTACKED : NOTE THE DARK OBJECT ON THE LEFT—THIS IS ONE OF THE CREW IN THE ACT OF BALING OUT

A DORNIER ON FIRE DURING AN AERIAL COMBAT : A PICTURE TAKEN BY THE ATTACKING BRITISH AIRCRAFT

Serving in RAF No. 609 Squadron, on September 15, Keith Ogilvie scrambled to meet a formation of Dornier bombers over London. Spotting a low-flying Dornier 215, Ogilvie dove and attacked it first from the side and then from behind, firing at the bomber's rear gunner. The battle ensued so low over the city that the *Daily Mirror* newspaper photographers captured the results—the bomber falling in flames (*top right*) as Ogilvie's Spitfire (*circled lower right*) swoops away, and the result-ing debris falling on Buckingham Palace and a city-centre railway terminus (*bottom*). Ogilvie later clipped out the newspaper story including frames of film from his gunsight; Ogilvie inscribed on the newsprint: "This one is taken from my film over London on Sept. 15, 1940, of a Dornier 215. It crashed on Victoria Station."

Never one to follow RAF protocol, Douglas Bader (*below*) nearly killed himself stunt flying in 1931 (losing both legs in the crash). He defied all odds when he worked his way back into RAF combat service, assuming command of No. 242 All-Canadian Fighter Squadron in June 1940. Quickly earning the Canadians' respect, Bader groomed his pilots into a crack force, all while campaigning to lead not just one squadron against Luftwaffe bombers but many at once for greater impact. His "big wing" (*above*) concept won favour with some RAF strategists, but not with ACM Hugh Dowding, who preferred to spread his limited resources across all of southern England, not just obvious targets.

"THE" POLISH SQUADRON

126 卐

Considered green recruits when they fled from Poland to the UK in 1939, Polish fighter pilots were grouped into an all-Polish squadron in the RAF. Their British commanders quickly learned the Poles' experience against the Luftwaffe provided insight to German bomber and fighter tactics. Shown in October 1940 are members of RAF No. 303 Fighter Squadron: (*left to right*) Mirosław Ferić, Johnny Kent, Bogdan Grzeszczak, Jerzy Radomski, Jan Zumback (with goggles atop his head), Witold Lokuciewski, Boguslaw Mierzwa, Zdzislaw Henneberg, Jan Rogowski, and Eugeniusz Szaposznikow. Over forty-two days of service in the Battle of Britain, Polish pilots shot down 126 German warplanes (*opposite bottom*), the highest-scoring squadron in the battle. One of their commanders, Canadian Johnny Kent, often said, "The Poles were playing the game for keeps far more than we were."

Once posted to an RAF squadron, Polish pilots needed training on British aircraft (*above left*). They had to learn to measure speed in miles per hour, not kilometres per hour, and fuel in gallons, not litres, as well as how to accelerate by pushing throttles forward, not back; and they had to get used to retractable undercarriages. Quickly, the Polish pilots (*top right*) inaugurated a squadron mascot, photographed with pilots Jan Zumbach and Mirosław Ferić, and began chalking up enviable records. In December Zumbach, Zdzislaw Henneberg (*below left*) and Ferić (*below right*) were awarded Distinguished Flying Crosses for their service in the Battle of Britain. Hugh Dowding commented, "Had it not been for the magnificent work of the Polish squadrons and their unsurpassed gallantry, I hesitate to say that the outcome of the battle would have been the same."

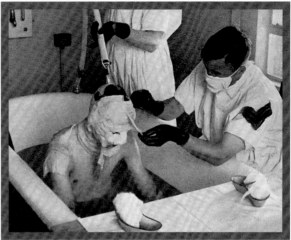

After completing his U of T medical degree in 1929, Dr. Albert Ross Tilley (*above left*) travelled abroad to the US and Europe to further his skill and knowledge in surgery. Back in Canada, in 1935, he opened a plastic surgery practice, but then the war intervened. His service as principal medical officer at RCAF HQ in London brought him to the attention of Dr. Archibald McIndoe (*middle, right, and below, seated next to pianist*) and his rehabilitation facility in East Grinstead. There, Tilley pioneered saline baths for patients (*above right*) in the Guinea Pig Club—servicemen severely burned in aircraft crashes and bailouts.

King George VI paid Caribou Squadron a visit on September 26. Dressed in his air marshal's uniform, the King moved along a line of air and ground crew offering his personal congratulations to each man.

Not only did the filming of the movie *Battle of Britain* incorporate a who's who of British film stars—Lawrence Olivier and Trevor Howard, and Susannah York (*third from right*)—seen here at the Duxford air base location in 1968, but it also attracted surviving members of the battle, including (*left to right*) Douglas Bader, Hugh Dowding (in wheelchair), Robert Stanford Tuck, Johnny Kent, Bolesław Drobiński, and Al Deere.

"By the time all the Hurricanes got up, we were all over hell's half acre," Christmas concluded.

"The Northolt Football Game,"[15] as their unrehearsed mass takeoff became known, was not one of the big wing's stellar moments. It may, however, have illustrated how time and experience had honed the quick-thinking and aerobatic skills of fighter pilots at Northolt, preparing them for whatever new twists the war might throw at them.

Not because of the mass scramble on September 21, but coincidentally, RAF Northolt received unexpected visitors during the final days of September. AM Billy Bishop arrived about tea time on September 25 so that members of RCAF No. 1 could share with him their fiftieth victory as a fighter squadron. A Canadian Press reporter was in tow to record the moment. The pilots assembled around a table in their dispersal hut and listened to P/O Otto Peterson and F/O Dal Russel describe their joint action earlier that day. They were carrying out a patrol along the south coast when they spotted a Dornier 215 below them. They both released bursts of machine-gun shells into the enemy aircraft before it plunged into the sea. Observer Corps spotters confirmed the claim,[16] and Bishop raised a glass in tribute. "To your continued success and glory," he said.[17]

Next day, King George VI arrived at Northolt and heard from the Canadian squadron leader that RCAF No. 1 pilots "have been shooting Nazi planes out of the sky or crippling them at a rate of more than one a day."[18] The King wore the uniform of an air marshal, while the Canadians wore off-duty uniforms; noticeably absent was the scarf that S/L Ernie McNab had been wearing to snub the RAF dress-code directive of "collars and ties" only.

"Your squadron is doing a fine job. Congratulations," said the King.

Next, the King visited the Polish pilots at the No. 303 end of the Northolt airfield. The Polish airmen showed their royal visitor a meticulously kept history of their service in the war, to which their flight commander, Johnny Kent, had added drawings illustrating the Battle of Britain phase. The King smiled in tribute and signed the book opposite Kent's sketches, "George R.I. September 26."[19] With their commanding officers translating, the Poles then revealed a few trophies from their sorties against the Luftwaffe: the bomb rack of a downed Dornier bomber, and bits of an Me 109 aircraft the Poles had shot down.

* * *

Adolf Hitler received no such souvenirs from his Luftwaffe crews or commanders in late September. At the Berghof, he weighed the impact of the past summer's *Adlerangriff* (Eagle Attack) against England, the suspension of Operation Sea Lion, and the prospect of further inconclusive attacks against the British. After six years of non-stop conquest and plunder across Europe, the führer had now suffered his first reversal, a lost opportunity to invade England. At least for the moment, his Directive No. 16 "to eliminate the English homeland as a base for the prosecution of the war against Germany" would not be met. But there was still territory for the taking, new battle plans to draw up for his generals, and even awards to present.

On September 25, the second-highest-scoring ace in the Luftwaffe, Adolf Galland, had arrived in Berlin to receive the *Eichenlaub* (Oak Leaves) award from Hitler. Just days earlier, during a heated exchange with the reichsmarschall, Göring had challenged his fighter pilots to come up with a solution to defeat the RAF. Germany's highest-scoring ace, Werner Mölders, had replied that he would like his Me 109s fitted with more powerful engines. Galland had gone one further. "I should like an outfit of Spitfires for my squadron," he'd said.[20] Göring was not amused. With equal temerity and now in the presence of the führer, Galland expressed his frustration with German press and radio for reviling the RAF, while he, Galland, admitted "the greatest admiration for the enemy across the water." Remarkably, Hitler did not disagree, suggesting "the English are a hundred years ahead of us,"[21] and that he regretted not being able to bring England and Germany together in a war against the Soviets.

Appreciation of the British, however, did not keep Hitler from sending hundreds more Luftwaffe bombers over the UK that very day. At 11 a.m., British radar towers detected a force of enemy aircraft approaching the south coast from the Cherbourg peninsula. Chain Home could not initially determine bomber strength or objective. But its presence, so distant from the previous attack forces bound for London, sparked a Fighter Command response. P/O Keith Ogilvie's No. 609 Squadron, inland from the Isle of Wight, was scrambled from Middle Wallop to break up a raid that seemed headed for the Royal Navy base at Portland.

"It was one hell of a big raid, I should think 200 bombers and fighter escort of all types, Dornier 17s and 215s, Heinkel 111s, Messerschmitt 110s and 109s," Ogilvie wrote.[22]

Over Portland, the bomber stream split into four fingers, one turning west to Plymouth, a second one east to Portsmouth, a third to Portland. The fourth force crossed the coast at Portland and disappeared, partly because all radar towers were aimed out to sea, but also because cloud cover obscured the bomber stream. The Royal Observer Corps was left to determine the speed and direction of the raid by listening for the sounds of the bombers outside their ground stations. They had no visual contact.

Soon there was no doubt that the target was the Bristol Aeroplane plant at Filton, the single-largest aircraft manufacturing facility in the world at the time, covering over 2.6 million square feet—it built the RAF's Blenheim and Beaufighter aircraft as well as their Hercules engines.

Ogilvie recalled the next few minutes, catching up to the bombers, as some of the most hectic he'd ever hope to experience. "Just over the big aircraft plant and obvious target, we came out [of the clouds] under the damn bombers," he wrote. "At this moment, the ack-ack [anti-aircraft guns] opened up . . . at the same time the bomb doors came open on the bombers and the whole flaming issue dropped their bombs at once. How none of us was hit [by either flak or bombs,] I'll never know."

Air raid sirens around Filton had preceded the raid by about fifteen minutes, so most of Bristol's huge workforce reached factory shelters in time. But at 11:48 a.m., in just forty-five seconds, the bombers in close formation dropped 168 bombs on the factory. Six semi-underground shelters took direct hits, and ninety-one men and women workers were killed; twenty-four others died in adjacent streets; while 315 people suffered wounds in the raid.[23] As the bomber force of fifty-eight Heinkels had turned for home, however, some forty RAF fighters engaged them.

In Red Section of No. 609, Ogilvie in his Spitfire attacked one bomber from the side. He broke away and attacked a second time. Both the bomber's engines were streaming glycol, a sure sign the Heinkels would go down. Then "there was a gigantic 'pow' and a fine big cannon hole appeared in my right wing," Ogilvie wrote. "A snappy glance in my rear mirror [was] full of a yellow-nosed 109. . . . I shook him but not before he put another up my tail, one through my fuselage, exploding in my wireless set behind my back, and, as a final souvenir, one in my port wing, puncturing my tire. Certainly my closest call to date."

The RAF lost four fighters and one pilot during the raid on Bristol. The Luftwaffe lost six bombers and eight aircrewmen; two more bombers crashed returning to France. The pinpoint attack on the factory prompted Air Ministry to assign No. 504 Squadron at RAF Filton to full-time protection of the facility. Two days later, when the Germans attempted a repeat raid on the factory, No. 504 was waiting and ten Me 110s were shot down.

Despite cold and blustery weather conditions on September 27, Albert Kesselring ordered another massive raid. He expected its proportions would rival the September 15 attack, but aircraft wastage was finally catching up to the Luftwaffe. Its bomber and fighter serviceability had fallen dramatically. Me 109 units were running at 70 percent of capacity. Bomber availability was even worse, below 65 percent. To compensate, Kesselring dispatched groups of Me 110s and Me 109s (the latter carrying single bombs from their fuselage bellies) over Kent and Surrey in an attempt to bludgeon their way to London and exhaust the RAF fighter defences along the way. Accompanying them were fifty-five Ju 88 bombers.

In answer, Keith Park scrambled his fighter squadrons in relays along the route to engage most enemy formations as they approached the coast and to harass them all the way to their intended targets, if not send them retreating to occupied France. For the Canadians of RCAF No. 1 Squadron, this would become the busiest, most successful day of the entire battle, led by one of the outfit's most innovative and experienced flight commanders, F/L Gordon McGregor.

Just after 9 a.m., the Canadians got the first of what would be three scramble calls that day. Their ground crew fired up a dozen Merlin engines, and the squadron's Hurricanes were rapidly airborne. Kesselring's Air Fleet bombers and escorts had already penetrated the first defence force between Maidstone and Tunbridge. Leading "A" Flight, at about 18,000 feet, F/L McGregor spotted thirty or more Ju 88 bombers escorted by as many Me 109s and 110s above them.

"I attacked an enemy bomber straggler," McGregor's combat report stated. "I broke off and . . . proceeded northwest after enemy bombers' formation which was still visible turning west from London. I delivered beam attack . . . on rearmost enemy aircraft. Machine jerked hard, port engine smoked heavily and machine went into steep left-hand spiral dive."[24]

It was a portent of the squadron's overall performance. Blue Section—led by S/L Ernie McNab, with wingmates F/O Bev Christmas and F/O Edward De Peyster Brown (from Coronado, California)—picked out one bomber and sent it diving into the ground. Regaining altitude, McNab joined Polish fighters from No. 303 Squadron to destroy an Me 110. Along the skirmish line, F/O Dal Russel in Caribou Squadron's Green Section was bounced by Me 109s, but quickly turned the tables and fired into one of the German fighters, and then did the same with a Me 110. P/O Pete Lochnan, also flying in Green Section, shared in the destruction of an Me 110 with a

Polish pilot. And Yellow Section F/Os Paul Pitcher and Bob Norris shared destruction of a Heinkel 111 bomber and an Me 110.

As the Canadians landed back at Northolt to rearm and refuel, F/L McGregor got confirmation that the Junkers bomber he'd sent spiralling down was his third victory of the battle, in his fiftieth combat sortie of the war.

The Canadians' banner day was barely beginning. At noon, with just eight serviceable Hurricanes available, RCAF No. 1 scrambled a second time to challenge twenty Me 109s over Gatwick on their way to London. When a Messerschmitt fighter *Schwarm* passed across McGregor's sight line, he fired one burst as his enemy cut left, and then a second when he cut right. The 109 fell away issuing smoke.

The leader of the German fighter escort, Oberstleutnant Ulrich Steinhilper, witnessed his command cut in half, to thirteen aircraft, for the last leg of the sortie. Then, from out of nowhere, he spotted thirty to forty Hurricanes and Spitfires racing toward his flight. He described it as "a wall of aircraft."[25] Steinhilper ordered those who could to evade the RAF fighters by climbing steeply to the point of stalling their Messerschmitts vertically. For those who followed Oblt Steinhilper, the manoeuvre worked; they escaped. The others, seven Me 109s, were shot down. The bomber stream, meanwhile, lost eight Ju 88s. The German sortie had turned into a disaster.

A third scramble at three o'clock put Caribou Squadron up against fifteen Dornier bombers flying at 5,000 feet and virtually overhead at Northolt. McGregor immediately fired into the leaders of the formation. On a second pass, he expended the remainder of his ammunition firing into another Dornier 215. "Starboard motor appeared to stop and return fire stopped.

E/a went into steep diving turn to right," stated his combat report. "I lost sight of the 215. Landed and re-armed at Biggin Hill where [intelligence officer] reported four enemy aircraft down from action in sight of the base."[26]

Even more impressive, RCAF No. 1, with a total of thirteen pilots available, had completed twenty-six sorties during three patrols of daylight operations. They had destroyed seven enemy aircraft, with probable destruction or damage to a further seven. Caribou Squadron had accomplished this while sustaining one injured pilot, one Hurricane destroyed, and two damaged.[27] When his fighter was hit, F/O Sprenger brought it down in a successful forced-landing. However, the morning sortie took the life of P/O Otto Peterson. One of the original RCAF fighter pilots who'd arrived in the UK back in June, Peterson had scored two enemy aircraft destroyed and two damaged in three months of No. 1's combat operations. In the morning debrief with the squadron intelligence officer and flight commanders, it was determined that Peterson had taken direct hits from Me 110s over Kent and died in the crash of his Hurricane.

Over the course of this day, six of No. 1's pilots—McGregor, Christmas, Pitcher, Russel, Yuile, and Brown—had each flown three sorties in seven hours. Among them, they accounted for twelve of the fifteen victories scored by the squadron.[28] By the end of the day, McGregor had recorded his fifty-third combat sortie. And, one day later, he celebrated his thirty-ninth birthday. He was the oldest RCAF fighter pilot in the Battle of Britain.

Earlier on the same afternoon, September 27, S/L Bader led a slightly diminished big wing of four squadrons, including No. 242's Canadians, in pursuit of twenty Me 109s over

Dover. With the sun at their backs, Bader's pilots surprised the German fighters and scattered their already haphazard formation. For the Luftwaffe, it was every man for himself.

The most successful combat report came from P/O John Latta, whose own aircraft had been hit. "My machine sustained damage to the tail and one wing [from] machine-gun fire, but I did not notice," Latta wrote. He latched onto the tail of a Messerschmitt whose pilot barely responded to the attack. "Enemy's idea of evasive tactics very poor—steep climbs and turns only ones noted."[29] Latta landed shells in the 109's fuel tank, and the plane went down in flames. Then he chased another cluster of 109s racing toward France and expended his ammunition knocking down his second enemy aircraft of the sortie.

As well as Latta's two victories, 242's Canadians claimed two more destroyed, one probably destroyed, and two damaged. In total, the wing claimed a dozen Me 109s destroyed. In addition to the German fighters, P/O Noel Stansfeld claimed a Junkers bomber. "I chased an Me 109 across Dover and lost sight of this e/a," he wrote in his report. "Then a Ju 88 crossed my sights and straightened out. I fired a burst at about 600 feet. . . . At about 50 feet my ammunition ran out (Damn it!). . . . I am convinced it had no chance of getting back across the Channel."[30]

Back on the ground at Coltishall station later in the day, the wing received a signal from Air Ministry that P/O Stan Turner and P/O Noel Stansfeld had been awarded DFCs. Willie McKnight would receive a bar to his DFC. Quite rightly, McKnight was proud of his record and bragged in a letter home: "I've got over twenty-one confirmed victories now, and if we keep up like this, hope to increase that before long.

The C.O. [Bader] was awarded the DSO last week . . . We're among the top three high-scoring squadrons in the service."[31]

By late September, McKnight had passed the seven-hundred-hour mark in his pilot's log, four hundred of them on Hurricanes alone. He concluded his letter to a friend in Calgary by boasting about Hurricanes being the best fighters in the RAF, and considered himself "an old timer in the flying game."*

Daylight operations had been a complete shambles for the Luftwaffe on September 27, with the loss of fifty-seven aircraft, including nineteen Me 109s, twenty-one Me 110s, and seventeen bombers. In total that day, the Luftwaffe had lost 133 aircraft, a number surpassed only on September 15 and August 15.[32]

Notified of the day's action and result, Prime Minister Churchill called it "the third great and glorious day for Fighter Command during the course of the Battle of Britain."[33]

* * *

The top fighter pilot on that "great and glorious day," Dal Russel, had destroyed two enemy aircraft, shared in the destruction of another, and damaged a fourth. His September 27 sorties marked the tenth straight day Russel and his squadron comrades had scrambled to meet the enemy in daylight operations. To an outsider, such prowess would suggest

---

* On January 12, 1941, during a series of "rhubarbs," low-level rapid strikes against German targets in occupied France, Hurricanes flown by P/O Willie McKnight and P/O John Latta were hit by anti-aircraft fire; neither pilot survived.

intense focus, extraordinary endurance, and, if nothing else, a killer instinct. Like most of the Canadians rushing up to face danger in the skies each day of the battle, however, theirs was a sense of duty, the result of accumulated experience, and an acute understanding that if they didn't do the job, nobody else would. Between September 28 and October 10, F/O Russel completed sixteen more ops, most uneventful, but still recording skirmishes. In a letter home, he revealed the toll all this was taking. "It is awfully hard to write when we are so darn busy, as we have been lately," he wrote, "as we get so very jittery and fogged out. My nerves are pretty well shot now."

Medical officers at Northolt got a strong reading of the way the jitters and fog played out among the front-line air and ground crew members. At best, they called it "battle fatigue." At worst, it was grounds for anxiety leave. A generation later, Russel's symptoms would have a new label—post-traumatic stress disorder—and be considered as debilitating and legitimate as flesh lacerations, fractured bones, or third-degree burns to the body. In early October, Russel wrote home again, but the letter took several days to complete: "Sorry I couldn't finish this two days ago, but we were called into the air and I have been so terribly tired since, that I just couldn't sit down and write. We have so many people either sick or wounded, that I have not had an hour off for over two weeks. . . . Today we were allowed to sleep in, for the first time in weeks."[34]

For a number of other Canadian aircrew that summer, recovery would require more than a full night's sleep. Fighter pilots Corbett, Hyde, and Desloges, who'd bailed out of burning aircraft during sorties on August 31, all remained in various states of recovery in London-area hospitals. Desloges had barely survived the attack on his Hurricane that day, when a Messerschmitt shell smashed through the Perspex of his fighter, tore his radio earphones, oxygen mask, goggles, and helmet from his head, burned his face, and sent shrapnel into one eye and down the side of his body. At 10,000 feet, the former University of Ottawa star athlete managed to extricate himself from the blazing cockpit, pull his ripcord, and come safely to earth near Gravesend.[35] Recovery would require numerous surgeries and specialized rehabilitation at Queen Victoria Hospital outside London.

Two years earlier, the RAF had appointed Dr. Archibald McIndoe as its principal consultant in plastic surgery, and transformed a one-time army hut behind Queen Victoria Hospital into the Centre for Plastic and Jaw Surgery. McIndoe's experience in pathological anatomy and reconstructive facial surgery put him in the front lines of treatment of pilots with severe combat burns and disfigurement.

In order for both Hurricanes and Spitfires to achieve a rapid rate of ascent, designers had positioned the fighter's fuel tank directly below and in front of the cockpit. In essence, the fighter pilot was sitting on hundreds of litres of fuel. Protective rubber or metal encasements around the tank added too much weight to the aircraft, cutting its maximum range by as much as 20 percent; and that kind of performance sacrifice RAF officials were not willing to make. When ignited by enemy fire, however, the resulting cockpit inferno left the pilot facing what they described as "orange death."[36]

The pattern of burn injury became so prevalent among aircrew patients that it received its own designation: airman's burn, "due to the sudden exposure of unprotected parts of the body to intense dry heat or flame as though the patient were thrust into a furnace for a few seconds and withdrawn."[37]

If they survived, pilots lost fingers, eyelids, hair, nose cartilage, jaw bones, and facial skin.

Apart from the medical challenges that McIndoe and his surgical team faced—pioneering ways to rebuild human faces and appendages—they also chose a new path in the psychological treatment of airmen who'd received severe wounds. They persuaded Air Ministry to waive the regulation that aircrew needing ninety or more days of treatment be discharged from the RAF. Inside the hospital, burn patients were allowed or encouraged to wear uniforms, but military rank was temporarily suspended so that pilots of various ranks could talk freely with peers. As much as possible, McIndoe's staff decided, the burn ward should feel like a clubhouse, with beer and sherry available and post-op nurses selected both for professional credentials and attractiveness.[38]

It took some adjusting for Nursing Sister Hilda Empey on her first shift in Dr. McIndoe's burn ward. Born in Germany in 1917 and having immigrated to Canada with her family in 1925, Empey became a trained nurse before the war. As a nursing sister posted overseas to Britain, she felt thrown into the deep end when assigned to the burn ward at Queen Victoria Hospital in East Grinstead. The first person she met was RAF patient Les Wilkins. Air combat burns had left him with no fingers, no nose, no mouth, and no eyelids. She nearly cried at the sight of him, but composed herself as he initiated the conversation.

"What's your name?" Wilkins asked.

"Nursing Sister Empey," she said.

"No. What's your first name?"

"Well, we don't know each other well enough," Empey improvised. She learned from him that in place of the fingers he'd lost in a burning airplane, Dr. McIndoe's surgeons had cut incisions farther up his hands beyond his knuckles to create new digits to give him some dexterity. When she turned to continue her rounds, she felt Wilkins pinch her behind with knuckled fingers that felt like a vice. Tears came to her eyes and she lost her temper. "Next time you do that, I'll punch you in the nose," she said.

"I ain't got one," Wilkins smiled.

"I can wait," she answered.[39]*

Later, the aircrew patients gave themselves the nickname "the Guinea Pig Club," creating a social support network for injured aircrew and their families. Their determination to keep their experience in perspective included such sardonic decisions as choosing a club secretary who "couldn't write because his fingers had been burned off," and a treasurer with such debilitating burns to his legs that "he couldn't abscond with [club] money."[40] The Guinea Pigs dubbed their masterful doctor "the Maestro."

Because of the growing number of Canadian patients treated at Dr. McIndoe's clinic, he eventually invited Canadian plastic surgeon Albert Ross Tilley to join the hospital staff. Born in 1904 in Bowmanville, Ontario, Tilley graduated from the University of Toronto's medical school in 1929 and furthered his surgical studies in Vienna, Edinburgh, and New York. He opened a private medical practice conducting plastic surgery in Toronto in 1935, while also serving as a reservist medical officer with the RCAF's City of Toronto Squadron.

---

* Forty years later, Hilda Empey (Moore) and Les Wilkins met during a reunion in Canada. She noted, "You've got a nose now. You'd better behave yourself." And they both laughed over memories of the pinching incident.

He had served as principal medical officer at RCAF head-quarters in London before joining McIndoe's staff at Queen Victoria Hospital treating burn victims of the Allied air forces.

Medical treatment of warriors wounded by burns had not changed significantly from methods used during the Great War. The principal approach was to apply a coagulating agent such as gentian violet or tannic acid to dry the wound and prevent infection. But that treatment often resulted in deformity and loss of function.

Tilley pioneered a three-phase form of burn management: *tulle gras* or atraumatic dressings (to preserve surfaces for grafting), saline bath (to clean wounds and keep them flexible), and sulphonamide dusting (to prevent sepsis or infection). With the wound healed and prepared for skin grafting, Tilley could reconstruct facial features, enabling patients to return to a normal state of existence.

"Only God can create a face," Tilley once said, but for scores of airmen disfigured by war burns, the doctor became a close substitute for God. He was particularly insistent on rebuilding ears, "else how could a man hold his glasses on?"[41]

Most reconstructions required between ten and fifty operations, or about eight surgeries per year, with patients coming and going to the hospital for several years. Tilley turned into a workaholic, dedicating himself both to operating rooms and the promotion of his patients' physical and emotional healing. Often, after performing intricate surgeries all day at the hospital, he would rest briefly at his living quarters before making his way back to the burn ward to check on his patients' progress.

Medical journals applauded Tilley as "a trailblazing pioneer of patient empowerment" for his view that the reconstruction of a patient's spirit was as important as rebuilding

275

his body.[42] Both McIndoe and Tilley believed that burn treatment had to include reintegration of patients to normal life. They encouraged the men they were treating to leave the hospital at will, and for local families to welcome the Guinea Pigs into their homes as guests. "Our biggest job wasn't taking out sutures or putting on bandages," Nursing Sister Empey said. "It was to get them out to the town, to the pub. . . . The people in town had them out to their homes. East Grinstead was known as the little town with the big heart."[43]

During the Second World War, doctors McIndoe and Tilley and the Queen Victoria Hospital burn clinic staff treated 649 Guinea Pigs, 176 of them Canadian airmen. Remembered Hilda Empey, "It was the highlight of my career."

In November 1940, the *Toronto Star* published a photograph showing five of the RCAF fighter pilots following their recovery from face and hand burns sustained in combat over Britain. Headlined "Fliers of 1st fighter squadron, come home,"[44] the story showed fighter pilots Bruce Millar, Jack Kerwin, Eric Beardmore, Jean-Paul Desloges, and Hartland Molson, all facing the camera. Their smiles likely said more about their relief at getting home than about the wounds they'd sustained. "There's nothing fatal about my wounds," Molson wrote about being shot down October 5, 1940. "A spread of small pieces of metal which burned me from shoulder to leg. . . . Otherwise, the damage was largely superficial."[45]

Such an attitude among the survivors served as a testament to the dedicated work of surgeons Archibald McIndoe and Ross Tilley.

* * *

The first days of October saw the Battle of Britain enter its final phase. At the Rominter Heide, the reichsmarschall's hunting reserve in East Prussia, Hermann Göring met with his star pilot, Major Adolf Galland. The Luftwaffe fighter ace reiterated his last conversation with Hitler. The Luftwaffe may have destroyed large numbers of British fighters, but its enemy had shown no decrease in strength nor hint of flagging morale. Just the opposite, the RAF had successfully beaten back waves of German bombers and fighters, blow for blow. The Luftwaffe's losses had more than doubled the RAF's losses since September 15. As an immediate consequence, Albert Kesselring declared an end to mass raids in daylight hours. Instead, he dispatched formations of thirty bombers during the day with escorts of two hundred to three hundred fighters.

F/L Johnny Kent was among the first to recognize the change in Luftwaffe tactics. He scrambled with his Polish wing-mates as well as some RCAF fighters on October 1, 1940. The Canadians were ordered to take on the fighter escorts, while Kent's No. 303 Squadron had orders to attack the bombers. Instinctively, Kent opened his throttle to attack with speed, and in a matter of minutes he had outdistanced his own squadron and fellow Canadians.

"It came as a distinct shock, when, just as I was closing with the enemy, which I'd recognized as [Me] 109s in an unusual formation, a stream of tracer bullets streaked past just above the top of my cockpit canopy."[46] The experienced flight commander broke to the right and down to avoid further enemy fire, and when he got reoriented, Kent realized he was all alone with a mass of enemy fighters. He kept turning and applying his rudder to skid his Hurricane across the sky, avoiding shells from the Messerschmitts. Suddenly, four of them conveniently passed in front of him. He fired a burst at the rearmost one and it went down with smoke pouring from its fuselage. A voice came over Kent's radio.

"Have you engaged enemy yet?" a controller asked.

"I think they're going to engage me at any moment," Kent reported back.

Strangely, few of the other enemy fighters seemed interested in taking him on. As he prepared for engagement from all angles, he sensed he had a distinct advantage. There were so many of them, maybe forty fighters, they had to be careful not to hit one another. On his side, he could fire at any aircraft he saw. He fired at another 109 and it disappeared in a sheet of flame. After several more bursts from his guns, the remaining Germans climbed, formed up, and headed east toward France.

Back at Northolt, the station commander, Stanley Vincent, had heard Kent's exchange with the controller on the radio and congratulated Kent for alerting the station to the sizeable fighter formation. He was credited with two Me 109 kills, bringing his total number of victories to four. His No. 303 Polish Squadron had stacked up an even more impressive score: in six hectic weeks that summer, the Poles had destroyed 126 enemy aircraft, a record unrivalled by any other squadron. Ten days later, Air Ministry told Kent he would be promoted to lead RAF No. 92 Squadron and receive a Distinguished Flying Cross. Of course, he was an old hand at award procedures at Buckingham Palace; he'd been there to receive his Air Force Cross in February 1939, which seemed a lifetime ago.

The tide of the battle had definitely ebbed. Douglas Bader, squadron leader for No. 242 and proponent of the big wing, was quick to realize it. The last thing he wanted for his Duxford Wing was less engagement with bombers and fewer dogfights with Messerschmitt fighters, but in October, Heinkels, Dorniers, and Junkers rarely appeared over the Thames Estuary. Instead, the Luftwaffe sent packs of 109s carrying small bombs in makeshift bomb-racks on their bellies. They arrived at top speed and high altitude, dropped their payloads, and just as quickly disappeared into those thick autumn clouds. With the German fighters flying above 25,000 feet, Bader's Hurricanes found it tougher to climb, catch, and challenge them.

Compared to the roar and fury of August and September, these fighter attacks, for Bader, were anticlimactic. One evening during that first week of October, however, he was leading the wing in a routine patrol over the estuary and discovered his radio had died. He signalled to his second to take over the patrol and peeled away for home. A few minutes later, a 109 emerged from a cloud about four hundred yards ahead and climbing. The enemy fighter levelled off, not noticing Bader on his tail. Nearly licking his lips, Bader closed to attack when another Hurricane dropped out of the clouds in front of Bader, right in his path, and fired a burst into the 109. There was a flash in the Messerschmitt cockpit as the enemy plane caught fire, rolled on its back, and plunged earthward. Bader flew alongside the Hurricane and recognized the interloper as friend and fighter comrade "Butcher" Barton from No. 249 Squadron. The Canadian had beaten Bader to the punch.*

---

* F/L Robert "Butcher" Barton was awarded a DFC on October 22, 1940. The citation applauded his leadership and "skill displayed on September 28, when his [No. 249] squadron destroyed twenty enemy aircraft . . . Barton destroyed four [of them]."

"When you decide to attack," Barton said, "it's like you're in a boxing match. You've got to be quick."[47] To add insult to injury, Barton lifted two rude fingers in a V with his palm facing inwards. It wasn't often anybody got away with an "up yours" to Douglas Bader.

In early October at Bentley Priory, Fighter Command headquarters, ACM Hugh Dowding finally felt sure his fighters were gaining superiority in British skies. Days were shortening and autumn cloud, fog, and rain were bringing the curtain down on further mass daytime raids, as well as Hitler's plans to invade England. Dowding had trusted his instincts that the battle would be won only "by science thoughtfully applied to operational requirements."[48] He also credited his master tactician, Keith Park, whose forces, although horribly outnumbered, had outwitted and outfought a determined German enemy. While Dowding was elevated to the position of Knight Grand Commander of the Bath, he would soon be retired and replaced by Sholto Douglas as commander-in-chief of Fighter Command. Likewise, Park would be replaced by Trafford Leigh-Mallory and relegated to Training Command. "The two victors thus realized the sad truth," wrote RAF fighter ace Peter Townsend, "that men are seldom grateful for their saviors."[49]

Far from achieving his objective of crushing the English homeland, Adolf Hitler now accepted that British resolve was intact. On October 12, he officially postponed the amphibious invasion of England, at least until spring. By doing so, the führer admitted that the UK would remain "a base for continued prosecution of the war," a safe harbour that would send Arctic convoys to keep the Soviet Union in the war, a launch point for fighting the German armies in North Africa, an aerodrome for Allied air forces that would bomb German industries and cities into ruins, and an armory that would eventually support an invasion of Europe and liberate it from Nazi occupation. Far from a defeated and occupied island, Britain would remain an aggravating thorn in Hitler's side and ultimately bring about his demise.

The first week of October brought word of overdue recognition for RCAF No. 1 Fighter Squadron. The station got word that S/L Ernie McNab would receive a Distinguished Flying Cross. Air Ministry announced that F/L Gordon McGregor and F/O Dal Russel would also receive DFCs. Despite the accolades, however, the squadron's mental and physical condition had bottomed out. On October 7, Captain John Nodwell of the Royal Canadian Army Medical Corps reported to his superiors on the exhausted condition of the pilots at RCAF No. 1. "There is a definite air of tension and they are unable to relax as they are practically on constant call," Nodwell wrote.[50]

The next day, Fighter Command informed the Canadians that they would be moving to a station at Prestwick, Scotland. On the afternoon of October 10, seventeen Hurricanes took off, heading north. Grounded by colds and a variety of other maladies, the commanding officer, F/O Paul Pitcher, and the intelligence staff were all loaded into cars to depart Northolt for the last time. With that, No. 1's front-line action in the Battle of Britain ended. Caribou Squadron had entered the battle on August 17, made its first kill on August 26, and in fifty-four days shot down thirty German planes, probably destroyed another eight, and damaged thirty-five. It had sustained the loss of three pilots (Edwards, Smither, and Peterson) killed-in-action, and ten wounded, mainly in flaming cockpits.

On their first night in Prestwick, the squadron diarist noted that living quarters were comfortable, the food excellent, and "the war seems very far away." Perhaps a more genuine indication of that distance was realized on November 8, when the squadron gathered at a local hockey arena for a friendly scrimmage. The game was billed as "Les Canadiens versus the Ayr Raiders" (Canadian civilians living in the nearby Scottish town).

"We were rather embarrassed . . . and outclassed," recorded the diarist. "However, after securing a lead of seven goals to one, the Ayr Raiders lifted the pressure in order to make the game interesting. Final score, 10 to 6."[51]

No casualties were sustained on either side.

CHAPTER ELEVEN

"THE BEST DAYS OF THEIR LIVES"

F EW CANADIANS WERE AS WELL TRAVELLED IN RAF SERVICE those first two years of the war as Johnny Kent. He'd been the youngest commercial pilot in Canada (licensed in 1935), but by the time the Battle of Britain ended, the seasoned aviator from Winnipeg had served as a test pilot, a photo reconnaissance pilot, a fighter pilot, and flight commander with RAF No. 303 Polish Fighter Squadron. In six hectic weeks, Kent had co-commanded the Polish squadron to the best combat record in the Royal Air Force. Kent himself had four victories and was awarded an Air Force Cross and a Distinguished Flying Cross. In October 1940, he was promoted to command of No. 92 Fighter Squadron in combat operations over Britain and eventually France.

Notwithstanding all this recognition, the Poles did him one better. Before Kent left No. 303, his Polish charges awarded "Kentowski" the ribbon of the *Krzyz Walecznych* (Cross of Valour), and insisted he have it sewn on his tunic as they celebrated. Equally impressive, Flight Lieutenant Kent survived his send-off party. "I managed to hold my own," he wrote, "and at three o'clock in the morning, the only two left on our feet were [Jan] Zumbach, my number two, and myself—and I saw him to bed, a feat which increased my reputation with the Poles quite considerably."[1]

After just three months with his new squadron, Kent reunited with his former comrades as wing leader of the Polish Wing at Northolt. He also found himself rubbing shoulders with celebrity on several occasions in 1941. In June, he received an invitation to Windsor Castle to meet the royal family. Later, he visited the prime minister at Chequers to discuss defending RAF airfields against airborne attacks. So intent on knowing how Allied aircrew would deal with such a threat, Churchill drove out to Kent's station at Northolt to discover its readiness for himself. At an inopportune moment, he gestured to the sky and shouted, "There are 5,000 paratroops coming down. What are you going to do?"[2]

"Sound the alarm, sir," said the guards major at the station.

"Well get on with it," the prime minister bellowed, before presenting himself at one of the No. 303 Polish Squadron's dispersal huts with Kent in tow. The squadron's pilots ignored the alarm and gathered around Churchill, whom they considered a god.

"What would these men be doing in an attack?" asked Churchill.

"They'd be in the air, sir," said Kent.

Less worried about defending the station than about capturing the moment with Churchill, Polish ace Jan Zumbach revealed the squadron's history book and asked their guest to autograph one of its pages.

"Why should I sign it?" Churchill snapped.

"Well, sir," said Kent, "His Majesty saw fit to sign it on the preceding page."

Churchill turned the page, acknowledged the "George, R.I." entry, and with an amused twinkle, said "All right" and signed.

In contrast to Kent's good standing in the eyes of RAF commanders, Air Ministry, and even the Prime Minister's Office, his squadron comrades, the Poles, never seemed to receive similar respect. Their 126 confirmed destroyed enemy aircraft versus fifteen Hurricanes lost (in forty-two days) was the best claim/loss ratio in the RAF in 1940.[3] And yet, back in the spring, RAF commanders had considered the Poles second-class recruits. They had to be retrained: how to measure speed in miles not kilometres, fuel in gallons not litres, and how to fly in traditional RAF vic formation in combat. "The British waste so much of our time with their childish exercises, when all of us had already won [our] wings," wrote Jan Zumbach.[4]

The RAF seriously underestimated the proficiency of the Polish fighter pilots. Most of those in No. 303 Squadron had flown combat operations over Poland (1939) and France (1940) and survived; of the three RAF officers (Ronald Kellett, Johnny Kent, and Athol Forbes) assigned to command and teach the Poles, none had actually seen the fierce combat their understudies had. What's more, unlike the training syllabus for air-to-air gunnery in the British Commonwealth Air Training Plan in Canada—with aircraft towing drogue targets at fixed speeds and altitudes for gunners to shoot at—Polish training flights involved chasing a weighted target tossed from a cockpit, firing at it in real time and in three dimensions, as both target and plane descended.

The RAF had also dictated that fighter aircraft harmonize wing-mounted guns into a cone of fire at four hundred yards ahead, and employ deflection shooting (anticipating where the target would be) when attacking enemy aircraft. Soon after their commanders declared their squadron operational, the Poles had their Hurricanes' guns harmonized to two hundred yards. That reduced the effect of gravity on the bullets' trajectory, allowed deeper penetration of German aircraft armour, and increased the number of hits per gun burst. Some called shooting at that range suicidal; the Poles called it hitting the target where it was, not where it might be. Finally, no one knew how long the war would last in 1940. And while the British could turn to their home population and the Commonwealth to replenish their fighter pilot losses, the Poles could not. In order to win, the Poles had to survive.* "Polish fighter pilot lives could not be given away cheaply," stated Mirek Szelestowski, later a flight commander with No. 303.[5]

In all, twenty-nine Polish fighter pilots lost their lives in the Battle of Britain. Yet when the war was won, even that sacrifice was insufficient to gain the Poles equality.

As plans gelled for a first anniversary VE Day parade in 1946, none of the organizers—Air Ministry, the RAF, not even the politicians at Westminster—chose to invite Polish pilots who'd served in the Battle of Britain, nor, for that matter, any of the Polish forces on the Allied side. At the Yalta summit in the summer of 1945, British prime minister Clement Attlee had agreed to recognize the Soviet Union's control and

---

* One additional survival record achieved by the Polish squadron: No. 303 was the only RAF single-seat fighter unit not to lose a CO or a flight commander killed or hospitalized during the Battle of Britain.

occupation of eastern Poland as the spoils of war. So as not to insult Soviet premier Joseph Stalin, British authorities chose to exclude the Free Polish forces from the parade. Air Force veterans in Britain and across the Commonwealth were outraged. They told Prime Minister Attlee that if the Poles didn't march in the parade, neither would they. Former Air Chief Marshal Hugh Dowding commented, "Had it not been for the magnificent work of the Polish squadrons and their unsurpassed gallantry, I hesitate to say that the outcome of the battle would have been the same."[6] And the wartime commanding officer of No. 303 Squadron Ronald Kellett added, "No squadron from the Empire could equal the courage and skill of our pilots, no bombing could daunt our airmen."[7]

In response to the uproar, British authorities agreed to allow some Poles to participate in the parade; they sent out twenty-five invitations. It was too little too late. None of Poland's formations, her soldiers, her tankers, her sailors, her airmen, marched in the parade. Canadian squadron leader Johnny Kent's estimation of his Polish comrades spoke volumes. "Britain must never forget how much she owes to the loyalty, indomitable spirit, and sacrifice of those Polish fliers," he wrote. "They were our staunchest Allies in our darkest days."[8]

* * *

Following his visit to the three squadrons sharing the airfield at RAF Northolt in late September 1940, Canadian air marshal Billy Bishop met in Mayfair with British parliamentary undersecretary for air Harold Balfour. "Our fellows are getting pretty tired," Bishop told him.

"I know," Balfour said. "But I'm afraid they'll have to stick it out a bit longer."[9]

Indeed, as Captain John Nodwell had noted in his October medical assessment, "The pilots go to work with forced enthusiasm and appear to be suffering from strain and general tiredness."[10] He also told his superiors that the pilots of RCAF No. 1 Squadron had received no official leave since their arrival in England nearly four months earlier.

The medical officer likely knew but did not share an important factor about the Canadians: their age. Caribou Squadron fighter pilots were generally older than the average age of those serving in other Allied air forces that summer. Flight Lieutenant Gordon McGregor had just celebrated his thirty-ninth birthday; he was the oldest Canadian in battle. S/L Ernie McNab was right behind at thirty-four, Flying Officer Deane Nesbitt at thirty, and F/L Vaughan Corbett at twenty-nine. F/O Paul Pitcher, at twenty-seven, was also well above the twenty-year average age of fighter pilots in the Battle of Britain.[11]

"We were old, untrained, and frightened," Pitcher recalled of his earliest sorties with the squadron. "Fatigue set in quickly. We were at it all the time."[12]

F/O Hartland Molson, at thirty-three, was also among the eldest combatants in the battle that summer.* "We called ourselves the Tired Businessmen's Squadron," Molson said.[13] He'd flown sixty-two sorties with No. 1 Squadron between August 17 and October 5, when he was shot down, barely escaping a burning Hurricane. Released from hospital in November, he was assigned duties at RCAF headquarters in Ottawa.

---

* Elsewhere in the RAF, in 1940, Douglas Bader was thirty, as was Sailor Malan, and Peter Townsend was twenty-six.

Tired businessmen maybe, but not retiring warriors. Canada's elder statesmen in the Battle of Britain still had plenty of service to give the war. F/L McGregor assumed command of a second RCAF fighter squadron, renumbered No. 402 in March 1941, leading the first Canadian fighter sweep in northern France on March 15. He would serve as director of RCAF Air Staff, command a wing in Alaska, be awarded an Order of the British Empire (OBE), command RCAF No. 126 Wing, and fly his last sortie (destroying an enemy locomotive) on March 28, 1945.

S/L McNab, the RCAF's first ace and first pilot decorated for combat, came home to lead the Eastern Air Command station at Dartmouth in 1941, and at the end of the war became a member of the Order of the British Empire.

F/L Corbett received a DFC in 1942, returning to Canada later that year. As group captain, he died in a flying accident in the winter of 1945. F/O Pitcher took command of RCAF No. 417 Squadron when it was posted to Egypt; he became the first to spearhead a Canadian fighter squadron in North Africa. After the summer of combat over the UK, F/O Deane Nesbitt commanded fighter wings in Alaska, Ottawa, and with the Tactical Air Force during the liberation of Northwest Europe, and in particular during the Battle of the Bulge.

F/O Dal Russel, decorated with a DFC at the same ceremony as McNab, led squadrons on both sides of the Atlantic for the rest of the war. He also made celluloid history in 1941 when Warner Brothers came to Canada to film *Captains of the Clouds*, a feature-length movie about Canadians' contribution to the British Commonwealth Air Training Plan; it starred Jimmy Cagney, Dennis Morgan, Brenda Marshall, and Billy Bishop (as himself). Russel's role in the movie was villainous.

Toward the end of the film, he piloted a Hurricane (masquer-
ading as a Messerschmitt) attacking Ferry Command bombers
en route to Britain. When the filming was over, for his own
amusement, Russel buzzed a few main streets in Halifax to see
if anyone was paying attention. The black crosses and swastika
markings on his fighter aircraft turned plenty of heads before
he disappeared into the clouds.

Even as the Battle of Britain phase of the war came to
an end, alumni of RAF No. 242 All-Canadian Squadron
stayed active and loyal to their commanding officer, Douglas
Bader. P/O Willie McKnight kept up his break-neck pace,
racking up six and a half destroyed enemy aircraft during the
battle. On November 5, while patrolling over Gravesend, he
broke away from the formation and climbed to chase Me 109s
above. His combat report revealed an unexpected twist. "One
Me 109 dived down and . . . I gave one burst from approximately
150 yards," he reported. The German aircraft began spew-
ing smoke and oil that covered McKnight's machine. Peering
through the debris, McKnight saw the enemy pilot waggle the
109's wings. "I flew up alongside and signaled him to land. He
however opened his hood and jumped out."[14]

The point of the message was apparently lost in translation.

No. 242 got one new Canadian acquisition, P/O Roland
Dibnah from Winnipeg. He'd formerly served with RAF No. 1
Squadron with one destroyed Me 110 among his nine claimed
victories. Perhaps Dibnah's most important win occurred in
early 1941, when he and his Hurricane survived a vicious
January snowstorm.

Bader's squadron suffered more than its share of losses
in the immediate aftermath of the long summer siege, however. On October 26, RAF searchers discovered the body of

P/O Neil Campbell, who had disappeared in action off Yarmouth in the middle of the month. P/O Norris Hart was shot down and killed on November 5.

In the new year, McKnight and P/O John Latta were lost to anti-aircraft fire during a rhubarb operation off the French coast. Between them, McKnight and Latta had destroyed twenty-plus enemy aircraft. McKnight had earned a DFC and bar, Latta a DFC. In February, P/O Marvin Brown was killed in a flying accident. Weeks later, after receiving a DFC from the King at Buckingham Palace, F/L Hugh Tamblyn was shot down over the sea; he survived the crash but died of exposure before rescuers could find him. Meantime, Bader himself was transferred away as squadron leader to RAF No. 145 Squadron. That stuck in Stan Turner's craw. "Look here, Sir," said Turner, poking his pipe stem into the chest of Air Vice-Marshal Leigh-Mallory, "you can't go and post our CO away, because we won't work for anyone else."[15]

Bader soon requested that Turner be posted with him at No. 145, which prompted Leigh-Mallory to say, "I'm glad you asked for Turner because he's getting to be a nuisance objecting to flying with anyone else."[16] Set in his ways, often prickly, but a savvy survivor, P/O Turner amassed a leading 1,125 hours and 35 minutes of combat time;[17] he fought in the war from start to finish.

As if S/L Bader's wartime career wasn't colourful enough, 1941 brought new and unexpected chapters. In the first eight months of the year, he flew sixty-two separate sweeps over France. His combat reports continued to bristle with victories. On August 9, during a dogfight over Le Touquet, the tail section of his Spitfire was virtually blown away. In his attempt to bail out, one of his prosthetic legs got wedged in the cockpit.

He released his parachute, which snapped the strap holding the prosthesis to his body. He was pulled free. Safely on the ground, but captured, he spent the rest of the war, three and a half years, in such notorious prisons as Stalag Luft III (home of the Great Escape) and Colditz Castle. He was liberated in May 1945.

Back home at war's end, Bader organized and led, on September 15, 1945, a flypast over London of the warbirds that had delivered the victory. It was the fifth anniversary of Battle of Britain Day. "Once over the city," wrote his biographer Paul Brickhill in *Reach for the Sky*, "[Bader] remembered the battle and nostalgically wanted to fight it again."[18]

* * *

Unlike Bader, none of the Millidgeville Trio survived the war. All three young aviators from New Brunswick, who'd earned their private pilots' licences at the Saint John Flying Club in the 1930s, saw action in the Battle of Britain. Duncan Hewitt, who'd travelled to the UK in 1936 and found work as an aero-engineer before receiving RAF training and a posting to No. 501 Squadron flying Hurricanes, died attacking a Dornier bomber on July 12. Harry Hamilton, whom the Saint John Flying Club's chief instructor had declared an "exceptional" pilot, died in an ambush while serving with No. 257 Fighter Squadron on August 29. And Pat Sclanders, who'd soloed at fifteen, becoming the youngest licensed pilot in Canada, died in action serving with Bader's Duxford Wing on September 9.

Hamilton was buried in Folkstone New Cemetery in Kent. Hewitt, whose body was never retrieved from the English Channel, is remembered on the Runnymede Memorial.

Sclanders's body was interred in the Commonwealth War Graves Commission graveyard at St. Luke Churchyard in Surrey.

Fifty years later, Frank Starmer—the boy who'd seen Sclanders's Hurricane come down near his Thames Haven family farm—by then in his sixties, led the Croydon Aviation Research Group to the crash site. Equipped with aircraft identity documents, a dig licence from the Ministry of Defence, and a metal detector, the archaeologists located Sclanders's Hurricane. They found airframe fragments, aluminum melt, Perspex fragments, and spent .303-inch cartridge cases. Finally, the crew found the aircraft ID plate for Hurricane P-3087. This was where P/O Pat Sclanders's final operation had ended. "There has never been a snappier, more determined crowd of fighter pilots," Bader said of the Canadians in No. 242, adding that it had been an honour to lead them.[19]

In the years following the fiftieth anniversary of Battle of Britain Day, eyewitnesses to those historic 113 days of aerial combat over the UK began to disappear. Simple arithmetic meant that any fighter pilot in his twenties or thirties in 1940 was in his eighties or nineties as the twenty-first century began. About that time, an Ontario-based businessman, and aviation book and artifact collector, named Michael Parry undertook a personal tribute to the memory of Canadians who'd served in the RCAF in the Second World War. When RCAF veteran and author Arthur Bishop wrote and published his book *The Splendid Hundred*, about Canadians who'd flown in the Battle of Britain, Parry committed to delivering copies to as many Air Force veterans as he could find. He hand-delivered autographed copies to a number of Canadian Battle of Britain vets, several of whom had served in RCAF No. 1 Fighter Squadron in 1940. Parry always stretched his visits with the vets into conversations over dinner or casual interviews on a backyard deck. When he delivered Bishop's book to Charles Trevena, who'd joined No. 1 Squadron in September 1940, Parry posed a request he often made to Air Force vets: "Tell me something I won't read in a history book."[20]

After some reflection, Trevena asked, "You ever heard of Otto Peterson?"

"Well, he, Ross Smither, and Bob Edwards, all with No. 1 RCAF, were shot down during the Battle of Britain," Parry said. "Return fire from a German bomber or fighter."

"No," Trevena said. "He was shot down by one of us."

"How do you know?"

"I was there at the debriefing."

Parry explained that Trevena carefully reconstructed the morning operation the Canadian squadron had conducted on September 27, 1940, perhaps the most hectic but successful sorties of the battle. "When you're dogfighting, your attention is on that plane you're trying to shoot down," explained Trevena. "You're aware of all other planes around you. Then, five minutes later it's all over. Everybody's gone."

Trevena said that during the morning sortie, F/O Molson was firing at a German fighter when Otto Peterson flew right into his gunfire stream. Details of the incident didn't become clear until the Canadians had returned to base and attended the normal post-op debriefing. There was chatter about this fighter destroyed, that one damaged, and so on. Then the squadron intelligence officer did a head count.

"Where's Otto Peterson?" he asked.

Trevena said Molson put up his hand and explained the accidental shooting. Within seconds, flight commander

Gordon McGregor was leading Molson into an adjoining room. With the door open so the rest of the squadron heard him, McGregor told Molson what happened: "You did *not* shoot Peterson down," he said emphatically. "He was shot down by Nazi fighters. That's what happened." And that's the way everybody would explain it from then on.

Sometime after he'd heard Trevena's account, Parry spent an evening with another close RCAF acquaintance, Paul Pitcher, who'd served with No. 1 Squadron throughout the Battle of Britain. He chose a quiet moment when the two of them were alone to corroborate the story. "Is it true that Otto Peterson was accidentally shot down by another Canadian fighter pilot?"

Parry said Pitcher took a long sip of the drink in his hand, looked him straight in the eye, and said, "Yes, it's true." Pitcher verified that Peterson had flown his Hurricane into a concentration of fire with devastating impact. It killed him outright. There was no radio transmission from him that he'd been hit. It was over in a second.

The official RCAF combat report stated, "Peterson . . . was shot down and killed."[21] It did not acknowledge friendly fire. Paul Pitcher and Michael Parry discussed how painful it had been for all members of Caribou Squadron to carry that memory around for a lifetime. They agreed it could have happened to anybody.

* * *

Early 1942 was a hectic time. The Americans were still dealing with the aftershock of the Japanese surprise attack on Pearl Harbor. The British were overwhelmed by the Japanese capture of Hong Kong and Singapore, as well as German

U-boats running roughshod over North Atlantic shipping convoys. Erwin Rommel's new offensive was playing out in North
Africa, Malta was under siege in the Mediterranean, and
Hitler's armies were at the gates of Moscow. In the midst of all
this, Prime Minister Churchill faced a vote of no confidence in
the British House of Commons. Defeat of the Luftwaffe in the
Battle of Britain seemed a faint memory. To bolster support for
his government, Churchill shuffled his war cabinet.

Among a number of changes, Churchill anticipated bringing Max Aitken, Lord Beaverbrook, in as minister of war
production. But Beaverbrook's physical health had deterior-
ated. One night, the two men convened at Churchill's Annexe
(above the Cabinet War Rooms) in London. The prime minister was vexed by a persistent noise. "Let someone go out and
stop that cat mewing," he complained.[22] He soon realized he
was hearing the ill effects of Beaverbrook's worsening asthma.
He noted in his diary that Beaverbrook was suffering from a
nervous breakdown. Only twelve days into his new cabinet
position, Beaverbrook resigned, describing his time serving
Churchill as "twenty-one months of high adventure."[23]

Indeed, during the Battle of Britain, Max Aitken had
worked at the sharp end of the war effort, keeping British
fighter aircraft production and repair ahead of the daily losses
in the skies over southern England. Described as aggressive,
argumentative, and brusque, Beaverbrook at the height of
the battle had increased fighter production targets by 15 percent, replaced management of plants that underperformed,
and ordered the cannibalization of all wrecked aircraft, about
2,000 in total, to put refurbished fighters back on the front lines
alongside new aircraft in record numbers and record time. He
helped win the Battle of Britain at the assembly-line level.

While they didn't always agree, Churchill and Aitken enjoyed a friendship forged by war. Some saw Beaverbrook's approach "more in common with a highwayman than an executive," but Churchill admired Beaverbook's buoyancy and vigour, declaring, "Some people take drugs. I take Max."[24]

In his letter of resignation, Beaverbrook downplayed his role. "I owe my reputation to you," he wrote to Churchill. "The confidence from the public really comes from you. And my courage was sustained by you."[25] Beaverbrook recalled his job in aircraft production as "the most glittering, glorious, glamourous era of my whole life."[26]

The Churchill-Aitken friendship persisted after the war. The former prime minister regularly stayed with the former war production minister at his villa La Capponcina, at Cap d'Ail in the south of France. It was there in August 1949 that Churchill experienced his first stroke. Beaverbrook abided by his friend's wishes and kept it secret. Beaverbrook died on June 9, 1964, just six months before Churchill's death on January 24, 1965.

* * *

For politicians such as Churchill and Beaverbrook, the Battle of Britain often came down to numbers: numbers of pilot casualties and aircraft replacements, numbers of urban streets decimated by the Blitz and rations distributed to keep survivors alive, and numbers of enemy losses to sustain your days in office. For most pilots and ground crew of Fighter Command, the battle meant not becoming a statistic and surviving to answer the call of the next scramble. For most British civilians who lived through it, Battle of Britain flashbacks involve trying to carry on a normal daily life amid the bombing.

Dorothy Firth, who lived through the Blitz in London, remembered the sounds of that summer. Overnights brought the noise of air-raid sirens and German bombing raids. Mornings it was the clatter of the fast commuter train into London to her clerk's job at Barclays Bank, eating lunch at her desk as quietly as possible because employees weren't allowed meal breaks. "There was always that feeling in the air, like a hum," she said, "when you heard the fighters up there doing their best to save us."[27]

Evenings, she donned her uncomfortable blue serge uniform for a volunteer shift with bucket and stirrup pump in hand as a fire-watcher dousing incendiaries in her neighbourhood. Or, when the Bill Nightingale concert group got the nod, she'd jump aboard a lorry to Richmond Park to perform skits, dances, and singsongs for the soldiers protecting the gun emplacements there.

One weekend, a cousin from Canada visited and Dorothy joined her at an impromptu party where she met George Marshall, a tank commander from Toronto. When the bombs started falling near the party venue, "We got down on the floor," she said. "George was lying next to me, trying to behave." When her Canadian beau returned from service in the Netherlands, the couple were married. In 1946, she boarded RMS *Queen Mary* with other war brides immigrating to Canada. But she never forgot the hum of that Battle of Britain summer.

Anne Elliott spent her first eight years living in north London. But when the Luftwaffe bombings in 1940 crept closer to her neighbourhood, the family had moved to Kent; her parents had actually smuggled her into the region (violating rules that prohibited children living in a potential German-invasion zone). Thus, they avoided the worst of the Blitz, but in 1944 the Germans began launching V1 and V2 flying bombs. All too often, they fell and exploded near the family's home in Kent.

Attempting to preserve some normalcy in Anne's childhood, Ethel Elliott signed her daughter up for piano lessons. The mother of a classmate in the community offered instruction in her home, insisting Anne always be on time. "When I arrived this day, I put my bike against the wall of her house, knocked on the door. No answer," Anne said. "I looked through her letterbox and there's her back garden. A flying bomb had left the front of the house standing, but the back was all gone. My school chum had survived, but her mother, the piano teacher, was killed."[28]

Anne Elliott later married a postwar RAF airman, Michael Reed, who wanted to continue service as aircrew in the RCAF. They immigrated to Canada in 1957.

Meanwhile, it took three attempts, but Jill Brown finally completed a transatlantic trip to Canada. Six years old when the war came to her hometown of Freshwater on the Isle of Wight, she had first travelled aboard the SS *Volendam*, which was torpedoed at sea, and later was booked on the ill-fated SS *City of Benares* but missed it when forced into quarantine. The Brown family ultimately chose to hunker down on the island for the duration of the war. When it ended, Jill emigrated to Canada permanently. "Hitler stopped me from moving to Canada," she said. "So, I did it on my own, arriving on August 23, 1958."[29]

* * *

They had less than twenty-four hours to prepare, but in the late fall of 1940, town councillors in Penticton, British Columbia, and the town's board of trade learned that one of their own was about to arrive home from overseas service. Overnight, they pulled out all the stops to honour Bruce Millar, a Battle of Britain veteran. Born in 1914, the son of a district Presbyterian minister in the South Okanagan town, Millar had studied at the University of British Columbia in Vancouver, excelling in basketball and aquatic competition. When the war came, he joined the RCAF's No. 110 Squadron. In 1940, he was shipped overseas and joined RCAF No. 1 Fighter Squadron at Northolt on August 31. During his first combat sortie, on September 9, his Hurricane was hit by enemy fire, and F/O Millar barely escaped the burning fighter as it disintegrated and crashed.

"Superficial and not considered serious," was how the telegram to the pilot's mother, Christina Millar, described his wounds.[30] He nevertheless required many weeks of hospitalization and treatment before he could travel home in November. There were interviews and papers to process in Toronto, and when word came that F/O Millar was aboard a westbound train home, Penticton sprang into action. By the time the town's Battle of Britain hero arrived, everything was ready. "Reaching down the full length of Eckhardt Avenue," the *Penticton Herald* reported, "organizations including the Canadian Legion, the B.C. Women's Service Corps, the Penticton Sea Cadets, Boy Scouts and others lined either side of the road."[31]

Three local bands, the Penticton Town Band, the Sea Cadets Band, and the Canadian Legion Band, marched, played, and led the procession. At the end of the parade, a police car escort, sirens blaring, preceded the final car carrying F/O Millar and his mother. The cars moved slowly so everybody could see and applaud the guests of honour. When the procession arrived at the municipal hall, students from both

Penticton elementary and high schools were waiting on the steps, waving flags, cheering, and calling out "Hello, Bruce!" As Millar stepped from his car, the Penticton Band played "O Canada," and Millar saluted. Town reeve Gordon Wilkins shook Millar's hand and read the official greeting: "This civic welcome which our fellow citizens, young and old, have extended to you on your return from the Battle of Britain is just a small token of our admiration of your war services. . . . You have lived up to the highest and best of Canada's traditions in your service overseas. Our pleasure having you back home is second only to that of your mother's."

With that, Reeve Wilkins presented a bouquet of flowers to Christina Millar. The audience applauded enthusiastically and, with his mother quietly stepping to her son's side for support, F/O Millar moved to the microphone. Briefly, and "with a trace of embarrassment in his voice," the *Penticton Herald* noted, "Millar expressed his appreciation for the enthusiastic welcome."

With the festivities complete, F/O Millar and his mother were delivered safely home for tea. Penticton had ensured that its native son received a triumphant homecoming, but it also recognized the scars, both visible and invisible, of his service in the Battle of Britain. Nine days later, he turned twenty-six. Bruce Millar retired from the RCAF as a wing commander in 1964 and died prematurely in 1969.

* * *

The scene was a dispersal hut at RAF Northolt, where pilots were receiving a dressing down. A none-too-happy squadron leader marched around the small room, fit to be tied. A dozen or so of his attentive flyers were taking a pasting for their performance in the air minutes earlier. Not all of the young fighters appeared to understand the reprimand.

"One. The RAF is not a flying circus!" the RAF commander barked.

An RAF pilot wearing Polish insignia and standing off to the side translated the reprimand.

"Two," continued the commanding officer, "strict R/T procedure will be observed at all times."

Another translation for the benefit of the Polish pilots.

"And it is never, repeat never, to be used for private Polish chit-chat!"

A pause as the Polish translator found the Polish equivalent of chit-chat.

"And finally, and God alone knows why, I've received the following signal," and he read from a paper telegram: "Congratulations! As of today, this squadron is declared operational. Signed Keith Park, Air Vice-Marshal AOC 11 Group."

Which needed no translation. The Poles cheered ecstatically.

A swell of patriotic musical orchestration accompanied the shift from this scene in the 1969 United Artists' epic movie *Battle of Britain* to another inside Fighter Command headquarters. Keith Park (played by Trevor Howard) conferred with his boss, Air Chief Marshal Hugh Dowding (played by Lawrence Olivier), and admitted, "I was wrong about the Poles. We also have a second squadron of Poles."

The two senior officers donned their caps and left the office together as Dowding recommended, "Make them operational."

"And the Canadians?"

"And the Czechs," Dowding says, "We need them all."[32]

The scene of Polish RAF pilots getting a tongue-lashing before being told their squadron is officially ready for combat, appears about ninety minutes into the motion picture. Like many segments of the movie, which compresses the 113-day Battle of Britain into two hours and thirteen minutes on the screen, the Polish pilot scene delivers a representation of what actually happened.

In his 1971 book, *One of the Few*, Battle of Britain veteran Johnny Kent described the August 30 sortie, in which he, as Canadian flight commander, is training his Polish charges over north London. Kent notes the language barrier, and accurately describes F/O Ludwik Paszkiewicz's decision to exit the training exercise to chase and single-handedly shoot down a Dornier bomber (as described in chapter six). The movie's scene in which actor Barry Foster, as the British RAF commander, chews out the Poles, and AVM Keith Park immediately dashes off a telegram of congratulations, takes a bit of artistic licence. In truth, Canadian flight commander Kent described the Poles going "cock-a-hoop" over Paszkiewicz's victory and requesting as a reward operational status, which was granted.

As for Trevor Howard's afterthought to Lawrence Olivier, "And the Canadians?" Well, inclusion of the Czechs, Poles, and Canadians as additional players in the movie's battle amounted to lip service. RCAF No. 1 Fighter Squadron had been operational for two weeks before the Polish incident. Of some 3,000 pilots—Winston Churchill's "few"—about 2,500 were British, 147 Polish, and 87 Czech. There were 105 Canadians, including 46 pilots from RCAF No. 1 Fighter Squadron, another 44 from RAF No. 242 Fighter Squadron, and individual CAN/RAF pilots serving in other RAF fighter squadrons. Those numbers did not include approximately two hundred RCAF ground crew serving at fighter bases in England.

While Canadian content is limited in *Battle of Britain*, the movie, it is not limited to that one Trevor Howard line. Were it not for Canadian-born Herschel "Harry" Saltzman, the film would have been without some of its principal backing. Born in 1915 in Quebec and raised in New Brunswick, Harry moved with his family to Cleveland before running away at age fifteen to join the circus. In the 1930s, studying in Paris, he fell in love with cinema, claiming a connection to film director René Clair. Back in North America, he managed the Gilbert Brothers Circus and, when war broke out, volunteered for the RCAF; he was medically discharged in 1943.

Theatre and film production drew him to Britain in the 1950s and 1960s. He was co-founder, with Albert Broccoli, of Eon Productions, the movie company that produced the early James Bond features *Dr. No*, *From Russia with Love*, *Goldfinger*, *Thunderball*, and *You Only Live Twice*. In 1966, when the Rank Organisation pulled out of its agreement with producer Bennie Fisz to fund a feature film about the Battle of Britain, Saltzman jumped in and arranged a new distribution deal with United Artists. Film director Anthony Mann described Saltzman's career path. "Harry used to make great pictures," he said. "Now he makes very successful ones."[33]

Much of the budget made available via Saltzman's newly formed Spitfire Productions helped underwrite the acquisition and modification of nineteen Spitfires and three Hurricanes from the UK Ministry of Defence. Under the supervision of RAF pathfinder veteran Group Captain T.G. Hamish Mahaddie, the later-model Spitfires received retro makeovers for an early 1940's look. Mahaddie, meanwhile, discovered that movie stand-ins for Luftwaffe fighters and bombers could be found in Spain. In mid-1966, he travelled to Tablada Airfield outside Seville where, to his surprise, the Spanish Air Force had thirty-two vintage Heinkel bombers on its operational flight line. Piled next to their air force hangars sat the airframes, propellers, tailplanes, and armament of twenty-five dismantled Messerschmitt 109s, minus their engines.[34]

The Nazis had delivered those Me 109s without engines to the Spaniards in the 1940s. After the war, the Spanish Air Force had explored the option of having modified Rolls-Royce Merlin engines installed in the 109s. The Spaniards flew the first Merlin-powered 109s successfully in 1954. Saltzman and Fisz acquired eighteen of the engine-less Spanish 109s (for $2,250 each) in an auction. They then negotiated a deal with the Spanish to fit Merlin engines into the eighteen 109s. The planes would be painted with wartime Luftwaffe colours and insignia, used in filming at Tablada Airfield, and then repainted in Spanish Air Force colours and returned to active service at Seville.

Another valuable prop came from the middle of Canada. In 1940, the Canadian Car and Foundry Company's aircraft assembly section, probably under the supervision of Can-Car engineer Elsie McGill, completed construction of Hurricane CF-SMI at its plant in Fort William, Ontario. Assigned to operational training exercises at stations in the British Commonwealth Air Training Plan in Canada, this Hurricane was decommissioned at the end of the war and disappeared. Until the day before the plane was to be scrapped.

The Hurricane was sitting in a farmyard outside Carman, Manitoba. Heavy rains postponed a junk dealer's visit to pick it up. Somehow, aircraft restorer Robert Diemert heard that this piece of aviation history was about to be demolished. He showed up just in time. "The basic metal was still good thanks to Manitoba's prairie dry weather," Diemert told a reporter. "Every kid in the neighbourhood had been through the plane. There was grass growing up through the airframe and loose wires hanging everywhere."[35]

Diemert invested thousands of dollars and 5,000 hours of labour in the reconstruction of the Can-Car Hurricane, and meanwhile learned to fly. He took lessons in Winnipeg and practised combat manoeuvres with the RCAF Golden Centennaires aerobatics team at Portage la Prairie, flying a wartime Harvard trainer he had purchased from Crown Assets. When the quarter-century-old Hurricane was finally air worthy, Diemert made a test flight.

"She flew like new," he said. It was after Diemert had flown his refurbished Hurricane in the 1967 Centennial Air Show in Ottawa that Hamish Mahaddie contacted him and asked if Spitfire Productions could hire him and his Hurricane to appear in the movie. Shortly before filming began, an RCAF C-130 Hercules transport delivered Diemert's Hurricane to RAF Henlow, where it was reassembled to join the other players in the movie.

In addition to a stellar lineup of vintage aircraft, Saltzman and Fisz had assembled an all-star cast, including Lawrence Olivier and Trevor Howard. The commanders and rank-and-file fighter pilots, if slightly older than the airmen they were depicting, were a who's who of the British acting community, including Michael Caine, Robert Shaw, James Cosmo, Edward Fox, David Griffin, Myles Hoyle, and Ian McShane. Key civilian roles were played by Ralph Richardson and Curt Jürgens, while Susannah York delivered the film's love interest, as the wife of RAF S/L Colin Harvey, played by Canadian actor Christopher Plummer.

"My role in the film was that of a Canadian squadron leader," Plummer wrote in his autobiography. "I'd asked that I be Canadian, as so many of my countrymen had done valiant RAF and RCAF service."[36] Plummer apparently emphasized the point by wearing a "Canada" shoulder-flash. While that was normal RAF practice later in the war—particularly with thousands of Canadians serving in forty-seven overseas squadrons as bomber, fighter, reconnaissance, transport, and training aircrew—wearing national identity flashes was uncommon at the time of the Battle of Britain.* Plummer noted that there were so many actors, filmmakers, and actual war heroes on the set each day that the atmosphere matched that of the actual battle. "The film was inundated with technical advisors, each of whom had been a top air-ace in the battle," including RAF fighter aces Ginger Lacey, Peter Townsend, Tom Gleave, Robert Stanford Tuck, Johnny Kent, and Douglas Bader.

A "Canada" patch on his RAF uniform was apparently the least of Plummer's worries on set. One morning, he arrived in his Mercedes automobile at a deserted airfield for his scene call and suddenly heard a lot of yelling from afar. He looked around and spotted an irate war veteran, Douglas Bader, lumbering on his prosthetic legs directly at Plummer's vehicle. "Get that filthy Kraut car out of here!" he yelled.

* RAF Spitfire ace Johnny Johnson became commander of Canadian No. 144 Wing in 1944. Soon after, Canadian fighter pilot Syd Ford presented Johnson with a pair of "Canada" shoulder flashes. "The boys would like you to wear these," he said. "After all, we're a Canadian wing and we've got to convert you." Johnson had them sewn on his uniform right away. (J.E. Johnson, *Wing Leader* [New York: Ballantine Books, 1957], 144.)

"Are you speaking to me, sir?" Plummer asked.

"You know bloody well I am," Bader fumed. "Now get that filthy thing out of here. Now!" To punctuate his outrage, Bader kicked the car with enough force that his prosthesis dented the Mercedes's rear end.

"I felt an enormous wave of sympathy for any Luftwaffe pilot who might have had the misfortune to come up against Air Commodore Bader," wrote Plummer.[37]

Filming began under director Guy Hamilton and director of cinematography Freddie Young at locations in Spain on March 13, 1968. Principal photography in the UK began on May 1. During the most intensive shooting in daylight hours through June and July, any or all of the armada of aircraft, including Spitfires, Hurricanes, Messerschmitts, Heinkels, Stukas, a helicopter, and a B-25 Mitchell customized photographic aircraft, could be airborne over the former RAF Duxford station.

To film each day's flying sequences required input from pilots from Spain, the US, the UK, and Canada; accommodation of the aircraft at RAF Henlow; RAF riggers and fitters to maintain the aircraft; military air traffic control; military air service companies; airfield safety services; and insurance services that covered non-flying aircraft for £5,000 each and flying aircraft for £10,000 each. Ultimately, the film crew accumulated 110 hours of pure flying scenes, which had to be edited down to forty minutes in the final cut of the movie. The *Battle of Britain* budget came in at $14 million.[38] Its box office gross was $13 million.

"I've never been in a film that received such coverage," Plummer wrote. "Each day there were so many journalists from all over the world on the set waiting for interviews, one could barely move. Harry Saltzman was a master marketeer."[39]

Saltzman had Leonard Mosley's book, *Battle of Britain: The Making of a Film*, serialized in a UK Sunday newspaper. On September 5, 1969, ten days before the annual Battle of Britain Day, Bader and Lacey attended the "switching on" ceremony of the annual Blackpool Illuminations light show. A documentary by Christopher Doll aired on ITV two nights before the premiere. On the evening of Monday, September 15, 1969, the Dominion Theatre on Tottenham Court Road in London premiered the movie with dignitaries, representatives of various Allied air forces, and 350 members of the Battle of Britain Fighter Association in attendance.

In spite of Saltzman's promotional blitz, critics generally panned the movie. The *Times* in London said that it was "tastefully done, not unintelligent, eminently respectable, and for the most part deadly dull." The *Guardian* said it was "neither a very good movie, nor a very formidable piece of history."[40] *New York Times* critic Vincent Canby wrote the movie was "one of those all-star non-fiction movies, of a somewhat lower order than *The Longest Day*."[41] Gene Siskel, in the *Chicago Tribune*, described it as "Harry Saltzman's 12-thousand-megadollar bomb,"[42] while Roger Ebert, reviewing for the *Chicago Sun-Times*, complained at suggestions that "Harry Saltzman, the producer, was only slightly less heroic than the guys who flew in the battle. They only died. He had to buy the planes."[43] In defence of the project, Saltzman told *Weekend Magazine* in Canada, "if we hadn't made the film when we did, we'd never get a second chance."[44]

Christopher Plummer attended the Royal Gala premiere screening at the Dominion in October 1969, when "the entire Royal Family turned up to salute not just us actors, but the hordes of decorated airmen [who] had squeezed themselves into their old uniforms weighed down by dozens of medals to sit back and watch a pretty authentic, well-researched and enormously ambitious reenactment of their very own glory days—the best days of their lives."[45]

* * *

Christopher Plummer's assessment rings Churchillian. Like the British prime minister's indelible words, "Never in the field of human conflict was so much owed by so many to so few," delivered in the British Parliament on August 20, 1940, Plummer's is perhaps a romanticized view of the Battle of Britain. Canadian feature writer Frank Lowe went further when he wrote: "For 113 days, lonely men in tiny single-engined aircraft fended off the mightiest war machine the world had ever seen. . . . The Canadians were there, as a minority, but as a potent and hard-fighting minority which gave a new lustre to the aerial reputation the country had won in a previous war through the daring of men such as [Billy] Bishop, [Raymond] Collishaw, and [Billy] Barker."[46]

Romantic or not, to have thwarted the world's most power-ful air force from exterminating the RAF and its defences must at least have given Fighter Command pilots who survived a great sense of accomplishment and relief. A more crucial after-effect might be what the battle achieved and how its result affected the next five years of the Second World War. In other words, how had Canada's "splendid hundred,"[47] as Arthur Bishop, Billy Bishop's son, described them, helped turn the tide?

Following the Dunkirk evacuation, Adolf Hitler's armies effectively occupied continental Europe; he had felt certain that by threatening an invasion of the British Isles, Britons would sue for peace, thus freeing German armies to push east to invade the Soviet Union. Meanwhile, buoyed by the Luftwaffe's victories in Spain, Poland, Norway, the Netherlands, Belgium, and France, Reichsmarshall Göring had promised he could sweep the RAF from the skies over Britain in a few weeks. Neither occurred. And what the German fighter and bomber aircrew ultimately faced across the Channel was not a cakewalk but a major air battle, one for which the Luftwaffe was neither designed nor prepared.

Leadership on both sides played a vital role in the results, too. Had it not been for ACM Hugh Dowding's brilliant generalship, and Göring's, Kesselring's, and Sperrle's lack of it (i.e., their failure to fashion more than a day-to-day strategy and their inability to identify the advantage that radar delivered to the British), the Germans might have succeeded in winning the Battle of Britain. If AVM Keith Park had not husbanded his fighter response as frugally, and if Göring had focused his full might on Britain's Chain Home radar, Fighter Command bases, and communications systems, it's likely the RAF could not have survived the onslaught. The Luftwaffe might then have crippled or dispatched Britain's Home Fleet and merchant shipping lifeline and opened the way for the German navy to deliver Operation Sea Lion, landing German armies on British soil unmolested.

That the Germans had no strategic plan for a lengthy air battle, that the Luftwaffe didn't concentrate on its real target, Fighter Command, and that it failed to recognize it needed to destroy the RAF's early-warning system, its command-and-control system, and then its pilots and aircraft, all spelled defeat. The Luftwaffe's checkerboard battle plan ultimately gave the RAF a chance to get up off the mat at the last moment, defeat the immediate threat in the skies, and prevent a potential invasion on the ground. The Germans were also wrong to assume that suddenly shifting their primary targets from military to civilian with the Blitz on London and other major cities would completely demoralize the British population. Perhaps most fatally, Göring completely underestimated the grit and ingenuity of Allied pilots (in combat) and their ground crews (in keeping their aircraft airborne). Canadian squadron leaders, flight commanders, individual pilots, and ground crewmen played key roles across some fifty-five squadrons of Fighter Command, contributing mightily to the frustration of German war aims.

Bottom line: the RAF did not defeat the Luftwaffe in the Battle of Britain. It did, however, inflict unacceptable losses—to the point that German armed forces could not accomplish the invasion of the British Isles that Hitler had directed. For the first time in a year of fighting, Nazi Germany had sustained a military setback. Perhaps more significant for Winston Churchill and Britons, the outcome of those 113 days helped sway American observers to the belief that Britain, given support, might just win the war.

As British military historian Richard Holmes put it: "Without Dunkirk and the Battle of Britain and the development of radar, there would be no D-Day. Without Britain, this unsinkable aircraft carrier, separated by that moat of defence from Europe, you cannot have an invasion of Europe. How do you bring American military power to bear on Europe without Britain? How do you mount a strategic bombing campaign without Britain? So, you cannot get anywhere without 1940."[48] In other words, Britain could not win the war alone, but at the end of the summer of 1940, she had refused to lose it.

Speaking later about September 15, 1940, the day acknowledged as Battle of Britain Day, Ernie McNab, the feisty Saskatchewan farm kid, who commanded RCAF No. 1 Fighter Squadron throughout the battle, reflected on the actions of his comrades. "We all felt that we had broken up Jerry's whole show and that he would never come back again in such numbers," McNab said. "He never did."[49]

* * *

In one of the very last sorties of the Battle of Britain, on November 1, 1940, S/L Johnny Kent and his fighter squadron had responded to a scramble call at 2:30 in the afternoon. First pursuing a patrol line from Biggin Hill to Hornchurch at 15,000 feet, his Hurricanes had no enemy contact. Turning north, the squadron of Polish fighter pilots was vectored toward Colchester in search of fifty Junkers bombers. Halfway across the Thames Estuary, Kent was distracted.

"I noticed four or five aircraft which I at first took to be our own fighters circling," Kent's combat report read. "I then noticed that they had bright yellow noses and immediately attacked."[50]

Overtaking an Me 109 from behind, Kent got a burst off and noted the enemy pilot manoeuvred well to evade his fire. The two opposing fighters nearly collided in the dogfight. The German dove away as Kent fired another burst and disappeared into clouds. By the time Kent reoriented himself, he was over the Channel. He turned for home and spotted more fighters, but turned away when British anti-aircraft fire came up to meet the intruders. He returned to base without incident. He'd expended his full ammunition allotment, 1,000 rounds, and had nothing to show for it.

Speaking later to an Air Force press relations officer, Kent quipped, "Never in the history of human conflict were so many bullets fired by one man with so little effect."[51]

A modest Canadian who had gone to Britain to become an officer and a fighter pilot, Johnny Kent was credited with four enemy aircraft destroyed in six weeks of aerial combat and for leading several squadrons on pivotal Battle of Britain operations. He had experienced the greatest air battle of the Second World War and was awarded an Air Force Cross, two Distinguished Flying Crosses, and the *Virtuti Militari*, Poland's highest military decoration for courage in the face of the enemy. But nothing made him prouder or more grateful than the simple fact he had been one of the few and survived.

CHAPTER ONE: FIGHT LIKE HELL TO GET INTO IT

1 J.A. Kent, *One of the Few: A Story of Personal Challenge through the Battle of Britain and Beyond* (London: William Kimber, 1971), 84.
2 Kent, *One of the Few*, 19.
3 Kent, *One of the Few*, 20.
4 Kent, *One of the Few*, 20–21.
5 Kent, *One of the Few*, 24 and 32.
6 Hugh Trenchard quoted in Andrew Boyle, *Trenchard: Man of Vision* (London: Collins, 1962), 340–44.
7 Trenchard quoted in Boyle, *Trenchard*, 340–44.
8 Hugh Dowding quoted in Peter Townsend, *Duel of Eagles: The Struggles for the Skies from the First World War to the Battle of Britain* (Richmond Hill, ON: Simon and Schuster, 1972), 126.
9 Kent, *One of the Few*, 86.
10 Kent, *One of the Few*, 86.
11 Kent, *One of the Few*, 88.
12 Adputor Savard correspondence with J.W.G. Clark, October 1, 1941. Floyd Williston files, Winnipeg, MB, courtesy of Norman Malayney.
13 Kent, *One of the Few*, 94.
14 Kent, *One of the Few*, 94.
15 Denis Richards, *Royal Air Force 1939–1945*, vol. I, *The Fight at Odds* (London: Her Majesty's Stationery Office, 1953), 122.
16 Peter Townsend, *Duel of Eagles*, 234.
17 Len Deighton, *Battle of Britain* (Toronto: Clark, Irwin, 1980), 71.
18 Kent, *One of the Few*, 98–100. Unless otherwise noted, all quotations in this section are taken from this source.
19 Winston Churchill quoted in Mark Hawkins-Daly, ed., *Speeches That Changed the World* (London: Quercus, 2005), 96.

CHAPTER TWO: APPETITE TO FLY

1 Neil Taylor, "The Flying Club Movement in Canada and Edmonton's Role," Alberta Aviation Museum, May 2019, https://albertaaviationmuseum.com/the-flying-club-movement-in-canada-and-edmontons-role/.

2 W.A.B. Douglas, *The Creation of a National Air Force: The Official History of the Royal Canadian Air Force*, vol. II (Toronto: University of Toronto Press, 1986), 73.

3 A.K. MacLean quoted in Leslie Roberts, *Canada's War in the Air* (Montreal: Alvah M. Beatty, 1942), 15.

4 Wayne C. McNeal, "General Aviation in Canada: A Study of Its Development and Policy" (master's thesis, University of British Columbia, 1969), 32.

5 Dal Russel quoted in "Wing Commander Blair Dalzell Russel, DSO, DFC and Bar," *Critical Moments: Profiles of Members of the Aircrew Association* (Aircrew Association, 1989), 260.

6 Tim Burke, "Fighter Pilot Looks Back to Days of Courage," *Montreal Star*, November 9, 1970.

7 "Democracy at War: Canadian Newspapers and the Second World War," Canadian War Museum, http://www.warmuseum.ca/cwm/exhibitions/newspapers/canadawar/royalairforce_e.html/.

8 Leslie Roberts, *Canada's War in the Air* (Montreal: Alvah M. Beatty, 1942), 17.

9 Russel quoted in "Wing Commander," 260.

10 Douglas, *The Creation of a National Air Force*, 148.

11 Eric Beardmore quoted in Arthur Bishop, *The Splendid Hundred: The True Story of Canadians Who Flew in the Greatest Air Battle of World War II* (Whitby, ON: McGraw-Hill Ryerson, 1994), 9.

12 "Flying Club Organized and Application Made to Ottawa for Charter," *London Free Press*, November 19, 1927.

13 Floyd Williston, "Charles W. Trevena—One of the Few," courtesy of Norman Malayney.

14 Paul Pitcher letter to David L. Bashow, Colorado Springs, CO, July 26, 1993 (Paul Pitcher files, with permission).

15 House of Commons, *Debates*, 4th session, 13th Parliament, June 30, 1920, 4553–56.

16 "United Kingdom Air Mission, Notes of a meeting on 31st October

[1939] with members of the Canadian War Cabinet," Directorate of History (DHist), Department of National Defence, 181.009 (D786).

17   F.J. Hatch, *Aerodrome of Democracy: Canada and the British Commonwealth Air Training Plan, 1939–1945* (Ottawa: Directorate of History, Department of National Defence, 1983), 12.

18   Charles Portal quoted in "Memorandum on the possibility of increasing training capacity in Canada for R.A.F." September 1939, Public Records Office, Air 2/3206; Charles Portal quoted in "Canadianization," Heakes Papers, DHist, Department of National Defence, 77/51.

19   Vincent Massey, *What's Past Is Prologue: The Memoirs of the Right Honourable Vincent Massey, C.H.* (Toronto: Macmillan, 1963), 303.

20   Massey, *What's Past Is Prologue*, 304.

21   Neville Chamberlain quoted in Hatch, *Aerodrome of Democracy*, 15.

22   Hatch, *Aerodrome of Democracy*, 15.

23   "Minutes of Emergency Council (Committee on General Policy) of Cabinet," October 31, 1939; secretary of state for external affairs to dominions secretary, November 3, 1939, Documents on Canadian External Relations (DCER), VII, 590, 598.

24   "United Kingdom Air Mission," DHist.

25   "Canada, Agreement Relating to Training of Pilots and Aircraft Crews in Canada and Their Subsequent Service between the United Kingdom, Canada, Australia and New Zealand, Signed in Ottawa, December 17, 1939" (Ottawa: King's Printer, 1941).

26   Arnold Heeney, "Air Training Scheme—Organization of Canadians in R.C.A.F. Units and Formations," Memorandum from undersecretary of state for external affairs to prime minister, December 13, 1939, DCER, VII, 642–45.

27   Undersecretary of state for external affairs to UK high commissioner, October 14, 1939, DCER, VII, pt. I, 860-1; UK high commissioner to Air Council, Oct. 16, 1939, PRO Air 2/3157.

28   Hugh Halliday, *242 Squadron, The Canadian Years: The Story of the RAF's All-Canadian Fighter Squadron* (Stittsville, ON: Canada's Wings, 1981), 13.

29   Bishop, *The Splendid Hundred*, 11.

30   "Percival Stanley 'Stan' Turner," Aviation During World War Two, n.d., http://www.century-of-flight.freeola.com/Aviation%20history/WW2/aces/Percival%20Stanley%20Turner.htm.

31   Hugh Halliday, *242 Squadron, The Canadian Years: The Story of the RAF's*

All-Canadian Fighter Squadron (Stittsville, ON: Canada's Wings, 1981), 16 and 20.

32 United Kingdom, *British Parliamentary Debates*, December 12, 1939, 1070.

33 Halliday, *242 Squadron*, 24.

34 Dave Lefurgey, "So My Son Will Know," *Air Force*, Spring 2007, 21.

35 F.W. Winterbotham, *The Ultra Secret* (New York: Dell, 1974), 24.

36 Winterbotham, *The Ultra Secret*, 21.

37 Ralph Barker, *Aviator Extraordinary: The Sidney Cotton Story* (London: Chatto & Windus, 1969).

38 Winterbotham, *The Ultra Secret*, 21.

39 Quoted in Lefurgey, "So My Son Will Know," 23.

40 Winterbotham, *The Ultra Secret*, 57.

41 Mackenzie King quoted in Roberts, *Canada's War in the Air*, 29.

42 King diary quoted in F.J. Hatch, "The British Commonwealth Air Training Plan," *Canadian Aviation Historical Society Journal* (Winter 1982): 100.

43 Ted Barris, *Behind the Glory: The Plan That Won the Allied Air War* (Toronto: Macmillan, 1992), 306.

44 Douglas, *The Creation of a National Air Force*, 192.

45 Marian Jones quoted in Jeff Bartkiewicz, "Calgary Flying Ace Lived Hard, Died Young," *Calgary Herald*, August 29, 2004.

46 Harry Pegler quoted in Bartkiewicz, "Calgary Flying Ace."

47 Pegler quoted in Bartkiewicz, "Calgary Flying Ace."

48 Halliday, *242 Squadron*, 28.

49 Pegler quoted in Bartkiewicz, "Calgary Flying Ace."

50 RAF No. 242 war diary quoted in Halliday, *242 Squadron*, 28.

51 Paul Henri Spaak quoted in Townsend, *Duel of Eagles*, 218 and 219.

52 Townsend, *Duel of Eagles*, 219.

53 Douglas, *The Creation of a National Air Force*, 150.

54 Douglas, *The Creation of a National Air Force*, 345.

55 Bishop, *The Splendid Hundred*, 11.

56 Bill Dunphy interview with author, Etobicoke, ON, April 17, 1991.

57 Dal Russel quoted in "Wing Commander," 260.

58 Andrew W. Hamilton, "McNab Gets First Kill During First Fight," *Globe and Mail*, August 16, 1940.

59 E.A. McNab, biographical file, DHist 75/360. Unless otherwise noted, all quotations in this section are taken from this source.

CHAPTER THREE: THE HURRICANE DRAIN

1   "Pat Sclanders Was Once Youngest Pilot In Entire Dominion: His 'Boy Scout' Act Startled Crowds at Maritime Exhibitions," *Telegraph-Journal* (Saint John), September 12, 1940.

2   "Pat Sclanders Was Once Youngest Pilot."

3   Ronald J. Jack, "Pat Sclanders—Boy Aviator," The Lost Valley, an Internet History of Saint John, N.B., December 6, 2017.

4   Floyd Williston, "The Young Boy from the St. [sic] John Flying Club," unpublished manuscript, courtesy of Norman Malayney.

5   Floyd Williston correspondence from friends Stan and Del (in UK), January 12, 1998, courtesy of Norman Malayney.

6   Larry Forrester, *Fly for Your Life: The Colorful Exploits of One of World War II's Greatest Fighter Aces* (Garden City, NY: Nelson Doubleday, 1973), 38.

7   Williston, "The Young Boy from the St. [sic] John Flying Club."

8   A.P.S. Wills quoted in Larry Forrester, *Fly for Your Life: The Colorful Exploits of One of World War II's Greatest Fighter Aces* (Garden City, NY: Nelson Doubleday, 1973), 42, 43.

9   Catherine Tucker (née Bramley-Moore) quoted in Floyd Williston correspondence from friends Stan and Del (in UK), January 12, 1998.

10 Floyd Williston, "044 Duncan Hewitt, RAF" profile, courtesy of Norman Malayney.

11 Floyd Williston, "043 Harry Hamilton, RAF" profile, courtesy of Norman Malayney.

12 Floyd Williston, *Hurricane Pilots in the Battle of Britain, Part III, The Millidgeville Trio*, 16, unpublished manuscript, courtesy of Norman Malayney.

13 Floyd Williston, *Hurricane Pilots, Part I*, 7, unpublished manuscript, courtesy of Norman Malayney.

14 Floyd Williston, *Hurricane Pilots, Part III*, 18, unpublished manuscript, courtesy of Norman Malayney.

15 Floyd Williston, "044 Duncan Hewitt, RAF" profile.

16 Norman Lee quoted in biography of James Duncan Smith, Floyd Williston files, courtesy of Norman Malayney.

17 Lee quoted in biography of James Duncan Smith.

18 James Duncan Smith quoted in correspondence with sisters, May–June 1940, Floyd Williston files, courtesy of Norman Malayney.

19 Peter Townsend, *Duel of Eagles: The Struggles for the Skies from the First*

World War to the Battle of Britain (Richmond Hill, ON: Simon and Schuster, 1972), 220.

20   Williston, *Hurricane Pilots. Part II* (unpublished manuscript), 8, courtesy of Norman Malayney.

21   Gordon Patterson quoted in Les Allison, *Canadians in the Royal Air Force* (Altona, MB: Friesen), 10, 11.

22   "Hilly's Button: Glenboro Man in R.A.F. Prizes Good Luck Token," Canadian Press, April 1, 1940.

23   RAF No. 1 Squadron Operations Record Book, France, May 1940. UK National Archives AIR27.

24   Mark Hilly Brown DFC citation quoted in Les Allison, *Canadians in the Royal Air Force.* (Altona, MB: Friesen. 1978), 6.

25   John "Max" Aitken quoted in Tony Holmes *American Eagles: American Volunteers in the RAF, 1937–1943* (Crowborough, UK: Classic Publications, 2001).

26   Paul Reynaud quoted in Townsend, *Duel of Eagles*, 229.

27   Hugh Dowding quoted in Townsend, *Duel of Eagles*, 232.

28   Hugh Dowding dispatch quoted in the London *Gazette*, September 10, 1946.

29   Duncan Hewitt June 1940 letter quoted in Williston, *Hurricane Pilots*.

30   Hermann Göring quoted in Townsend, *Duel of Eagles*, 239.

31   Admiralty quoted in Richards, *Royal Air Force 1939–1945*, vol. I: *The Fight at Odds*, 130.

32   David L. Bashow, *All the Fine Young Eagles: In the Cockpit with Canada's Second World War Fighter Pilots* (Toronto: Stoddart, 1996), 19.

33   John Latta combat report quoted in Halliday, *242 Squadron*, 57.

34   Jocho Helbig quoted in Townsend, *Duel of Eagles*, 247.

35   Spencer Dunmore, *Above and Beyond: The Canadians' War in the Air, 1939–45* (Toronto: McClelland & Stewart, 1996), 44.

36   Al Deere quoted in Deighton, *Battle of Britain*, 73.

37   Williston, *Hurricane Pilots*.

38   Duncan Hewitt June 1940 letter quoted in Williston, *Hurricane Pilots*.

39   Bashow, *All the Fine Young Eagles*, 23.

40   Stan Turner quoted in "The Black Spring," *The Canadians at War 1939–45*, ed. Andrew R. Byers (Montreal: Reader's Digest, 1995), 34.

41   DHist., Public Relations Release No. 561, July 12, 1942.

42   Neil Campbell correspondence home to Canada quoted in Halliday, *242 Squadron*, 78.

43 Stan Turner quoted in Byers, ed., "The Black Spring," 34.

44 Neil Campbell correspondence home to Canada quoted in Halliday, *242 Squadron*, 78.

45 Stan Turner quoted in Byers, ed., "The Black Spring," 34.

CHAPTER FOUR: A TOUGH BUNCH

1 Norman Longmate, *How We Lived Then: A History of Everyday Life during the Second World War* (London: Hutchinson, 1971), 105, 106.

2 King George VI quoted in Dunmore, *Above and Beyond*, 52.

3 Winston Churchill quoted in Mark Hawkins-Daly, ed., *Speeches That Changed the World*, (London: Quercus Publishing, 2005), 95.

4 David Low, "Very well then, alone!" (cartoon) *Evening Standard*, June 18, 1940.

5 Jill Mason (née Brown) interview with author, Whitby, ON, May 1, 2023.

6 Allan Bullock, *The Life and Times of Ernest Bevin*, vol. II: *Minister of Labour, 1940–45* (London: Heinemann, 1967).

7 "Broomstick Army Who Won a Special Place," *1939–1940: The People's War*, ed. Nigel Peake (Portsmouth: Portsmouth Publishing, 1989), 66.

8 Anthony Eden quoted in Vera Lynn, *We'll Meet Again: A Personal and Social History of World War Two* (London: Sidgwick & Jackson, 1989), 39.

9 Lynn, *We'll Meet Again*, 40

10 Longmate, *How We Lived Then*, 106.

11 Jill Mason (née Brown) interview with author, May 1, 2023.

12 Bill Brydon interview with Alex Barris, July 13, 1993, Montclair, NJ.

13 Lance Cole, *Secrets of the Spitfire: The Story of Beverley Shenstone, The Man Who Perfected the Elliptical Wing* (Barnsley, UK: Pen & Sword Books, 2012), 30.

14 Wayne Saunders, "A Magnificent Contribution," *Airforce* 34, no. 1 (2010): 14.

15 Beverley Shenstone quoted in Jonathan F. Vance, *High Flight: Aviation and the Canadian Imagination* (Toronto: Penguin Canada, 2002), 100.

16 Beverley Shenstone (using pseudonym Brian Worley), "Fighter Fundamentals," *Aeronautics* 2, no. 2 (March 1940), 69.

17 Shenstone, "Fighter Fundamentals," 110.

18 Shenstone, "Fighter Fundamentals," 114.

19 "A Short History of Sir Sydney Camm CBE, FRAeS, 1893–1966," Royal Windsor Web Site, updated January 2007, http://www.thamesweb.co.uk/windsorpeople/SirSydneyCamm.html.

20 Beverley Shenstone quoted in Saunders, "A Magnificent Contribution," 16.

21 Jonathan Glancey, *Spitfire—The Biography* (London: Atlantic Books, 2006), 61.

22 Chris McNab, *The Luftwaffe 1933–45: Hitler's Eagles* (New York: Chartwell, 2014), 183–85.

23 Hannes Trautloft diary quoted in Chaz Bowyer and Armand van Ishoven, *Hurricane & Messerschmitt at War* (Enderby, UK: Promotional Reprint, 1993), 187.

24 Hannes Trautloft diary quoted in Bowyer and van Ishoven, *Hurricane & Messerschmitt at War*, 187.

25 Townsend, *Duel of Eagles*, 136.

26 Erhard Milch quoted in Townsend, *Duel of Eagles*, 138.

27 Len Deighton, *Fighter: The True Story of the Battle of Britain* (St. Albans, UK: Triad/Panther Books, 1979), 108.

28 Deighton, *Fighter: The True Story of the Battle of Britain*, 127.

29 Paul Brickhill, *Reach for the Sky: The Story of Douglas Bader* (London: Collins, 1954), 17.

30 Andrew Brookes, *Crash! Military Aircraft Disasters, Accidents and Incidents* (London: Ian Allan, 1991), 36, 37.

31 Douglas Bader diary quoted in Brickhill, *Reach for the Sky*, 151.

32 Douglas Bader quoted in Brickhill, *Reach for the Sky*, 159.

33 Brickhill, *Reach for the Sky*, 175.

34 Trafford Leigh-Mallory quoted in Brickhill, *Reach for the Sky*, 177

35 Brickhill, *Reach for the Sky*, 179.

36 Walter Beisiegel quoted in Brickhill, *Reach for the Sky*, 178.

37 Bader and Turner quoted in Dunmore, *Above and Beyond*, 54.

38 Laddie Lucas, *Flying Colours: The Epic Story of Douglas Bader* (London: Random Century, 1981), 110.

CHAPTER FIVE: TWISTING TURNING MÊLÉE OF FIGHTERS

1 Robert Wright, *Dowding and the Battle of Britain* (London: Macdonald & Co., 1969), 142.

2   Wright, *Dowding and the Battle of Britain*, 144.

3   Denis Richards, *Royal Air Force, 1939–1945,* vol. I, *The Fight at Odds* (London: Queen's Printer, 1953), 149 and 150.

4   R.V. Jones, *Most Secret War: British Scientific Intelligence 1939–1945* (London: Penguin, 2009), 92–95.

5   Galeazzo Ciano quoted in Len Deighton, *Fighter: The True Story of the Battle of Britain* (St. Albans, UK: Triad/Panther Books, 1979), 33.

6   Deighton, *Fighter*, 36.

7   Hermann Göring quoted in Len Deighton, *The Battle of Britain* (Toronto: Clark, Irwin, 1980), 81.

8   Richards, *Royal Air Force 1939–1945*, 161.

9   Stephen Bungay, *The Most Dangerous Enemy: A History of the Battle of Britain* (London: Aurum, 2000), 33.

10 Chris McNab. *The Luftwaffe, 1933–45: Hitler's Eagles.* (New York: Chartwell, 2014), 59.

11 John Boileau, "Canada's Merchant Navy: The Men That Saved the World," *Legion,* July 14, 2010.

12 Winston Churchill quoted in Mark Hawkins-Daly, ed., *Speeches That Changed the World* (London: Quercus, 2005), 96.

13 Jill Mason (née Brown), interview with author, May 1, 2023, Whitby, ON.

14 Werner Kreipe quoted in Deighton, *The Battle of Britain*, 109.

15 Hans-Ekkehard Bob quoted in Joshua Levine, *Forgotten Voices of the Blitz and the Battle for Britain* (London: Ebury, 2006), 168.

16 H.R. Hamilton Combat Report, July 30, 1940, courtesy of Norman Malayney.

17 Hans-Ekkehard Bob quoted in Levine, *Forgotten Voices of the Blitz*, 168.

18 Duncan Hewitt, July 1940 letter quoted in Floyd Williston, *Hurricane Pilots in the Battle of Britain, Part II, The Millidgeville Trio*, unpublished manuscript, courtesy of Norman Malayney), 10.

19 Harry Hogan correspondence, Floyd Williston files, Winnipeg, MB, courtesy of Norman Malayney.

20 Deighton, *The Battle of Britain*, 112.

21 Williston, *Hurricane Pilots in the Battle of Britain*, 12.

22 Duncan Hewitt, July 1940 letter quoted in Williston, *Hurricane Pilots in the Battle of Britain*.

23 Hugh Dowding quoted in Wright, *Dowding and the Battle of Britain*, 142.

24 "The Airmen's Stories: P/O R.A. Horley," Battle of Britain London Monument," n.d., https://www.bbm.org.uk/airmen/Howley.htm.

25 Hannes Trautloft quoted in Peter Townsend, *Duel of Eagles* (Richmond Hill, ON: Simon and Schuster, 1972), 294.

26 Ian MacDougall quoted in Townsend, *Duel of Eagles*, 295.

27 Stephen Bungay, *The Most Dangerous Enemy: A History of the Battle of Britain* (London: Aurum, 2000), 157.

28 "Adolf Hitler's Address to the Reichstag (19 July 1940)," in Max Domarus, ed., *Hitler. Speeches and Proclamations, 1932–1945, The Chronicle of a Dictatorship*, vol. 3: *1939–1940*, (London: Bloomsbury), 2062.

29 Winston Churchill, *The Second World War*, vol. II, *Their Finest Hour* (Cambridge, MA: Houghton Mifflin, 1949), 259.

30 Norman Longmate, *How We Lived Then: A History of Everyday Life during the Second World War* (London: Hutchinson, 1971), 108.

31 "Warum" propaganda leaflet printed by His Majesty's Stationary Office, March 1940.

32 Ellin Bessner, *Double Threat: Canadian Jews, the Military, and World War II* (Toronto: University of Toronto Press, 2018), 159.

33 Patrick Otter, *Yorkshire Airfields in the Second World War* (Newbury, UK: Countryside Books, 1998), 82.

34 *Canadian Jews in World War II: Part I, Decorations* (Montreal: Canadian Jewish Congress, 1947), 29.

35 Richards, *Royal Air Force, 1939-1945*, 159.

36 Bill Nelson letter quoted in *Canadian Jews in World War II: Part I, Decorations*, 29.

37 Deighton, *Battle of Britain*, 119.

38 "Adolph Hitler's Directive No. 17," Battle of Britain Historical Society, 2007, https://www.battleofbritain1940.net/document-27.html.

39 Martin Sugarman, "World War II: Jewish Pilots and Aircrews in the Battle of Britain," Jewish Virtual Library, A Project of American-Israeli Cooperative Enterprise.

40 Robert Wilson letter quoted in Floyd Williston, "P/O Robert R. Bob Wilson of Treble One" (unpublished manuscript, courtesy of Norman Malayney).

41 Robert Wilson letter quoted in Floyd Williston, "P/O Robert R. Bob Wilson of Treble One."

42 Edith Wilson letter to son Bob Fitzsimmons, September 1986, quoted in Floyd Williston, "P/O Robert R. Bob Wilson of Treble One."

43 Jack Nissen with A.W. Cockerill, *Winning the Radar War: A Memoir* (Toronto: Macmillan, 1987), 88.

44 Dialogue quoted in Townsend, *Duel of Eagles*, 325 and 326.

45 Stephen Bungay, *The Most Dangerous Enemy: A History of the Battle of Britain* (London: Aurum, 2000), 141.

46 "Leave It to Us, Sonny," Dudley S. Cowes (artist), Imperial War Museum, London, https://www.iwm.org.uk/collections/item/object/5694.

47 Mason, interview with author. Unless otherwise noted, all quotations in this section are taken from this source.

CHAPTER SIX: OUR NATIONAL DUTY RESTS TERRIBLE AND CLEAR

1   Garfield Weston quoted in Graham Chandler, "The Gift of Air Power," *Legion* magazine, September 15, 2012.

2   Lord Beaverbrook quoted in Len Deighton, *Fighter: The True Story of the Battle of Britain* (St. Albans, UK: Triad/Panther Books, 1979), 183.

3   Lord Nuffield and Lord Beaverbrook quoted in J.F. Willock, "The Castle Bromwich Aircraft Factory," paper published Warwickshire Industrial Archaeology Society, January 2021.

4   Denis Richards, *Royal Air Force, 1939–1945*, vol. I, *The Fight at Odds* (London: Queen's Printer, 1953), 152.

5   Tim Clayton and Phil Craig, *Finest Hour: The Battle of Britain*, (New York: Simon & Schuster, 1999), 229.

6   Deighton, *Fighter*, 183.

7   Richard I. Bourgeois-Doyle, *Her Daughter the Engineer: The Life of Elsie Gregory MacGill* (Ottawa: NRC Research Press, 2008), 26.

8   Crystal Sissons, *Elsie Gregory MacGill: Engineering the Future and Building Bridges for Canadian Women, 1918–1980* (PhD diss., University of Ottawa, 2008), 46.

9   Elsie MacGill quoted in "Women on the Wing," *Chatelaine* magazine, August 1931.

10 Bourgeois-Doyle, *Her Daughter the Engineer* 149.

11 Caption of photo entitled "Hurricanes Made in Canada," *Standard Photonews*, Montreal, July 20, 1940.

12 Elsie MacGill, "Aircraft Engineering in Wartime Canada," *Engineering Journal* (November 1940): 470–71.

13 "Queen of the Hurricanes: Elsie MacGill," *True Comics*, No. 8 (January 1942), 17–21.

14 Elsie MacGill, "Aircraft Engineering in Wartime Canada," *Engineering Journal* (November 1940): 470–71.

15 Bev Christmas interview by Cameron Falconer, University of Victoria, Special Collections, Military Oral History Collection (SC104), Beverley Evans Christmas, CBE_028.

16 Bev Christmas interview by Cameron Falconer, University of Victoria, Special Collections, Military Oral History Collection (SC104), Beverley Evans Christmas, CBE_028.

17 Historical Section of the Royal Canadian Air Force, *The R.C.A.F. Overseas*, vol. 1: *The First Four Years* (Toronto: Oxford University Press, 1944), 10.

18 "History of the Battle of Britain: The New Tactics," RAF Museum, London.

19 "History of the Battle of Britain: The New Tactics," RAF Museum, London.

20 Ernest McNab combat report quoted in *The R.C.A.F. Overseas*, vol. 1, 12.

21 Spencer Dunmore, *Above and Beyond: The Canadians' War in the Air, 1939–45* (Toronto: McClelland & Stewart, 1996), 67.

22 "Beaverbrook Builds R.A.F. Planes While Son Destroys the Germans,'" Canadian Press, August 16, 1940.

23 Peter Townsend, *Duel of Eagles* (Richmond Hill, ON: Simon and Schuster, 1972), 346.

24 Hugh Dowding quoted in Peter Townsend, *Duel of Eagles*, 351.

25 Richards, *Royal Air Force, 1939–1945*, vol. 1, 170.

26 Deighton, *Battle of Britain*, 137.

27 Adolf Galland, *The Battle of Britain* (UK: Air Historical Branch, Air Ministry, AHB6, February 1953), 1.

28 Deighton, *The Battle of Britain*, 155.

29 Adolf Galland, *The First and the Last (Die Ersten und die Letzen)* (London: Methuen, 1954).

30 Paul Deichmann, *Spearhead for Blitzkrieg Luftwaffe Operations in Support of the Army, 1939–1945* (New York: Ivy, 1996).

31 Deighton, *Fighter*, 229.

32 Hermann Göring quoted in Townsend, *Duel of Eagles*, 345 and 365.

33 Winston Churchill, *The Second World War:* vol. II, *Their Finest Hour* (Cambridge, MA: Houghton Mifflin, 1949), 324.

34 British House of Commons, Hansard, 5th Series, Volume 364, cc 1167, August 20, 1940.

35 J.A. Kent, *One of the Few: A Story of Personal Challenge Through the Battle of Britain and Beyond* (London: William Kimber, 1971), 104.

36 Paul Pitcher letter to author David L. Bashow, July 1993, copy in Paul Pitcher papers, courtesy of Jerry Vernon, Canadian Aviation Historical Society.

37 Bill Sprenger combat report quoted in William Arthur Bishop, *The Splendid Hundred: The True Story of Canadians Who Flew in the Greatest Air Battle of World War II* (Toronto: McGraw-Hill Ryerson, 1994), 38.

38 McNab quoted in Bishop, *The Splendid Hundred*, 40.

39 Anne Reed (née Elliott), interview with author, May 1, 2023, Whitby, ON.

40 Winston Churchill, *The Second World War:* vol. II, 342.

41 Martin Middlebrook and Chris Everitt, *The Bomber Command War Diaries: An Operational Reference Book: 1939–1945*, (New York: Viking, 1985), 76 and 77.

42 Adolf Hitler quoted in Vera Lynn, *We'll Meet Again: A Personal and Social History of World War Two* (London: Sidgwick & Jackson,1989), 66.

43 Ludwik Paszkiewicz quoted in Mariusz Gasior, "The Polish Pilots Who Flew in the Battle of Britain," Imperial War Museum, n.d., https://www.iwm.org.uk/history/the-polish-pilots-who-flew-in-the-battle-of-britain.

44 J.A. Kent, *One of the Few: A Story of Personal Challenge through the Battle of Britain and Beyond* (London: William Kimber, 1971), 105.

45 "Kentowski" nickname appears in Lynne Olson and Stanley Cloud, *A Question of Honor: The Kosciuszko Squadron, Forgotten Heroes of World War II* (New York: Knopf, 2003), 120.

46 Ernest McNab, "R.A.F. Is Well Prepared To Meet Nazi Hordes," third of four articles written May 5, 1941, https://flyingforyourlife.com/pilots/ww2/mc/mcnab/.

47 *The R.C.A.F. Overseas,* vol. 1, 14.

48 Bev Christmas interview by Cameron Falconer. Unless otherwise noted, all quotations in this section are taken from this source.

CHAPTER SEVEN: SAFE IN YOUR HANDS

1 Len Deighton, *Fighter: The True Story of the Battle of Britain* (St. Albans, UK: Triad/Panther Books, 1979), 241.

2 F/L H.N. Hamilton Combat Report (G 89367), August 18, 1940. Floyd Williston files, Winnipeg, MB, courtesy of Norman Malayney.

3 F/L H.N. Hamilton Combat Report (G 89375), August 26, 1940. Floyd Williston files, Winnipeg, MB, courtesy of Norman Malayney.

4 Peter Townsend, *Duel of Eagles* (Richmond Hill, ON: Simon and Schuster, 1972), 371.

5 Peter Townsend, *Duel of Eagles* (Richmond Hill, ON: Simon and Schuster, 1972), 372.

6 Floyd Williston, *Hurricane Pilots in the Battle of Britain, Part III, The Millidgeville Trio*, 26, unpublished manuscript, courtesy of Norman Malayney.

7 Peter Townsend, *Duel of Eagles* (Richmond Hill, ON: Simon and Schuster, 1972), 392.

8 Derek Wood and Derek Dempster, *The Narrow Margin* (Barnsley, UK: Pen and Sword, 2003), 314.

9 Floyd Williston, "He Was Full of Courage and Dash," *Times Globe* (Saint John, NB), September 14, 2000.

10 Floyd Williston, *Hurricane Pilots in the Battle of Britain, Part III, The Millidgeville Trio*, (unpublished manuscript, courtesy of Norman Malayney), 15.

11 Trafford Leigh-Mallory quoted in Paul Brickhill, *Reach for the Sky: The Story of Douglas Bader* (London: Collins, 1954), 198.

12 Trafford Leigh-Mallory quoted in Brickhill, *Reach for the Sky*, 198.

13 Hugh Halliday, *242 Squadron: The Canadian Years, The Story of the RAF's All Canadian Fighter Squadron* (Stittsville, ON: Canada's Wings, 1981), 92.

14 "Hamilton Pilot Vanquishes Nazi Raider in Scrap," *Hamilton Spectator*, September 1940.

15 Halliday, *242 Squadron*, 84.

16 Halliday, *242 Squadron*, 91.

17 Alfred Woodhall quoted in Brickhill, *Reach for the Sky*, 203.

18 Halliday, *242 Squadron*, 93.

19 George Christie quoted in Halliday, *242 Squadron*, 93.

20 Noel Stansfeld quoted in Halliday, *242 Squadron*, 95.

21 Willie McKnight combat report quoted in Halliday, *242 Squadron*, 94.

22 McKnight letter to Harry Pegler, September 22, 1940, quoted in Jeff Bartkiewicz, "Calgary Flying Ace Lived Hard, Died Young," *Calgary Herald*, August 29, 2004.

23 Deighton, *The Battle of Britain* (Toronto: Clark, Irwin, 1980), 150.

24 Cyrill Newall quoted in Halliday, *242 Squadron*, 96.

25 Bader and Woodhall quoted in Brickhill, *Reach for the Sky*, 206.

26 Dowding quoted in Robert Wright, *Dowding and the Battle of Britain* (London: Macdonald & Co., 1969), 180.

27 Deighton, *The Battle of Britain*, 151 and 159.

28 Historical Section of the Royal Canadian Air Force *The R.C.A.F. Overseas*, vol. 1: *The First Four Years* (Toronto: Oxford University Press, 1944), 15.

29 Robin Hill, "The Man Who Fell to Earth," Essex Historic Aircraft Collection, Ingatestone, September 1940, www.aviationmuseum.co.uk.

30 Roy Sweeting quoted in Hill, "The Man Who Fell to Earth.

31 "Town Of Sackville Mourns with University President on Death of Pilot Officer," New Brunswick newspaper, September 7, 1940.

32 John Greenwood letter to Floyd Williston, c. 1990, courtesy of Norman Malayney.

33 Paul Pitcher correspondence with Floyd Williston, June 16, 1997. Williston files, Winnipeg, MB, courtesy of Norman Malayney.

34 Ernest McNab, "Initial Fight with Enemy Is Memory That Remains" third of four articles written, May 5, 1941, https://flyingforyourlife.com/pilots/ww2/mc/mcnab/.

35 Sam Robertson, "'Scramble Angels' Is Signal For R.C.A.F. Unit To Soar," Canadian Press, September 4, 1940.

36 Townsend, *Duel of Eagles*, 409.

37 Robert "Butcher" Barton interviewed by Norm Christie, Hedley, BC, 2004, for *King & Country* TV series (with permission).

38 Stephen Bungay, *The Most Dangerous Enemy, An Illustrated History of the Battle of Britain* (London: Aurum Press, 2010), 202.

39 Wood and Dempster, *The Narrow Margin*, 212 and 213.

40 Deighton, *The Battle of Britain*, 163.

41 Deighton, *Fighter*, 253.

42 Townsend, *Duel of Eagles*, 293 and 410.

43 Winston Churchill, *The Second World War:* vol. II, *Their Finest Hour* (Cambridge, MA: Houghton Mifflin, 1949), 312.

44 Norman Longmate, *How We Lived Then: A History of Everyday Life during the Second World War* (London: Hutchinson & Co., 1971), 111.

45 Terry Copp, "Standing Up to the Blitz: Army, Part 4," *Legion,* January 1, 1996.

46 R.S. Gilmour quoted in Denis Richards, *Royal Air Force 1939–1945*, vol. I, *The Fight at Odds* (London: Her Majesty's Stationery Office, 1953), 187.

47 William L. Shirer, *The Rise and Fall of the Third Reich, A History of Nazi Germany* (New York: Simon and Schuster, 1959), 1022 and 1023.

48 Hugh Dowding quoted in Wright, *Dowding and the Battle of Britain*, 184.

49 Deighton, *The Battle of Britain*, 169.

50 Hermann Göring quoted in Deighton, *Fighter*, 270 and 271.

51 Adolf Galland, *The Battle of Britain* (UK: Air Historical Branch, Air Ministry, AHB6, February 1953), 2.

52 Adolf Galland quoted in John Zentner, *The Art of Wing Leadership and Aircrew Morale in Combat*, Vol. Cadre Papers (Maxwell, AL: Air University Press, 2001), 33 and 34.

53 Bader and Woodhall quoted in Brickhill, *Reach for the Sky*, 209.

54 Bader and Woodhall quoted in Brickhill, *Reach for the Sky*, 211.

55 Vera Lynn, *We'll Meet Again: A Personal and Social History of World War Two* (London: Sidgwick & Jackson, 1994), 67.

56 Townsend, *Duel of Eagles*, 428.

57 P/O Hugh Tamblyn Combat Report, September 9, 1940, quoted in Hugh Halliday, *242 Squadron, The Canadian Years: The Story of the RAF's All-Canadian Fighter Squadron* (Stittsville, ON: Canada's Wings, 1981), 102.

58 McKnight letter to Harry Pegler, September 22, 1940, quoted in Bartkiewicz, "Calgary Flying Ace."

59 "Matching Faces to a Few of the Names," *Battle of Britain Remembered* (magazine), 219.

60 Stephen Bungay, *The Most Dangerous Enemy: A History of the Battle of Britain* (London: Aurum, 2000), 214.

CHAPTER EIGHT: JUST SORT OF GOT USED TO IT

1 Vera Lynn, *We'll Meet Again: A Personal and Social History of World War Two* (London: Sidgwick & Jackson, 1994), 67.

2 Lynn, *We'll Meet Again*, 69.

3 Stephen Bates, "Blitz 70th Anniversary: Night of Fire That Heralded a New Kind of War," *The Guardian*, September 6, 2010.

4 Lynn, *We'll Meet Again*, 68.

5 Dorothy Marshall (née Firth) correspondence with her daughter Helen Beauchamp, Toronto, ON, November 3, 2023.

6   Dorothy Marshall (née Firth) interview with author, Toronto, ON, May 25, 2023.

7   "Fire Watchers and Fire Guards," Firefighters' Memorial Trust, https://firefightersmemorial.org.uk/research/fire-watchers-and-fire-guards/

8   Simon Fowler, *Richmond at War, 1939–1945* (Richmond, UK: Richmond Local History Society, 2015).

9   Marshall (née Firth) correspondence, November 3, 2023.

10 Marshall (née Firth) interview, May 25, 2023.

11 Lynn, *We'll Meet Again*, 127.

12 Keith C. Ogilvie, *You Never Know Your Luck: Battle of Britain to the Great Escape, the Extraordinary Life of Keith "Skeets" Ogilvie* (Stotfold, UK: Fighting High Publishing, 2016), 63.

13 Ogilvie, *You Never Know Your Luck*.

14 Ogilvie, *You Never Know Your Luck*, 1 and 64.

15 Ogilvie, *You Never Know Your Luck*, 53.

16 Spencer Dunmore, *Above and Beyond: The Canadians' War in the Air, 1939–45* (Toronto: McClelland & Stewart, 1996), 68.

17 Denis Richards, *Royal Air Force 1939–1945*, vol. 1, *The Fight At Odds* (London: Her Majesty's Stationery Office, 1953), 186.

18 Ogilvie, *You Never Know Your Luck*, 73 and 74.

19 J.A. Kent, *One of the Few: A Story of Personal Challenge Through the Battle of Britain and Beyond* (London: William Kimber, 1971), 111 and 112.

20 Kent, *One of the Few*, 114.

21 Jan Zumbach, *On Wings of War: My Life as a Pilot Adventurer* (London: Deutsch, 1975).

22 J.E. Johnson, *Wing Leader* (New York: Ballantine Books, 1957), 138.

23 Kent, *One of the Few*, 120 and 121.

24 Mathias Joost, "The Unsung Heroes of the Battle of Britain: The Groundcrew of No. 1 (RCAF) Squadron," *RCAF Journal*, 2015.

25 Jay Warner interview with author, Antonito, CO, USA, February 5, 2023.

26 Thomas A. Lawrence quoted in "Aviators of Hudson Strait," National Film Board of Canada, 1973.

27 "Wing Commander Arthur Hicklin Warner," Government of Canada, 2013, https://www.canada.ca/en/department-national-defence/maple-leaf/rcaf/migration/2013/wing-commander-arthur-hicklin-warner.html.

28 Edwin Reyno correspondence with Swannell, July 18, 1980, from Floyd Williston files, courtesy of Norman Malayney.

29 Edwin Reyno, "Personal Reflections of a Pilot," *The Roundel*, September 1960.

30 Ernest McNab, "Initial Fight with Enemy Is Memory That Remains" third of four articles written May 5, 1941, https://flyingforyourlife.com/pilots/ww2/mc/mcnab/.

31 Otto Peterson letter home to Saskatchewan, September, 1940, quoted in "One Helped to Rescue Leader, Gives His Own Life for Empire," *Halifax Chronicle*, September 11, 1940.

32 Norman Longmate, *How We Lived Then: A History of Everyday Life during the Second World War* (London: Hutchinson & Co., 1971), 105 and 106.

33 Frank Lowe, "20 Years Ago, They Broke The Luftwaffe," *Weekend* magazine, *Montreal Gazette*, vol. 10, no. 37, September 10, 1960, 6.

34 Reyno correspondence with Swannell, July 18, 1980.

35 Ernest McNab, "Pilot Needs Oxygen for Fighting at Great Heights," second of four articles written May 5, 1941, https://flyingforyourlife.com/pilots/ww2/mc/mcnab/.

36 W.P. Coward letter quoted in "Winnipeg Pilot Tells of Reactions During Air Battle with Germans," *Winnipeg Tribune*, July 31, 1940.

37 Winston Churchill, *The Second World War:* vol. II, *Their Finest Hour* (Cambridge, MA: Houghton Mifflin, 1949), 331.

38 Churchill, *The Second World War*, vol. II, 329 and 330.

39 Ernest McNab, "Pilot Needs Oxygen." https://flyingforyourlife.com/pilots/ww2/mc/mcnab/

40 Deighton, *The Battle of Britain* (Toronto: Clark, Irwin, 1980), 168.

41 Lowe, "20 Years Ago, They Broke The Luftwaffe," 6.

42 *Völkischer Beobachter* quoted in Peter Townsend, *Duel of Eagles* (Richmond Hill, ON: Simon and Schuster, 1972), 431.

43 Erich Raeder and Adolf Hitler quoted in Peter Townsend, *Duel of Eagles* (Richmond Hill, ON: Simon and Schuster, 1972), 437.

44 William L. Shirer, *The Rise and Fall of the Third Reich: A History of Nazi Germany* (New York: Simon and Schuster, 1959), 1026 and 1027.

45 Reinhard Heydrich quoted in Shirer, *The Rise and Fall of the Third Reich*, 1028.

CHAPTER NINE: A SINGLE SAVAGE PURPOSE

1   Anne Reed (née Elliott) interview with author, May 1, 2023, Whitby, ON.

2   Paul Pitcher letter to David L. Bashow, July 1993, Paul Pitcher papers, courtesy of Jerry Vernon, Canadian Aviation Historical Society.

3   Michael Bywater, "Our Forgotten Freedom Fighter: Why the Unsung Hurricane Is the True Ace of the Battle of Britain," *Independent* (London, UK), January 17, 2011.

4   Pitcher to Bashow, July 1993.

5   Tom Gleave quoted in Chaz Bowyer and Armand Van Ishoven, *Hurricane and Messerschmitt* (Leicester, UK: Promotional Reprint Co., 1974), 36 and 37.

6   Pitcher to Bashow, July 1993.

7   Hermann Göring quoted in Bowyer and Van Ishoven, *Hurricane and Messerschmitt*, 176.

8   Hans-Ekkehard Bob quoted in Joshua Levine, *Forgotten Voices of the Blitz and the Battle for Britain* (London: Ebury, 2006), 184.

9   Stephen Bungay, *The Most Dangerous Enemy: A History of the Battle of Britain* (London: Aurum, 2000), 319 and 219.

10 Adolf Galland, *The Battle of Britain*, unpublished (translated) manuscript, Air Ministry, Air Historical Branch, February 6, 1953, 21.

11 "Interview with Hans-Ekkehard Bob," Griffon-Merlin, n.d., https://www.griffonmerlin.com/wwii-interview/hans-ekkehard-bob/.

12 Winston Churchill, *The Second World War:* vol. II, *Their Finest Hour* (Cambridge, MA: Houghton Mifflin, 1949), 332.

13 Keith Ogilvie diary quoted in Keith C. Ogilvie, *You Never Know Your Luck: Battle of Britain to the Great Escape: The Extraordinary Life of Keith "Skeets" Ogilvie* (Stotfold, UK: Fighting High Publishing, 2016), 67.

14 Bungay, *The Most Dangerous Enemy*, 218.

15 Deane Nesbitt quoted in "Pilots of the RCAF and RAF in the Battle of Britain," *Toronto Star*, September 15, 1965.

16 J.D. Smith Combat Report, R.A.F. Form 1151, September 15, 1940, quoted in "Part played by Canadian fighter pilots on 15 September 1940," (unpublished manuscript), Floyd Williston files, Winnipeg, MB, courtesy of Norman Malayney, 16.

17 Douglas Bader quoted in Peter Townsend, *Duel of Eagles: The Struggles for the Skies from the First World War to the Battle of Britain* (Richmond Hill, ON: Simon and Schuster, 1972), 440.

18   Hugh Halliday, *242 Squadron, The Canadian Years: The Story of the RAF's All-Canadian Fighter Squadron* (Stittsville, ON: Canada's Wings, 1981), 103.

19   Paul Brickhill, *Reach for the Sky: The Story of Douglas Bader* (London: Collins, 1954), 221.

20   Townsend, *Duel of Eagles*, 390.

21   John Weal, *Jagdgeschwader 54 Grünherz*, vol. 6 (Oxford: Osprey, 2001), 286–89.

22   Hans-Ekkehard Bob quoted in Levine, *Forgotten Voices of the Blitz*, 192.

23   Keith Ogilvie diary quoted in Ogilvie, *You Never Know Your Luck*, 67.

24   Keith Ogilvie diary quoted in Ogilvie, *You Never Know Your Luck*, 68.

25   Queen Wilhelmina correspondence quoted in Ogilvie, *You Never Know Your Luck*, 70.

26   Queen Elizabeth quoted in Vera Lynn, *We'll Meet Again: A Personal and Social History of World War Two* (London: Sidgwick & Jackson, 1994), 74.

27   Blitz victim quoted in Norman Longmate, *How We Lived Then: A History of Everyday Life during the Second World War* (London: Hutchinson & Co., 1971), 133.

28   Statistics and epitaph quoted in Longmate, *How We Lived Then*, 133 and 134.

29   George Levesque quoted in Frank Lowe, "The Few: 20 Years Ago, They Broke the Luftwaffe," *Weekend* magazine 10, no. 37 (*Montreal Gazette*), September 10, 1960.

30   Ron Lowman, "The Battle of Britain: September 1949," *Toronto Star*, September 9, 1990.

31   Townsend, *Duel of Eagles*, 442.

32   Alfred Price, *Battle of Britain Day: 15 September 1940* (London: Greenhill Books, 1990), 80.

33   Adolf Galland, *The First and the Last (Die Ersten und die Letzen)* (London: Methuen, 1954).

34   Larry Forrester, *Fly For Your Life: The Colorful Exploits of One of World War II's Greatest Fighter Aces* (Garden City, NY: Nelson Doubleday, 1973), 153 and 154.

35   Robert "Butcher" Barton interviewed by Norm Christie 2004, Hedley, BC, for *King & Country* TV series, with permission.

36   Dal Russel quoted in "Wing Commander Blair Dalzell Russel, DSO, DFC and Bar," *Profiles of Members of the Aircrew Association*, (Aircrew Association, 1989), 263.

37 Gordon McGregor quoted in "Group Captain Gordon R. McGregor: OBE, DFC, Croix de Guerre, Cdr. Order of Orange Nassau" (Aircrew Asscociation, 1989), 203.

38 Paul Pitcher RCAF No. 1 Squadron combat report, September 15, 1940, Floyd Williston files, Winnipeg, MB, courtesy of Norman Malayney.

39 Bob Norris RCAF No. 1 Squadron combat report, September 15, 1940, Floyd Williston files, Winnipeg, MB, courtesy of Norman Malayney.

40 "Canadians continue success in air against Nazi flyers," Canadian Press cable, September 26, 1940.

41 Ernie McNab quoted in Tim Woods, "A few Canadians..." *Canada Today* 27 (Commemorative Issue), Canadian High Commission, Canada House, London, UK, September 1990, 3.

42 Churchill, *The Second World War:* vol. II, 336.

43 Halliday, *242 Squadron*, 104.

44 John Terraine, *The Right of the Line: The Royal Air Force in the European War, 1939–1945* (London: Hodder and Stoughton, 1985), 211.

45 Michel Lavigne, "Part Played by Canadian Fighter Pilots on 15 September 1940," (unpublished manuscript), Floyd Williston files, Winnipeg, MB, courtesy of Norman Malayney, 37 and 38.

46 Douglas Bader quoted in Derek Wood and Derek Dempster, *The Narrow Margin: The Battle of Britain and the Rise of Air Power* (London: Tri-Service Press, 1990), 122.

47 Price, *Battle of Britain Day*, 86–92.

48 J.A. Kent, *One of the Few; A Story of Personal Challenge through the Battle of Britain and Beyond* (London: William Kimber, 1971), 115.

49 Kent, *One of the Few*, 116.

50 Joss Meakins, "Polish Pilots and the Battle of Britain," Historic UK, n.d., https://www.historic-uk.com/HistoryUK/HistoryofBritain/Polish-Pilots-the-Battle-of-Britain/.

51 Halliday, *242 Squadron*, 102.

52 Harold Bennett, ed., *Bawdy Ballads and Dirty Ditties of the Wartime RAF* (Bognor Regis, UK: Woodfield, 2000).

53 Peter O'Brian, No. 152 Combat Report quoted in Michel Lavigne, "Part played by Canadian fighter pilots on 15 September 1940," (unpublished manuscript), Floyd Williston files, Winnipeg, MB, courtesy of Norman Malayney, 37.

54 Lavigne, "Part played by Canadian fighter pilots," 37.

55 Lynn, *We'll Meet Again*, 70.

56 Len Deighton, *Battle of Britain* (Toronto: Clark, Irwin, 1980), 202.

57 Bungay, *The Most Dangerous Enemy*, 225.

58 Townsend, *Duel of Eagles*, 444.

59 Albert Kesselring quoted in Townsend, *Duel of Eagles*, 445.

60 Kriegsmarine report quoted in Townsend, *Duel of Eagles*, 445 and 446.

61 Denis Richards, *Royal Air Force, 1939–1945*, vol. I, *The Fight at Odds* (London: Her Majesty's Stationery Office, 1953), 186 and 187.

62 Hitler's Directive No. 16 quoted in Townsend, *Duel of Eagles*, 292.

63 Terraine, *The Right of the Line*, 212.

64 F.W. Winterbotham, *The Ultra Secret* (New York: Dell, 1974), 58 and 59.

65 W. Ewart Cockram correspondence with Smither family quoted in "In the Struggle for Liberty And Justice," *London Free Press*, September 1940.

CHAPTER TEN: GREAT AND GLORIOUS DAY

1 Keith Ogilvie diary quoted in Keith C. Ogilvie, *You Never Know Your Luck: Battle of Britain to the Great Escape, The Extraordinary Life of Keith "Skeets" Ogilvie* (Stotfold, UK: Fighting High Publishing, 2016), 73.

2 Keith Ogilvie diary quoted in Ogilvie, *You Never Know Your Luck*, 74 and 75.

3 Bev Christmas interview by Cameron Falconer, University of Victoria, Special Collections, Military Oral History Collection (SC104), Beverley Evans Christmas, CBE_028.

4 Tim Clayton and Phil Craig, *Finest Hour: The Battle of Britain* (New York: Simon & Schuster, 1999), 185 and 186.

5 Bev Christmas interview by Cameron Falconer.

6 Frank Lowe, "The Few: 20 Years Ago, They Broke The Luftwaffe," *Weekend* magazine 10, no. 37 (*Montreal Gazette*), September 10, 1960.

7 Arthur Bishop, *The Splendid Hundred: The True Story of Canadians Who Flew in the Greatest Air Battle of World War II* (Toronto: McGraw-Hill Ryerson, 1994), 90.

8 Hartland Molson quoted in Shirley E. Woods, *The Molson Saga: 1763–1983* (Toronto: Doubleday, 1986).

9 Douglas Bader quoted in Hugh Halliday, *242 Squadron, The Canadian*

Years: The Story of the RAF's All-Canadian Fighter Squadron (Stittsville, ON: Canada's Wings, 1981), 107.

10 RCAF No. 1 Squadron diarist quoted in Bishop, *The Splendid Hundred*, 86.

11 Historical Section of the Royal Canadian Air Force, *The R.C.A.F. Overseas*, vol. I, *The First Four Years* (Toronto: Oxford University Press, 1944), 20.

12 Bev Christmas interview by Cameron Falconer.

13 Gordon McGregor quoted in "Group Captain Gordon R. McGregor: OBE, DFC, Croix de Guerre, Cdr. Order of Orange Nassau" (Aircrew Asscociation, 1989), 203.

14 Hartland Molson correspondence with Floyd Williston, June 13, 1997, Floyd Williston files, courtesy of Norman Malayney.

15 Bev Christmas interview by Cameron Falconer.

16 *The R.C.A.F. Overseas*, 20.

17 "Air Marshal Bishop Visits Canadian Fliers," Canadian Press cable, Toronto CP Office, September 26, 1940.

18 Ernie McNab quoted in "Canada's Airmen Visited By King," Canadian Press cable "Somewhere in England," Toronto CP Office, September 26, 1940.

19 "Canada's Airmen Visited By King," Canadian Press cable "Somewhere in England," Toronto CP Office, September 26, 1940.

20 Adolf Galland quoted in Philip Kaplan, *Fighter Aces of the Luftwaffe in World War II*, (Auldgirth, Dumfriesshire, UK: Pen and Sword Aviation, 2007), 10.

21 Adolf Hitler quoted in Peter Townsend, *Duel of Eagles: The Struggles for the Skies from the First World War to the Battle of Britain* (Richmond Hill, ON: Simon and Schuster, 1972), 450.

22 Keith Ogilvie diary quoted in Ogilvie, *You Never Know Your Luck*, 77 and 78.

23 Mark Beckwith, "45 Seconds," Making History, February 6, 2022, https://making-history.ca/2022/02/06/wednesday-25th-september-1940/.

24 Gordon McGregor combat report, September 27, 1940, quoted in *The R.C.A.F. Overseas*, 23.

25 Ulrich Steinhilper quoted in Stephen Bungay, *The Most Dangerous Enemy, An Illustrated History of the Battle of Britain* (London: Aurum, 2010), 230.

26 Gordon McGregor combat report, September 27, 1940, *The R.C.A.F. Overseas*, 26.

27 *The R.C.A.F. Overseas*, 27.

28 *The R.C.A.F. Overseas*, 27.

29 John Latta combat report, September 27, 1940, quoted Halliday, *242 Squadron*, 109.

30 Noel Stansfeld combat report, September 27, 1940, quoted Halliday, *242 Squadron*, 109.

31 Willie McKnight correspondence, September 22, 1940 quoted in Hugh Halliday, "No. 242 Canadian Squadron revisited," *RCAF Journal*, 4, no. 2 (September 12, 2017).

32 Bungay, *The Most Dangerous Enemy*, 231.

33 Winston Churchill quoted in Bishop, *The Splendid Hundred*, 91.

34 Dal Russel correspondence quoted in "Wing Commander Blair Dalzell Russel, DSO, DFC and Bar," *Profiles of Members of the Aircrew Association* (Aircrew Association, 1989), 266 and 267.

35 "Flight-Lieut. Jean Paul Desloges Invalided Home," *Toronto Star*, January 1941.

36 Kevin Mowbrey, "Albert Ross Tilley: The Legacy of a Canadian Plastic Surgeon," *Canadian Journal of Plastic Surgery* 21, no. 2 (Summer 2013): 102–6.

37 A.H. McIndoe, "Total Reconstruction of the Burned Face," *British Journal of Plastic Surgery* 26 (1983): 410–20.

38 Will Chabun, "Lionel Hastings—A Proud Guinea Pig," *Regina Leader-Post*, November 9, 2001.

39 Interview with Hilda (Empey) Moore, "Treating Severe Burns Victims: Heroes Remember," June 7, 1997, https://www.veterans.gc.ca/eng/video-gallery/video/4595.

40 Lionel Hastings quoted in Chabun, "Lionel Hastings," *Regina Leader-Post*.

41 Ross Tilley quoted in Peter Wilton, "WWII Guinea Pigs Played Crucial Role in Refining Plastic Surgery in Canada," *Canadian Medical Association Journal* 159 (1998): 1159.

42 W.R. Feasby, *The Official History of the Canadian Medical Services, 1939–1945*, (Ottawa: Department of National Defence, Directorate of History and Heritage, 1956), 363–66.

43 Interview with Hilda (Empey) Moore, "Treating Severe Burns Victims: Heroes Remember," June 7, 1997.

44 "Fliers of 1st Fighter Squadron, R.C.A.F., Come Home," *Toronto Star*, November 1940.

45 Hartland Molson letter to Floyd Williston, July 3, 1997, courtesy of Norman Malayney.

46 J.A. Kent, *One of the Few: A Story of Personal Challenge through the Battle of Britain and Beyond* (London: William Kimber, 1971), 124.

47 Robert "Butcher" Barton interviewed by Norm Christie, 2004.

48 Hugh Dowding quoted in Townsend, *Duel of Eagles*, 455.

49 Townsend, *Duel of Eagles*, 455.

50 R.J. Nodwell quoted in Dave McIntosh, *High Blue Battle: The War Diary of No. 1 (401) Fighter Squadron, RCAF* (Toronto: Stoddart, 1990), 41.

51 RCAF No. 1 war diary (November 8, 1940) quoted in McIntosh, *High Blue Battle*, 46.

CHAPTER ELEVEN: THE BEST DAYS OF THEIR LIVES

1 J.A. Kent, *One of the Few: A Story of Personal Challenge through the Battle of Britain and Beyond* (London: William Kimber, 1971), 127.

2 Exchange between Winston Churchill and Kent recounted in Kent, *One of the Few*, 161–63.

3 Richard King, "Battle of Britain Legend—303 (Polish) Squadron," Key.Aeor, January 24, 2024, https://www.key.aero/article/battle-britain-legend-303-polish-squadron.

4 Jan Zumbach quoted in Mariusz Gasior, "The Polish Pilots Who Flew in the Battle of Britain," Imperial War Museum, https://www.iwm.org.uk/history/the-polish-pilots-who-flew-in-the-battle-of-britain

5 Mirek Szelestowski quoted in Richard King, "Battle of Britain Legend—303 (Polish) Squadron," https://www.key.aero/article/battle-britain-legend-303-polish-squadron.

6 Hugh Dowding quoted in Mariusz Gasior, "The Polish Pilots Who Flew in the Battle of Britain," Imperial War Museum, n.d., https://www.iwm.org.uk/history/the-polish-pilots-who-flew-in-the-battle-of-britain.

7 Ronald Kellett quoted in Richard King, "Battle of Britain Legend."

8 Johnny Kent quoted in Paul Collins, "John Alexander Kent and the RAF's Polish Fighter Pilots," Canada.ca, September 12, 2019, https://www.canada.ca/en/air-force/services/history-heritage/battle-britain/profiles/john-alexander-kent-and-raf-s-polish-fighter-pilots.html.

9 Billy Bishop and Harold Balfour quoted in Arthur Bishop, *The Splendid Hundred: The True Story of Canadians Who Flew in the Greatest Air Battle of World War II* (Whitby, ON: McGraw-Hill Ryerson, 1994), 98.

10 R.J. Nodwell quoted in Dave McIntosh, *High Blue Battle: The War Diary of No. 1 (401) Fighter Squadron, RCAF* (Toronto: Stoddart Publishing, 1990), 41.

11 "The Few: Battle of Britain Aircrew," Bentley Priory Museum, n.d., https://bentleypriorymuseum.org.uk/bentley-priory-and-the-battle-of-britain/the-few/#:~:text=The%20defence%20of%20Britain%20during,was%20just%2020%20years%20old.

12 Paul Pitcher quoted in Tim Woods, "A Few Canadians," *Canada Today* 27 (Commemmorative issue, September 1990): 2.

13 Hartland Molson quoted in "A Few Canadians," *Canada Today*, 2.

14 Willie McKnight combat report, November 5, 1940, Floyd Williston files, Winnipeg, MB, courtesy Norman Malayney.

15 Stan Turner quoted in "Percival Stanley 'Stan' Turner," Century of Flight, n.d., http://www.century-of-flight.freeola.com/Aviation%20history/WW2/aces/Percival%20Stanley%20Turner.htm.

16 Trafford Leigh-Mallory quoted in "Percival Stanley 'Stan' Turner."

17 Bishop, *The Splendid Hundred*, 115.

18 Paul Brickhill, *Reach for the Sky: The Story of Douglas Bader* (London: Collins, 1954), 361.

19 Douglas Bader quoted in *Toronto Star*, February 13, 1941.

20 Michael Parry interview with author, Port Perry, ON, January 22, 2023.

21 Historical Section of the Royal Canadian Air Force, *The R.C.A.F. Overseas: The First Four Years*, (Toronto: Oxford University Press, 1944), 24.

22 Winston Churchill, *The Second World War*, vol. IV, *The Hinge of Fate* (Cambridge, MA: Houghton Mifflin, 1949), 75.

23 Lord Beaverbrook correspondence, February 26, 1942, in Churchill, *The Second World War*, vol. 4. 85.

24 Winston Churchill quoted in Bradley Tolppanen, "Great Contemporaries: Max Aitken, Lord Beaverbrook" The Churchill Project, Hillsdale College, Mississippi, June 17, 2016.

25 Beaverbrook correspondence, February 26, 1942, in Churchill, *The Second World War*, vol. IV, 85.

26 Lord Beaverbrook quoted in Tolppanen, "Great Contemporaries."

27 Dorothy Marshall (née Firth) interview with author, Toronto, ON, May 25, 2023.

28 Anne Reed (née Elliott) interview with author, May 1, 2023, Whitby, ON.

29 Jill Mason (née Brown) interview with author, May 1, 2023, Whitby, ON.

30 Telegram quoted in "Bruce Millar Wounded in Air Battle," *Penticton Herald*, September 12, 1940.

31 "Flying Officer Bruce Millar Given Warm Welcome by the Citizens of Penticton," *Penticton Herald*, December 5, 1940.

32 *Battle of Britain*, Spitfire Productions, Harry Saltzman and Bennie Fisz, 1969.

33 Anthony Mann quoted in Pearl Sheffy, "The Man Who Got the Bond Going," *Calgary Herald*, January 29, 1966.

34 Robert J. Rudhall and Dilip Sarkar, *Battle of Britain: The Movie—The Men and Machines of One of the Greatest War Films Ever Made* (Yorkshire: Ramrod Books, 2000), 17.

35 Robert Diemert quoted in "A Canadian and His Rebuilt Hurricane," *Weekend Magazine* 30 (*Montreal Gazette*), 1968, 13.

36 Christopher Plummer, *In Spite of Myself: A Memoir* (Toronto: Alfred A. Knopf, 2008), 475.

37 Plummer, *In Spite of Myself*, 475.

38 Tino Ballo, *United Artists: The Company That Changed the Film Industry* (Madison: University of Wisconsin Press, 1987), 272.

39 Plummer, *In Spite of Myself*, 477.

40 "Battle of Britain's Mixed Reviews in London, Hot B.O., Notables Attend," *Variety*, September 24, 1969, 6.

41 Vincent Canby, "Screen: Army of Stars Wages the Battle of Britain," *New York Times*, October 21, 1969, 42.

42 Gene Siskel, "The Movies," *Chicago Tribune*, November 4, 1969, 5.

43 Roger Ebert, "Battle of Britain" (review), *Chicago Sun-Times*, November 3, 1969.

44 Harry Saltzman quoted in Bruce Moss, "A New $12 Million Film Relives This Decisive Air Battle of World War II," *Weekend Magazine* 30 (*Montreal Gazette*), September 1968, 12.

45 Plummer, *In Spite of Myself*, 477.

46 Frank Lowe, "20 Years Ago, They Broke The Luftwaffe," *Weekend* magazine, (*Montreal Gazette*) 10, no. 37 (September 10, 1960): 4.

47   Bishop, *The Splendid Hundred*, 4.

48   Richard Holmes, "Normandy 1944," lecture to Defence Electronics History Society, May 11, 2006, Shrivenham, UK.

49   Ernie McNab quoted in Michel Lavigne, "Part played by Canadian fighter pilots on 15 September 1940," (unpublished manuscript), Floyd Williston files, Winnipeg, MB, courtesy of Norman Malayney, 39.

50   Johnny Kent, RAF No. 92 Fighter Squadron combat report (Form F), November 1, 1940. Floyd Williston files, Winnipeg, MB, courtesy of Norman Malayney.

51   Johnny Kent quoted in Adputor Savard correspondence with J.W.G. Clark, October 1, 1941, RCAF Headquarters (Great Britain).

SOURCES

AUTHOR INTERVIEWS
All interviews conducted in the preparation of this book are included in the Notes section.

UNPUBLISHED SOURCES

McNab, E.A. Biographical file, Directorate of History (DHist), Department of National Defence, 75/360.

McNeal, Wayne C. "General Aviation in Canada: A Study of Its Development and Policy." Master's thesis, School of Community and Regional Planning, University of British Columbia, 1969.

Savard, Adputor. Correspondence with J.W.G. Clark, RCAF Ottawa, October 1, 1941.

Sissons, Crystal. "Elsie Gregory MacGill: Engineering the Future and Building Bridges for Canadian Women, 1918–1980." PhD diss., University of Ottawa, 2008.

Williston, Floyd. "Hurricane Pilots in the Battle of Britain, Part II, The Millidgeville Trio." Unpublished manuscript.

———. *The First of the Few*, partial unpublished manuscript.

———. "Hurricane Pilots in the Battle of Britain, Part III, The Millidgeville Trio." Unpublished manuscript.

———. "P/O Robert R. Bob Wilson of Treble One." Unpublished manuscript.

———. "The Young Boy from the St. [*sic*] John Flying Club." Unpublished manuscript.

PUBLISHED SOURCES

BOOKS

Allison, Les. *Canadians in the Royal Air Force*. Altona, MB: Friesen, 1978.

Ballo, Tino. *United Artists: The Company That Changed the Film Industry*. Madison: University of Wisconsin Press, 1987.

Barker, Ralph. *Aviator Extraordinary: The Sidney Cotton Story*. London: Chatto & Windus, 1969.

Barris, Ted. *Behind the Glory: The Plan That Won the Allied Air War*. Toronto: Macmillan, 1992.

———. *The Great Escape: A Canadian Story*. Toronto: Thomas Allen, 2013.

Bashow, David L. *All the Fine Young Eagles: In the Cockpit with Canada's Second World War Fighter Pilots*. Toronto: Stoddart Publishing, 1996.

Bennett, Harold, ed., *Bawdy Ballads & Dirty Ditties of the Wartime RAF*. Bognor Regis, UK: Woodfield, 2000.

Bessner, Ellin. *Double Threat: Canadian Jews, the Military, and World War II*. Toronto: University of Toronto Press, 2018.

Bickers, Richard Townshend. *The Battle of Britain*. London: Salamander Books, 1990.

Bishop, Arthur. *The Splendid Hundred: The True Story of Canadians Who Flew in the Greatest Air Battle of World War II*. Whitby, ON: McGraw-Hill Ryerson, 1994.

Bishop, Edward. *Book of Airmen's Obituaries*. London: Daily Telegraph, 2002.

Bishop, Patrick. *Fighter Boys: Saving Britain 1940*. London: Harper Press, 2004.

Bourgeois-Doyle, Richard I. *Her Daughter, The Engineer: The Life of Elsie Gregory MacGill*. Ottawa: NRC Research Press, 2008.

Bowyer, Chaz, and Armand van Ishoven. *Hurricane & Messerschmitt at War*. Leicester, UK: Promotional Reprint Co., 1993.

Boyle, Andrew, *Trenchard: Man of Vision*, London: Collins, 1962.

Brickhill, Paul. *Reach for the Sky: The Story of Douglas Bader*. London: Collins, 1954.

Brookes, Andrew. *Crash! Military Aircraft Disasters, Accidents and Incidents*. London: Ian Allan, 1991.

Bullock, Allan. *The Life and Times of Ernest Bevin*, vol. II: *Minister of Labour, 1940–45*. London: Heinemann, 1967.

Bungay, Stephen. *The Most Dangerous Enemy: A History of the Battle of Britain*. London: Aurum, 2000.

Byfield, Ted, ed. *Alberta in the 20th Century*, vol. 8, *The War That United the Province*, 1939–1945. Edmonton, AB: United Western Communications, 2000.

Churchill, Winston. *The Second World War*, vol. II: *Their Finest Hour*. Cambridge, MA: Houghton Mifflin, 1949.

———. *The Second World War*, vol. IV: *The Hinge of Fate* Cambridge, MA: Houghton Mifflin, 1949.

Clayton, Tom, and Phil Craig. *Finest Hour: The Battle of Britain*. New York: Simon & Schuster, 1999.

Cole, Lance. *Secrets of the Spitfire: The Story of Beverley Shenstone, the Man Who Perfected the Elliptical Wing*. Barnsley, UK: Pen and Sword, 2012.

Deichmann, Paul. *Spearhead for Blitzkrieg Luftwaffe Operations in Support of the Army, 1939–1945*. New York: Ivy Books, 1996.

Deighton, Len. *Battle of Britain*. Toronto: Clark, Irwin, 1980.

———. *Fighter: The True Story of the Battle of Britain*. St. Albans, UK: Triad/Panther Books, 1979.

Domarus, Max, ed. *Hitler. Speeches and Proclamations 1932–1945*: *The Chronicle of a Dictatorship*, vol. 3: *1939–1940*, London: Bloomsbury.

Douglas, W.A.B. *The Creation of a National Air Force: The Official History of the Royal Canadian Air Force*, vol. II. Toronto: University of Toronto Press, 1986.

Dunmore, Spencer. *Above and Beyond: The Canadians' War in the Air, 1939–45*. Toronto: McClelland & Stewart, 1996.

Feasby, W.R. *The Official History of the Canadian Medical Services 1939–1945*. Ottawa: Department of National Defence, Directorate of History and Heritage, 1956.

Forrester, Larry. *Fly for Your Life: The Colorful Exploits of One of World War II's Greatest Fighter Aces*. Garden City, NY: Nelson Doubleday, 1973.

Fowler, Simon. *Richmond at War, 1939–1945*. Richmond, UK: Richmond Local History Society, 2015.

Galland, Adolf. *The Battle of Britain*. UK: Air Historical Branch, Air Ministry, AHB6, 1953.

Galland, Adolf. *The First and the Last (Die Ersten und die Letzen)*. London: Methuen, 1954.

Glancey, Jonathan. *Spitfire—The Biography*. London: Atlantic Books, 2006.

Greenhous, Brereton, Stephen J. Harris, William C. Johnston, and William G.P. Rawling. *The Crucible of War, 1939–1945: The Official History of the Royal Canadian Air Force*, volume III. Toronto: University of Toronto Press. 1994.

Halliday, Hugh. *242 Squadron: The Canadian Years, The Story of the RAF's "All Canadian" Fighter Squadron*. Stittsville, ON: Canada's Wings, 1981.

Hatch, F.J. *Aerodrome of Democracy: Canada and the British Commonwealth Air Training Plan, 1939–1945*. Ottawa: Directorate of History, Department of National Defence, 1983.

Hawkins-Daly, Mark, ed. *Speeches That Changed the World*. London: Quercus, 2005.

Holmes, Tony. *American Eagles: American Volunteers in the RAF, 1937–1943*. Crowborough, UK: Classic Publications, 2001.

Johnson, J.E. *Wing Leader*. New York: Ballantine Books, 1957.

Jones, R.V. *Most Secret War: British Scientific Intelligence, 1939–1945*. London: Penguin, 2009.

Kaplan, Philip. *Fighter Aces of the Luftwaffe in World War II*. Auldgirth, UK: Pen and Sword, 2007.

Kent, J.A. *One of the Few: A Story of Personal Challenge through the Battle of Britain and Beyond*. London: William Kimber, 1971.

Levine, Joshua. *Forgotten Voices of the Blitz and the Battle for Britain*. London: Ebury Press, 2006.

Longmate, Norman. *How We Lived Then: A History of Everyday Life during the Second World War*. London: Hutchinson, 1971.

Lucas, Laddie. *Flying Colours: The Epic Story of Douglas Bader*. London: Random Century, 1981.

Lynn, Vera. *We'll Meet Again: A Personal and Social History of World War Two*. London: Sidgwick & Jackson, 1989.

Massey, Vincent. *What's Past Is Prologue: The Memoirs of the Right Honourable Vincent Massey, C.H.* Toronto: Macmillan, 1963.

McIntosh, Dave. *High Blue Battle: The War Diary of No. 1 (401) Fighter Squadron, RCAF*. Toronto: Stoddart, 1990.

McNab, Chris. *The Luftwaffe, 1933–45, Hitler's Eagles*. New York: Chartwell, 2014.

Middlebrook, Martin, and Chris Everitt. *The Bomber Command War Diaries: An Operational Reference Book, 1939–1945*. New York: Viking, 1985.

Mosley, Leonard. *The Battle of Britain: The Making of a Film*. London: Weidenfeld and Nicolson, 1969.

Nissen, Jack, with A.W. Cockerill. *Winning the Radar War: A Memoir*. Toronto: Macmillan, 1987.

Ogilvie, Keith C. *You Never Know Your Luck: Battle of Britain to the Great Escape, the Extraordinary Life of Keith "Skeets" Ogilvie*. Stotfold, UK: Fighting High Publishing, 2016.

Olson, Lynne, and Stanley Cloud. *A Question of Honor: The Kosciuszko Squadron, Forgotten Heroes of World War II*. New York: Knopf, P, 2003.

Otter, Patrick. *Yorkshire Airfields in the Second World War*. Newbury, UK: Countryside Books, 1998.

Plummer, Christopher. *In Spite of Myself: A Memoir*. Toronto: Knopf, 2008.

Portugal, Jean E. *We Were There: The R.C.A.F. and Others—Volume 7, A Record for Canada*. Toronto: Royal Canadian Military Institute Heritage Society, 1998.

Price, Alfred. *Battle of Britain Day: 15 September 1940*. London: Greenhill Books, 1990.

Profiles of Members of the Aircrew Association. Aircrew Association, 1989.

Richards, Denis. *Royal Air Force, 1939–1945*, vol. 1: *The Fight at Odds*. London: Her Majesty's Stationery Office, 1953.

Roberts, Leslie. *Canada's War in the Air*. Montreal: Alvah M. Beatty, 1942.

Rudhall. Robert J., and Dilip Sarkar. *Battle of Britain: The Movie—The Men and Machines of One of the Greatest War Films Ever Made*. Yorkshire UK: Ramrod Books, 2000.

Shirer, William L. *The Rise and Fall of the Third Reich, A History of Nazi Germany*. New York: Simon and Schuster, 1959.

Terraine, John. *The Right of the Line: The Royal Air Force in the European War, 1939–1945*. London: Hodder and Stoughton, 1985.

The R.C.A.F. Overseas: The First Four Years. Toronto: Oxford University Press, 1944.

Townsend, Peter. *Duel of Eagles: The Struggles for the Skies from the First World War to the Battle of Britain*. Richmond Hill, ON: Simon and Schuster, 1972.

Vance, Jonathan F. *High Flight: Aviation and the Canadian Imagination*. Toronto: Penguin, 2002.

Weal, John. *Jagdgeschwader 54 Grünherz*, vol. 6. Oxford: Osprey, 2001.

Williston, Floyd. *Through Footless Halls of Air: The Stories of a Few of the Many Who Failed to Return*. Burnstown, ON: General Store Publishing, 1996

Winterbotham, F.W. *The Ultra Secret*. New York: Dell, 1974.

Wood, Derek, and Derek Dempster. *The Narrow Margin*. Barnsley, UK: Pen and Sword, 2003.

Woods, Shirley E. *The Molson Saga, 1763–1983*. Toronto: Doubleday, 1986.

Wright, Robert. *Dowding and the Battle of Britain*. London: Macdonald & Co., 1969.

Wynn, Kenneth G. *Men of the Battle of Britain: A Who Was Who of the Pilots and Aircrew, British, Commonwealth and Allied, Who Flew with the Royal Air Force Fighter Command July 10 to October 31, 1940*. Norwich, UK: Gliddon Books, 1989.

———. *Men of the Battle of Britain: Supplementary Volume*. Norwich, UK: Gliddon Books, 1992.

Zentner, John. *The Art of Wing Leadership and Aircrew Morale in Combat*. Cadre Papers, Air University Press, College of Aerospace Doctrine, Education and Research, 2001.

Zumbach, Jan. *On Wings of War: My Life as a Pilot Adventurer*. London: Deutsch, 1975.

NEWSPAPERS, PERIODICALS, PRESS AGENCIES, BROADCASTS, MOVIES, PARLIAMENTARY PAPERS, WEBLOGS

"A Canadian And His Rebuilt Hurricane," *Weekend Magazine* 30 (*Montreal Gazette*), 1968.

Aeronautics 2, no. 2 (March 1940).

"A Few Canadians . . ." *Canada Today* 27. Commemorative Issue. Published by Canadian High Commission, Canada House, London, UK, September 1990.

"Air Marshal Bishop Visits Canadian Fliers." Canadian Press cable, London, September 26, 1940.

Aviators of Hudson Strait (documentary. National Film Board of Canada, 1973.

Bartkiewicz, Jeff. "Calgary Flying Ace Lived Hard, Died Young." *Calgary Herald*, August 29, 2004.

Bates, Stephen. "Blitz 70th Anniversary: Night of Fire than Heralded a New Kind of War," *Guardian*, September 6, 2010.

"Battle of Britain." https://en.wikipedia.org/wiki/Battle_of_Britain.

Battle of Britain (movie). Spitfire Productions, Harry Saltzman and Bennie Fisz, 1969.

"Battle of Britain Day." https://en.wikipedia.org/wiki/Battle_of_Britain_Day.

Battle of Britain Remembered magazine. "Matching Faces to a Few of the Names."

"*Battle of Britain*'s Mixed Reviews in London, Hot B.O., Notables Attend." *Variety*. September 24, 1969.

"Beaverbrook Builds R.A.F. Planes While Son Destroys the Germans." Canadian Press, August 16, 1940.

Beckwith, Mark. "45 Seconds." *Making History* (newsletter), February 6, 2022.

"Bob, Hans-Ekkehard." https://en.wikipedia.org/wiki/Hans-Ekkehard_Bob

Bob, Hans-Ekkehard. Quoted in interview on Griffon-Merlin website. https://www.griffonmerlin.com/wwii-interview/hans-ekkehard-bob/.

Boileau, John. "Canada's Merchant Navy: The Men That Saved the World." *Legion*, July 14, 2010.

"Broomstick Army Who Won a Special Place." *1939–1940: The People's War, Yesterday* magazine. Portsmouth: Portsmouth Publishing, 1989.

"Bruce Millar Wounded in Air Battle." *Penticton Herald*. September 12, 1940.

Burke, Tim. "Fighter Pilot Looks Back to Days of Courage." *Montreal Star*, November 9, 1970.

Byers, Andrew R. ed.. "The Black Spring," *The Canadians at War 1939–45*. Montreal: Reader's Digest, 1995.

Bywater, Michael. "Our Forgotten Freedom Fighter: Why the Unsung Hurricane Is the True Ace of the Battle of Britain." *Independent*, January 17, 2011.

Canadian Jews in World War II, Part I, Decorations. Montreal: Canadian Jewish Congress, 1947.

Canada, Agreement Relating to Training of Pilots and Aircraft Crews in Canada and Their Subsequent Service between the United Kingdom, Canada, Australia and New Zealand, Signed in Ottawa, December 17, 1939. Ottawa: King's Printer, 1941.

"Canada's Airmen Visited By King." Canadian Press cable, "Somewhere in England." September 26, 1940.

Canby, Vincent. "Screen: Army of Stars Wages the Battle of Britain." *New York Times*, October 21, 1969.

"Canadians Continue Success in Air Against Nazi flyers." Canadian Press cable. September 26, 1940.

Carr, Bill. "The Battle of Britain: The Canadians." Gatineau, QC. Vintage Wings of Canada, 2015.

"Ceremonies Yesterday Mark City as One with Leading Air Centres of the World." *Free Press* (London, ON). August 25, 1928.

Chabun, Will. "Lionel Hastings—a Proud Guinea Pig." *Regina Leader-Post*, November 9, 2001.

Chandler, Graham. "The Gift of Air Power." *Legion*, September 15, 2012.

Collins, Paul. "John Alexander Kent and the RAF's Polish Fighter Pilots."

September 12, 2019. https://www.canada.ca/en/air-force/services/
history-heritage/battle-britain/profiles/john-alexander-kent-and-raf-
s-polish-fighter-pilots.html.

Copp, Terry. "Standing Up To The Blitz: Army, Part 4." *Legion*, January
1, 1996.

Ebert, Roger. "Battle of Britain" (review). *Chicago Sun-Times*, November
3, 1969.

Evening Standard. London, June 18, 1940.

"Fire Watchers and Fire Guards." Firefighters' Memorial Trust. https://
firefightersmemorial.org.uk/research/fire-watchers-and-fire-guards/.

"Fliers of 1st Fighter Squadron, R.C.A.F., Come Home." *Toronto Star*.
November 1940.

"Flight-Lieut. Jean Paul Desloges Invalided Home." *Toronto Star*, January 1941.

"Flying Officer Bruce Millar Given Warm Welcome by the Citizens of
Penticton." *Penticton Herald*. December 5, 1940.

Galland, Adolf. https://en.wikipedia.org/wiki/Adolf_Galland.

Gasior, Mariusz. "The Polish Pilots Who Flew in the Battle of Britain."
Imperial War Museum, https://www.iwm.org.uk/history/the-polish-
pilots-who-flew-in-the-battle-of-britain.

Halliday, Hugh. "The Battle of Britain: Air Force, Part 17," *Legion*, September
1, 2006.

———. "Battle of Britain: Canadians in the Royal Air Force." *Skies*,
September 11, 2019.

———. "Battle of Britain: Canadian Pilot Biographies." RCAF Association,
2024. https://www.rcafassociation.ca/heritage/1914-1945/battle-of-
britain/.

Hamilton, Andrew W. "McNab Gets First Kill During First Fight." *Globe
and Mail*, August 16, 1940.

"Hamilton Pilot Vanquishes Nazi Raider in Scrap." *Hamilton Spectator*,
September 1940.

"Hawker Hurricane." https://en.wikipedia.org/wiki/Hawker_Hurricane.

Heeney, Arnold. "Air Training Scheme—Organization of Canadians in
R.C.A.F. Units and Formations." Memorandum from undersecretary
of state for external affairs to prime minister, December 13, 1939.

Hill, Robin. "The Man Who Fell to Earth." Essex Historic Aircraft
Collection, Ingatestone, September 1940. www.aviationmuseum.co.uk.

"Hilly's Button: Glenboro Man in R.A.F. Prizes Good Luck Token."
Canadian Press. April 1, 1940.

Howley, Dick. Battle of Britain Monument. https://www.bbm.org.uk/air-men/Howley.htm

"Hurricanes Made in Canada." *Standard Photonews* (Montreal). July 20, 1940.

"In The Struggle For Liberty And Justice." *London Free Press.* September 1940.

Jack, Ronald J. "Pat Sclanders—Boy Aviator." *Telegraph-Journal,* December 6, 2017.

Joost, Major Mathias. "The Unsung Heroes of the Battle of Britain: The Groundcrew of No. 1 (RCAF) Squadron." *RCAF Journal* (Battle of Britain edition, 2015).

"Kanalkampf." https://en.wikipedia.org/wiki/Kanalkampf

King, Richard. "Battle of Britain Legend—303 (Polish) Squadron." Key Aero. https://www.key.aero/article/battle-britain-legend-303-polish-squadron.

Lefurgey, Dave. "So My Son Will Know." *Airforce,* Spring 2007.

London Gazette, September 10, 1946.

Low, David. "Very well then, alone!" (cartoon caption) *Evening Standard,* June 18, 1940.

Lowe, Frank. "20 Years Ago, They Broke The Luftwaffe." *Weekend* magazine 10, no. 37 (*Montreal Gazette*), September 10, 1960.

Lowman, Ron. "The Battle of Britain: September 1949: An Anxious World Watched as a Desperate Nation Fought for Freedom." *Toronto Star,* September 9, 1990.

MacGill, Elsie. "Aircraft Engineering in Wartime Canada." *Engineering Journal* (November 1940).

McIndoe, A.H. "Total Reconstruction of the Burned Face." *British Journal of Plastic Surgery* (1983).

McNab, Ernest. "Canadians Played Big Part In Decisive Air Battle" (fourth of four articles written May 5, 1941). https://flyingforyourlife.com/pilots/ww2/mc/mcnab/.

———. "Initial Fight With Enemy Is Memory That Remains" (third of four articles written May 5, 1941). https://flyingforyourlife.com/pilots/ww2/mc/mcnab/.

———. "Pilot Needs Oxygen for Fighting at Great Heights" (second of four articles written May 5, 1941). https://flyingforyourlife.com/pilots/ww2/mc/mcnab/.

———. "R.A.F. Is Well Prepared to Meet Nazi Hordes" (first of four articles written May 5, 1941). https://flyingforyourlife.com/pilots/ww2/mc/mcnab/.

Montagnes, James. "Girl Designs New Trainer: Elizabeth MacGill Is Only Woman Aeronautical Engineer in Canada." *New York Times*, October 13, 1940.

Moss, Bruce. "A New $12 Million Film Relives This Decisive Air Battle of World War II." *Weekend Magazine* 30 (*Montreal Gazette*), September 1968.

Mowbrey, Kevin. "Albert Ross Tilley: The Legacy of a Canadian Plastic Surgeon." *Canadian Journal of Plastic Surgery* (Summer 2013).

"Nickelling." https://en.wikipedia.org/wiki/RAF_Dishforth. https://premierrelics.com/new-products-62/wwii-era-1940-airborne-heavy-bomber-dropped-british-propaganda-leaflet-dropped-on-germans.

"One Helped to Rescue Leader, Gives His Own Life for Empire." *Halifax Chronicle*. September 11, 1940.

"Parents Proud." Canadian Press. August 16, 1940.

"Pat Sclanders Was Once Youngest Pilot in Entire Dominion: His 'Boy Scout' Act Startled Crowds at Maritime Exhibitions." *Halifax Chronicle*, September 12, 1940.

"Percival Stanley 'Stan' Turner." *Aviation During World War Two, Century of Flight*. http://www.century-of-flight.freeola.com/Aviation%20history/WW2/aces/Percival%20Stanley%20Turner.htm.

"Pilots of the RCAF and RAF in the Battle of Britain." *Toronto Star*. September 15, 1965.

"Queen of the Hurricanes: Elsie MacGill." *True Comics* 8 (January 1942).

RAF No. 74 Squadron. http://74sqdn.tk/squadron-history.

Reyno, Edwin. "Personal Reflections of a Pilot." *The Roundel*, September 1960.

Robertson, Sam. "'Scramble Angels' Is Signal for R.C.A.F. Unit to Soar." Canadian Press cable, September 4, 1940.

Saunders, Wayne. "A Magnificent Contribution." *Airforce* 34, no.1 (Spring 2010).

Sheffy, Pearl. "The Man Who got the Bond Going." *Calgary Herald*, January 29, 1966.

Shenstone, Beverley (using pseudonym Brian Worley). "Fighter Fundamentals." *Aeronautics* 2, no. 2 (March 1940).

Siskel, Gene. The Movies. *Chicago Tribune*, November 4, 1969.

Sugarman, Martin. "World War II: Jewish Pilots and Aircrews in the Battle of Britain." Jewish Virtual Library, A Project of American-Israeli Cooperative Enterprise.

"Supermarine Spitfire." https://en.wikipedia.org/wiki/Supermarine_Spitfire.

Taylor, Neil. "The Flying Club Movement in Canada and Edmonton's Role." *From rhe Hangar*. Edmonton: Alberta Aviation Museum, May 2019.

"The Airmen's Stories—F/O R. Smither." Battle of Britain London Monument Archive, 2007.

"The Few: Battle of Britain Aircrew." Bentley Priory Museum. https://bentleyprAiorymuseum.org.uk/bentley-priory-and-the-battle-of-britain/the-few/

Tolppanen, Bradley. "Great Contemporaries: Max Aitken, Lord Beaverbrook." Churchill Project. Hillsdale College, Mississippi, June 17, 2016.

"Town Of Sackville Mourns with University President in Death of Pilot Officer." *Telegraph-Journal* (Saint John, NB). September 7, 1940.

"Treating Severe Burns Victims: Heroes Remember." Interview with Hilda (Empey) Moore, June 7, 1997, Victoria, BC. https://www.veterans.gc.ca/eng/video-gallery/video/4595.

"Turner, Percival Stanley." *Century of Flight*. http://www.century-of-flight.freeola.com/Aviation%20history/WW2/aces/Percival%20Stanley%20Turner.htm.

"Wing Commander Arthur Hicklin Warner." Department of National Defence, Canada. https://www.canada.ca/en/department-national-defence/maple-leaf/rcaf/migration/2013/wing-commander-arthur-hicklin-warner.html.

Warum leaflets. https://premierrelics.com/new-products-62/wwii-era-1940-airborne-heavy-bomber-dropped-british-propaganda-leaflet-dropped-on-germans.

Williston, Floyd. "He Was full of Courage and Dash." *Times Globe* (Saint John, NB), September 14, 2000.

Willock, J.F. "The Castle Bromwich Aircraft Factory." Paper published by Warwickshire Industrial Archaeology Society, January 2021.

Wilton, Peter. "WWII Guinea Pigs Played Crucial Role in Refining Plastic Surgery in Canada." *Canadian Medical Association Journal* (1998).

"Winnipeg Pilot Tells of Reactions During Air Battle with Germans." *Winnipeg Tribune.* July 31, 1940.

"Women on the Wing," *Chatelaine*. August 1931.

PHOTO CREDITS

Dust Jacket

FRONT: RCAF No. 1 Fighter Squadron with Hurricane CH 1733: Imperial War Museum (IWM). BACK: Vapour trails over Westminster: Department of National Defence DND PL 106650.

First Photo Section

PAGE 1: Bristol Bulldog aircraft and Kent at Buckingham Palace: Polish Institute and Sikorski Museum (PISM) London; Johannesson Flying Service hangar and Konrad Johannesson in RFC: Brian Johannesson and Cathie Eliasson with permission.

PAGE 2/3: Chain Home radar tower: National World War II Museum, New Orleans; Radar operator CH 15332: Imperial War Museum (IWM); Douglas Bader and RAF No. 242 Fighter Squadron CH 1413: IWM.

PAGE 4: German bomber over Thames C 5422, and Hermann Göring HU 4481: IWM.

PAGE 5: Hugh Dowding portrait D 1417: IWM; Scramble of RAF No. 242 Fighter Squadron pilots: Library and Archives Canada (LAC) DND PL 3055.

PAGE 6: Patrick Sclanders and plane: Floyd Williston files, courtesy Norman Malayney; Beverley Shenstone: David Fleury and Mary Shenstone with permission.

PAGE 7: Elsie MacGill portrait, Hurricane assembly at Canadian Car and Foundry, MacGill and Can-Car officials looking skyward: courtesy Richard Bourgeois-Doyle.

PAGE 8: London in the Blitz, and Firewatcher D 5007: IWM; Dorothy Firth portrait: Helen and Terry Beauchamp, with permission.

Second Photo Section

PAGE 1: RCAF No. 1 Fighter Squadron boarding RMS *Duchess of Atholl*: Paul Pitcher papers, with permission.

PAGE 2/3: Max Aitken Lord Beaverbrook HU 88386, John Max Aitken CH 14129, and RCAF No. 1 Fighter Squadron CH 1733: IWM.

PAGE 4/5: Images of RCAF No. 1 Fighter Squadron at RAF Northolt: Paul Pitcher papers, with permission.

PAGE 6/7: John Burdes and fellow ground crew aboard RMS *Duchess of Atholl*: LAC DND PL 535; Re-arming Hurricane with inbound aircraft overhead: National Air Force Museum of Canada; all other ground crew images: Paul Pitcher papers, with permission.

PAGE 8: Winston Churchill surveys Blitz damage in London H 3978: IWM; Jill Brown and Teddy bear, courtesy Jill (Brown) Mason; Anne Elliott and bicycle, courtesy Anne (Elliott) Reed.

Third Photo Section

PAGE 1: Keith Ogilvie: courtesy Keith C. Ogilvie, with permission; Johnny Kent: PISM; Scramble: IWM HU 49253.

PAGE 2: Images of Keith Ogilvie shooting down Dornier bomber: courtesy Keith C. Ogilvie, with permission.

PAGE 3: Hurricane aircraft in formation CH 1500, and Douglas Bader seated on aircraft CH 1406: IWM.

PAGE 4/5: RAF N0. 303 Fighter Squadron pilots walking to camera CH 1535; Polish Squadron victories in Battle of Britain: IWM.

PAGE 6: Polish pilots inside aircraft in training CH 1150; Jan Zumbach and Miroslaw Feric Polish squadron with mascot CH 1537: IWM; three-shot of Zdzislaw Henneberg, Johnny Kent, and Miroslaw Feric in battle dress CH 1531: IWM.

PAGE 7: Ross Tilley portrait and Guinea Pig Club members in treatment and gathered inside and outside East Grinstead: East Grinstead Museum.

PAGE 8: King George VI visits RCAF No. 1 Fighter Squadron at Northolt: Paul Pitcher papers, with permission; Actors and veterans on set for filming of *Battle of Britain* movie 1968: PISM.

Index

ab initio, 20
ace, 10, 23, 52, 53, 64, 69, 71, 72,
    145, 167, 246, 262, 263, 277,
    280, 284, 289, 307, *307n*.
Adlerangriff (Eagle Attack), 16, 130,
    146, 147, 169, 178, 187,
    262.
Adlertag (Eagle Day), 146, 147.
Admiralty (Royal Navy), 69.
Advanced Air Striking Force (AASF),
    10, 46, 60, 61-63.
Aero Digest, 53.
aero-engine mechanic (fitter), 20,
    23, 48, 103, 189, 199, 207-209,
    211, 228, 308.
Aeronautical Research Committee
    (UK), 37, 93.
Air Board (Canada), 18, *19n*.
Air Council (UK), 67.
aircraft
    (Armstrong Whitworth) Atlas, 49.
    (Armstrong Whitworth) Siskin,
        31, 49, 50, 52.
    (Armstrong Whitworth) Whitley,
        12, 13,
    (Avro) 504, 85, 98.
    (Avro) Tutor, 98.
    (Boulton Paul) Defiant, 107, 122,
        123, 171.
(Bristol) Blenheim, 8, 35, 44, 47,
    65, 107, 122, *136n*, 157, 158,
    160, 178, 185, 264.
(Bristol) Bolingbroke, 47.
(Bristol) Bombay, 61
(Canadian Vickers) Canso, 47.
(Curtiss) Hawk, 50.
(de Havilland) Cirrus Moth, 2.
(de Havilland) Gypsy Moth,
    52-54.
(de Havilland) Tiger Moth, 10,
    17, 19, 47, 53, 58.
Dornier 17 and 215, 63, 71, 74,
    99, 116-118, 121, 129, 146,
    147, 150, 160, 162, 165, 173,
    179, 182, 188,192, 204, 209,
    227, 230-234, *232n*, 236-238,
    243, 253, 261-263, 267, 279,
    292, 303.
(Douglas) Digby, 47.
(Fairchild) PT-19 Cornel, 47.
(Fairey) Battle, 35, 60-62, 75, 97,
    99, 221.
(Fleet) Finch, 21, 47.
(Fokker) Universal, 207, 208.
(Gloster) Gauntlet, 4.
(Gloster) Gladiator, 35.
(Gotha) bomber, 160.
(Hawker) Fury, 4, 87

(Hawker) Hart, 54, 55, 87.

(Hawker) Hurricane, 6, 9, 11-15,
35, 38, 41, 42, 43, 44, 46-48,
51, 52, 57, 60, 61, 64-69, 71,
72-75, 77, 88, *88n*, 91, 97, 99,
100, 103, 104, 107, 118, 119,
121, 128, 129, 136, *136n*, 138,
140-145, *143n, 144n*, 147,
150-152, 156, 157, 159-174,
176-183, 188-192, 201-204,
207, 209-211, 214, 215,
221-223, *223n*, 227-230, 232,
232n, 235, 237-246, 258-261,
266-272, *270n*, 277, 279, 281,
285, 286, 288, 290, 292, 293,
295, 300, 304-306, 308, 313.

(Heinkel) He 111, 65, 68, 73, 75,
89, 92, 99, 147, 151, 167, 173,
174, 214, 215, 236-241, 243,
248, 263-265, 267, 279, 305,
308.

(Heinkel) 51 biplane, 153.

(Heinkel) 59 float plane, 120.

(Junkers) G-38, 85.

(Junkers) Stuka dive bomber Ju
87, 64, 65, 68, 70, *70n*, 71, 114,
129, 147, 153, 155, 308.

(Junkers) Ju 88, 71, 127, 154, 158,
203, 230, 256, 265-267, 269.

(Lockheed) Electra, 36-38.

(Lockheed) Hercules C-130, 306.

(Lockheed) Hudson, 47.

(Luftschiffbau) Zeppelin, 82.

(Messerschmitt) Me 109, 9, 10,
46, 61-65, 68, 71, 90, 91, 122,
126, 127, 129, 146, 153, 161,
163, 165, 167, 168, 180,
187-189, 191, 192, 200, 201,
203, 205, 206, 209, 210, 214,
215, 221-224, 227-229, 231,
233, 237-241, 243, 246, 256,

258, 262, 263, 265-270,
277-279, 290, 305, 313,

(Messerschmitt) Me 110, 35, 64,
65, 68, 71, 119, 126, 127, 146,
147, 150, 154, 172-174, 180,
181, 188, 189, 191, 192, 200,
204, 209, 224, 227, 228, 238,
263, 265-268, 270, 290.

(Miles) Magister, 35.

(North American) Harvard, 22,
35, 306.

(North American) B-25 Mitchell,
308.

(Rothmere) bomber, 8.

(Supermarine) S.6, 88.

(Supermarine) Spitfire, 6, 8-11,
33, 35, 38, 57, 72, 73, 75, *85n*,
87, 90, 91, 97-101, 107, 124,
126, 127, 136-139 *136n*, 145,
152, 153, 159, 161, 167, 168,
171, 173, 176-178, 185, 189,
191, 193, 199-202, 212, 213,
221-223, *223n*, 227, 229,
230, 232, 237, 242, 243, 245,
248, 253, 257, 263, 264, 267,
272, 291, 304, 306, *307n*,
308.

(Supermarine) Stranraer, 47.

(Supermarine) Type 224, 88.

(Supermarine) Type 300, 89.

(Vickers-Armstrong) R100, 19,
21n.

(Vickers) Vidette, 84.

(Westland) Lysander, 12, 23, 35,
47.

Air Fighting Development Unit
(AFDU), 144.

Air Force Cross (AFC), 1, 7, 8, 13,
202, 278, 283, 314.

airframe mechanic, 8, 86, 189, 207,
208, 293, 305, 306.

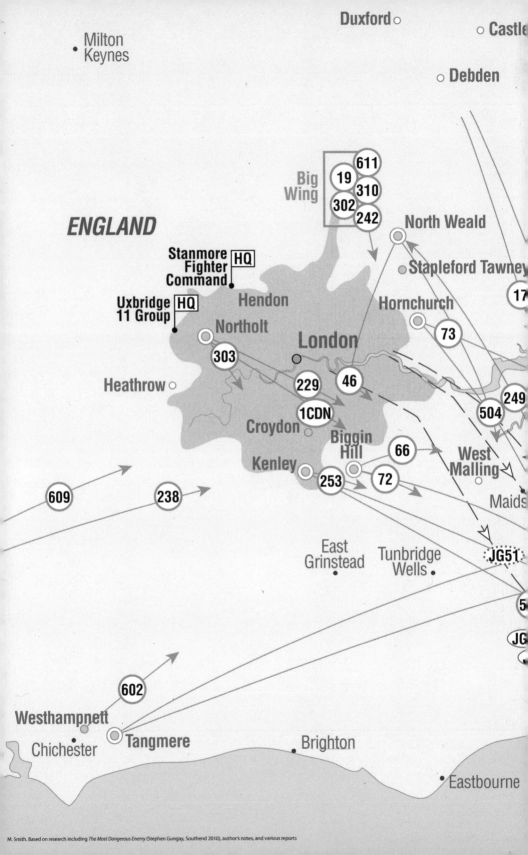

Duxford ○ ○ Castle

○ Debden

ENGLAND

Milton Keynes

Big Wing

611
19
310
302
242

North Weald

○ Stapleford Tawney

Stanmore Fighter Command [HQ]

Hendon

Hornchurch

17

73

Uxbridge 11 Group [HQ]

Northolt

London

303

Heathrow ○

229

46

1CDN

249

504

Croydon

Biggin Hill

66

West Malling

Kenley

253

72

Maids

609

238

East Grinstead

Tunbridge Wells

JG51

5

JG

JG

602

Westhampnett

Chichester Tangmere

Brighton

● Eastbourne

M. Smith. Based on research including *The Most Dangerous Enemy* (Stephen Gungay, Southend 2010), author's notes, and various reports